THE

REMAINS

OF THE

REV. JAMES MARSH, D. D.

KENNIKAT PRESS SCHOLARLY REPRINTS

Dr. Ralph Adams Brown, Senior Editor

Series on

LITERARY AMERICA IN THE NINETEENTH CENTURY

Under the General Editorial Supervision of
Dr. Walter Harding
University Professor, State University of New York

THE

REMAINS

OF THE

REV. JAMES MARSH, D. D.

LATE PRESIDENT,

AND

PROFESSOR OF MORAL AND INTELLECTUAL
PHILOSOPHY,

IN THE

UNIVERSITY OF VERMONT;

WITH A

MEMOIR OF HIS LIFE.

Compiled by
JOSEPH TORREY

KENNIKAT PRESS
Port Washington, N. Y./London

12809

THE REMAINS OF THE REV. JAMES MARSH, D.D.

First published in 1843
Reissued in 1971 by Kennikat Press
Library of Congress Catalog Card No: 77-122659
ISBN 0-8046-1308-7

Manufactured by Taylor Publishing Company   Dallas, Texas

~~~~~~~~~~~~~~~~~~~

" Sunt qui scire volunt eo fine tantum ut sciant, et turpis curiositas est. Et sunt qui scire volunt ut sciantur ipsi, et turpis vanitas est. Et sunt item qui scire volunt, ut scientiam vendant, verbi causâ, pro pecuniâ, pro honoribus, et turpis quæstus est. Sed sunt quoque qui scire volunt, ut ædificent, et charitas est; et item qui scire volunt, ut ædificentur, et prudentia est. Horum omnium soli ultimi duo non inveniuntur in abusione scientjæ, quippe qui ad hoc volunt intelligere, ut benefaciant."—*St. Bernard. Flores cap.* 196.

~~~~~~~~~~~~~~~~~~~

PREFACE.

As to my own share in the work here presented to the public, I should be disposed to say nothing, were it not proper for me to give some account of the manner in which I have endeavored to discharge a delicate office of friendship.

The late Dr. Marsh, near the close of his life, committed his papers to my care, with the request, that I would select from them such as I might think suitable, and cause them to be published. He hoped they might be not without use to the world; at least, that they would prove acceptable to his friends, and perhaps a source of some little benefit to his children. A few of these writings were already designed for the press by himself; but none of them had, as yet, undergone that revision and that careful correction, which doubtless he would have chosen to bestow on them, had his life and health been spared.

The papers consisted of letters, comprising a voluminous and interesting correspondence; of translations, chiefly from German writers on phi-

1*

losophy ; of lectures and fragments relating to the several subjects which entered into the author's course of instruction; and of sermons and addresses, written by him on various occasions, ordinary and extraordinary.

Of the letters, I have inserted several entire, and extracts from many more, whenever they served to assist me in drawing up the biographical memoir. The translations, I have wholly omitted, as not coming within the purpose of the present publication. Some of the lectures and more important fragments have been introduced, and such of the discourses, as seemed most fully to embody the author's views on subjects in which he felt the deepest interest.

In the arrangement of these papers, I have followed the same order which the author was accustomed to observe in the instruction of his classes ; and I think the careful reader will find no difficulty in tracing in it somewhat of a logical connexion. The first in the series is the fragment of a letter, begun in compliance with the request of a literary friend, but I believe never completed, or sent to its destination ; and to which I have given its present place, as furnishing an appropriate introduction to the following essays. The tract on physiology claims no other merit or importance than that of presenting, in a distinct and lucid manner, the main principles which Dr. Marsh regarded as lying at the basis of that important science, with which he was in the habit of commencing his course of philosophy. The views are the same

which may be found hinted at in the writings of
Coleridge, and which are more fully exhibited in
the works of Carus, and other German authors.

The lectures on psychology, which follow, are
complete, so far as they go. I ought, perhaps, to
say, that the author was never quite satisfied with
them in their present shape ; and that he was on
the point of recasting them in an entirely different
form, when he was arrested by the sudden attack
of the disease which brought him to the grave. It
was owing, no doubt, to this dissatisfaction with
the first part of the lectures, that he could never
prevail on himself to finish out the sketch as he
had begun. The latter part of the subject, relating to the feelings and to the will, was certainly
not the least interesting to himself; nay, on some
accounts, was considered by him as the most important of all, from its near connexion with morals
and religion. I have endeavored, in a measure, to
supply the deficiency, by inserting the letters
which come next ; wherein, as also in several of
the discourses, the views held by the author on the
subject of the Will, and on the connexion of the
understanding with the active powers, are discussed, and set forth as distinctly as the narrow limits
he allowed himself, would permit.

On Metaphysics, or philosophy properly so called, where the eminent and peculiar power of Dr.
Marsh, as an expounder of the highest truths of
science, chiefly appeared, nothing unfortunately has
been left by him, except scattered hints, on loose
scraps of paper, not to be reduced to any form,

even of aphorisms, which would render them intelligible to the general reader. In his lectures, Dr. Marsh seldom made use of notes, but chose rather to trust himself to the fulness of his own mind. I have selected the discourses out of a larger number, which were written, for the most part, to be delivered in the College chapel. They contain his views on most of the important subjects, respecting which it is desirable that the views of such a man should be known. The sermon on Conscience, and the two or three discourses on Sin, I think it must be acknowledged, contain a developement of principles, fundamental in their nature, and direct in their bearing on the most essential questions of theology.

As to the biographical memoir, it aims at nothing beyond a sketch of the simple incidents in the life of an unpretending scholar and christian. I have attempted neither to trace the development of his mind, nor to give an exposition of his philosophical system. The one I leave to some abler pen, and refer for the other to his own writings. It is enough for me, if I have succeeded in presenting the humbler traits of his meek and gentle character, without disparaging its worth by the smallness of my offering.

J. TORREY.

June 1, 1843.

CONTENTS.

		Page.
Preface,	- - - - - - - -	5
Memoir,	- - - - - - -	13
Entrance at Dartmouth College,	- - - -	15
Religious Experience,	- - - - -	17
Entrance at Andover,	- - - - - -	20
Appointment as Tutor at Dartmouth,	- -	20
Short Residence at Cambridge,	- - - -	29
Return to Andover,	- - - - -	30
Review of Ancient and Modern Poetry,	- -	50
Translation of Bellerman,	- - - -	51
Journey southward; introduction to Dr. Rice,	-	52
Visit to Dr. Rice at Richmond,	- - -	57
Employment at Hampden Sidney College,	- -	58
Return to New England,	- - - -	62
Second Residence at Hampden Sidney,	- -	65
Return to New England,	- - - -	71
Appointment as Professor at Hampden Sidney, Ordination and Marriage,	- - - - -	73
Appointment as President of the University of Vermont,	- - - - - - - -	76
His Views of Collegiate Education,	- - -	78
Exposition of the Course of Instruction and Discipline in the University,	- - - -	84
Death of Mrs. Marsh,	- - - - - -	86
Review of Professor Stuart's Commentary on the Epistle to the Hebrews,	- - - -	87
Publication of Coleridge's Aids to Reflection,	-	91

Page.

Publication of Selections from the old English Writers on Practical Theology, - - - - 103
Second Marriage, - - - - - 104
Resignation of the Presidency, and Acceptance of the Chair of Moral and Intellectual Philosophy, - 105
Publication of Herder's Spirit of Hebrew Poetry, 110
Studies and Plans as Professor, - - - - 110
Theological Views, - - - - - 119
Opposition to Evangelism, - - - - - 125
Loss of his second Wife, - - - - 128
Sickness and Death, - - - - - - 130
APPENDIX.
Letter to S. T. Coleridge, - - - - 135
——— to a Young Clergyman, - - - - 139
——— to Rev. S. G. W. - - - - 140
——— to J. M. - - - - - - 143, 148
——— from Dr. Rice, - - - - - 149
——— from Dr. Follen, - - - - - 151
——— from Mr. Gillman, - - - - 153
——— from H. N. Coleridge, - - - - 156
——— from Dr. Green, - - - - - 158

Outlines of a Systematic Arrangement of the Departments of Knowledge, with a View to their Organic Relations to each other in a General System, - 187
Space, - - - - - - 188
Time, - - - - - - 190
Geometry, Chronometry, Permutations, - 193
Metaphysical Principles of Natural Philosophy, 194
The Dynamic Theory, - - - - 195
Distinguishable Powers of Nature, and Laws of Action, - - - - - - 197
Light and Heat, - - - - - 204
Electricity, - - - - - - 205
Crystalization, - - - - - - 206
Organic Life, - - - - - 206

Page.

Remarks on some of the leading points connected with Physiology, - - - - - - - 211

    Tendency of Inorganic Matter to Spherical Forms, - - - - - - 214

    Crystallization, - - - - - 216

    Organic Life, - - - - - 218

    Vegetable and Animal Life distinguished, - 224

Remarks on Psychology.

    Chapter 1. Limits and Method of Psychological Inquiry, - - - - - 239

    Chapter 2. Preliminary Facts and Distinctions, - - - - - - 248

    Chapter 3. Additional Remarks on the Nature and Aim of the present Inquiries. Distinction of the Powers or Faculties of the Soul, 259

    Chapter 4. Cognitive Faculties, Consciousness, and Self-consciousness, - - 274

    Chapter 5. The Powers of Sensation, - 286

    Chapter 6. Distinction between Empirical and Pure or Mathematical Intuitions of Sense; and between what belongs to Sense and what belongs to the Higher Powers of Understanding and Reason, 302

    Chapter 7. Continuation of the same subject. The Inner Sense, and its Objects, - 316

    Chapter 8. Memory, and Power of Association, - - - - - - - 327

    Chapter 9. Recapitulation, - - - 342

    Chapter 10. Peculiar Function of the Understanding, - - - - - 354

    Chapter 11. General Conception of Reason, and its relation to the Understanding, 360

On the Will, as the Spiritual Principle in Man. *A Letter to a Friend,* - - - - - 368

On the Relation of Personal Existence and Immortality to the Understanding and the Reason, - 391

Discourse on Conscience, - - - - 398

Necessary Relation of our Real Purposes to their Le-

Page.

gitimate Results, under the Divine Government.

A Sermon on Hypocrisy, - - - - 423

Three Discourses on the Nature, Ground, and Origin of Sin.

 Discourse 1,   -   -   -   -   -   439

 Discourse 2,   -   -   -   -   -   468

 Discourse 3,   -   -   -   -   -   487

Discourse on the True Ground in Man's Character and Condition, of his Need of Christ,   502

Address at the Inauguration of the Author as President of the University of Vermont,   -   -   556

Discourse at the Dedication of the University Chapel, on the Necessary Agency of Religious Truth in the Cultivation of the Mind, - - - - - 585

Tract on Eloquence,   -   -   -   -   -   611

Tract on Evangelism, - - - - - - 629

MEMOIR

OF THE

LIFE OF JAMES MARSH, D. D.

JAMES MARSH, the author of the following Remains, was born in Hartford, Vermont, July 19th, 1794. His father, Mr. Daniel Marsh, was a respectable farmer, a man of plain good sense, and the same native sincerity and candor which formed so beautiful a trait in the character of his son. Joseph Marsh, Esq., the grandfather of James, was one of the most active and intelligent among the early settlers of Vermont. He came from Lebanon, in Connecticut, and established himself at Hartford, about the year 1772, shortly after the first beginning of the settlements in that quarter of the country. Being a man of talents and enterprize, he soon took a prominent part in the political concerns of the State, which was then engaged in its disputes with the various foreign parties that claimed the right of jurisdiction over the

2

territory. He was a member of that convention
at Westminster, which declared, in the name of
the people, the independence of Vermont; and
which afterwards assembled at Windsor, and formed the original Constitution of the State. On the
adoption of this constitution, and the organization
of the Government, in 1778, he was chosen the
first Lieutenant Governor; an office which he continued to hold, at intervals, for a number of years.
James Marsh was born in the house of his grandfather, a pleasant mansion in the retired valley of
Otta Quechee river. As it was intended that he
should follow the occupation of his father, he
spent here the first eighteen years of his life in
the hardy labors of the field. With this arrangement of his parents he was not only satisfied, but
well pleased. No man was ever more strongly
attached to the place of his birth; and the independent life of the farmer had a charm for him,
which never lost its hold on his imagination. In
his letters, he often speaks of those woods and
meadows in which he had spent so many pleasant
days; and, even at the close of his professional
studies, thought seriously of returning to his father's farm, where he hoped to find that leisure and
freedom for the activity of his mind, which he did
not expect to enjoy in more immediate contact
with the world. His elder brother, who was destined for college, having, for some reason, been
diverted from his purpose, James was induced to
take his place; and accordingly, at about the age
of eighteen, turned his attention for the first time

to the preparatory studies. Having completed these, under the care of Mr. William Nutting, who was then preceptor of the Academy at Randolph, he was admitted as a member of Dartmouth College, in the autumn of 1813.

The college at this time, or soon after, became involved in those notable difficulties, which finally resulted in the establishment of a rival University, whose brief existence began and ended, I believe, within the period of Mr. Marsh's residence at Hanover. Such a state of things, it might easily be supposed, could hardly tend to any advantage of the young men whose fortune it was to be then connected with the institution. The troubles, however, were mostly outward ; within the bosom of the college, the strictness of discipline and regularity of studies never suffered any serious interruption. Some of the best scholars ever educated at Dartmouth went through the worst of these days. In fact, the several departments of instruction were never better filled than they were at precisely that time, and the whole was under the direction of that wise and excellent man, President Brown, whose premature removal, in the full vigor of his power and highest promise of usefulness, inflicted on the college the severest loss it was ever called to sustain.

Under these favorable influences, Mr. Marsh soon gave evidence of the fine parts with which he was endowed. The late period when he began to study, subjected him, at first, to some inconvenience ; but the disadvantage of an imperfect preparation operated with him only as a stimulant to greater exertion, and was in fact compensated, in no slight degree, by that maturity of mind and those industrious habits he had brought with him from the farm. The same free and enterprizing spirit which afterwards formed his distinguishing character as a student, manifested itself in him from the first. Without being ambitious to shine in any particular branch of learning, he seemed intent on exploring the whole field of knowledge, and exercising his faculties in every right direction. This expansive tendency of his mind did not lead him, however, to overlook the importance of thorough and exact discipline. He aimed at becoming an accurate and profound as well as general scholar, and never allowed himself to be satisfied with superficial attainments. Although a great devourer of book, he was not in the habit of reading at random, and as fancy led him, but was uniformly guided by a leading purpose, which he had distinctly conceived and settled in his own mind.

If he had a decided preference at this time for any particular class of studies, it was perhaps for the ancient languages and literature; especially the Greek, which he did not cease to study and admire as long as he lived. His proficiency in these languages, while at college, was very respectable; his skill in them consisted chiefly in an ability to read them with ease and fluency, and with a discriminating sense of their beauties of style and expression. Neither his time nor his means allowed him to do much more. In connection with these studies, he pushed his inquiries to a considerable extent in literary history and criticism. The only writings of his college days which have been preserved, relate almost entirely to these subjects. In the mathematics and the severer sciences, he was patient and thorough, shrinking from nothing that was abstruse or difficult, but rather taking delight in whatever served to task his powers and rouse them to their utmost exertion. His lighter reading was, of choice, confined, for the most part, to the old English writers, whose fulness of thought and fresh vigorous language furnished a more pleasurable excitement to his mind, than the tamer productions of more recent times. Yet there was no period of the English literature which he did not make it a point to study, in its best authors.

In the spring of 1815, Mr. Marsh was for a while interrupted in these studious pursuits by an important event, which gave the decisive turn to his whole future life. During a season of uncommon attention to the subject of religion in the college, in which most of the students participated, his own mind became interested in that subject, and his serious reflections resulted in a change of views and feelings, which he ever afterwards regarded as the commencement of a new life in his soul. Among his earliest papers, is one which contains a full account of the progressive steps by which he was led, after many severe inward conflicts, to place his hope on what he considered to be a sure foundation. He says he had been instructed from childhood in the great things pertaining to another world ; but his first serious impressions were now almost entirely forgotten. His mind was recalled to them by hearing that one of his fellow-students had become serious. A few days afterward, being present at a religious meeting, where the individual just mentioned offered some remarks and a prayer, his attention was completely arrested, and fixed upon his own personal condition. He went home, laid aside his studies, and applied himself to the reading of religious books and to reflection. His first effort was to commit himself to God, in a voluntary and conscious act of surrendering up every thing to him, as his rightful Lord and Sovereign. But every attempt of this kind only convinced him the more of the great distance and alienation of his heart from the source and centre of all good. He remained in this state of feeling for some days. When he found he was making no progress in the performance of what he conceived to be his first duty, he became alarmed, and began to fear lest he should return back to his former indifference and unconcern. The horrible suspicion arose in his mind, that he was given over to hardness of heart, which threw him into a state bordering on despair. "I envied those around me (he says) whom I looked upon as in a more hopeful condition than myself, and my heart rose in opposition to the divine sovereignty. Yet I struggled with my misery, and was in the greatest fear, lest I should be left to blaspheme the name of my Creator. Filled with dismay, and almost overcome by the suggestions of a rebellious heart, I went to visit one whom I knew to be, like myself, in great darkness and depression, in order to join with him in lamenting our wretched state." Here, during the interview with his friend, he first found relief from these dismal apprehensions. The opposition of heart with which he had been so long struggling, seemed to give way for the admission of better feelings; although for several days he scarcely ventured to hope the change was of that radical and permanent nature, which he felt to be necessary for his peace. But gradually his views became more clear and decided. "The things of another world (he says) completely filled my mind, and God appeared to me to be all in all. I have no apprehension that I experienced any remarkable displays of his character; I saw no particular application of his mercy to myself; but he appeared infinitely glorious, and I felt that if I had ten thousand souls, I could with confidence commit them to his mercy and care. I experienced no fears respecting my own situation, and no particular joys or exulting hopes; but a calm and tranquil peace of mind, such as the world could neither give nor take away."

These feelings, however, did not continue long without suffering some abatement; and his faith was soon subjected to a variety of trials. "At one time in particular," he notices, "after being engaged in meditation, I took up a proposition of

Euclid. As I proceeded in the demonstration, all my faith in things invisible seemed to vanish, and I almost doubted the reality of my own existence. By degrees, my convictions became more settled and less dependent on circumstances. I could pursue my studies with calmness, proceeding, as I hope, from a belief that it was my duty, and a confidence that God was able to preserve me. At times, however, I have feared that my peace arose rather from the decay of religious affections, than from true evangelical faith. Yet I thought, from self-examination, that I discovered some marks of a growing principle of Christian life. I thought my desires after holiness and an increase of the Christian graces, together with the sense of my own sinfulness and the imperfection of my best performances, were becoming more strong, and furnished some evidence of a state of grace."

Under these impressions, Mr. Marsh took an early opportunity to make a public profession of religion; and on the 7th of August in the same year, united with the church at Dartmouth College. After recording this event, he says: "With the members of this church, and under the instruction of our beloved pastor, the Rev. Professor Shurtliff, I now enjoy the most favorable and agreeable means for improvement in christian knowledge, and for growth in the christian life. That I may have grace to improve these distinguishing blessings to the glory of the great Giver of every good and perfect gift, to the honor of that Redeemer who was delivered for our sins and

raised for our justification, to the good of the
church in this place and the upbuilding of the
church universal, and, finally, to my own spiritual
and everlasting welfare, is, so far as I know my
own heart, my most sincere and ardent prayer."

It is impossible, as it seems to me, for any one
to read this account, without being satisfied that
Mr. Marsh himself was fully convinced he had experienced, at this time, a great and decided change
in his religious character; had passsd a crisis in
his spiritual life, different from any thing he had
ever before known, and worthy of being held by
him in perpetual remembrance. That he might
be mistaken on this point, is possible; as who may
not be, in regard to a thing so deceitful as his own
heart? But, at all events, he felt that this was to
him the beginning of a new life. Henceforth his
aims were fixed and all his powers consecrated to
one great object. His studies, which had been
for a while interrupted by this all-engrossing subject, were now resumed, and pushed forward with
unabated ardor. The change in his religious character had neither contracted his mind nor diminished his enthusiasm in the pursuit of knowledge.
It rather stimulated him to greater exertion; his
mind expanded with the more ennobling principle
by which its energies were now directed; and instead of contracting his aims, and seeking to content himself with humbler attainments in human
science, he felt himself bound, more than ever, to
cultivate, to the utmost possible extent and in
every direction, the powers which God had given
him.

With these enlightened views of his duty under the present circumstances, he went on to complete what he had already so successfully begun, in laying the foundations of a thorough and truly liberal education. Without neglecting the regular tasks required of him, he was led, by his own indefatigable zeal, to venture far beyond the beaten track, and to push his inquiries into every part of the field where the human mind has left any monuments of its power. Thus he became a general scholar, in the worthiest sense; not a mere smatterer, possessing the show without the substance of learning, but profound, systematic and clear, as well as comprehensive, in all his views. This was the character with which he left college; and few have acquired it more fairly, or have sustained it with greater constancy, than he did, through the whole of his subsequent life.

Having finished his collegiate studies, Mr. Marsh was at no loss to decide as to the choice of a profession. He was inclined to Theology by the native bent of his mind, as well as by his religious feelings; and he had no reason to doubt that this was the course marked out for him by divine Providence. Accordingly, in November, 1817, he entered the Theological school at Andover, with a view to prepare for the sacred ministry. Here he remained about one year, when he received and accepted an invitation to become a tutor at Dartmouth College.

In this situation he spent two of the happiest, and in many respects most profitable years of his

life. Being in a good degree familiar with the
branches of science in which he was called to in-
struct, and at full liberty to take his own course,
as to the employment of his leisure hours, he had
ample opportunity, which he did not fail to improve, of giving greater extent, as well as solidity,
to the foundations which had been already so
broadly laid. His studies, at this time, went over
a wide range, but they were regular and severe.
He cultivated more general and familiar acquaintance with the great writers of antiquity ; studying
the various forms of the ancient languages, at their
purest sources ; and perhaps he might now say, as
Milton did of himself at the same age, that he had
not merely wetted the tip of his lips in the stream
of these languages, but in proportion to his years,
swallowed the most copious draughts. But what
he chiefly aimed at was, to make himself familiar
with the spirit of the ancient literature ; to pene-
trate to the ground of all its diversified forms, and
to master the secret of the mighty charm by
which it binds all hearts that come within its influence. While investigating this subject, in which
he was led to compare the spirit of the ancient literature with the modern, he became interested in
the study of the middle ages, and read every thing
he could get access to on this important period,
which, as containing within itself the germ of
modern cultivation, he thought deserving of more
attention than it usually received. After the same
manner, he studied the literature of more recent
times, endeavoring everywhere to look beneath the

surface and the mere form, and to find out the pervading spirit which characterized each particular author, and his age. In all this he never lost out of sight, the great practical end of self-culture. In contemplating the efforts of other minds, and searching for the causes of their failure or success, he was aiming to develope his own. Freedom, boldness, and vigor of thought, were the qualities by which he was most strongly attracted. He preferred those writers above all others for their influence on his own taste and habits of thinking, who possessed most of what he considered the peculiar characteristics of modern genius, profound moral sentiment, and intensity of feeling. In a letter written at this time, wherein he speaks of the style of thinking that belongs to different classes of literature, and to different persons, according as their tastes and characters are formed by one or the other, he adduces Pope and Byron, the one as an example of a cold and unfeeling style, the other of a style characterized by immense power of thought, feeling and expression. Of Byron, he says, " you will soon be tired of him as an example, but he seems to me to *live* more than other men. He has conceived a being in his imagination of stronger powers, of greater capacity for suffering and enjoying, than the race of mortals, and he has learned to live in him. ' It is,' he says,

> ' to create, and in creating live
> A being more intense, that we endow
> With form our fancy.'

How vastly does every thing of a religious nature swell in importance, when connected in our minds with a being of such capacities as Byron seems to us to be! When I speak as I do of this author, I know you will not imagine that I can ever intend to approve his moral feelings, or commend the moral tenor of his works. But why should not the disciple of Christ feel as profoundly, and learn to express as energetically, the power of moral sentiment, as the poet or the infidel? It is this, that I aim at in my devotion to Byron. I love occasionally to hold communion with his spirit, and breathe its energy. It gives me new vigor, and I seem in reality to live a being more intense." Such was Mr. Marsh's literary creed at the present time; afterwards it became somewhat modified.

In the same letter, he speaks of his tutorship as a drudgery, which he would be glad to be rid of. This was written near the close of the first year he spent in that office, but he consented to remain for another. The fact that he was requested to do so, proves that his services were acceptable, at least that he was chargeable with no serious neglect of his duty. To the students, he could scarcely fail to be other than a pleasant and profitable instructer, though his mode of teaching, and his habits of familiar intercourse with his pupils, were quite different, I suspect, from what had been customary before. "There are some," he says, in a letter written after he had left Hanover, "who seem to know no way of managing young men,

4

but by the terror of authority ; but such a method
tends to break down all the independent spirit
and love of study for its own sake, which I thought
it of so much importance to cherish." Perhaps he
then carried his notions on this subject a little too
far ; perhaps his own method of allowing and encouraging young men to use an unlimited freedom
in the choice of their studies, would have proved
incompatible with any regular system of discipline
calculated on the average wants of the youthful
mind. But if he was in an error here, it was from
judging of others by himself, and too charitably
presuming that none would be tempted, in such a
case, to turn their liberty into licentiousness.
However that might be, a mind so deeply imbued
as his was, with the true spirit of the scholar,
could not fail to infuse a portion of his own zeal
into those who were under his care ; and his influence at Dartmouth, was, I doubt not, in the highest
degree salutary. One effect at least, it must have
had, namely, to raise the tone of scholarship, and
inspire higher aims, than those connected with the
mere task-work of the recitation room.

His devotion to these labors, and to his other
literary pursuits, did not prevent him from cultivating, as he had opportunity, the social affections
of his nature. Although a real student, he was as
far as possible from being a recluse. No man had
a stronger love for cultivated society, nor understood better what such society ought to be. He
had a constant longing after more freedom of intellectual intercourse, and thought the benefit to

be derived from such intercourse incomparably greater than could be gained from books alone and solitary studies. "Not that I would like," he says in one of his letters of this period, "the unrestrained intercourse of French petits-maitres or petittes-maitresses; but surely there can be no objection to the free and hearty expression of friendship, or to that easy and familiar interchange of thought, which we find in the letters of Cowper and his correspondents, and, indeed, of all the literary men of the last century, as Shenstone, Gay, &c. Such a state of society seems to me to promise much more exercise of social feelings and sympathies, than our constrained, cautious and freezing reserve. Where a prohibition is put upon the expression of all the social affections, and we dare not give proof of their existence, there is great reason to fear they do not exist long. A fire may indeed live for a time, if buried in ashes; but if buried too long, we look in vain for the cheering flame or the glowing embers. We rake off the ashes, and all is gray."

The society which he found at Hanover must doubtless have been exceedingly pleasant to him, and perhaps contributed, more than any thing else, to reconcile him to the long suspension of his professional studies; for love had some influence here, as well as literature. He had fixed his affections on a young lady of the place, in all respects most worthy of his choice; and as the inclination proved to be mutual, an affair of the utmost importance to his future happiness was thus settled. This person, whom he afterwards married, was Miss Lucia Wheelock, daughter of James Wheelock, Esq., and a niece of the former President. Many of the extracts which I shall hereafter introduce, are taken from letters of Mr. Marsh, addressed to her. But besides the agreeable circle into which he was thus drawn, he enjoyed the intimacy of several literary friends, men of the same age and of like spirit with himself, in whose society he found the most constant excitement to intellectual activity. They formed a club, of which I have often heard him speak, as one of the best schools of discipline to which his mind had ever been subjected. They met together, I believe, once a week, for literary discussion, the reading of original pieces, and the criticism of each other's performances. In preparing himself for these meetings, Mr. Marsh was accustomed to lay out his whole strength. The free, unrestrained interchange of thought which was here encouraged, fell in completely with his own views; and the lively debates of the club gave an impulse to his mind, the effects of which were not soon forgotten.

On many accounts, the two years which Mr. Marsh spent as a tutor at Hanover, were among the most memorable of his life, and had the most important influence upon his future character, both as a scholar and a theologian. Perhaps he had employed his time in the best possible manner, to prepare himself for the sphere of action to which he was looking forward, as the ultimate aim of his labors. If, instead of devoting his leisure to more general objects, to the study of ancient and modern learning, to the cultivation of his taste and the discipline of his reasoning powers, he had undertaken to pursue and complete his theological studies, with an impatient zeal to be engaged in the active duties of his profession, he might have accomplished something; though less, I apprehend, than many in the same situation. A man who took nothing for granted, but felt himself bound to know the grounds of every thing he professed to understand and believe, could never have satisfied himself by such a superficial preparation, and must have felt constantly embarrassed by the inadequacy of his own views. As it was, he took the right course for a mind constituted like his; and the result was such as might have been predicted by any one who knew the comprehensiveness of his intellect and the sincerity of his aims.

In the autumn of 1820, Mr. Marsh returned to Andover, for the purpose of completing his professional studies. But before he sat down to his books, he concluded to spend a short time at Cambridge, partly for the sake of social relaxation, and partly for the purpose of becoming better acquainted with the literary advantages of the place. He was aware that this step might be misinterpreted, and expose him to the risk of some jealousy and disapprobation; but, conscious of the uprightness of his motives, he was not to be deterred by any fears of that sort from gratifying so rational a wish. " I hope to learn," he said, " how to defend my religious principles (which, I am more and more

confident, will never differ essentially from those I
have been taught to believe) with more enlarged
views, and on more philosophical grounds, than I
should be able to do with the advantages offered
at Andover." With these advantages, however,
he was well satisfied. At Andover, he found
means and opportunities for prosecuting his theological inquiries as ample as he could desire; and
he intended neither to disparage nor to neglect
them. But he wished to extend his acquaintance
with men as well as books, and with other minds
than those who had been trained in the same
school with himself. From such intercourse he
expected to derive the advantage of which he
speaks above, and thought it would be of importance to him in his future studies.

It was his intention to remain at Cambridge
about two months; but for some reason or other,
he shortened his stay, and was at Andover again
in the middle of November, where he soon found
himself settled completely to his mind. "I would
tell you, he says in a letter of this date, "how
favorably I am situated here. I room with our
old acquaintance, Mr. M., which particular you
will be apt to think not very favorable. But he
being a rough body, I shall be sure, I think, to get
one of the benefits that my Lord Bacon proposeth
from intercourse with friends. For though the
first fruits of friendship be to divide care, and the
second to gain counsel, yet even without these, 'a
man learneth of himself, and bringeth his own
thoughts to light, and whetteth his wits as against

a stone, which itself cuts not.' I board in commons, and room in college ; partly from necessity, but principally from choice. I have begun a very Pythagorical mode of living, and if I devour less beef than my fellows, I hope to devour more books, which I can command better here than any where else."

Mr. Marsh entered upon the work now before him with the zeal of an indefatigable student, but with the seriousness also of one who felt how much was depending on the issue. Writing to a friend, he says : " The commencement here of a permanent system of labor impresses it upon me more strongly than I have ever felt it before, that I am engaging, and at my own risk, in the serious business of life. In a word, I begin to think, as if it were time to be in earnest, and to do with my might what my hands find to do. It is much easier—and I am aware it is much better suited to my inclination—to feel one's self free from responsibility, and at liberty to be governed by the impulse of the moment, than to be a man among men, to form and maintain a character on elevated, uniform and consistent principles. There are many, it is true, whose characters and conduct are uniform and consistent, because they are unconsciously governed by habits, and perhaps principles, impressed upon them from infancy. There are comparatively few who sustain with uniformity a character of their own formation, who *consciously* govern themselves by principles tried and approved at the tribunal of their own reason and

conscience. To form and support a character in this way, on noble and just principles, should and will ensure a more enviable reputation than all the accomplishments and acquirements of mere intellectual greatness."

His private journal, as well as many of the letters he wrote during this period, show how uniformly and how conscientiously he sought to govern himself by these pure principles, and how completely he subordinated the love of learning and the ambition of the scholar, to the higher aims of the christian. In this respect, I am sorry to say, his character was often grossly misapprehended. Many seemed to consider him as a "mere scholar," a man given wholly to books and to speculative inquiries; one in whom the life of religion was smothered by his too much learning, and who could feel no interest or sympathy in any thing except what was purely intellectual. Nothing gave him more pain than to find himself so misunderstood. But he saw no way of correcting the mistake, except by steadfastly pursuing his own course, and leaving it to correct itself. It was for this reason, doubtless, he felt somewhat disappointed at first, in the social privileges at Andover. For the purpose of mutual benefit, he chose to associate with a few whose views of the objects and aims of study seemed most nearly to correspond with his own. These excellent young men, too, fell into the common mistake of considering him as a mere scholar, and he was compelled to feel, he said, that his intercourse and conversation

with them must be nothing more nor less than a continual trial of strength and comparison of intellectual acquirements. This, for a while, gave him great uneasiness. But, as his true character came to be better known by his friends, the unnatural constraint of such sort of intercourse gave way to more cordial feelings; and the friendships which he formed at Andover, were among the most pleasant recollections of his life.

The impression, however, was never wholly removed from the minds of all, that Mr. Marsh was too much given to study, and not sufficiently attentive to other more practical duties. In one respect, this was true. He did feel, I may say, an aversion to every thing that is formal and merely outward in religion. Perhaps he carried his notions on this subject to a fastidious extreme. At any rate, I shall not attempt to defend them. But if the record of his private feeling can be trusted, he was a man who habitually held communion with his heart in secret, and kept an altar there to the living God, whose fires were never suffered to go out. Speaking, in one of his letters, of the means enjoyed for religious improvement at Andover, he says: "Our general intercourse is less familiar than it might and ought to be, in this as in other things; and from what I have told you of my habits, you might suppose that I should derive little assistance from others, in regard to religious feelings. Such has, indeed, been the case; but though far too unfeeling and indifferent, I hope still that I have learned something about the way

5

of life. There are frequent conferences and class meetings; but I have attended few of them, simply because I did not find them profitable. It might be my own fault; but they seemed too formal, and not sufficiently familiar to allow the natural play and expression of feeling. When that is the case, and when there is not some particular cause to raise the general tone of feeling above the restraint of forms, nothing is more profitless to me than the constantly recurring routine of formal assemblies of any kind." It would be wrong to infer, however, from what he has said here, that Mr. Marsh felt an objection to such meetings generally, or thought that they could not be made profitable, even to himself. Soon after this, he speaks of a club or association which was about to be formed, for the purpose of familiar and free conversation on practical religion. "We shall make it an object," he says, "to remove all formality and restraint, as far as possible; and it will become, I hope, a kind of religious *levee*. If so, I have no doubt it may be highly useful in many respects. It will introduce more freedom of intercourse, and, I hope, a higher tone of conversation, both in style and matter, than any thing we have here now. To myself, I hope it will be profitable, by directing my mind more to practical and experimental religion. I confess, too, I have some wish to remove an impression, which, I fear, has been too correct, that I was a mere scholar, and had little regard for any thing but merely speculative inquiries. The impression, in fact, I found, a few weeks since, was so strong, as to justify anxiety on my part to remove it; and I believe I have done so, in a great measure. I have asserted, and must try to prove by example, that diligence in the pursuit of study is compatible with religious feelings. Pray for me, my dear friend, that I may not be deceived, in circumstances which so much expose me to the sophistry of my own heart."

The plan which Mr. Marsh proposed for himself, in resuming his theological course at Andover, was comprehensive, beyond any example which could have come within his own observation; and embraced a more extensive circle of studies, than it would be thought useful or expedient for most men to undertake. It is by no means my wish to hold him up, in this respect, as a model for any one's imitation. The humbler plan, which experience seems to approve, as best adapted, in the majority of cases, to secure the ends of a professional education, is, to lay its foundation deep, rather than broad; and to aim at thoroughness and accuracy in a few things which the profession requires to be well known, rather than at a general and superficial acquaintance with many. But there are some minds which will not be so confined; which are borne onward, by a sort of irrepressible impulse, to extend their energies beyond the absolute demands of their profession; which, in fact, cannot pursue a particular branch of science, without seeking to trace its connexion and its relations with every thing that can be known. Such minds are apt to know their own wants, and

to understand, better than others can tell them,
how to shape their course, so as to fulfil the destiny to which they are appointed, and to effect the
greatest good of which they are capable in their
day and generation.

In a journal, which Mr. Marsh now began for
the purpose of noticing in it the progress of his
daily inquiries, he lays out the course of study
which he meant to pursue, under the following
heads:

"1. A general system of ancient history and
literature, to commence with Hebrew Geography,
Natural History, Chronology; and so to the character, and civil and religious fortunes of the people.

"2. With a view to prepare myself earlier than I
should, for coming to the historical sense of the
New Testament, I begin with the history of the
Jews, at the return from captivity.

"3. I connect, with both these, partially, the
studies in Professor Stuart's department; namely,
the critical study of the Old and New Testament.
The sum and final result of these several courses
will be the right understanding of the doctrines of
the sacred Scriptures, in Dr. Wood's department.
I must, of course, feel myself, at present, very
poorly prepared for these last investigations. So
far as they proceed on the ground of natural religion, I can prosecute them effectually. It will
afford a useful, though severe exercise of abstract
thought; and I shall add to the pleasure of it, by
associating it, as far as practicable, with the his-

tory of natural religion, as it exists in fact in the writings of the pagan philosophers.

"4. In addition to these, I must contrive, if I can procure the means, to pursue modern literature one hour a day." All the studies which he mentions here, if we except the last, were within the sphere of his profession, and strictly conformable to the course at the Seminary. But he pursued them according to his own method, as a voluntary exercise, in addition to the prescribed course of studies, to which at the same time he meant to devote all needful attention. Of his method, as well as of the wide range of his inquiries, I shall have occasion to speak more particularly hereafter. In connexion with these more strictly professional studies, he contrived to find time for acquiring a good knowledge of two or three modern languages, and for investigating to some extent, at the original sources, the history and literature of the middle ages. It may seem difficult to conceive how he could be employed, at one and the same time, in so many different pursuits, without losing himself entirely in the multiplicity of his objects, and defeating his own end, by grasping after so much at once. In his journal, however, he never complains of being distracted or hindered by the variety of his studies; but often takes occasion to notice the evidence of his success. February 21, 1821. He makes the following entry: "Of my progress in the German language, I have been more conscious than ever before, and begin to feel as if I had conquered it. On Saturday in the

forenoon, I read in the regular course of my studies about fifty pages, and read it well.   In Span-
ish, too, I have done something, and shall conquer
it within the year.   My Hebrew I have had some
fears about, but think I shall master it."   The
whole record of this day, which happens to be
more full than usual, furnishes, perhaps, as faithful an account as could be given of the manner in
which he was accustomed to employ his time.

   "At the club on Friday, [this was an association of students, formed chiefly by his own means,
for the familiar discussion of subjects connected
with their studies,] I was rather surprised to find
that though I had devoted but half a day to the
subject, (the Apostolic Fathers,) my knowledge of
them was as good as any one's.   I do not make this
record from vanity, but the fact is to me a proof
of the superiority of my system of study.   The
question was started about the rise of the Gnostic
sects; and as I was not very fully acquainted
with it, spent some time afterwards in looking
into eastern philosophy, in order to trace back
their principles.   Read forty pages in Heeren's
Ideen, respecting the religion of Zoroaster.   He
considers the authenticity of the Zendavesta, as
the record of that system, to be established; and
from the contents of the work, proves the religion
to have been first set up in the Bactro-Median
kingdom, east of the Caspian, at least one hundred years before the reign of Gustasp, or Darius
Hystaspes, in whose reign it is generally thought
Zoroaster lived.   It was transferred to Persia, and

made the court religion of that empire by Cyrus.
I took an abstract of the system, and shall say
no more of it here.

"I have made some progress in Dr. W's. department during the week, and some in the critical
knowledge of the New Testament. I have learnt,
too, how to connect this study more with the cultivation of practical piety, by reflecting carefully
on the subject or the chapter which I have studied,
and applying it directly to my own heart; I may
mention, too, in this place, the fair prospects of
the club noticed in my last record; [this was
another club, and the same that he alludes to in
one of his letters, quoted a few pages back;] the
objects of which I must endeavor to connect somehow systematically with this subject.

"For two or three days my attention has been
principally turned to the Hebrew Sacrifices, the
subject for our club next week. I must try to
write on it, and connect it with the sacrificial rites
of pagan nations.

"To-day spent two hours in reflecting on this
subject, before I rose. In the forenoon, studied
pretty faithfully the six or seven first chapters of
Leviticus, which contain the substance of the
whole matter, and will require yet more thought.
Read several pages in John, and am nearly prepared to mark out the plan of a dissertation.

"Spent an hour on the subject of chronology,
and nearly two hours in reading twice over Horace's Epistle to Augustus, containing 270 lines.
It has much interesting matter, relating to the

tastes of the Romans, the state of literature among
them at that time, and many opinions which are
interesting, as the opinions of Horace. Reading
it again with my pupil [a young gentleman from
Yale College, who had been placed under his care]
will make me master of all that is valuable in it.

" Wrote a letter to my friend B., and read 30
pages of Hallam's dissertation on the state of society in the middle ages. He does not seem to be
acquainted with the opinions of De Stael and
Schlegel ; or if he is, he does not, in my opinion,
give them the right influence in forming his notions
of the human mind in the decline of the Roman
Empire. I learned from him some interesting
facts, about the state of the Latin language in the
provinces. In addition to what I already mentioned, with a view to Gnosticism, I read 10 or 12
pages of Muenscher, who traces it to the emanation system, through the medium of the Jewish
sects."

Mr. Marsh speaks, in the above extract, of his
system of study. He seldom read any authors in
course, but for the most part simply consulted
them on the subjects which interested him, and
aimed to make himself master of their leading
thoughts. By this practice, he acquired a habit of
looking through a book, and seizing its most valuable contents, which surprized those who were not
acquainted with his peculiar method. In reading
an author for the first time, he gave but little
attention to his language, but endeavored to enter
fully into his meaning, and to get at the scope of

his views. After this, he would seek to express
the same thoughts in his own language, and then
compare what he had done with the original. This
was a very frequent exercise with him ; and he
maintained that while it tended gradually to elevate and refine his own style, it gave him a much
clearer perception of the precision and elegance of
the writer's language, than he could obtain in any
other way. He was also accustomed to make
copious abstracts from the more important works
which he studied, and several of these remain
among the fragments of his early writings that
have been preserved. Close thinking, he said,
often superseded, with him, the use of books. It
was in this way he usually prepared himself for the
daily recitations ; and he sometimes found that he
had thus anticipated nearly all that was said, and
moreover, could connect the different subjects together, so as to make a more simple system, than
was practicable with one who read much without
reflection.

With the more dry and scholastic studies of this
period, he was in the habit of intermingling a
lighter kind of reading, particularly poetry. He had
now, in a great measure, lost his admiration of
Byron, and became attached to Wordsworth, and
other poets of the same class. He thought they
breathed more of the true sublimity, the settled
elevation and purity of christian sentiment, than
could be found in many other writers. " There
is in them," he says, in one of his letters, "a
power of thought that enlarges and strengthens the
6

intellectual power, while it elevates the whole soul, and fixes it in calmer seats of moral strength. It is the poetry that, of all, I would prefer to make my habitual study. Nor would I study it as I used to study poetry, but with a direct practical purpose, to nurse my own faculties, to imbibe its spirit, to breathe its purity, and recurring constantly to the Gospel, the still purer fountain from which it derives its characteristic excellencies, to form that exalted character which should be the aim of every christian.

Into the various knowledge which he was thus accumulating, Mr. Marsh strove from the first to introduce a principle of unity, which should reduce it to one harmonious system in his own mind. This effort was no less characteristic of the man than his continued thirst for new acquisitions; and it was the ground of that deep interest which he always felt in philosophical studies. In the early part of his journal, he mentions Dr. Brown's treatise on cause and effect, as a work which he had read, with great attention, and unbounded admiration of the author as an acute and powerful reasoner. "I find myself," he says, "too strongly inclined to admit his theory, independently of the reasoning by which it is supported, from the simplicity which it introduces into all our speculations on the phenomena and powers of nature." Very different was the opinion which he came afterwards to entertain of this writer and his theory. Even now he felt altogether dissatisfied with the old method of the Scotch and English philosophers,

which he thought too formal, cold and barren.
They did not, he said, keep alive the heart in the
head. He wanted something which could meet
more completely all the facts of his own consciousness, and explain the deeper mysteries of his spiritual being. For this reason the writings of St.
Paul seemed to him superior to all worldly philosophy. " I have studied," he says, in his journal,
" the eighth chapter of Romans, with much intensity and much satisfaction. I find the only way
to understand St. Paul is to analyze his argument,
and get at the scope of his thoughts, by close and
profound attention. It is the best introduction to
the only life-giving philosophy, to enter with congenial feelings into those views of man which he
everywhere developes." At this time he was in
the habit of studying a good deal the works of
Coleridge, particularly the " Sketches of his Literary Life and Opinions." With the aid of Coleridge and Madame de Stael, he began, moreover, to
consult Kant's Critique of the Pure Reason, then
a perfect *terra incognita* to American scholars. If
I mention that in addition to this, he undertook to
read through the works of Plato, and make a copious analysis of each dialogue, without meaning to
neglect any of his regular and more appropriate
studies; many, I fear, would be disposed to think
he had altogether overrated his own powers, and
undertaken what he could not possibly perform to
any good purpose. But he thought differently of
it; and in truth, his simple style of living, his
Pythagorical diet, as he termed it, gave him a

great advantage ; so that with clear and definite views as to what he would accomplish, he was enabled to do more than most men would think possible, without either sacrificing his health, or being overburthened and oppressed by the variety of his pursuits.

He had a simple aim in all this. It was, as I have before said, to satisfy the instinctive desire of his mind after unity in all his knowledge. But with this, he was endeavoring, also, to obtain deeper insight into the grounds and nature of that faith, which he felt to be the life of his soul. The real difficulties in those great questions which had been called up in recent controversies, lay deeper, as he conceived, so far as they properly came within the province of speculation, than the parties on either side had as yet reached. He was desirous of searching to the bottom of them, and was willing to undergo all the labor and painful suspense which such an investigation must necessarily involve. The following letter, addressed to the friend of his heart, at Hanover, seems to have been written while he was thus engaged.

Andover, July 1st, 1821.

MY DEAR L. — I rejoice to hear of the more interesting attention to religion on the Plain, and among the students; and am the more ready to make an apology for my own loss of a letter, because, in such a situation, the time that would have been devoted to me, may have been, and, I presume, has been, more profitably employed. For

your heart is engaged, I am aware, more than mine
has been, in this most interesting and important of
all subjects; though I hope you do not think me
wholly indifferent to experimental piety. I trust
I am far from it; though I have, for some time,
been in the habit of contemplating it with perhaps
too much of the coolness of the speculative scholar.
It is the almost unavoidable consequence of devotion to study, and of any thing like a comprehensive view of the vast field which religious controversy now embraces. The simple, unlearned
christian, who knows only his Bible, and daily reads
that with an unquestioning confidence in the more
simple truths which he reads, and which he that
runs may read, may well be, in some respects, the
envy of the puzzled though learned man of books.
He goes on in the even tenor of his way, with his
head at ease, and his heart unmoved, but by the
feelings of penitence and love. He knows nothing
of the ten thousand distracting questions, the har-
rowing doubts and maddening skepticism, that dry
up the heart and seethe in the brain of the unfortunate student, who has ventured to pass the consecrated limit of his traditional faith, and look back
upon it with the cool eye of critical investigation.
Few, indeed, let me assure you, even of those who
undertake, as professional men, to examine and establish the principles of their faith, know any thing
of this. Their principles are, in fact, fully established in their own minds, before they begin to examine them. They will boast, perhaps, of having
dived into the very quagmire of skepticism, and

fathomed its hidden depths; when, if the truth were known, they have probably floated along the surface, or coasted the shores of this mighty deep, in the cock-boat of their own opinionated self-confidence. They see that all below is dark and dreamy; and fancy, like Chateaubriand upon the Dead Sea, they can hear the groans of Sodom and Gomorrah beneath them. No wonder they choose the upper air, and leave unruffled the abyss below. They now see the light, and are resolved to rejoice in it. But wo to the daring and ill-starred adventurer who plunges into the metaphysic depths of controversial theology! Well may he ponder his voyage; for it is little less difficult than that of our great adversary, when he passed

> "the throne
> Of chaos, and his dark pavilion spread
> Wide on the wasteful deep."

He will soon find himself in

> "A gulf, profound as that Serbonian bog
> Betwixt Damiata and Mount Casius old,
> Where armies whole have sunk."

The man, to speak in plain language, who at this day undertakes to settle for himself the various systems of theology, must not only unravel the mysteries of "fate, free-will, foreknowledge absolute, &c., without getting lost in their mazes, but while floundering in an everlasting 'hubbub wild' of ancient learning crazed, and made to dance, like Epicurus' atoms, to the 'harmonious discord' of some German metaphysical bagpipe, he must be careful to keep his balances nicely adjusted, and weigh with statistical accuracy the " hot, cold, moist and dry " of these " embryo atoms." He must meet the theories of the philologist and the theories of the philosopher. He must silence, says one, every whisper of emotion, and let reason teach him. Listen to the heart, says another ; it is the very sanctuary and the oracle of truth. And then, in a situation like mine, how many struggling propensities of the heart withdraw it from the simple feeling of the gospel truth ! The love of popularity and the love of independence, the pride of knowledge and the pride of ignorance, the pride of liberality and the pride of orthodoxy, put up and let down the mind on one side and on the other ; while, to use a figure of Luther, like a drunken man on horseback, it goes plunging and reeling onwards. Truly, a man in such a course, if like Dante he has his Beatrice, or divine love for a guide, may arrive at heaven at last ; but, like Dante, he must do it by first going through hell and purgatory. I do not mean to say that I have any serious doubts in regard to the system of faith which we professed together before the altar ; nor have I quite enough of Cæsar's courage to say that I am rather telling you what is to be feared than what I fear ; for I see difficulties in every system, enough to confound the weakness of human reason. But *this* I know, that such an abstraction from the things of this world, and such a devotion to the things of God and the

things of an invisible future, as are the fruits of
our New England revivals, are most rational in
themselves, and most suitable to the character of
immortal beings. Let us earnestly hope and pray
that the revival will extend through the place and
the college."

It would be wrong, however, to infer from anything he has said in this rather imaginative and
playful letter, that he ever allowed himself to be
so absorbed in these speculations, or carried away
by them, as to forget the humble and docile temper which it became him to cherish, as a disciple
and learner at the feet of his divine Master. " I
may allow myself," he says in his journal, " to
speculate with some boldness on points of dogmati-
cal theology ; I may question—my duty impels me
to question—on what grounds every received article of faith is rested by those who defend it. I may
question the origin and authority of the Scriptures ;
but when I have admitted their divine original, I
have only to ask what they teach. And O may I
ever ask with an honest, humble heart. The
teachings of the divine Jesus I cannot question,
even if I would. I am compelled, after all my
speculations, to bow down to him with most unquestioning submission and confidence. How
much, how very much is contained in the simple
expression of his honest disciple, ' He taught as
one having authority, and not as the Scribes.'
Yes, his instructions have more in them than all
the ingenious speculations of Jewish or Grecian
doctors, and they come with authority from on

high. It is not by bold speculation these are to be learned, or their spirit imbibed. 'He that doeth the will of my Father shall know of the doctrine.' An honest simplicity of heart will lead to the understanding of mysteries which the wise men of this world have not known, even the mysteries of the soul—of love and faith, and hope and trust in God, and that peace that passeth all knowledge. Most fervently would I pray for that poverty of spirit, that meekness and lowliness of mind, that guides to the knowledge and imitation of Christ.

In this spirit of Christian simplicity of heart, combined with the enthusiasm and independence of a true scholar, Mr. Marsh prosecuted and completed his theological education at Andover. Nor should I fail to mention, that he felt, during all this time, the same interest which he ever afterwards continued to manifest, in the great benevolent enterprizes of the day. Thus he says in one of his letters, dated April 14th, 1822: " I am more and more convinced,—indeed, I was convinced long ago,—I *feel* more and more, that whatever is contrary to the highest religious elevation and purity, is not only sinful, but disgraceful. In other words, my philosophy and my habitual feelings coincide more, I trust, with the spirit of religion ; and it is not self-denial, but pleasure to engage in its duties. You may think this a roundabout way of telling you a simple fact ; but in my mind it is not so simple as it may seem. I have thought more than ever, of late, on the great efforts made

7

to evangelize the world, and of the exceeding
desirableness of that great object. It is the cause
of God, and my prayers shall daily ascend for its
prosperity. In one way or another, too, I hope I
may yet do something for a cause so grand, where
it is an honor to add but one stone to the mighty
structure. I know not, and have for myself but
little choice, in what way it may be, whether with
my voice or my pen; but I could not die in peace
without the consciousness of having at least attempted something, as a co-worker with the holy
men, who are honored as the instruments of God
in doing his own glorious work. I have always,
indeed, approved it as the glory of the age, but
have not had my enthusiasm enkindled in regard
to it, as a work in which *I* wish to engage.
Henceforth my voice and my influence, whatever
may be my situation, will, I hope and believe, be
most decidedly on the part of all that is godlike
and benevolent. I am beginning to prepare myself for the active duties of a minister, and am
ready to believe I shall find more pleasure in it
than I have ever done in my studies."

I should mention, that some time during his
last year at Andover, he wrote an article, which
made its appearance in the July number for that
year of the North American Review, and contained the results of his studies for some time past
in the favorite branches of taste and criticism.
It is a review of an Italian work by Gattinara di
Breme, and bears the running title of " Ancient
and Modern Poetry ; " but it was the writer's

design to point out the distinguishing features of modern genius as compared with the ancient; and more particularly to show how much, in the peculiar character of modern art, is due to the influence of Christianity in giving a more spiritual direction to the powers of the human mind. The subject was one upon which he had read extensively, and reflected still more than he had read. This is evident on every page of the essay, which, so far from bearing any of the marks of a new and unpractised hand, might easily be mistaken for the production of a veteran critic. The performance did him great credit in the estimation of all whose good opinion he was most anxious to win.

About the same time, he engaged in another literary enterprize, of somewhat greater moment. In connexion with a friend then residing at the Seminary as a licentiate, he undertook to translate and prepare for the press, the German work of Bellerman, on the Geography of the Scriptures. The great want, which he felt to exist, of a standard work in the English language on this important branch of Biblical learning, rather than any hopes of profit or fame, was his chief inducement in employing himself upon so dry a task ; nor did he desist from it, until, on his part, it was fully completed.

The effect of this intense and continuous application of mind began now, for the first time, to manifest itself upon his health ; and, by the persuasion of his friends, he was induced to throw aside his studies for the present, in order to try the

benefits of a short sea voyage, and of a visit to
the South. He embarked at Boston, on board a
coaster bound for New York, with the intention,
when he arrived there, of shaping his course in the
way that promised to be most agreeable. After
spending a short time among the friends whom he
found in New York, he proceeded to Princeton,
where he arrived in the first days of May, when
nature was in full bloom, and, as he expresses it,
" the air filled with fragrance and with poetry."
Writing from Princeton, he says : " In general, I
find myself, thus far, much better pleased with this
country, than with New England ; partly from the
climate, and partly from the more social character
of the people ; and, were it not for my friends,
might be strongly tempted to forget the land of
my fathers. I am aware that much of the pleasure I now feel, however, is to be attributed to circumstances that are not permanent, and so my estimate may be unfair ; and very probably may be
changed, when I arrive again in our delightful val-
lies. Horace has somewhere said, that change of
place does not change the mind ; but really, I believe he was mistaken, for I find mine changing
with every scene." This journey, which he undertook simply for the restoration of his health,
was the means of introducing him to many new
and valuable friends, some of whom had an important influence in deciding the course of his future
life. It was at Princeton he first became acquainted with that excellent man, the Rev. Dr.

Rice, by whose means he was led, eventually, to direct his steps to Virginia.

Having spent several weeks in this tour to the South, which he extended as far as Philadelphia, he returned home by the way of New Haven. Here he passed some days in the family of the venerable Dr. Morse, who took a strong interest in his behalf, and urged him, after the completion of his professional studies, to establish himself in that town, as the editor of a religious periodical review. This plan, though in the end it issued in nothing, long occupied a place in Mr. Marsh's thoughts; who never wholly relinquished it, indeed, until he had finally concluded to take up his residence at the South. After a short visit to his friends in New Hampshire and Vermont, he was enabled, in June, to resume his studies, which he prosecuted with unabated vigor till the following September, when he left the Seminary, to enter upon the more untried scenes of active life.

To many young men, especially those of a retiring disposition, there is no period of life more trying and full of anxieties and depressions, than that which intervenes between the attainment of a profession and the fixing on a place for settlement in the world. There are some, who seem to fall naturally into their proper position; others are put there by powerful or influential friends. Not a few are left to find it as they can; and the best of these must often struggle the hardest, and toil through many a year of wandering, before they can arrive at the field which Providence has al-

lotted them. This proved to be a long and painful season of suspense to Mr. Marsh. He had
many reasons for wishing to be soon settled in life.
It was a torment to his active mind, to be left
without any definite object; while, moreover, his
outward relations and engagements seemed to urge
upon him the necessity of fixing, with the least
possible delay, upon his sphere of action.

He had looked forward to this necessity with a
sort of shrinking dread; for although conscious
of possessing talents and qualifications which fitted
him for eminent usefulness, yet he had little or no
confidence in himself, as possessing those exterior
advantages which are soonest to strike the eye of
the world; and the very idea of soliciting patron-
age, or subjecting himself, in any way, to a condition of servility or dependence, was most abhor-
rent to all his feelings. Hence, as I have before
observed, he proposed, at first, on leaving his studies at Andover, to live, for a while, on his father's
farm. "It is very essential," he said, in addressing the person most interested in his decision, "it
is very essential to my happiness and usefulness,
to be able to pursue my objects in my own way;
and, with the independence and leisure which I
may hope to secure, I have little doubt that I shall
bring to pass more in five years, than I shall with
the perplexity that is likely to attend any public
employment which is open to me."

The few friends at Andover, to whom he dis-
closed his plans, thought it a romantic scheme,
much fairer in prospect, than it would prove to be

in the actual trial : and assured him, that at all events, he would not be suffered to remain long in his retreat. Some of them believed that he would find reasons for abandoning his plan before he left the Seminary. There appears to have been some ground for this conjecture ; for shortly after, the prospect was held out to him from a quarter where it was not altogether unexpected, of an active employment, quite agreeable to his wishes. An effort had been made, I believe, by his friends at Princeton, to procure him a place as an assistant to Dr. Rice, in the editorship of a theological and literary magazine, to be published at Philadelphia. Assured of the friendship of Dr. Rice, and the favorable opinion which that gentleman entertained of his qualifications to write for a public journal, he thought it not unlikely that he might soon hear from him on the subject. Thus he was "hung up for a while," as he expresses it, "between Philadelphia and the farm, and vibrating with a very irregular motion."

About this time, Dr. Green left the presidential chair of Nassau Hall College, in New Jersey, and Dr. Rice was elected his successor. In a letter to Mr. Marsh from one of his Princeton friends, it is intimated that Professor Lindsey, who was then connected with the same college, might perhaps be chosen to the place left by Dr. Green ; and that, in this case, Mr. Marsh would be strongly recommended to the vacant Professorship. But however that may have been, the unsettled position of his friend Dr. Rice, destroyed all the prospects of Mr. Marsh for the present at the south, and he made up his mind to go home to the farm.

How he employed himself there, I have no means of ascertaining, from his letters or journal: except that a month or two after his return home, he appears to have been engaged on the translation of Bellermann, which he finished in December, having despatched five hundred pages in a fortnight. He was now without an object to detain him at home ; and, harrassed with doubt and perplexity, he at last resolved to throw himself into the scenes of life, where exertion would be called for, and struggle to perform what the providence of God should seem to point out as his duty in the world. So on the 6th of January, 1824, he left his father's house, in compliance, as it would seem, with an invitation from Dr. Rice, and arrived at Princeton in the middle of the same month.

From Princeton he writes home, as follows: "Of my future prospects, I can tell you nothing new at present. Dr. Rice has not declined the presiding here, and the whole matter is yet in a state of uncertainty. Dr. R. was still sick at Hampden Sidney College, three or four weeks since, but was improving, and is probably at Richmond before this. From what I can learn, my business there will be principally with the magazine ; and whether anything permanent is to be expected, here or there, is yet entirely in the dark. But if I gain nothing else, I have an opportunity to try the strength of my own faith and patience, and I hope the occasion will not be lost. If what *is* lost, in worldly prospects, is gained in firmness and consistency of christian character, the loss will be great gain. You see that I am in a serious mood, and look upon life with very sober feelings; but do not think that I am discouraged or unhappy. I trust I have too much philosophy, and above all too much faith, to have my feelings very greatly depressed by any such vicissitudes as may happen to me. If we have still to learn that happiness is not to be sought in worldly prospects, a severe lesson may not be useless."

He proceeded onward to visit Dr. Rice at Richmond, and was received by that noble-hearted man and his excellent lady, with a frank and cordial welcome. The doctor himself was but just recovered from a most distressing and tedious sickness, which had reduced him to the very brink of the grave. Mr. Marsh gives an interesting account of his first appearance in public, before his people, which shows in a most favorable light the amiable character of the man with whom the destinies of his life seemed now about to be connected. " He yesterday attended meeting in the morning; and after service by another (for he was unable to preach), he slowly climbed into the pulpit and appeared to his people, for the first time in public. He alluded in the most impressive manner to his sickness, and in reference to the deep interest and earnest prayer of his people, said, I stand before you as one prayed back from the brink of eternity. The people were all in tears, and I was never more interested than at such an expression of feel-

ing between a pastor and his people, especially
when, trembling with agitation, he leaned upon the
desk, while the whole congregation united in singing the doxology, with tears in their eyes."

In this amiable family, and in the pleasant society of Richmond, Mr. Marsh spent several weeks,
before any thing was decided as to his future employment. "The family," he says, "have treated
me with the greatest friendship, and I feel more
attached to them than I could have believed I
should in so short a time. Their affectionate kindness, indeed, makes me ashamed of my constitu-
tional coldness and reserve; for I can find neither
language nor gestures to make a suitable return
for the attentions which I continually receive.
Mrs. R. especially treats me with the confidence
of a sister; and she seems resolved to think that
the doctor and I shall somehow fall pretty near together, wherever our lot is fixed in the world. He
is now balancing between Princeton and Hampden Sidney; and the strong attraction here keeps
him at present from falling either way. We have
both been struck with the coincidence of our views
and feelings on almost all the important subjects
on which we have conversed; and I know few
things that would be more desirable to me in set-
tling, than to be connected with him. But it will
be hard, I am aware, to break off the ties that
hold us to New England." At length it was decided that Mr. Marsh should go to Hampden Sidney, but with what prospects, or in what capacity,
seems to have been left somewhat doubtful. In

announcing this, Mr. Marsh says, " I have no doubt, though he has not said it in so many words, that Dr. Rice has some view to his own decision in sending me there. The worst circumstances is, that my duty is so undefined, that I shall be in danger of doing nothing to my satisfaction ; but I hope to do some good." The following was his first letter from Hampden Sidney, and is interesting as giving his first impressions of the scene of his future labors.

" *H. S. College, Feb.* 25, 1823.

" I am once more seated in a solitary room, and at leisure to let my thoughts wander at will, at least for a few moments. But they very soon reach the place of their destination, though it is far away. No sooner do I seat myself alone, and look upon the magic characters that are written in the fire, than I feel as if mounted upon " the wondrous horse of brass," and am transported in a moment's time to the fairy land of our own green hills and greener meadows. I can scarcely see, so swift is the motion of the " bridleless steed," the vast regions that vanish behind me, till I reach the little retreat where I have so often wandered. I know when I approach it, by the green hills and mountains ; and even the snow that covers the whole, with its sparkling uniformity, cannot deceive me. The moment I look from the fire, the charm is dissolved. The little naked, whitewashed room, the fireplace without furniture, the face of the country all around, the woolly-headed

servants, and the recollection of many a tedious
mile, remind me that the comforts of a New England *home* are far from me. But I do not mean
to give you a very sad picture of Virginia, lest I
should have occasion to varnish it over again.
But if you should ever be inclined to come here,
I can tell you something of what you will meet
with. You will find the whole household establishment on a most wretched footing. The
houses of the most respectable families in this
country are not so well provided with what we
call conveniences of life, as those of ordinary farm-
ers in New England. Every thing is left to the
servants, and every thing is out of order. But
the Virginians hate trouble, and so concern themselves little about it. They never make any apol-
ogies, but welcome you kindly and heartily to such
as they have. The servants are generally negligent, and a day behind-hand, (a Yankee phrase,)
and a stranger, at first, fares among them but
poorly. Here I live quite in college style; have a
room by myself in friend Cushing's house, and
board with him and three other young gentlemen,
(students,) quite in an old bachelor way. No
woman is connected with the establishment, but a
black cook, in another building. I have a few
Hebrew scholars, and meet with the theological
society of students, and preach occasionally. Dr.
Rice is still deliberating about coming here to
establish a theological seminary. If he comes, as
he probably will, he will wish me to be connected
with him. But whether he will have sufficient

means to support an assistant, and whether, if he does, it will be my duty to make a longer stay here than I contemplated, are questions that I cannot decide at present. We must leave our concerns with Providence, and I pray that I may be prepared to do what that shall direct, with submission, if not with cheerfulness.

" I have found good people here, and am in the room which the good Dr. Hoge occupied as his study. The names of Drury, Lacy, and of Dr. Alexander, are written about the windows and walls. The shadows of many good men, indeed, seem to rise up around me, and exhort me to do with my might what my hands find to do. Pray for me, that I may be a faithful servant of the Lord Jesus."

Mr. Marsh found many friends in the pleasant neighborhood of Hampden Sidney; but the nature of the employment in which he was now engaged, as well as the entire uncertainty of his future prospects, depressed and discouraged him. He expresses these feelings in his next letter. " Good as the people are," he says, " and well as I am treated, I feel myself alone. In a word, I was never made for society. The feelings that might flow spontaneously in solitude with my friends, are chilled, and all powers of sympathy destroyed, by the intercourse of the world. I have not learned, and never can learn, to throw myself into the bustle of society and enjoy the unrestrained intercourse of feelings. Either my heart is not sufficiently susceptible by nature, or I have loaded it too much with the lumber of learning, and kept it mewed up too long in the cell of the student. It has strong and permanent attachments, and I feel their strength now more than ever ; but the lighter spirits that float nearer the surface of the soul, and are ready to flash out on every occasion, are exhausted by the midnight lamp, or more probably were never there. I am sometimes almost resolved to give up this vain attempt to act in public, and devote myself to study, till an opportunity to be useful as a literary man shall present itself. I am satisfied that I shall never do any thing valuable in any other way ; and the attempt only leaves such a feeling of discouragement and dissatisfaction with myself, as makes me unhappy, and in the end unfits me for doing any thing."

The acting in public, to which he alludes above, was preaching ; a duty for which, even under the most favorable circumstances, he never thought himself well calculated ; and which must have been peculiarly irksome and painful in the present depression of his mind. One of his correspondents at Hampden Sidney afterwards good-humoredly alluded to his "attempts" of this sort, and thought them by no means so bad. "The *sinks*," he says, "you used to make at college, are frequently spoken of. This should encourage you to do better, if you still continue to preach, which, I hope, is the case."

Tired, at length, of the suspense and uncertainty, from which he saw no prospect of being very soon relieved, Mr. Marsh determined to abandon all expectations of being usefully employed at the South, and turned his steps towards home, where he arrived some time in the month of May. The little success, which he imagined he had met with in his pulpit essays in Virginia, led him to turn his attention, more seriously than ever, to other fields of exertion; and he now resolved to devote himself to literary labors, provided the way should be opened for his doing it with the prospect of usefulness to his fellow men. He thought he saw an opening of this sort at New Haven, where an editor was wanted for the Christian Spectator. Accordingly, he wrote a letter of inquiry to a friend; and, while waiting for the answer, which was delayed long beyond his hopes, addressed the following consolatory lines to Miss Wheelock, now in Maine, who naturally sympathized in all the trials with which he was himself so perplexed and embarrassed. "There are many things which we look upon as blessings, that are incompatible with each other, from their own nature or ours; and it is very probable that, after comparing what we possess with other things that we wish for, we should find such to be the case with them, and deliberately prefer our present condition. The different parts of our fortune must be consistent with each other; and wealth and worldly prosperity are not often found joined with the meek and patient temper, which I hope we may both cherish and love more than any outward distinctions. 'Let Euphorion (says Bishop Tay-

lor,) live quietly with his old rich wife; and remember, thou canst not have his riches, unless you
have his wife too.' Now, for myself, I know few
with whom I would exchange circumstances, on
the whole, poorly as I think of some of mine. But
the most trying thing to our pride, after all, is, to
admit that we need consolation. The very idea
of it, as of being pitied, is humiliating; and it is
more natural to harden ourselves against disappointment, and take refuge in self-confidence and
pride, than meekly to study wisdom and contentment by such reflections. This is especially the
case, when our fortune seems to depend chiefly
upon ourselves; and to keep one's feelings calm
and unruffled, to be patient and humble, in such
circumstances, is itself a great victory. You will
think, from this style, that I am in very low spirits,
and looking on every side for support; but it is not
the case. I am studying with some diligence;
and hope, as soon as a door of usefulness is opened,
to engage with some zeal and success. In the
mean time, my dear L., let us employ the means
of happiness and usefulness in our power; and, in
whatsoever state we are, therewith be content
ourselves, and diffuse peace and contentment
around us."

The answer from his friend at New Haven at
last arrived, and the prospect, of which he never
had very high notions, proved so much more indefinite and discouraging than he feared, that he immediately wrote to decline any further action under the conditions proposed. It was a great pity

that Mr. Marsh's application, in this case, met with no better success; for no man could have been found, who would have entered with a more genial spirit into the management of such a work; and, undoubtedly, no efforts would have been spared by him, to render it such as he had marked out in his imagination. About this time, some of his friends, without his own knowledge, used their influence to find a place for him at Cambridge; and one or two of the Professors, to whom the subject was mentioned, spoke favorably of the plan. But before any thing definite could be done, the sky began to break in another quarter; and Mr. Marsh was summoned to meet Dr. Rice, whose plans were now matured, and who was recruiting his health at Saratoga Springs. Mr. Marsh lost no time in complying with the invitation of that noble and well-tried friend; and soon wrote back from Troy, with the good spirits of a man who had found, at last, what he had almost learned to give up in despair.

"I met Dr. Rice," he says, "yesterday, in Albany, and have spent part of the day with him and Mrs. Rice, at Dr. Chester's. I find every thing arranged as I had wished; and the course of my own future labors is at last so defined, that I know what I have to do, and can begin to act with a view to a connected and regular plan. I begin to feel, *indeed*, as if the field of my labor was spread before me, and the horrors of suspense and doubt and indecision are losing their hold. My efforts, for the present, will be divided between the College and the Theological School; but the instruction will all be in departments in which I am much interested, and for which I am, perhaps, best qualified."

Before setting his face to the South, however, Mr. Marsh made a journey through the White Hills, to Saco, in Maine, for the purpose of visiting his friend and the destined companion of his labors in the field he was about to visit. From thence he went to Boston, and soon after took passage, in a coaster, for Norfolk, where he arrived safely on the last of November.

The passage was a stormy one; and Mr. Marsh, who was the only person in the cabin free from sickness, found employment enough in taking care of the passengers who were not so well off. Among the rest was a little black-eyed Jewess of fifteen, who spoke and wrote German, Dutch, French and English, and read Hebrew. "You may well suppose," he says, "that I would be a good deal interested in this fine daughter of Abraham, as well from her origin, as her personal character. She seems a very inexperienced and simple girl, though she has been in several of the European capitals, and resided in most of the principal cities in this country. She has been so sick, too, all the way, as scarcely to be able to help herself at all; and, some of the time, could not even hold up her head; so that I was compelled, though, indeed, no compulsion was necessary, in a case of so much helplessness and distress to place myself by her side, and afford all the support and assistance in my power, in the midst of confusion and sometimes of terror." The young Jewess was the only other passenger in the ship, besides himself, bound for Richmond; and when they arrived, introduced her friendly companion and protector to her father's family, and a host of Jewish acquaintances. The next morning, he went to the Synagogue, and was much gratified with the opportunity to witness their religious service. When this was over, "several of the congregation came to me at once," he says, "and spoke to me, and seemed much gratified to have observed that I read the Hebrew with points. Some very interesting looking boys, especially, seemed anxious to talk with me; and I had several quite polite and even pressing invitations to call on them. I am the more pleased, as they, in fact, know little of Hebrew, and seem anxious to learn; and I hope I may be of some service to them." These details are so characteristic of the man, that I could not forbear, though at some risk of being tedious, inserting them in this place.

At Richmond he soon had the pleasure of meeting Dr. Rice and his lady, who arrived from Boston by land, not an hour after himself. Here he had another opportunity of witnessing the strong attachment of the people to their former pastor. "I felt," he says on this occasion, "as if I was too much a stranger, and had too little sympathy with the strong feeling that was expressed. One company had hardly dried their tears, till others of the good doctor's people came in, and some of them sobbed aloud, as they hung upon Dr. and Mrs. Rice, and kissed them. In short we were all very happy to be together in Richmond."

His happiness was not less, when he found himself, at last, quietly settled and engaged in the interesting and important duties of his calling, associated with such a man as Dr. Rice, whose excellent qualities of mind and heart opened more and more upon him, on better acquaintance. "Taking him all in all," he said, "I value his character more than that of any man whom I have yet known, decidedly. He is a great and good man, with the devotion of a primitive saint, and the enthusiasm of a scholar." Thus pleasantly situated, with a definite object before him, and the prospect of more extended usefulness, Mr. Marsh soon regained the vigor and elasticity of mind to which he had been long a stranger, and entered with an ardor which he inspired in all around him, into his cherished but long neglected studies. "I was kept up last night," he says in a letter which he wrote soon after commencing his duties at Hampden Sidney, "till 12 o'clock, by a discussion in a society we have formed here, and which, by the excitement and interest it is producing, reminds me of Hanover more strongly than any thing of the kind I have enjoyed since the days of my tutorship." I cannot forbear to remark here, that the excitement and interest of which he speaks, was a contagion caught from his own mind, and which seldom failed to be spread by his simple, earnest words, whenever he spoke upon any sub-

ject with which his own mind was full. This was
one among many other causes of his great power
and success as a teacher. " I slept but little," he
continues, " and dreamed of 'auld lang syne.'
And I am never more happy, than in that state of
feverish excitement, in which the mind is too
much roused to admit of sleep. I feel then the
superior dignity and worth of mind, too serious
for anything volatile or playful, and my thoughts
fix on great and serious subjects. I feel, too, a
consciousness of intellectual strength, that may
have something of pride mixed with it, but which
still I would not lose, because it prompts me to
worthy enterprizes. You perceive I am getting
my thoughts and feelings aroused here, and acquiring self-confidence once more. I *am* doing so:
and I see here a field of labor, large enough for all
the powers I ever had the vanity to think myself
possessed of." There was but one perplexing difficulty to be encountered, and one which, even to
the candid and liberal mind of Mr. Marsh, ever
ready to make the largest allowance for habits of
thinking and feeling different from his own, seemed insurmountable. " Slavery," he says, " presses
upon this southern country with an intolerable
weight. In whatever direction I turn my thoughts,
to devise plans for the intellectual and moral improvement of the people, slavery and its necessary
accompaniments stare me in the face, and mock
me with the fruitlessness of my efforts. The simple and obvious fact, that men who have from fifty
to a hundred slaves, must have large plantations to

support them, and must consequently live scattered at a distance from each other, presents, of itself, insuperable difficulties in the way of any high degree of cultivation."

The particular employment of Mr. Marsh, in his connexion both with the college and with the theological school, was the teaching of languages; but he meant by no means to confine himself to that comparatively limited sphere. Some of his friends were anxious that he should preach; and were at a loss to see why so good a talker might not talk in the pulpit as well as elsewhere. But he looked upon the matter in a different light. "I have," he says, "an unconquerable inclination to a course of thinking, and habits of mind, which are almost or quite incompatible with preaching; and in following which, I hope to be more useful than I could ever hope to be as a public speaker. Every man who can wield a pen and write to the purpose, and who sees the state and prospects of this country, ought to feel himself called on to use it in the promotion of moral principles and right views of religious and moral improvement. Shall I tell you,—I would aim, if I could hope to produce even a little effect, to influence the views of intelligent men, and rouse all who have the capacity, to something of enthusiasm in promoting the solid and permanent moral interests and the highest happiness of this free and happy country, to wipe away the dark stain of slavery, and become, in the language of Milton, the soberest, wisest, and most christian people of these latter days."

In the theological school especially, to the establishment of which Dr. Rice had consecrated his life, Mr. Marsh took the deepest interest, as an institution most intimately connected with all those objects which he thought it most desirable to promote. But like the great and good man who had given himself wholly to it, he was for placing it on the broadest foundation, and for having it devoted to no other interest than simply Christ and the church. "What is wanted here," he said, " is a school as free as possible from sectarian feelings, with liberal plans, and primitive zeal and devotion. I most sincerely desire that such an one may be built up; and could I be useful in accomplishing it, would do almost any thing in my power to do, but shall never sacrifice my independence of opinion, or labor upon the paltry littleness of any human system."

It was with this school Mr. Marsh expected to be ultimately connected as Professor of the Oriental languages. This was the wish of Dr. Rice; and the presbytery who had the oversight of the Institution, cordially concurred in it. As the funds, however, did not at present suffice for the full support of a Professor in that department, Mr. Marsh was solicited to remain for a time on a somewhat different footing, but which would make him sure of an adequate support. Every thing seemed now prepared for his permanent settlement in life. Accordingly, in the summer of 1824, he set out on his return to New England, for the purpose of being married, and making such other arrangements as were suited to his present plans.

Instead of taking the direct route and travelling in the speediest way, Mr. Marsh chose to improve this opportunity to visit, at his leisure, whatever was most remarkable and interesting in the State which he had now adopted as his own. Accordingly he started on horseback, and directed his course towards the West. I have heard him speak of this journey as one of the most pleasant and interesting he ever made. He saw much that was new in men and manners, as well as in the face of nature, and tried life in some of its strangest forms. One night he reached, almost dead with fatigue, the log-hut of a German widow, near the highest point of the Capen mountains. The sons were out hunting bears; but the old lady said she never turned any body away, and it was five miles to another house. " So," says he, " I waited upon myself, or, in the woman's dialect, ' gave some truck to my critter,' and after a frugal supper of apples and milk, climbed the ladder, and went to bed, among all sorts of lumber and all kinds of four-footed beasts and creeping things." The garret, however, he observes, was well aired, and he could see, as they revolved around, all the hosts of heaven. At another time, he passed the Sabbath in the family of an old Scotch Presbyterian, who possessed all the strong peculiarities of his race, and with his broad accent spent nearly

the whole day in giving him his light on many
passages of the Bible. He had lived there, in
the very heart of the Alleghany, for thirty years,
with very few neighbors, and those mostly ignorant Germans ; and when a stranger called upon
him who seemed able to receive the light, he
felt himself called upon to let it shine for the
benefit of the world. His wife was from the
neighborhood of Washington, with the manners
and education of a lady. Our traveller marvelled
somewhat, and was very much interested to meet
with such a family in that mountainous wilderness. At Brownsville, on the banks of the Mo-
nongahela, he visited his brother, who had been
settled there for several years ; and the three hundred miles which he had travelled on horseback
having fully satisfied his inclination, he now sold
his horse, and performed the rest of the journey
by the way of Lake Erie, and down the canal to
Albany.

As soon as he had arrived among his friends at
the north, he received the notice of his appointment to a Professorship in Hampden Sidney College. At Hanover, on the 12th of October, he
was ordained to the sacred office of a christian
minister ; on the 14th was married, and immediately thereupon set out with his wife for their new
home, which they reached in health and safety, on
the 30th of the same month. While at the north,
some of his friends had predicted that he would
not be suffered to remain long out of New England. He smiled at the well meant compliment ;

10

but saw no reason to complain of his lot, or to suppose that it might be changed. The department assigned to him in the college, was not the one he would be likely to have chosen for himself. He was conscious of being better fitted for another sphere. In the knowledge of languages, it is true, both ancient and modern, his attainments were extensive; but he had studied them rather for his own use, than with any view or expectation of teaching them to others. To the minute accuracy of a well trained grammatical scholar, he made little pretension; perhaps his habits would never have allowed him to become a great proficient in that branch of learning. But his idea of what constitutes a philologist was both just and adequate; and, as it now seemed evidently to be the design of Providence that this should be the business of his life, he set himself earnestly to the task of preparing himself thoroughly for his duties, gathering around him for this purpose, all the means he could find at hand, and sending abroad for such necessary books as he could not obtain nearer home. At the same time he exerted himself to excite a greater interest in classical studies, and to correct the popular notion, which had already crept into some of the schools of learning, that such studies are useless, and ought no longer to have a place in our systems of education. On this subject his opinion was very decided; and it may not be out of place to insert here, some of the views which he shortly afterwards embodied in an able article published in the Christian Spectator. "It

is not merely," he maintained, " as forming habits
of mind, the benefits of which are to be afterwards
enjoyed, that the employment of months and years
in the study of language is to be defended. It
must, from the nature of the case, be the most direct and effectual method, if faithfully pursued, of
developing our own minds, and hastening our intellectual growth. This will be the result, to some
extent, whatever language be the object of attention, if it be studied critically, and its principles
fully comprehended. But for the purposes of general instruction, it is our duty to employ, as the
instruments of cultivation, those languages which
exhibit the most regular and the most perfect developement of the human mind. In making ourselves masters of these, as contained in their clas-
sic authors, * * we do indeed appropriate to ourselves the intellectual treasures of many generations. In the organization of a language, philo-
sophically contemplated and understood, we have
the human mind itself, as it were, exhibited to our
view in its complex and diversified operations. In
studying a language like the Greek, containing a
regular structure and systematic developement
from its own radical forms, we trace the gradual
and progressive evolutions of thought ; we follow
the mind in the history of its advancement ; and
often in investigating the derivative forms of a single root, and observing the relations and transitions
of thought which they exhibit, we obtain views
and secure a knowledge of the human mind, of
more interest to the philosopher than the history

of an Oriental dynasty." While thus laboring to
promote a spirit of classical learning in the College, he did not forget the other duties which de-
volved on him, in his connexion with the Theological School. He made it a point to read every
day a portion of Hebrew, and he began to study
the Aramaic and Syriac languages. He now commenced also the translation of Herder's Spirit of
Hebrew Poetry, the first parts of which were published in several successive numbers of the Christian Repository at Princeton. At the same time
he kept up an active literary correspondence with
scholars, both at the north and the south, and with
some of our missionaries among the Indians, from
whom he drew much curious information respecting the forms and structure of the languages
spoken by those southern tribes.

From first to last, Mr. Marsh was connected
with Hampden Sidney College about three years;
a time hardly sufficient to enable him fully to realize any of his plans. But when he was called,
as he so soon was, into another field, he left behind
him an impression of his competency to fulfil the
highest expectations of his friends; and during
that short period, many young minds took from him
a direction which decided their characters for life,
as was long afterwards, in several cases, gratefully
acknowledged.

In October, 1826, Mr. Marsh was appointed
President of the University in his native State. It
was not the first time he had been thought of, as
a suitable person to fill that responsible office. As

early as 1821, while a theological student at Andover, he had been consulted about becoming a
candidate for the place, which happened then to
be vacant. But, by the advice of his friends, he
prudently declined making any positive engagement; and such, indeed, was the condition of the
college, and so uncertain were its prospects, that
the corporation proceeded no farther, on that occasion, than to appoint a temporary head; leaving it
in the power of the faculty to suspend, at any moment they pleased, the course of public instruction.
The affairs of the college were now in a somewhat better condition. Since the time I have just
spoken of, the old college edifice, it is true, had
been destroyed by fire; but this misfortune, which
was already, in a measure, repaired by the erection
of new buildings, had been the means of calling
forth an expression of public sympathy which au-
gured well, inasmuch as it evinced the interest still
felt in the State for the preservation of its oldest
institution of learning. In other respects, however, there was not much that could be considered
very hopeful or inviting. The students were few
in number; the funds not wholly free from embar-
rassment; the library and apparatus a mere name;
and besides, an impression seemed to prevail with
many, that an institution doomed to so many
strange calamities, was never destined to succeed,
and had better be given up by its friends.

All these circumstances were well known to Mr.
Marsh; nor had he failed to measure his own
strength, and to consider how far he was prepared

to contend with such difficulties. The situation, as he states in his journal, was not one for which he supposed himself, in all respects, best qualified. But he thought that, on the whole, the way of his duty was clear, and resolved to undertake the responsible trust, hoping, as he expressed it, that, by the Divine assistance, he should be able to conform his habits to the duties required of him, and to act with energy and effect. To re-establish in the public confidence and favor an institution which seemed on the very verge of extinction, appeared to him an object worthy of his highest efforts; and he saw, moreover, an opportunity, the most favorable that could be desired, for introducing such improvements in the system of discipline and instruction, as were called for by the wants of the age. This was the great business to which he first directed his energies; and no sooner was the faculty reorganized, than he brought it forward as a matter for thoughtful inquiry and earnest discussion.

I need not say that, on the whole subject of education, Mr. Marsh's views were liberal and enlarged. It would be out of place for me here to enter into a full exposition of his opinions on the collegiate systems of this country. He had studied them faithfully, and compared them with those of the old world. I shall content myself with a brief statement of what he considered to be the chief defects in the prevailing systems, and of the means by which he thought these defects might be at least partially remedied, without any wide

departure from the spirit and essential character of
our institutions.

It was his opinion, that in our colleges generally, the rules for the admission of students were
too limited and inflexible. Admitting the principle, he said, in its fullest sense, that the business
of education is to develope the mind, and to make
it conscious of its own powers; and that a certain
course of studies must be insisted on, as, on the
whole, best adapted to this end; yet, why exclude
any who may be unfortunately prevented from embracing the whole of this course, from the privilege of taking that part of it which lies within
their means? There seemed to him to be no good
reason for this. The best system, he maintained,
is, after all, but partial in its effect; it cannot give
a full developement to every capacity of the mind,
nor fit it alike for all the various pursuits of life.
Why, then, in aiming exclusively at an object
which is in itself unattainable, forget others which
also have their importance? It is better to have
a partial education, than none at all; it is better
to get this at a college, furnished with ample and
liberal means of instruction, than at inferior schools,
where no such means are enjoyed. So he rea-
soned; and he believed that the evils, which, it
might be feared, would result from thus extending
the privileges of collegiate instruction, were either
imaginary or could easily be obviated. There was
no necessity implied in it of lowering the standard
of education, or of encouraging young men to pur-

sue a partial course, whose circumstances allowed
them to do more.

He was also for allowing considerable more lat-
itude to the native inclinations and tendencies of
different minds. It was absurd to expect every
young mind to develope itself in just the same
way; and equally absurd to confine each one to
the same kind and quantity of study, as if it were
possible for all to receive alike. Wherever a right
tendency appeared, he thought it should be encouraged, and allowed the freest room to unfold itself;
and that to set up any particular system of study
as an absolute law, from which there could be no
departure, was to forget the true business of education, and sometimes the surest way to frustrate
its end. But the independence for which he contended was not an unlimited one. He would still
have a regular, systematic course of studies for the
general guidance; and as this would be adapted to
the average wants of the students, all might be
required to conform to it, without preventing or
discouraging any who might be disposed to push
their studies in other directions, to whatever extent they pleased.

He thought the methods of instruction in use
too formal and inefficient. There was not enough
of actual teaching, and too much importance was
attached to text-books. He wanted to see more
constant and familiar intercourse between the
mind of teacher and learner. The student, he
held, should be required, not merely to exercise
his talents in apprehending the ideas of others,

but should have his mind brought in contact with those of his instructers, and his own powers of thought and judgment invigorated and sharpened by competition with theirs. In his opinion, there was a want of free and familiar discussion, and of such actual trial of the scholar's powers, as would give him the habit of applying them with promptitude and effect, and impart that knowledge of one's own resources, which is so important in the business of life.

In regard to morals and formation of character, he did not consider that to be necessarily the best system which secures the most minute and strict observance of college rules, or even of the external requisitions of morality; but that which most effectually unfolds and exercises correct principles of action in the mind of the individual scholar. The virtue which is practised from a love of it, he said, and from the dictates of a growing moral principle, is of more value than that which proceeds from a fear of college censures. The one affords permanent security for the future character of the individual; the other may leave him exposed to temptation, which he has no means of resisting, the moment he ceases to feel his accustomed restraints. And the same principle he would apply to every department of intellectual cultivation. The mind, he said, whose powers, by whatever course of study, are thoroughly awakened and exercised in the proper manner, is prepared to act with promptitude in every emergency, and can readily acquire the particular

11

knowledge necessary in the peculiar circumstances in which it may be placed. The scholar, for example, who has successfully cultivated his reasoning powers, and accustomed himself to the independent exercise of his own judgment in the use of them, will be able to reason correctly, whether at the bar or in the senate ; but he who has merely learned Euclid without studying for himself and putting in practice the principles of reasoning, may be lost the moment he traverses beyond the book, and in the practical duties of life, may show himself a dunce. To develope and cherish, then, those great principles which are to form the character of the student in his intercourse with the world, to call into vigorous and habitual exercise those powers which are the elements of all intellectual power, and to do this by employing, as the means, departments of knowledge which will in themselves be of the greatest practical utility, he considered to be the true aim of education, which ought never to be lost sight of in a minute attention to less important matters.

Many evils, as he conceived, were connected with the mechanical system at present adopted in the classification of students ; and he thought it in the highest degree desirable to fix upon some method which should pay more respect to the real abilities and attainments of scholars, and which would allow them to pass from one division to another, according to the degree of proficiency or promise which they actually manifested. But he was fully aware of the practical difficulties which must attend every plan of this sort which could be proposed ; and therefore never urged this point, except as one that he rather wished than ever expected to see fully accomplished. In a word, he thought the whole collegiate system of study, as existing in this country, too much of a mechanical routine, wherein each individual who had taken the prescribed number of steps and gone through all the forms, might be sure of his degree in the arts at the end of the course ; it mattered little whether he had been idle or industrious. The mere formal examinations which were then deemed sufficient at many of the colleges, appeared to him to be, on the whole, rather worse than useless. Examinations rightly conducted, on the other hand, he considered of the utmost importance, both as furnishing a powerful incentive to study, and a very fair means of determining the real attainments and merit of the scholar.

The improvements he proposed may be briefly summed up under the following heads : First, as to the rules for the admission of students, he would have them so modified as to extend the privileges of collegiate instruction, under certain regulations, to those whose necessities would limit them to a part only of the general course. Secondly, as to the system of discipline, he would have a mode of government more entirely parental, and more exclusively confined to the exertion of moral and social influence, and where this failed, would prefer simply to exclude the unworthy individual from the enjoyment of his privileges. Thirdly, as to the

method of instruction, he would have it uniformly
directed in all its branches to the ultimate result
of a full and manly developement of the individual,
without thwarting or coercing the native tendencies of his mind.   Fourthly, as to the system of
classification or subdivision, he would have it such
as at least to encourage those who showed themselves able and disposed to do more than accomplish the prescribed course, to pursue other additional studies under the advice and direction of the
faculty.   Fifthly, he proposed to have all designa-
tions of rank and of scholarship proceed on the
absolute instead of the relative merit of the student, and to be determined on a close examination,
by appropriate marks, to be recorded at the end
of each year.

These views and opinions, which I have taken
partly from my own recollections and partly from
the original paper submitted by Mr. Marsh to the
corporation of the University, were after being
fully discussed by the faculty and by that body,
adopted as the ground-work of a change in the
whole system of the institution, afterwards made
known to the public in a pamphlet drawn up by direction of the faculty, and entitled "An Exposition
of the Course of Instruction and Discipline in the
University of Vermont."   The pamphlet was sent
to such as it was thought would be likely to take
an interest in the subject of which it treated.
Several of the Presidents and Professors connected
with other colleges in New England, were pleased
to express their approbation of the main features

in the plan, and thought there could be little doubt that the experiment would ultimately prove a successful one. As to its actual success, it may be remarked, that the system has thus far fulfilled every reasonable expectation of its friends; though it must be allowed, that, owing to various circumstances, it has been unavoidably subjected to some essential modifications.

Having accomplished this object, in effecting which, I may observe, he had the cordial co-operation of his fellow officers in the faculty, and having thus established his character as an enterprising and efficient President, Mr. Marsh now turned his attention to other matters, more immediately connected with his favorite pursuits. From the first, he had been accustomed to take an active part in the business of instruction. The department to which he chiefly confined himself in teaching, was intellectual and moral philosophy, the same which afterwards became his more exclusive field of labor. Philosophy was with him a far more comprehensive, more deeply seated and vital interest, than many seem willing to regard it. It had occupied his most earnest thoughts, ever since he could call himself a student; and on all the important questions and principles which it embraces, he had already attained to a clear knowledge, both of what the human mind had done, and what still remained to be accomplished. The problem which now interested him, and to which he chiefly directed his inquiries and meditations, was to fix definitely the true and only legitimate method of scientific in-

quiry; such a method as would involve in its own
very nature the necessity of progress, and which
would vindicate the result to which it led, by being
one and identical with the constitution of the human intellect itself. To the want of this, he
thought, might be attributed most of the errors and
deficiences of the prevailing systems. He felt it
to be the first duty which he owed to those whom
he was to guide in the study of philosophy, to take
care that they should receive no direction from
him which he had not ascertained, to his own satisfaction, to be the way prescribed by reason and
truth. But the clear and conscious knowledge of
a truly philosophical method, not merely in its general outlines, but in all its wide details and applications, as it is one of the most important, so it is
one of the most difficult, and therefore slowest
attainments of a meditative mind. It was not till
after many years, that Mr. Marsh succeeded in so
far realizing his object as to be quite satisfied —
not with his leading principles, for these had long
been well settled in his mind — but with the entire form of his system, as containing within itself
the unity of an organic whole.

Early in the year 1828, an event occurred in his
family which diverted his attention entirely from
these matters, and for many months engrossed all
his feelings and thoughts. This was the sickness
of his wife; which, gradually assuming a more
and more threatening character, at length took the
form of a settled decline, and resulted in her death
on the 18th of August, in the same year. Thus

were his hopes of happiness cut off, as he remarks
in his journal, in the only place where he expected
to find it — the domestic circle. They had been
connected in marriage a little less than four years;
their hearts had been united for a much longer
period. The pure and devoted attachment of Mr.
Marsh to this excellent woman shone mildly forth
in all their intercourse with each other, while together, and remains embalmed, I may say, in an
enduring form, for his friends, in the letters he
wrote her from Andover and from the south;
letters in which the warmth of true affection is expressed with a noble simplicity, as it gushes unconsciously from the depth of christian principles.
This was the first of his domestic calamities, and
on this account, if no other, doubtless the most
severe of all he was ever called to experience.
But he was enabled to endure it with christian for-
titude and resignation.

As soon as he had recovered from the first shock
of this heavy affliction, he returned to his studies,
with a determination to turn them to some practical account; and the following year of his life was
one of uncommon activity. During the next winter and the spring of 1829, he published, in the
Vermont Chronicle, a series of papers, signed
" Philopolis," on the subject of popular education.
He also wrote, for the Christian Spectator, a long
and elaborate review of Professor Stuart's Commentary on Hebrews. This article, which contains the germ of some of those thoughts the writer afterwards more fully unfolded, is chiefly val-

uable on account of the clear and distinct manner
in which he has defined the particular province
and pointed out the true use of grammatical interpretation, as applied to the Scriptures. "The
Jews," he says, "had no need of learned criticism
and a large apparatus of antiquarian lore, to understand the words of our Saviour or of Paul. They
required but the ordinary exercise of the understanding; and if they did not discern the deep
spiritual import of the words addressed to them, it
was because they were earthly minded, and had
not the Spirit. Now it is the precise and appropriate aim of such criticism as that of Professor
Stuart, to give us the same advantages which they
enjoyed; to place us in the same relative condition
for apprehending spiritual truths, in which they
were placed. It is to clear away the *incidental*
obstacles to our right discernment, that the principles and the apparatus of criticism are employed.
The duty of the critical and grammatical inter-
preter is, to show us precisely and definitely the
notions which a writer's words must naturally have
conveyed to the understanding of those to whom
they were addressed. It is simply to accomplish
this, that it becomes necessary to investigate the
laws and usus loquendi of the language employed;
and so fully to occupy our minds with all that was
peculiar and important in the habit and condition
of the people addressed and of the writer, as to be
able, as it were, to see with their eyes and hear
with their ears. If the critic enables us to do this,
or, having done it himself, gives us, with clearness

and fidelity, the result of his labors, it will then depend, as in the case of the Jews, upon the state of our own spiritual being, how far we shall apprehend the things of the Spirit." Speaking of the prejudice which existed against this sort of learning, since it had been abused in Germany to the purposes of infidelity, he goes on to remark that "we have more fear of injury to the cause of religion from the influence of superficial modes and systems of philosophizing, than from the principles of criticism. It is the surreptitious introduction of false philosophy alone, that gives any just ground to fear the results of interpretation; and to this we are exposed far more in the application of criticism without principles, than of that which is guided by the laws of language and the principles of right reason. It is, in short, the evil heart of unbelief, that we have reason to fear, as the perverter and misinterpreter of the truth. Free us from this, and we fear not the dangers of critical inquiry. We are of the number of those who believe that, in the legitimate and conscientious employment of our understandings and rational powers, we are bound to follow truth with our whole hearts; and that in so doing, even though we might not attain it, we could not be at war with it. If we thus study the word of God with an humble and believing spirit, the more largely and deeply we explore it, the richer will be our harvest of truth and righteousness. If, in following after, we still obey the truth, we can never be led astray. The law in the conscience bears wit-

12

ness to the thunderings of Mount Sinai, as the voice of God. That which he has revealed in his word, can in no case be at variance with what he has written in our hearts. It may be *at war* with our *passions* and selfish purposes; it may be above the comprehension of our understandings; but it cannot *contradict* the unbribed and unequivocal voice of reason."

Simple and true as all this may now seem, it was strange language for the time in which it was uttered; and placed the right interpretation of Scripture on far different and higher grounds, than what had commonly been contended for. Instead of making it to rest, ultimately, on certain ingenious rules of human invention, as if the living truth of God's word could be determined and settled by such fallible means alone, he insisted upon the necessity, also, of a coincidence between what is in our own spirit, and what God has revealed in his word; and maintained, that there is no light which can guide us to a right and full understanding of the Scriptures, except that which first shines in our own hearts. So, in another place, he says: "Wherever the subject treated is of a spiritual nature, we must have, in addition to all these outward helps, the exercise and developement of the corresponding spiritual acts and affections in our own consciousness. How is it possible, otherwise, for us to understand the words, or to refer them to the things designated? We may have a notion of their effects and relations; but the words, in this case, mean more than these; and more must be

known, before the meaning of the writer can be
fully apprehended. We must sit at the feet of our
divine Master, and learn of him, and obey his
commands, before we can know of his doctrine,
before we can fully understand or believe in the
name of Jesus." In a word, the prevailing doctrine of the day was, Understand, and then believe; while that which Mr. Marsh would set forth,
not as any thing new, but as the old doctrine of
the church from the earliest times, was, Believe,
that ye may understand. Fides enim debet præ-
cedere intellectum, ut sit intellectus fidei premium.
"Such views," he adds, "may not, indeed, be
learned from the superficial philosophy of the Pa-
leian and Caledonian schools; but the higher and
more spiritual philosophy of the great English divines of the seventeenth century abundantly teaches
them, both by precept and by practice." For these
old English divines, he entertained the highest regard and deepest veneration. He had already determined in his own mind, when he wrote the
above, to publish a selection from their best pieces,
with an introduction and occasional notes of illustration. Such a work, he hoped, might contribute
somewhat to diffuse a better taste than seemed
generally to prevail, with regard to religious books,
and to direct the attention, especially of young
men, to the almost forgotten "treasures of ancient
wisdom." About this time, he received a copy of
Coleridge's "Aids to Reflection;" and was struck,
not so much with the coincidence of that author's
views with his own, as with the adaptedness of the

work to the very end which he had himself proposed. With Coleridge's other writings, he had,
as I have before intimated, been long familiar, and
esteemed him highly, both as a profound metaphysician and the highest English master for clearness
and precision of philosophical language. It was
with no small delight, he now saw the genius of
that remarkable man employed to illustrate one of
his own favorite authors; and the opportunity
which thus offered itself, of introducing both Leighton and Coleridge to the American public, was
one, he thought, which ought not to be neglected.

Coleridge was known on this side the Atlantic,
chiefly as a metaphysician and a poet. His " Lay
Sermons" might have led a few curious readers to
suspect that he sometimes ventured also on the
discussion of theological questions; but these productions were generally regarded, I imagine, as
having more of a political than a religious bearing.
The only work of his that had as yet been published, in this country, was his " Literary Life and
Opinions;" and from this work many gathered
that the writer belonged to that eccentric class of
transcendental philosophers, with the deep mystery
of whose metaphysical doctrines no man of sense
would think it worth his while to perplex himself.
In short, " Coleridge's Metaphysics" had become
a sort of bye-word for something pre-eminently
obscure and unintelligible. To set up such a writer as a guide to serious reflection, on the most
important of all subjects, and to secure for him
that respect and confidence, without which no

author can be read to any profitable purpose,
might have been justly considered a presumptuous
undertaking, had it been attempted by any man
without that deep insight into the aim of the
work, and that clear conviction of its power to
work its own way into notice, if but once fairly
brought before the public, which Mr. Marsh possessed. As it was, we may well suppose, he had
some misgivings of his own ; for besides the prejudice mentioned above, there was another to be
encountered, of still greater magnitude, in the ob-
stinacy of long established opinions, of opinions
"unassailable even by the remembrance of a
doubt." Earnest reflection upon ourselves and
the laws of our inward being, would lead us to
feel, according to Mr. Coleridge, the utter incom-
patibility of the system of philosophy commonly
received, with the doctrines of a spiritual religion,
and even with our own necessary convictions. We
should see the necessity of taking other grounds,
and of resorting to other distinctions than any to
be found in the popular system of the day, in order
satisfactorily to account for some of the most common facts of our consciousness, as well as to reconcile faith with reason, and thus justify the ways of
God to man. The tendency of his work was,
therefore, to undermine the only foundation which
many a favorite theory had to build upon, in recent days, both in metaphysics and theology.
There was some hazard in attempting to push into
public notice, a work which so boldly attacked the
system which, as to its leading principles, was

adopted in this country by a sort of tacit consent, as the only true philosophy of the human mind. Mr. Marsh felt this to be so. "In the minds of our religious community especially," he says, " some of its important doctrines have become associated with names justly loved and revered among ourselves, and so connected with all our theological views of religion, that one can hardly hope to question their validity without hazarding his reputation, not only for orthodoxy, but even for common sense. To controvert, for example, the prevailing doctrine with regard to the freedom of the will, the sources of our knowledge, the nature of the understanding as containing the controlling principles of our whole being, and the universality of the law of cause and effect, even in connection with the arguments and the authority of the most powerful intellect of the age, may even now be worse than in vain."

But besides his own conviction of the goodness of his cause, there was one other consideration which encouraged him to proceed with his undertaking : " I have reasons for believing," he says, " there are some among us, and that their number is fast increasing, who are willing to revise their opinions on these subjects, and who will contemplate the views presented in this work, with a liberal and something of a prepared feeling of curiosity. The difficulties in which men find themselves involved by the received doctrines on these subjects, in their most anxious efforts to explain and defend the doctrines of spiritual religion, have led many to suspect that there must be some lurking error in the premises. It is not that these principles lead us to *mysteries* which we cannot comprehend ; they are found, or believed at least by many, to involve us in absurdities which we can comprehend.

In regard to the number of this class who were dissatisfied with the prevailing theories, and who were prepared to listen, with somewhat more than a feeling of curiosity, to views professedly drawn from a deeper insight into human nature, Mr. Marsh had not deceived himself. It might be said to comprise every earnest and reflecting mind not already committed to some system. The time, indeed, was quite ready for the appearance of such a work ; it was only necessary to secure for it a favorable impression, and to fix the attention of thinking men upon the real points of interest, the important doctrines and distinctions it aimed to set forth.

These were the objects which Mr. Marsh had in view in writing his " Preliminary Essay,"—a befitting introduction to the noble work which it recommends, designed more especially, in the first instance, for the purpose of making an application of the doctrines therein contained, " to opinions and discussions (then) prevailing among ourselves," but conceived in so large a spirit, and with such a grasp of the whole field of inquiry, embracing as it does questions of the deepest and most enduring interest, as might well challenge for it the attention of this or any other age.

I shall here quote a considerably long passage from this valuable performance, as serving to show better than any thing that could be said, the thoughtful and considerate manner in which he went about his undertaking, and the mingled hopes and fears with which he looked forward to its result. " In republishing the work in this country," he says, " I could wish that it might be received by all for whose instruction it was designed, simply as a didactic work, on its own merits and without controversy. I must not, however, be supposed ignorant of its bearing upon those questions which have so often been, and still are, the prevailing topics of theological controversy among us. It was indeed incumbent on me, before inviting the attention of the religious community to the work, to consider its relation to existing opinions, and its probable influence on the progress of truth. This I have done with as severe thought as I am capable of bestowing on any subject, and I trust, too, with no want of deference and conscientious regard to the feelings and opinions of others. I have not attempted to disguise from myself, nor do I wish to disguise from the readers of the work, the inconsistency of some of its leading principles with much that is taught and received in our theological circles. Should it gain much of the public attention in any way, it will become, as it ought to do, an object of special and deep interest to all who would contend for the truth and labor to establish it upon a permanent basis. I venture to assure such, even those of

them who are most capable of comprehending the
philosophical grounds of truth in our speculative
systems of theology, that, in its relation to this
whole subject, they will find it to be a work of
great depth and power, and, whether right or
wrong, eminently deserving of their attention. It
is not to be supposed that all who read, or even
all who comprehend it, will be convinced of the
soundness of its views, or be prepared to abandon
those which they have long considered essential
to the truth. To those whose understandings by
long habit have become limited in their powers of
apprehension, and, as it were, identified with certain *schemes* of doctrine, certain *modes* of contemplating all that pertains to religious truth, it may
appear novel, strange, and unintelligible, or even
dangerous in its tendency, and be to them an occasion of offence. But I have no fear that any earnest or single-hearted lover of the truth as it is in
Jesus, who will free his mind from the idols of
preconceived opinion, and give himself time and
opportunity to understand the work by such reflection as the nature of the subject renders unavoidable, will find in it any cause of offence or any
source of alarm. If the work become the occasion
of controversy at all, I should expect it from those
who, instead of *reflecting* deeply upon the first
principles of truth in their own reason and conscience, and in the word of God, are more accustomed to *speculate*—that is, from premises given
or assumed, but considered unquestionable, as the
constituted point of observation, to look abroad
13

upon the whole field of their intellectual visions,
and *thence* to decide upon the true form and dimensions of all which meets their view. To such
I would say, with deference, that the merits of
this work cannot be determined by the merely
relative aspect of its doctrines, as seen from the
high ground of any prevailing metaphysical or theological system. Those, on the contrary, who
will seek to comprehend it by reflection, to learn
the true meaning of the whole and of all its parts,
by retiring into their own minds, and finding there
the true point of observation for each, will not be
in haste to question the truth or the tendency of
its principles. I make these remarks because I
am anxious, as far as may be, to anticipate the
causeless fears of all who earnestly pray and labor
for the promotion of the truth, and to preclude
that unprofitable controversy that might arise from
hasty or prejudiced views of a work like this. At
the same time I should be far from deprecating
any discussion which might tend to unfold more
fully the principles which it teaches, or to exhibit
more distinctly its true bearing upon the interests
of theological science and of spiritual religion. It
is to promote this object, indeed, that I am induced, in the remarks which follow, to offer some
of my own thoughts on these subjects, imperfect I
am well aware, and such as, for that reason as
well as others, worldly prudence might require
me to suppress. If, however, I may induce reflecting men, and those who are engaged in theological inquiries especially, to indulge a suspicion

that all truth which it is important for them to know is not contained in the systems of doctrine usually taught, and that this work *may be* worthy of their serious and reflecting perusal, my chief object will be accomplished." From some particular expressions, as well as from the general tenor of these remarks, it would seem as if the writer supposed that the publication might possibly be an occasion of engaging him in controversy. Though he deprecated this, he did not dread it. Had he been called forth by a worthy antagonist in defence of his author's views, on any important topic, he would doubtless have obeyed the summons, and we might have seen, under the excitement of dispute, a still more masterly exposition than any he has given, of what he considered the only true spiritual philosophy.

The able manner in which he acquitted himself, in this case, of his undertaking, established his reputation as a good scholar and profound metaphysician, both at home and abroad. But what was of more consequence in his own view, since he had been induced to engage in the enterprize out of no regard to himself, but from the simple love of truth and the strong interest he felt in the spread of sounder principles of philosophy, was to see the work producing its silent but sure effect. Though no notice was taken of it, so far as I remember, in the more important periodical journals, it met with a rapid sale, and found readers among all classes and sects. If all did not approve the doctrines it taught, few could deny

the great moral and intellectual power which it
every where exhibited. There were some professed scholars, indeed, men of elegant taste and
clear understandings, rather than of deep and earnest thought, who affected a sort of contempt for
such obscure speculations, which they looked upon
as useless, if not wholly unintelligible. Others
there were who seriously doubted whether the
introduction into practical religion of habits of
thinking so metaphysical and abstract, could well
consist with fervent piety and a zeal to do good;
while a few believed that some of the doctrines
advanced were erroneous in themselves and dangerous in their tendency. But far greater was the
number of those who thought that by this timely
publication, good service had been done to the
cause of religion and of true philosophy; and
many were the letters of congratulation and of
inquiry which Mr. Marsh received on this occasion
from various parts of the land. In a word, the
interest excited by the work went quite beyond
the modest expectations of its editor, and he flattered himself that the good effected by it would
be not less extensive.*

* Soon after the publication of the Aids to Reflection, Mr.
Marsh received the degree of Doctor of Divinity from Columbia
College in the city of New York. In 1833, the same honor was
conferred on him by Amherst College in Massachusetts. Partly
for confirmation of what I have said above, and partly for the sake
of the valuable remarks they contain, which I should be sorry to
have lost, I have introduced into this note a few extracts from various letters, received by Mr. Marsh on this occasion. The excellent writers, whose names I withhold, will pardon the freedom I
take, in consideration of my motives. 1. " I thank you very sin-

Mr. Marsh sent his edition of the "Aids" to Coleridge, accompanied with a letter, which I shall

cerely for your kindness in sending me a copy of ' Aids to Reflection.' I have delayed writing, till I should have read the book. And it is, I must say, with no ordinary interest I have read it. In the first place, the author, or as he oddly enough calls himself, the editor, exhibits everywhere a mind of mighty grasp. The conceptions and reasonings of such a mind, cannot but make a strong impression. Though occasionally eccentric, I cannot look at them without pleasure, nor seriously attend to them without profit. I love once in a while to be roused by something new. Secondly, the author's taste is congenial with mine, as to the old English writers. Leighton has for many years been as favorite an author with me as with Coleridge. The same of the other English books he refers to, so far as I have read them. And I wish most heartily, that our young men, especially young ministers, might form their taste and their habits of thinking on the model of the old authors, rather than those of a modern date. I could name some ten or a dozen old writers that I would not give up, for all that have lived the last two or three generations. Thirdly, Coleridge goes much farther than I expected he would, in maintaining what I consider fundamental principles, as to the christian religion. Most of his practical views — I mean his views of the nature of Christian piety and of the Christian life, seem to me scriptural and excellent; and I have fewer objections to make to his doctrinal opinions, than I supposed I should have when I read your preface. And this fact leads me to think, either that you have somehow misapprehended the prevailing sentiment of the orthodox in New England, or else that I differ from them more than I am aware. As to many things which Coleridge asserts on the philosophy of religion, (if I am so happy as to understand him) I hold the same; though it would seem that both you and he regard those things as at war with what Calvinists believe. But in some of these cases, he appears to me to have adopted a mode of thinking and writing, which makes plain things obscure, and easy things difficult. I am able, if I mistake not, to take some doctrines, which he holds forth, or rather covers up, with hard, abstruse and almost unintelligible phraseology, and to express them in language which shall carry them to the mind of every enlightened Christian and philosopher with perfect clearness. Now I acknowledge it is a good thing to make men *think*, yea, and to *compel* insert in the Appendix.   To this letter he never received any answer; but the state of the author's

them to it, if that is necessary. But it would be a serious question, whether this can be most effectually done by investing moral and philosophical subjects in obscurity, — or by covering them with light. For myself, I wish as little of abstruseness and unintelligibleness in books as may be. I am conscious of too much of this in regard to many, if not most subjects, as they lie in my own mind; and I am always glad to find myself relieved by luminous thoughts and luminous language in others." — 2. " Your remarks in the Introduction to Aids to Reflection, are deemed by some rather heretical, and they even have been quoted, on the other side, as proofs, that there is a declension from the stiffness of former days. But on one great point, that of human *power*, — so essentially connected with the sense of accountableness, — I have, for some years, been inclined to adopt what I suppose are also your own views, — and have occasionally given such instruction to the senior class; that is, have stated, that motives are not efficient causes; and therefore a volition is not accounted for by ascribing it to motives; — a *determiner* must be found; and that determiner, unless some other spirit, is our own spirit. Our own mind is the originator, the cause. Here is power; and we could have no idea of power in God, unless we first found it in ourselves. The denial of this, makes God the universal agent — and comes to Spinozism in fact — destroying the sense of responsibleness." — 3. " As Columbia College has at the late commencement added your name to its list of honorary graduates, you may perhaps read with some interest the discourse which you will receive with this letter. Permit me, at the same time that I request your acceptance of the pamphlet, to express to you the very great gratification which I have received from your preface and notes to your reprint of Coleridge. He is an author to whom I owe much in the formation of my opinions, and whom I have always regarded with a sort of affection. You have double claim upon the thanks of the American public, as well for making known to them so excellent a work, as for adding to its value and utility by your own exposition of his object and meaning." — 4. " Will you pardon the liberty, which, though a stranger, I take in asking of you the favor of a letter to Mr. Coleridge in England. The Aids to Reflection, which you have been the means of bringing before the American public, have excited in me a strong desire to see their author. The

health, taken in connection with his well-known
carelessness about his own productions, sufficiently
accounted, perhaps, for this seeming neglect. It
is the concurrent testimony of all the Americans
who subsequently visited Coleridge, and of whom
I have had an opportunity to inquire, that he never
expressed himself otherwise than as gratified with
what had been done for the spread of his writings
on this side the Atlantic. From the most intimate
friends of that excellent man, from Mr. Henry
Nelson Coleridge, Mr. Gillman and Dr. Green,
Mr. Marsh received many letters, expressing how
highly his labors were appreciated ; and, as farther
proof of this, his essay was prefixed, by Coleridge's nephew and executor, to the last London
edition of the Aids, in 1839. I have thought it
right, for reasons which it is not necessary now to
state, to introduce several of these letters in the
Appendix to this Memoir.

The first American edition of the Aids to Reflection was published in November, 1829; and
was followed, in May, 1830, by the first volume of
" Selections from the old English writers on Practical Theology ;" a work which did not meet with

views which he presents, and which are so happily sustained in
your introduction, are views, many of which I have held some
years; and I cannot but hope that their promulgation, under such
auspices, is destined, in this country at least, to effect a new era
in Moral and Metaphysical Philosophy." — To these extracts from
letters of eminent men, in church and state, many others might be
added of the like kind and import ; but these are enough to show
the impression which was produced by the work through which
the subject of this memoir first became generally known to the
public as an author.

sufficient success to encourage the editor to proceed with the undertaking. After all that has
been said in praise of the solid and sterling qualities peculiar to the eminent divines of those earlier times, every attempt, I believe, to give them
general currency, at least in this country, has
proved rather a failure. The craving of the present age seems to be after aliment of a different
sort, lighter and more easily digestible; but whether
better adapted to promote the growth and developement of a truly spiritual life, each must judge
for himself from his own experience. The tracts
published by Mr. Marsh were, Howe's " Blessedness of the Righteous," and Bates' " Four Last
Things." He thought of the former, that " for
depth of insight, combined with practical efficiency
in its appeals to the heart, it was at least one of
the best things in the language." But there were
now other matters which claimed and engrossed
his whole attention.

He had, by this time, succeeded in furnishing
himself with most of the helps which he thought
it necessary to have around him, in order to the
successful prosecution of his philosophical studies.
He had also formed a new marriage connexion,
with the sister of his former wife; and the breach
in his domestic circle being thus happily repaired,
he would have felt himself more at liberty, than at
any previous time, for his favorite pursuits, had it
not been for the discouraging condition of things
in the college whose interests were confided to his
care. It was a remark he dropped in one of

his letters to a friend, and I have heard him repeat the same myself, that "during the great part of his life, he had found himself chained in situations where he felt paralyzed in the exertion of his powers, and vainly longed for freedom." This casual expression gave utterance to a feeling, which those who knew him and his circumstances will best know how to appreciate. Nothing could be more foreign from the native gentleness of his spirit, as well as from the christian principles by which he habitually governed himself, than the indulgence of any thing like a fretful, impatient temper. He meant simply to state what was indeed most true, in regard to his experience of life, that outward circumstances were generally against him; and the aspirations of his mind, instead of being quickened and encouraged by what did not depend on himself, met with constant checks and occasions of diversion. He was sensible of a certain incongruity between the situation in which he was placed and the kind of duties to which he was called, and the decided inclination and bent of his intellectual energies. Hence he accounted for it, that so little had been done by him, compared with what he might have accomplished, in a situation more favorable for the realizing of his own plans and wishes.

There was no time, perhaps, when he had a more painful sense of this, than at the present juncture of affairs in the University. When he took the presidential chair, it was with no expectation of being called upon to perform any thing

14

beyond the common duties of the station. For
these, he felt himself competent; and so indeed
he was. In the business of instruction, no man
could excel him; and the deep paternal interest
which he felt for the right developement of the
young minds that came under his care, gave an
influence to his advice, and an authority to his
government, most salutary and effectual. For the
details of business, for financial concerns, and
whatever else belongs to the outward relations of
a college, he did not think, himself, that he was so
well fitted. These were matters with which he
always chose to have as little to do as possible.

But a crisis had now arrived in the affairs of the
University, which seemed to call for this sort of
activity in its presiding officer, more than for any
other. The revolution which had been effected
in the system of studies and of discipline, while it
added to the respectability of the institution
abroad, left it to struggle, with narrow means, under the many disadvantages of a new experiment.
The number of students, instead of being increased
by the change which opened the doors to a class
of young men never before permitted to share in
the advantages of collegiate instruction, on the
whole, rather diminished. Every thing had been
done that could be, to place the institution on the
best footing, as to its internal concerns and arrangements; nothing remained but to satisfy the
public, on which it depended for its support, that
the advantages secured and offered were worth enjoying. Dr. Marsh was clearly convinced of the

necessity of this course ; he saw no other way left, of bringing the system, upon which so much labor had been bestowed, to the test of a fair experiment, and thus securing the prosperity of the institution whose interests he had identified with his own. But without disparagement of his character, whose excellence lay in quite another direction it may be said that neither he nor his friends had any confidence in his qualifications for a business of this sort. His friends doubted whether their president could enter with any comfort to himself, or any reasonable prospect of success, on the formidable undertaking which the present emergency seemed to require. These doubts were not held back, and they were responded to with equal frankness and good feeling on the part of the president. It was a matter, he said, which had long lain with weight on his own mind, whether he was in the situation best suited to the habits of his mind, or for the realization of those objects which he had most at heart. He had little doubt that he might employ his energies with greater satisfaction to himself and usefulness to the world, in a sphere that would allow more opportunity and scope for the free action of his mind in its own chosen direction. The details of business were occupying all his time, and unfitting him for those higher pursuits, which, if he might judge by his own experience and feelings, constituted the true business of his life. The duties of the presidency had become irksome to him, and he was anxious to be relieved from its burthensome honors. As an effort was about to be made for the pecuniary relief of the college, he wished to take that opportunity of leaving his place, with a view either to assume the duties of a professor, or to retire from public life altogether.

To the latter of these propositions, no friend of his or of the institution, which was so indebted to him for its substantial worth and character, could listen for a moment. At the same time, it could hardly be expected of him to take a step perhaps without a precedent, and seemingly risk his character for firmness and self-respect, by voluntarily assuming a lower station in the institution over which he had once presided. Of any ordinary man this could not be expected. But Dr. Marsh was exempt from that vulgar pride which is always ready to sacrifice to a miserable self-esteem the sense of duty and the highest apparent good. With a true greatness of soul, which few men ever possessed or exhibited in an equal degree, in relinquishing his place as president, he determined to comply with the earnest wishes of his friends, and still retain his connexion with the university. Had he done the former without the latter, it would have been looked upon as a very ordinary transaction. But by simply changing his relations, while he showed a noble disregard to himself, he consulted the best interests of the institution, which was looking to his decision. Let it not be understood by any thing here said, that Dr. Marsh was not considered by those who best knew him an excellent president. On the contrary, he was eminently qualified for his station in every most important respect. It was a peculiar crisis in the affairs of the college, which alone, in his own view and that of others, justified the change and led him to take a step that created at first, as was to be expected, some surprise and wonder ; but as soon as the whole truth was known, gained for him on all sides that heartfelt respect and esteem, which in the end are sure to be awarded to a great action.

This event of his life I find recorded in his diary, with a few remarks, expressed with characteristic modesty : " During the year 1833 a change took place in my public relations, which must not be wholly unnoticed in this faithful, though so often interrupted journal. I had never considered myself so well qualified for the office which I had previously held, as for some other station ; and this feeling was expressed in this journal at the time of my entering upon its duties. It brought me in contact with the world more than suited my taste, and required a kind of action for which, indeed, I was unqualified, and for which it was fighting against nature to qualify myself. The institution was undoubtedly, as things were, suffering at the time from the want of more active exertion to avail ourselves of the position which we had gained in the confidence of the public in respect to our course of instruction and internal management. As the best method, therefore, of meeting all the wants of the institution, I withdrew from the presidency and took the chair of Moral and Intellectual

Philosophy, using my influence to bring in Mr.
Wheeler in the place which I had before occupied."

In the course of the same year, 1833, he found
time to complete and publish in two volumes
12mo. the work of Herder on the " Spirit of Hebrew Poetry." The first dialogues were transla-
ted while he was at Hampden Sidney, and given
to the public, as I have already mentioned, in the
Christian Repository. This work of Herder's,
although considered one of his best performances,
and ranking as a classical and standard production
among his countrymen, has never attained, I believe, to any great degree of popularity among ourselves. It contains many bold opinions, and novel
interpretations of scripture, quite at variance with
the more sober views, and as I think, more correct
taste, that prevails in our own religious community.
Dr. Marsh was disposed, at first, to qualify some
of the more objectionable passages, by means of
accompanying notes, but he soon gave up that
plan. " My belief is," he says, " that such is the
character and spirit of the work, taken as a whole,
as to give it an influence highly beneficial to the
cause of truth and of sound Biblical learning among
us, if only it be read in the spirit that dictated it,
and to correct in the general result, whatever individual errors of opinion it may contain." So he
left it to stand or fall on its own merits.

The important change in his public relations,
which freed him from those responsibilities and
disturbing cares of business, he had found to be so

incompatible with a continuous and proper devotion of his mind to the subjects which chiefly interested him, was not followed immediately by the result which he and his friends had anticipated. He found himself assailed by doubts, which he could not at once entirely overcome, whether the step he had taken would be rightly interpreted by all; whether he had paid sufficient respect to the feelings and interests of his family; whether, after all, he could properly remain with an institution whose prosperity might seem to some to be connected with the fact of his leaving the presidency; and by other scruples of the like nature. These preyed upon his mind for a time, and unfitted him even for his favorite studies. In itself, the change was most desirable to him; he felt it a relief to be quit of those tiresome honors, which he had not coveted before they were conferred, nor for their own sake cared for afterwards. But he felt that his character was of some consequence; and had a dread of being thought weak, in doing what no weak man, no man without a moral courage like his own, would ever have ventured to do. But these feelings gradually wore away; and vanished entirely, when it became evident that his motives were every where rightly appreciated, and that none were disposed to view his conduct in any other light than one which reflected honor on himself, and confirmed the propriety of his decision in so important a matter. The four or five succeeding years were devoted by him, almost without interruption, to a course of laborious study, in

which, as he says in his journal, it was his grand
object to prepare himself, by reading and reflection, for taking a comprehensive view of all the
parts of knowledge, as constituting a connected
and organic whole, and to understand the relations
and relative importance of the several parts. "This
systematic view," he observes, "being once clearly attained, I cannot but think, it will be comparatively easy to write instructively, and to develope
the truth, in various departments of learning, with
reference to fixed principles."

He has here expressed what were indeed the
leading aims of his whole life — scire ut ædificat,
scire ut ædificetur — but aims to which the short
remainder of it was devoted, with a more exclusive and continuous attention. This would be a
proper place to exhibit to my readers some account
of the method which he pursued in his inquiries, as
well as of the system of philosophy out of which
it grew, or in which it resulted ; but the contracted limits of my plan will not allow me to enter into any copious detail. From his familiarity with
the writings of Coleridge, and the high respect
which he ever felt and expressed for Coleridge's
authority in matters of this sort, it has been hastily
inferred that he was no more than a disciple of
that great master. It would be a mistake, however, to suppose that the opinions of Dr. Marsh
were taken up immediately from any particular
author or school. Submission to the authority of
great names was something wholly alien from the
character of his mind : although no man was more

modest in the estimation of his own powers, or more ready to confess his obligations, in all cases where he had been benefitted by others. It may be said of him with greater justice than of many who have laid far higher claims to originality, that his system was the result of his own profound meditation, and one to which he was irresistibly led, in endeavoring to construct for himself a consistent and connected whole, out of the materials of his knowledge. He acted upon his own maxim, laid down at the beginning of the "Preliminary Essay," that "it is by self-inspection only, we can discover the principle of unity and consistency, which reason instinctively seeks after, which shall reduce to a harmonious system all our views of truth and being, and destitute of which, all the knowledge that comes to us from without, is fragmentary, and in its relation to our highest interests as rational beings, the patch-work of vanity.

In seeking for this principle of unity within himself, he became early convinced, even from the first, that the ultimate views of truth and grounds of conviction could be placed no where within the domain of sense or of the speculative understanding. The distinct and appropriate offices of these powers, the one to present the mere elements of knowledge, the other to limit and define, to generalize and arrange, precluded, in his view, the possibility of arriving by their means at the ultimate ground of all knowledge and reality. The senses furnish us with nothing but the phenomenal aspects of being, in their inconstant, fluctuating

15

and endless variety. The human understanding, an important instrument, but not a source of knowledge, can do no more than to analyze and combine, under the form of conceptions, what has thus been presented ; and the highest unity it can arrive at by this process, is but a generalization of particulars, an abstraction, which may again be analyzed and recombined without end. Giving up the search for a principle of unity in this direction, he found himself forbidden again, in the depth of his moral convictions, to rest in the conclusions of the mere speculative reason. The unity thus arrived at, or rather assumed in the first place, as a necessary hypothesis to a consistent scientific whole of knowledge, betrayed its radical defect, by confounding the Creator with his creatures ; and thus conflicting with the demands of our moral being. It might please the mere man of intellect, led on by no other interest than an aimless thirst for knowledge, but must ever fail to satisfy the still deeper wants of the spirit, when but once fully awakened to a sense of what it needs. Both as a philosopher and as a christian, Dr. Marsh felt that the ultimate ground of truth must also be a living ground. The soul, as a living and life-giving principle, could not be satisfied with abstractions, nor its hollow cravings be stilled with unsubstantial shadows and barren formulas.

The great question with him was not alone what is truth ? but, what is that which imparts to truth its living reality ; which connects knowing with being ; and in the clear perception and contemplation of which, the whole aggregate of our knowledge begins to reduce itself to the form, not merely of a systematic, but of an organic unity? He would find this no where but in the mysterious union of the contemplative and the moral, of freedom and necessity, in the self-consciousness of the spirit; in that act of freedom by which the spirit affirms the reality of its own being, and in this sees the ground of its knowledge of all else that is real. The will, the moral part of our being, is here placed in supremacy, the practical raised in honor above the merely contemplative; but at the same time, both are in one, in the being of the spirit itself.

It would be wholly foreign from my object, even if it were in my power, to go at large into all the explanations which might be deemed necessary for the elucidation of this point, so fundamental in that system of philosophy, which, for the sake of distinction, has sometimes been called the spiritual, and which Dr. Marsh not merely advocated, but, so to speak, identified with all his habits of mind. I will observe, however, that, according to this view, no living and actual knowledge can be arrived at simply by speculation. The man must become what he knows; he must make his knowledge one with his own being; and in his power to do this, joined with the infinite capacity of his spirit, lies the possibility of his endless progress.

This was the kind of progress which Dr. Marsh consciously aimed at, in all his studies; and hence the wide scope and liberality of his method. Hence the fearlessness with which he pushed on his inquiries far beyond the limits of ordinary speculation, safe in his fundamental position, that nothing could be true for him which was contradicted by " the interests and necessities of his moral being." Hence the discriminating judgment which he always evinced in his choice of books and of authors; the course of his reading being invariably directed with a view to the great end which he never lost sight of, the developement of his own spiritual being. With respect to the fortunes and fates of different philosophical sects, he had but little curiosity. I doubt if he ever read a single author, merely for the purpose of gratifying an idle wish to know what opinions he entertained, and what influence he exerted on his particular age. The only interest which he felt was for the truth, ever one and the same, under all its different manifestations; and when he had found an author who showed marks of deep and earnest thought, he used him, not as a transient companion, but as a bosom friend, to consult and hold communion with on all fit and necessary occasions. Few persons, I apprehend, ever studied the two master spirits of the Grecian philosophy with a deeper insight into their meaning, or a keener perception and relish of their respective excellencies. Plato was his favorite author, whom he always kept near him. With some of the works of Aristotle, particularly his Treatise on the Soul, and his Metaphysics, he was scarcely less familiar. Of the old English writers on philosophical subjects, I need not say that his knowledge was most intimate and thorough.

But his reading and reflection were by no means confined to matters strictly philosophical. He took a deep and lively interest in the discoveries of modern science, particularly in all those which have contributed to throw more light on the great processes and agencies of nature, through the whole of her vast domain. In all these discoveries, truly deserving to be called such, he saw the tendency of science to dismiss the material conceptions hitherto so prevalent, and to become more dynamic. The contemplation of nature, as presenting an ascending series of distinguishable powers, acting by laws correlative to ideas contained potentially in our own minds, and thus serving to reveal what is within us to ourselves, was one on which he delighted to dwell, as leading to the most intelligible view "of the relation of our finite spirits to nature on the one hand, and to *the* spirit, as their own proper element, on the other." He has given us some of his views on this subject in the letter on the Will, which I have inserted in the present volume.

The zeal with which he labored, however, in the true vocation of the scholar, striving continually to turn his knowledge to account as a means of self-developement, did not lead him to forget or to overlook the duty which required him to employ his powers also for the benefit of others. He had a strong desire to be useful, and studied diligently to know how he might use his talents and

acquisitions so as best to subserve, in his own
proper sphere, the glory of God and the good of
mankind. Several works, of more or less importance, were projected by him in the course of his
public life, and some of them partially executed.
Two of these deserve to be mentioned, since he
had bestowed on them considerable thought, and
never wholly given up the purpose, which in regard to one of them was publicly announced, of
sending them before the world. The first was a
system of logic, the plan of which he drew up as
early as 1832, or earlier. It was to follow, in its
general divisions and arrangement of matter, the
German work of Fries on the same subject.* The
" novelties in terminology necessary to a thoroughly scientific system " seems, from one of his
letters, to have been what chiefly delayed him in
the execution of this work. He was waiting,
moreover, in hopes of deriving some assistance in
respect to language from Coleridge's promised
"Elements of Discourse." Dr. Marsh has left
nothing in manuscript on this subject except a
free translation of Fries' work, which he seems to
have made a sort of preparatory exercise to his
own. The other work which he had in contemplation, but never found time to execute, was a
treatise on Psychology. The few chapters on this
subject, contained in the present volume, were
written without any view to publication, for the
use of the classes which he instructed in that department of science.

* See Dr. Follen's Letter in the Appendix.

To these labors he was prompted simply by the interest he took in the cause of education, and by his desire to supply, so far as lay in his power, a defect which he conceived to exist in the common text-books, relating to those important parts of intellectual discipline. The same wish to be useful wherever he could, led him sometimes to engage in still humbler services in literature, and he thought himself not unworthily employed in translating and preparing for the press the little German work of Hedgewisch on the elements of chronology. But these matters, however important in their place, had no other interest for him but as they were connected with the business of education, and subsidiary to higher ends. His more serious thoughts were habitually directed to the great truths and studies which belong especially to man's moral and religious nature. The knowl-edge of ourselves, of that which constitutes our distinctive humanity, and of our relations to that higher world which is the proper home of our spirits, was in his view the science of sciences, without which all the rest would be without a basis and without meaning. The position of Cole-ridge, that the Christian faith is the perfection of human intelligence, was one which he adopted from the fullest conviction of its truth. Hence, instead of making the distinction which many do, between faith and philosophy, as if they were at irreconcilable war with each other, as if it were impossible for the same individual to have them both together, but the possession of the one neces-

sarily implied the abandonment of the other, he
held it to be our duty as Christians, " to *think* as
well as to act rationally, and to see that our convictions of truth rest on grounds of right reason."
"What is not rational in theology," he maintained, " is of course irrational, and cannot be of
the household of faith." Not that reason is competent to teach us the peculiar doctrines of Christian revelation. This certainly lies altogether beyond its province. Not that it can give us those
experiences or states of being which constitute
experimental or spiritual religion. These rest
on other grounds. But neither the doctrines nor
experiences of true religion can contradict the
clear convictions of right reason. He thought it
a point of great moment, and well worthy of consideration, that it is not the method of the genuine
philosopher to separate his philosophy and religion,
and, adapting his principles independently in each,
leave them to be reconciled or not, as the case
may be. A thinking man "has, and can have
rationally, but one system, in which his philosophy
becomes religious, and his religion philosophical."

It is no part of my design to speak at any length
of Dr. Marsh's religious creed, which indeed dif-
fered in no essential respect from that professed
and taught by the early reformers; but I may observe that the points on which he insisted with
peculiar earnestness, as being immediately connected with the feeling of responsibleness, and
with right views of moral evil, and as most liable,
at the present day, to be perverted, were those of

the freedom of the will, and of human dependence. As to the former, his views are well-known. In regard to the latter, he said that he could not conceive of a more irrational dogma, or more contradictory to the inward experience of the Christian, or one that involves more inconvenient consequences, than that which teaches the existence of a *self-regenerative* power, and places the seat of moral evil *out of the will.* The whole seemed to him to be mistaking and misrepresenting the great fact on which Christianity itself is based, as the antecedent ground of its necessity,—the fact of original sin. "Those writers and teachers," he said, "who think in this way to make the subject more clear, do in fact so lean to their own understanding as to insist on comprehending it in a sense in which it is incomprehensible, and of course misconceive it to the extent of making it no sin at all. Hence, of necessity, if consistent, they must also misconceive the doctrine of redemption, and indeed make both the disease and the remedy a very superficial affair, and very *easily understood.*"

On the point last mentioned, the doctrine of redemption, he had the misfortune to find that his views, owing perhaps to the different position from which he was accustomed to look at the subject, were very frequently misapprehended. Those with whom he conversed on this point were apt to take partial statements, which could not be understood without a knowledge of the whole system to which they pertained, and give them an

16

undue importance. Thus, when, in speaking of
the atonement, he confessed his ignorance of the
objective nature of the work, he was sometimes
understood as denying the doctrine altogether ;
than which nothing could be farther from his
thoughts. Alluding in one of his letters to a conversation of this sort, in which his views appear to
have been perversely misapprehended, he says :
" I did not deny even the vicarious nature of
Christ's death. I held it to be *essential* to the
work of redemption ; but as to the precise relations of it, and the mode in which it is effective to
that end, I could not dogmatize as confidently as
many others are prepared to do." There is a remark of his on this point, which he made in his
last illness, and which is quoted in the discourse
preached at his funeral by President Wheeler, so
beautiful and pertinent that I cannot forbear to
transcribe it in this place : " If I speculated on
this subject," said he, " it was only to place it
within the necessary limits of systematic contemplation. I never dreamed of removing a single
feature of light or shade from it as it stands, and
must stand, to the common faith, and for the common salvation, of all believers. And what I may
have said or think, no more impairs its use for the
purposes of spiritual life, peace and joy, to myself
and others, than the analysis, which the chemist
makes of water, destroys it for common use."

Once he received a letter from a divine of some
note, with whom he had corresponded on this
topic, in which the writer, after lamenting the per-

version of his great learning and talents, charitably
quoted, as applicable to his case, some of the most
pointed texts of Scripture about " philosophy and
vain deceit," "profane babblings," "making ship-
wreck of the faith," and other passages of like
import. What reply he made to that individual,
or whether he ever made any, I have no means of
knowing ; but he observed in general, with regard
to those who were so fond of misrepresenting him,
" Whether I or *they* lean more to our own understanding, and trust more in human wisdom and
philosophy falsely so called, is not perhaps for me
to decide. If I were disposed to controversy, it
would, I suppose, be very easy for me to make a
noise in the great Babel ; but they make enough
without my help."

So far was he, indeed, from being in any sense
carried away by his philosophy from the Christian
faith, that it was from the religious point of view,
and by the Christian standard, he was accustomed to judge of the character, bearing, and influence of everything that came under his notice,
whether in the religious, political or literary world.
Without enlarging on this, I will simply introduce
here an extract from one of his letters to a valued
correspondent, in which he touches upon the current literature of the day. " How little," he says,
" of the literature that falls in the way of young
people, and of that which is most fascinating, is
what we could wish in this respect, (viz. its religious influence.) The works and life of Sir Walter
Scott leave the reader, to say the least, indifferent

to religious principle ; those of Charles Lamb are certainly no better ; and with all the high aspirations of Wordsworth, there is much in his writings that is more favorable to an undefined naturalism or pantheism, than to the truth of the gospel. The fact is, I fear, that the Christian world has, of late, enjoyed too much worldly prosperity for the spiritual interests of the church itself, and our Christianity hangs so loosely upon us, that we are in danger of forgetting and denying both the Father and the Son. We want men, who, comprehending the philosophy and the spirit of the age, have at the same time the spirit, the active zeal and the eloquence of Paul. The young men about Cambridge and Boston among Unitarians, and to some extent among others, I have no doubt, will adopt the " spiritual philosophy," so called, against Locke and Edwards ; and will they stop with the Eclecticism of Cousin ? As the young men of education go, so goes the world. The popular religious works, and the general style of preaching among all classes and denominations, have too superficial and extraneous a character to protect speculative minds at all against the philosophical dogmas and criticisms with which our popular literature is so abundantly furnished. We need either a deeper and more heartfelt and heart-protecting practical piety, or else a more vigorous and profound philosophical spirit, in the interest of truth, and armed for its defence. We ought indeed to have both ; but how are we to obtain them ? "

In all efforts for the promotion of the great
interests of humanity, for the increase of true religion and piety among ourselves, and for the general spread of Christianity through the world, Dr.
Marsh took a deep and lively interest. He looked
upon such efforts as the glory of the age, and felt
it a privilege to co-operate in them as far as his
means and opportunities would allow. But while
he heartily approved of all the great objects which
in these latter days have enlisted the feelings and
called forth the activity of Christian benevolence,
he could not always approve of the measures re-
sorted to for promoting them. He had little faith
in the efficacy of any other means to reform the
world, than the simple power of gospel truth.
Expedients of mere human cunning and contrivance, whatever might be their immediate effects,
appeared to him rather an injury to the cause they
pretended to advance, and the more so in the same
proportion as they departed from the noble simplicity of the gospel. He was astonished at the
ease with which even good men sometimes allowed
themselves to be deceived in this matter ; and he
could no longer be still, when he observed whole
communities rushing thoughtlessly into innovations,
wrong in principle and unsafe in practice, which,
whatever they might promise at first, could scarcely fail to result otherwise than in injury to the
cause of true religion, and destruction to the peace
and order of the churches. On one occasion in
particular, he felt himself called upon to take an
open and determined stand against an innovation

of this sort, which, under the sanction and patron-
age of influential men, in and out of the State,
was threatening to become the universal order of
the day.   Sometime in the year 1836, an itinerant
minister, or evangelist, by the name of Burchard,
came on a visit to the State of Vermont, and was
employed to preach in some of the churches.   He
was a man of considerable address and power over
the passions, with a quick perception of individual
character, and great tact in adapting a set of measures to bring the community into a certain state
of feeling, and then make the public feeling react
upon the minds of individuals.   The seeming success that attended his labors inspired a very general confidence both in the man and in his measures ; and the new system of making converts by
rudeness of language, joined with a certain tact-
ical skill, threatened to supplant, at least for a
time, the more orderly and quiet means of winning
souls to Christ by the power of the truth.   Dr.
Marsh looked upon the whole movement with suspicion from the first ; but when the scenes came
to be enacted before his own eyes, he felt compelled to employ his pen and the whole force of
his personal influence in opposition to a system so
palpably mischievous and absurd.   Its friends and
advocates were in the habit of appealing to experience, and thought the propriety of the measures,
revolting as they might be to the unbiased sensi-
bilities of the pious heart, was still sufficiently
confirmed by their surprising results.   He could
not listen to such language ; his great objection to

the whole system was its confessedly empirical character. "Are we to be told," said he, "when a novel system of measures for the promotion of religion is proposed, that with the Bible in our hands, and all that we know, or ought to know, of the principles of the gospel in their application to the conscience, we must not pass our judgment upon it *till we have tried it*; and whatever may be our objections to it beforehand, its apparent good results must silence them? But who is to judge the nature of the results, and how long a time is to be allowed for proving that what appears to be good, is truly so? If immediate appearances of good are to be taken as an unanswerable argument in favor of a novel system of doctrines and measures, and the majorities in our churches are to judge and decide on those appearances, uncontrolled by that knowledge and insight into the deeper principles of religious truth, which can be expected only as the result of mature reflection in those who are set for the defence of the gospel, what limit can there be to new experiments, and how long will our churches sustain themselves under influences so radically subversive of whatever is fixed and permanent, whether in doctrines or the institutions of religion?" The representations and remonstrances of Dr. Marsh, through the press, before associations of ministers, and wherever he could get access to the public mind, were not without their effect; and the evil which threatened to deluge the religious community, and against which he was the first to lift up a standard, gradually subsided and died away from this part of the land.

I have nothing more to relate in regard to matters connected with the public life of this truly great and good man. The remainder of his days were passed in the silent pursuits of study, in the faithful discharge of his professional duties, and in the patient endurance of great privations and the severest domestic trials. In 1838, he lost his second wife; and in consequence partly of this event, and partly of pecuniary embarrassments, found himself under the unpleasant necessity of disposing of his house, and of breaking up his family. The last entry which he made in his private journal relates to these melancholy and painful reverses:

"*Aug*. 20. How much have I gone through, in the providence of God, since the last record was made here! Again am I left alone, and my children motherless. My dear wife, after a lingering decline since March last, was taken to her final rest on Sunday morning, the 12th of this month, at about three o'clock, just ten years, within twenty-four hours, since the like affliction befel me. What lessons of instruction, what excitements and encouragements to the service of God, have I not received in the life and death of these beloved companions! What examples of simplicity and purity of heart, of self-denial and devotion to their domestic duties, to their friends, to the cause of truth and to God! Dear L., with all her sincere and hearty devotion, and her warm affection as a

wife and mother, gone, too, from a world of trial
to a world of rest and blessedness! Thanks be to
God for all that she was while she lived, and especially for that consolation which she has left in
the assurance that a spirit so meek, so devoted,
and so acquiescent in the will of God, cannot but
be blessed wherever it is conscious of the presence
and government of God.

"*Sept.* 16. After an absence of three weeks at
Hartford, partly to dispose of my children, and
partly to recover from fatigue and exhaustion of
spirits, I returned yesterday. And oh to what a
place have I returned! How changed from what it
used to be, when on returning, I was received here
with open arms and bounding hearts? — I no
longer have a family around me, nor the endearments of a home. My mother-in-law is with
another daughter at Montpelier, my children are
dispersed, so that I am now here literally alone.
Oh that my time may be consecrated to the truth,
and to God, that when I have accomplished my
task, I too may go to my rest with the same com-
posure and holy confidence in God, as were exhibited by the dear companions of my past years.

"*Sept.* 30. During the past fortnight I have
done little but make arrangements for my accom-
modation, and prepare to enter again upon my
professional duties. Alas! how can I again become interested in those pursuits which I have so
long prosecuted with the cheering smiles of companions, and amid the endearments of a home,
now so desolate. I am here in my solitary rooms,

17

and look around in vain for her to whom I loved
to go when the labor of the day was done. To
whom now can I go for comfort when I am sad,
and to what rejoicing heart can I run, when my
own heart is animated with new views of truths,
with new hopes and more cheerful prospects?
What does not remind me that I am alone and
desolate? But why do I dwell upon such reflections? Let me rather gird my mind for the duties
of life, and spend my remaining days as a pilgrim,
still and ever looking, while I labor on, for that
rest which remaineth for the people of God."

The physical constitution of Dr. Marsh was
never very robust, and several years before the last
attack of the disease which brought him to the
grave, bleeding at the lungs, he had been visited
in the same manner, and for a time felt somewhat
alarmed for himself. But he soon recovered, and
enjoyed his usual health till the winter of 1841-2,
when, after taking a slight cold, he was suddenly
seized in the night-time, while on his bed, with a
recurrence of the complaint, but not so as to give
him at first much uneasiness. In a few days,
however, the bleeding returned, with an increase
of violence, and it soon became evident, both to
his friends and to himself, that there could be no
expectation of his permanent recovery.

This gave him no other solicitude than it would
be natural for one to feel, who was conscious
within himself of great and useful plans which he
had long been preparing to carry into execution,
but which must now, to all appearances, fail of

their accomplishment. With the returning Spring, he indulged a feeble hope that he might so far recover as to be able to make a journey to the South, in quest of the temporary relief—which was all he looked for — to be obtained from a milder climate. But this hope also was soon abandoned; when he cheerfully surrendered himself to the will of God, and directed his thoughts to the great work of preparing for the inevitable event which was so near before him. Through his whole illness, he enjoyed remarkable clearness and serenity of mind; and those of his friends who were privileged to sit by him and listen to his heavenly discourse, will never forget the impression left on their minds by those sadly pleasing interviews. His sickness was attended with but little pain or uneasiness, except what arose from an occasional difficulty of breathing. He died on Sunday morning, July 3, 1842, at the house of his brother-in-law, David Reed, Esq., in Colchester, in the 48th year of his age. His funeral was attended with every demonstration of respect by a large and friendly concourse of the citizens of Burlington, of clergymen from the neighboring towns, and of the members of the University to which he belonged; and a discourse, which has been published, was pronounced on the occasion by the Rev. Dr. Wheeler, President of the University. To that discourse I refer my readers for a faithful portraiture of the man, as well as for many of the beautiful sayings that fell from his lips, and expressed

the peace, serenity and christian trust, with which
he awaited his approaching change.

In the personal appearance of Dr. Marsh, there
was nothing which would strike or interest a common observer; but few there were, perhaps, who
sooner won upon the respect and esteem of strangers, even on the slightest intercourse, so gentle
were his manners, so sensible and yet so unpretending the style of his conversation. " I know
not," says one of the best judges, " that I ever
met with a person for whom I felt so deep a reverence on so short an acquaintance. But he carried a character in his face not to be mistaken —
in which, except in one other instance, I never
saw so legibly written *the peace of God*. The
moral beauty which was so striking in his expression, had an elevation in it, from its connexion
with his mind, that I have rarely seen. And how
winning the simplicity of his manners! You could
not for a moment doubt, that they were the necessary growth of a pure heart, and no common order
of intellect."

His feeble and tremulous voice disqualified him
for making an impression as a public speaker; but
in the lecture-room in the College chapel, and in
other places where he had " fit audience though
few," the depth of his thoughts, the calm earnestness of his manner and the felicity and appropriateness of his language never failed to interest his
hearers, beyond all power of a more fluent but
superficial eloquence.

His habits of living were temperate and abste-
mious, almost to a fault. Without being fastidious
or particular about his diet, he confined himself, of
choice, for the most part to vegetable food, and
seldom ate or drank beyond a very moderate
allowance. He was fond of walking, and once
travelled on foot, in a direct course, over mountain
and valley, from Burlington to Hartford, his
native place. As a student, he was regular and
severe, seldom allowing any day to pass without
its appointed task, and often noting down in his
journal what books he had read, and the impression they had left on his mind. He devoted much
time also to meditation and to writing, and with
all his other duties and labors, maintained an extensive and learned correspondence, in which he
poured out the treasures of his intellect without
stint or measure. If his letters could be collected,
they would form, I have no doubt, a most interesting and instructive volume.

His life was cut short, before he could realize,
as he wished and intended to do, the objects to
which so many hours of laborious study and profound reflection had been devoted. But who will
say that he lived in vain; that he has done nothing
for the promotion of a right philosophical spirit,
nothing for the advancement of moral and religious
truth, and nothing in giving an impulse and direction to other minds, whose influence may be felt
hereafter? Some may doubt the soundness of his
philosophy, and perhaps the orthodoxy of his
creed. But none can question the nobleness of

his aims, the purity and disinterestedness of his motives, and the untiring diligence of his endeavors after all that is praise-worthy and true. May there be many others to rise up and follow in his steps.

APPENDIX.

[To S. T. Coleridge.]

Burlington, Vt., U. S. A., March 23, 1829.

DEAR SIR: — The motives which lead me to hazard the presumption of addressing you, I hope will appear, in the course of this letter, to be such as may justify me to your sense of propriety. Although a stranger to literary reputation, and never likely to be known to you by other means than by sending you my name, I venture to believe you will give me credit for higher aims than the gratification of literary vanity in so doing. I should probably expose myself to a more deserved imputation of the sort, if in a country where they are not very generally known, I should claim such an acquaintance with your works, and such a sympathy with their spirit, as would entitle me to seek an intercourse with yourself. But I do not mean to claim for myself so much as this; and only say, that from my past knowledge of your "Literary Life," some ten years ago, I have sought, as my opportunities would permit, a more intimate acquaintance with your writings, and with your views on all the great and important subjects of which you have treated. If I have not been benefitted by so doing, and those with whom I have been associated, it is not your fault; for I have long been convinced, that though "there are some things hard to be understood," and though your views are not, in the works which we have, unfolded from first principles in a manner suited to the novice in philosophy, yet it is in consequence of the false and superficial notions to which the world is accustomed, rather than to their inherent difficulty, that your philosophical writings have been so generally considered mystical and unintelligible. I trust, however, that I have derived some degree of profit and of clearer insight from the study of your writings, and have sometimes ventured to hope that they would acquire an influence in this country which would essentially benefit our literature and philosophy. You probably know, nearly as well as I can tell you, the state of opinions among us, in regard to every department of intellectual effort. We feel here so immediately the changes in these matters which take place in England and Scotland, that important discussions on questions of general interest to literary men and christians, when started there, soon draw attention here, and are followed up with similar results. The miscalled Baconian philosophy has been no less talked of here than there, with the same perverse application. The works of Locke were formerly much read and used as text books, in our colleges; but of late have very generally given place to the Scotch writers; and Stewart, Campbell and Brown are now almost universally read as the standard authors on the subjects of which they treat. In theology, the works of Edwards have had, and still have, with a large portion of our thinking community, a very great influence; and we have had several schemes of doctrine, formed out of his leading principles, which have had each its day and its defenders. You will readily see the near affinity that exists between his philosophical views and those of Brown; and yet it happens, that the Unitarians, while they reject Edwards, and treat him with severity for his Calvinism, as it is here called, give currency to Brown for views that would seem to lead to what is most objectionable in the work on the Freedom of the Will. There has lately risen some discussions among our most able orthodox divines, which seem to me likely to shake the authority of Edwards among them; and I trust your "Aids to Reflection" is, with a few, exerting an influence that will help to place the lovers of truth and righteousness on better philosophical grounds.

The German philosophers, Kant and his followers, are very little known in this country; and our young men who have visited Germany, have paid little attention to that department of study while there. I cannot boast of being wiser than others in this respect; for though I have read a part of the works of Kant, it was under many disadvantages, so that I am indebted to your own writings for the ability to understand what I have read of his works, and am waiting with some impatience for that part of your works, which will aid more directly in the study of those subjects of which he treats. The same views are generally entertained in this country as in Great Britain, respecting German literature; and Stewart's History of Philosophy especially has had an extensive influence to deter students from the study of their philosophy. Whether any change in this respect is to take place, remains to be seen. To me, it seems a point of great importance, to awaken among our scholars a taste for more manly and efficient mental discipline, and to recall into use those old writers, whose minds were formed by a higher standard. I am myself making efforts to get into circulation some of the practical works of the older English divines, both for the direct benefit which they will confer upon the religious community, and because, in this country, the most practical and efficient mode of influencing the thinking world, is to begin with those who think from principle and in earnest; in other words, with the religious community. It is with the same views, that I am aiming to introduce some little knowledge of your own views, through the medium of a religious journal, which circulates among the most intelligent and serious clergy, and other christians. It is partly with a view to this, that I venture to address you, and to request the favor of an occasional correspondence with you. In the last number of the Journal alluded to, the "Christian Spectator" for March 1829, published at New

Haven, Connecticut, I have a review of Prof. Stuart's Commentary on Hebrews, in which I have given a view of the Atonement, or rather Redemption, I believe nearly corresponding with yours, and indeed have made free use of your language. In a note, I had also given you credit for it, but the note was omitted by the publishers, and a few paragraphs of their own remarks added. If you should have the curiosity to see the use which I have made of your works, the journal can be found, I presume, at Millers' American Reading Room, or at the office of the Christian Observer. It has been my intention to write an article, or perhaps more than one, for the same journal, on your "Aids to Reflection;" but my other duties will probably prevent it for the present. I shall send you, with this, an Address delivered by me on coming to my present place, in which also you will find free use made of your works; and I cannot resist the inclination also to refer you to an article on Ancient and Modern Poetry in the North American Review for July 1822, which I wrote while pursuing professional studies at Andover, Massachusetts. If you should impute to me some weakness in thus referring you to some few things which I have written, I can only say, that as you seemed, in your Literary Life, to be gratified with the use made of your political essays in this country, I have also a farther motive in the supposition that you might be gratified with knowing that your philosophical writings are not wholly neglected among us. If, after reading the pieces to which I have referred, Sir, you should think the seed which you have been sowing beside all waters, is likely to bring forth any valuable fruits in these ends of the earth, I beg that you will pardon my boldness, and write as suits your convenience, to one who would value nothing more highly than your advice and guidance in the pursuit of truth, and the discharge of the great duty to which I am called, of imparting it to those who are hereafter to be men of power and influence in this great and growing republic.

With sentiments of the highest esteem,

Your very obedient servant,

JAMES MARSH.

[To a young Clergyman.]

Burlington, March 9, 1837.

My Dear Sir : — I have some experience, as you suggest, in regard to such thoughts and speculations as you
are busied with at present. I have occupied a great deal
of time, and expended a great deal of thought, in conceiving what I could do in different circumstances from those
in which I was placed ; and could I have followed my own
inclinations, and have had a farm to go to, I should at one
period very certainly have rusticated myself, and quit public life altogether. For a great part of my life, I have felt
myself chained to situations in which I felt myself paralyzed in the exertion of my powers, and vainly longed
for freedom. But I now feel that had I yielded less to
such feelings, and without any reflective reference to what
I could or could not do, gone on to do my utmost, more or
less, in the sphere of duty in which I found myself placed,
I should have saved myself vast trouble, and done the
world more good. I am convinced that the views you
have in regard to the union of farming, or any other business of that sort, with the higher duties of one who means
to exert an extended influence on the intellectual and
moral and religious character of those about him, however
fair at a distance, are not easily realized in practice.
There is a continual tendency to merge the higher ends
in the lower, and very few would do more than to hold
their own, in regard to intellectual power and resources.
One, too, is exposed to more injurious imputations in regard to motives, and his authority and influence with others are more weakened, by their taking such a course, than
in preaching for a salary ; and I know no way of avoiding
this evil any where, but by a life so consecrated to the
discharge of duty, so laborious and self-denying and holy,
that we may appeal, with the apostle, to every man's conscience, for the simplicity and godly sincerity of our conversation. I would say, in a word, if you will allow me to
speak freely my own mind, do not allow your powers to
be relaxed and their effect paralyzed, by reflections upon

other possible conditions of usefulness; but consider yourself as called of God to preach the gospel where you are, till his Providence shall plainly call you elsewhere, and, making that your first and great object, "make full proof of your ministry." In the mean time your mind will be enlarged, and you will be better prepared to do good to your own people, as a religious teacher, if you keep before you all the interests of humanity, in their widest extent, and so labor for these, that your weekly routine of parochial duty shall become at length but a subordinate part of your labors for the great cause of truth and of righteousness. R—— told me, when here, that your people were more and more pleased with your style of preaching, and that your prospect of usefulness was every way good. As the matter appears to me, therefore, I would say, think of nothing else for the present, but of doing your utmost in the sphere of duty that surrounds you. I could give you a long talk upon the various points in your letter, and an earnest one, if it were worth while; but you see my drift, and can readily supply the rest. I will only add, with emphasis, do not waste time and energy, as I have done, by thinking what you could do in other circumstances; but let the only question be, how can I do most here, where the providence of God has placed me, for accomplishing the great ends to which my life is consecrated, making the proper duties of your station the first and starting point of all.

Very sincerely, yours, &c.,

J. MARSH.

[To the Rev. G. S. W., Sackett's Harbor, N. Y.]

Burlington, Feb. 2, 1838.

MY DEAR SIR:—I am sorry your letter has been so long unanswered, and that I should have seemed so negligent of your claims. But I assure you it has not been as it may have seemed in the case, for indeed I have written the amount of three or four letters, at different times ; but in my attempt to bring a great subject within the compass of a letter, have so perplexed it that I cannot send what I have written. So, as I have not time to try again, and if I did, should probably succeed no better, I must do at last what I might have done at first, send you a brief and hasty reply. You do not, in fact, need any *help* from me, to follow out the problem upon which you have been at work, and I am glad to see that you are so obviously on the right track. What I aimed at, in what I wrote, was to show some of the more general and philosophical principles which connect your view of the identity of subject and object with the grounds of philosophical truth universally. But the subject is too extensive and too difficult for a letter. I will only say here, then, that the doctrine, in its practical bearing, as you apply it to the leading doctrines of the gospel, is nothing more than a philosophical expression of what is implied in numerous passages of Scripture, as understood by the old divines, and as they must be understood, if we would find in them any spiritual meaning. I live, yet not I, but Christ liveth in me. Only so far as this is true, and I have the inward experience of the crucifying of the old man and of the awakened energies of a new and spiritual life ; i. e., only so far as I am crucified with Christ, and risen with him, by that power of Christ which effectually worketh in them that believe; only so far, I say, is Christ any thing *for me*, either in his death or his life. We may, indeed, know him after the flesh, as we know our fellow-men ; i. e., historically and from outward experience, but not inwardly and spiritually. He is, and can be recognized as, my Redeemer and Saviour, only as by the living power of his Spirit he has become the inward and actual life of my life, so that by virtue of his gracious inworking, my enslaved will is freed from the bondage of nature, empowered to overcome the propensities of nature, to abjure the evil principle of self-will, or the law of nature, and freely to obey the universal law of truth and holiness.

But this statement even, I am aware, seems mystical when presented in this naked way; and should I attempt to enlarge here, I should only make it worse. But there is a way, I believe, of developing the subject, and of exhibiting the relation of the subjective to the objective, in the successive gradations of powers, from those of organic life in its lowest forms, upward to the development of the supernatural or spiritual, that would throw light on the relation of our spiritual being to nature and to the spiritual. I can only say here, that as the powers of our natural life have their correlative objects in the natural world, so that which is spiritual in us must seek and find its correlatives in the spiritual world; and that universally the subjective is the measure of the objective, each necessarily presupposing the other, as the condition of its actual manifestation. Thus the correlative of *conscience* is *God*, and with the awakening or *actuation* of the subjective, there is a necessary presentation of the objective, and a commensurate conviction of its reality. In other words, God is the objectivity and reality of the conscience, and in proportion as the conscience is awakened, does it become impossible to doubt the existence of God. In like manner, we may say that where the principle of spiritual life is awakened, it has its correlative object, *Christ*, in the fulness of his divine nature, as that which it presupposes, in the same sense that the principle of organic life presupposes the world of sense, as its necessary condition and correlative.

But not to leave you with these vaguenesses for the sole answer to your letter, after so long delay, I will direct one of our recent graduates at Rochester to send a manuscript to you, which is in his hands, and was originally sent to Mr. Dana, of Boston. It may help you to carry out your thoughts in some particulars, and even in theological matters, though it is not itself properly theological. I will thank you to return it to me as soon as convenient.

Yours, truly,
JAS. MARSH.

[To Mr. J. M.]

Burlington, April 2, 1838.

My Dear Sir : — I rejoice, and hope I am truly thankful to the God of all grace, for such news as your letter contains. I rejoice with you, in your experience of the blessedness of trusting in him, and of looking to that Lamb of God, which taketh away the sin of the world. If there is joy in heaven over one sinner that repenteth, there is surely cause of joy and gratitude for us, when, as we have reason to hope and believe, our friends are brought from darkness to light; and in addition to the general causes of rejoicing, there is also that arising from our personal relations. We have all here felt much interest in your religious feelings and character, and anxious not only on your own account, but that to your other qualifications for acting well your part in a world that so much needs both thinking and good men, you might have also that of a fixed religious principle, that of *faith* in *God* and *faith* in the *truth*. We may now, I trust, cherish with confidence the belief that in whatever outward sphere of action your judgment, and the advice of friends, may lead you to seek the ends of living, they will always be worthy ends, and subordinate to the great end of glorifying God. Where there is not a principle of religious faith, you will understand now how it is that, while we hope for the best, we cannot feel assured for our young men, that they will always be found walking in the truth, or that they will not become the prey of a worldly and selfish ambition. But when a man's will is brought in subjection to the law, or rather inwardly actuated by the living power of conscience, as God working in it both to will and to do, and when the understanding is illuminated by that inward light, which shineth more and more unto the perfect day, this power and light we can trust with implicit confidence, not only as securing the man himself amidst the buffetings of temptation, but as having a diffusive energy, and exerting a controlling influence upon the world around. I hope and pray that in and through you, as a chosen instrument

of God, they may be manifested for the promotion of every
good word and work, and for the salvation of many souls.
As to the sphere of action in which you shall seek to serve
God in your generation, I hardly dare give advice, but will
mention some of the considerations which seem to me to
pertain to the question.   I take it for granted, that a Christian, animated by the ardor of love to Christ and to the
souls of men, will most naturally seek to engage in labors
immediately promotive of the glory of the one, and of the
salvation of the other.   I have no doubt, moreover, that
he will find more satisfaction, more that is *congenial* to his
feelings, in preaching the gospel of Christ, and striving to
win the souls of men unto obedience to its law of love,
even with all the hardships and self-denial which the
ministry of the gospel involves, than in any other sphere
of duty.   Yet it could not be inferred that it is the duty of
every man, even of every one qualified for it, to engage
directly in the labors of the ministry.   Constituted as our
Christian communities are, requiring, as they do, the power of truth and religious principle in every department,
requiring indeed to be pervaded by the spirit of truth,
there is no regularly constituted sphere of duty, where the
most enlightened and warm-hearted Christian may not
find ample scope for the exercise of all his powers and all
his graces.   In reference to the interests of education and
to the political interests of the country, connected as they
so obviously are with the interests of the world, and rest-
ing ultimately for their security on the diffused influence
and power of truth, as I have no doubt you now very clearly perceive, how often have I wished for men in our public
councils, who could see things from the higher point of
view to which you allude !   How much do we need men,
who, seeing things from that vantage ground, could and
would advocate the cause of truth and right with the eloquence of Burke and Chatham, combined with that inner
soul and spirit of eloquence, which the writings of Paul
the Apostle most adequately express !   What soul so vast
in its conceptions, or so exuberant in the overflow of Christian affections, as not to find objects large enough, and

interests sufficiently dear, for the full employment of mind and heart, among those which every day demand the labors of the pen and the press, of the pulpit and the halls of legislation. But I see I am giving you little help in deciding the question of employment, unless you should be led to look at objects more immediately connected with the exertion of Christian influence than the study and practice of law, which it seems to me you will find too far insulated to meet the promptings of your own heart. And yet I should not think it time misspent, to employ a year or so in the study of legal principles and matters connected with them. Theology I would at all events study, in some form; if not with a view to preaching, yet as necessary to the higher objects, which I trust you will, at all events, aim at in life. But you must come down here and talk of this matter more at large. At present, your thoughts will be chiefly occupied with the more immediate spiritual interests of yourself and those around you; and it is best they should be so. You will find, probably, that you still know but in part, and that the depths of evil in your own heart, its self-flattering devices and consequent dangers, with the corresponding depth and height of the exceeding love and preventive grace of God, are learned but by degrees The more you know of the one, the better will you understand the other.

We are anxious to have you come and mingle with your former companions here, in the hope that you may be the means of good to them. There is, we trust, rather more than the usual sobriety and susceptibility to religious impressions among the students, and I hope that our new arrangement for religious worship may be made a blessing. I am glad you read Cudworth, and wish you would join with his writings those of John Howe and Leighton. Howe's Blessedness of the Righteous, for depth of insight combined with practical efficiency in its appeals to the heart, is at least one of the best things in the language.

Very affectionately and truly yours,

J. MARSH.

19

Burlington, Oct. 2, 1840.

MY DEAR SIR : — I have but this moment received your letter, and too late, I fear, for you to get an answer before tomorrow morning. However, I will do my best to have it reach you. I shall not probably have occasion to use the long discourse which you have, within a few weeks, and you are quite welcome to keep it. The sermon which I inquired for, has appeared, so that I shall not need to ask for your copy.

I fear I can hardly give, in a letter and in so much haste, a series of subjects for discussion, that will be of much service to you. I will, however, give an outline, that may be filled up afterwards. It will be connected, as you will see, with the philosophical views, which must of necessity determine the method of a theological system; but at the same time I would discuss each topic, under the practical aspect which it assumes in the word of God.

1. Anthropology. Man, as a created, a dependent, a responsible, and therefore a free or self-determined, a spiritual and personal being; his relation to the absolute and universal law of truth and duty, his primitive or ideal character and condition as formed in the Divine image, his fallen condition by nature, and relation of the finite free will to an individual nature on the one hand, and to the redemptive power of the Word and Spirit of God on the other.

In connection with these topics, study carefully the Epistles of Paul, especially that to the Romans, with Usteri's Paulinische Lehrbegriff, Tholuck's Commentary on Romans, Heinroth's Anthropologie and Psychologie, Coleridge, and I will venture to add, my sermons. Right views of these subjects are indispensable to all that follows, as pertaining to the Christian system.

2. The doctrine of a revelation, of inspiration, &c., and the true idea of these as connected with anthropology and psychology. The whole subject connects itself with our

views of the relation of the understanding to the reason on the one side, and to sense on the other. You will find valuable helps in the latter part of both works of Heinroth to which I referred above, as well as in Coleridge. Coleridge's work on Inspiration is not yet published. The common works, your teachers can refer you to. Nordheimer and Henry can probably help you to the German books.

3. The doctrine of Redemption. Distinguish its subjective and objective necessity. The former, as already considered under the first head. The latter is a vexed question, and you will do well to study it as presented by different systems of Theology, and as treated by Tholuck and Coleridge, neither of whom, however, is very explicit. See Tholuck's Commentary on Romans, 5th chapter. This is, of course, closely connected with the work of Redemption in the same relations as subjective and objective, or relative to the subject redeemed, and to the necessary requisitions of the law and character and God. The common method is to treat first, as connected with this whole subject, of the person and character of Christ, his relation to man and to God, and so to the several offices which he bears, as connected with the work of redemption.

4. The effects wrought in the redeemed — regeneration, faith, repentance ; and so all the fruits of the Spirit. This will involve, again, the relation of the believer to Christ, and the agency of the Spirit of God. The doctrines of justification and sanctification, and their relation to each other, you will find points of much controversy, and requiring careful study. Read St. Paul for yourself, and with all the help you can get. This topic lies at the bottom of some great divisions among theologians, and is connected, as you will see, with the main topic under the previous head.

The church, or the relation of believers to each other, as one in spirit, and to Christ, as their common head, and as constituting the *spiritual* church, governed by a spiritual law, and co-operating to a spiritual end. The visible church, as grounded on and deriving all its life and power and authority from this, and so a mere lifeless and spiritless and unmeaning semblance, except as it expresses the actual and living presence and power of Christ in his members — his body, which is the church.

The future state of believers and unbelievers, future rewards and punishments, the spiritual world, the judgment and its consequences, &c. Theology in its limited sense, — the rational idea of God — grounds of a rational conviction of his existence — mode of existence — personality, triunity, relation to nature or the material universe, and to the spiritual world, or spiritual existences.

But I have made out a longer list than I intended; yet I could think of no better way, than to put the subjects in the form of a systematic outline. Many things, however, are left out, as you will perceive, which are necessary to a complete system. I believe you will find what I have given, to be subjects that have a systematic relation to each other, and you can take up more or less, and more or less minutely, as you choose. For the purposes of the pulpit, I would discuss everything in a practical form, and carry nothing there simply speculative. My own more elaborate sermons are not such as I would approve for common use. There is so much of speculative interest in all our schools, that the plain, practical preaching of the gospel is likely to be lost sight of. Pray you rise above this; and let your sermons breathe and utter forth the solemn earnestness and the yearning love for the souls of men, that characterize the gospel itself. Whatever may be the character of my own sermons, the exhibition of such a spirit is, in my deliberate judgment, the only preaching.

Yours truly,

J. MARSH.

LETTERS FROM CORRESPONDENTS.

[From Dr. Rice.]

Union Theological Seminary, April 14, 1829.

MY DEAR SIR : — I have felt badly, that none of us answered the very interesting letter written by you, just after your great bereavement. I wish you to know the circumstances, which prevented my writing. Your letter came to hand just as I was preparing a sermon to preach on a particular occasion. As soon as this preparation was made, I had to leave home, and was laboriously engaged during a tour of six weeks. On my return, I had all the cares of the commencement of the session. By that time, your letter, in being handed about among the neighbors, was lost. I do most fully concur with you in opinion as to the importance of getting into circulation the writings of the great men who lived in the seventeenth century. And if you can succeed in your design, a benefit of incalculable value will be conferred on New England. The *theological taste* has been too long formed on the model of metaphysics. Systems and sermons are moulded into this form. Rhetoric is extinct. Eloquence, instead of being like the garden of Eden, bright in celestial light, and breathing the airs of heaven, is a very *Hortus Siccus*, with every flower labelled and pasted on blank paper; the colors all faded, the fragrance gone, and "behold all is very dry." There must be a new model. But it will never be framed by our teachers of Sacred Rhetoric. Indeed I have no doubt, but that they will impede the progress of Reformation. Something may be expected from an increased study of the Bible. If it were studied *right*, great improvements would of course follow. For the spirit of that inimitable composition cannot be breathed into a man, without an awakening of something in him corresponding to its sublimity, its pathos, its overpowering eloquence. The men whom we agree in admiring were made what they were, in a great degree, by the Bible. Instead of sitting down to study it with a system of metaphysics to control their philology, they brought themselves to its sacred pages, that they might feel the *vis fulminea*, and breathe the heavenly *aura* of divine truth. Convinced that it was an emanation from the Eternal Source of truth, they entirely gave themselves up to its influences, and were borne by it *extra flamantia moenia mundi.*

How different the writers of the present day! But I need not stay to point out the contrast. You have especially marked the difference in regard to religious feeling. It is true that the present age requires action. But certainly religion is getting to be too much, in some places, an affair of business. It is becoming cold and calculating. And should the present excitement wear off, I apprehend the church will be left in a deplorably desolate and barren condition. I could wish indeed the activity of Christians to be increased a thousand fold; but I wish to see them borne on by that profound, deep-toned feeling which pervaded the inmost souls of such men as Leighton, Baxter, and Howe. But as to the business part of your undertaking, I hardly know what opinion to give. I should think that you would do well to have a subscription sufficient to cover your expenses. Selections have generally sold badly. The prevailing taste is for other things. Such poetry as Mrs. Hemans's, is more popular than Milton's. A *souvenir* in polite literature, and a sermon of *cut and dry metaphysics,* or *cut and dry rhetoric,* is all the rage. I think that there have been several English editions of Leighton. His whole works then would scarcely do well. Howe, Baxter, etc., are too voluminous for general reading, and would afford very good opportunity for selection. Bishop Hopkins is one of my favorites of the old school I could wish you to take something from him. Jeremy Taylor has been republished in this country. Some extracts from Thomas Browne's Religio Medici would furnish a choice morceau—nor would I neglect the "silver-tongued Bates." Barrow has vast force, but not much feeling. He has no rhetoric. If these hasty hints should give you any pleasure, I shall be glad.

Mrs. Rice unites with me in most affectionate remembrances, and best wishes for your health and usefulness.

Yours most truly,

JOHN H. RICE.

To the Rev. James Marsh, Burlington, Vermont.

~~~~~~~~~~~~~~~~~~~~~~

<div style="text-align:center">[From Dr. Follen.]</div>

<div style="text-align:right"><em>Cambridge, April</em> 14, 1832.</div>

DEAR SIR: — Your very kind letter, which assured me of your favorable reception of the views of German philosophy which I had given in my Inaugural Discourse, has been a source of great satisfaction to me. I have delayed answering your letter in the hope to find some leisure hours, in which I could express to you more fully my sentiments on those topics of deep interest which you touch upon, and do my best to answer your questions. But as the desired time for a long letter may not arrive, I will in a few lines give you my views of what seem to me, from a very limited and recent experience in this country, to be the most desirable steps to be taken in order to infuse life and intelligence into the clay of our present philosophical literature and instruction. Your edition of Coleridge, with the excellent prefatory aids, has done and will do much to introduce and naturalize a better philosophy in this country, and particularly to make men perceive that there is much in the philosophy of other nations, and that there is still more in the depths of their own minds that is worth exploring, and which cannot be had cheap and handy in the works of the Scotch and English dealers in philosophy. Still there is a want of good text-books, of works in which that spirit of a better philosophy is carried into each of its special branches. And here the important question arises, which of the various disciplines which constitute the highest department of human knowledge, should be selected to begin the work of reformation. There are two on which I rest my hopes as the pioneers in philosophy. In a community which is deluged with superficial discussions on momentous questions which can be settled only by philosophic principles, I look upon Psychology and the history of Philosophy as the parents of a new race of thoughts and modes of reasoning. Those, therefore, who would dispose and prepare the public mind for the reception of philosophy in all its branches, who would lead men not only to use, but to understand their own reason, should lend the whole weight of their intellectual eminence to those two sciences. The one makes men acquainted with the ideas of others on the subject of philosophy, the other teaches them its realities in their own minds; the one leads their understandings abroad to become acquainted with the intellectual world without them, the other guides them home to its living springs within them. I am not acquainted with a thorough work or a good text-book on either of those sciences in English; and in German literature, rich as it is in valuable works in these departments, I know no one of which a mere translation would meet the wants of the community, though they furnish excellent materials. Thus, in the philosophy of the human mind, the Anthropology of Kant, and the Psychologies of Carus, Fries, and others, would greatly aid an able compiler, but neither of them would of itself, probably, succeed in supplanting the genteel and palatable philosophy of Brown. In the history of philosophy, an extract from Tenneman's great work, considerably larger than his own synopsis of it, I should think would be the most suitable undertaking. A truly philosophical logic seems to me the third great desideratum; and it was with great pleasure that I heard from our mutual friend, Mr. Henry, that you had actually announced one on the basis of Fries, whose work I consider the best on that subject. Among the German works on logic, in your possession, you do not mention that of Schulze, (the author of Aenesidemus,) which he used as a text-book in his lectures in Gottingen, and that of Tasche, compiled from the notes taken of Kant's lectures on logic. If these books should be of any service to you, I should be happy to lend them to you, and will send them in any way you may point out. There are many other topics on which I wish to communicate with you, particularly the plan of Mr. Henry to publish a philosophical journal, which seems to me a very desirable object. But I must conclude now, with the expression of my hope that this summer will not pass away without bringing me the pleasure of a personal acquaintance with you. At any rate, I earnestly hope for a frequent exchange of thought with you upon subjects of such deep interest to us both.

With the highest esteem,

Your friend and servant,

CHARLES FOLLEN.

To President James Marsh, Burlington, Vermont.

～～～～～～～～～～

[From Mr. Gillman.]

Highgate, Feb. 24th.

DEAR SIR: — Although your kind and sympathizing letter has remained unanswered, it gave me unfeigned satisfaction, as I felt it a mark of regard for myself, and an affectionate testimony of love for the memory of one of the best of human beings. Sorrow and sickness have, ever since we lost him, followed so closely on each other, that I have left many things undone which I yet never lost sight of; and among them was the assurance I owed you of my sense of the value of those feelings which induced you to address me. I am sorry I cannot give you any information respecting the writings Coleridge has left. But Mr. Henry Nelson Coleridge intends himself the pleasure of forwarding the new works, entitled " Literary Remains," published since his death, by the Bishop of

20

Vermont, who has offered to convey any parcel to you. I
am obliged by your introduction of that gentleman to me;
we were highly pleased with his manly simplicity, and interesting appearance and manners. I beg your acceptance,
my dear Sir, of the first volume of Coleridge's Life. The
second volume is not yet finished, but it will, I think, be
the most interesting of the two, as it will contain so many
notes and memoranda of his own. How much I wish you
could have known, or even have seen him! I enclose the
copy of an epitaph I wrote for a very humble tablet, which
I put up in our church at Highgate; and also a copy of his
will, which latter will no doubt interest you deeply; a copy
too, of the last thing he wrote, ten days before he breathed
his last, and when in his bed and suffering greatly. I must
now, my dear Sir, beg you to accept my cordial regard, and
to rest assured of the sentiments of esteem with which I
am   Yours, faithfully,

JAMES GILLMAN.

To Dr. Marsh.

SACRED TO THE MEMORY

OF

SAMUEL TAYLOR COLERIDGE;

POET, PHILOSOPHER, THEOLOGIAN;

This truly great and good man resided for the last nineteen
years of his life,

In this Hamlet;

He quitted "the body of this death,"

July 25th, 1834,

In the Sixty Second year of his age.

Of his profound learning, and his discursive genius, his
literary works are an imperishable record.

To his private worth,

His social and christian virtues,

JAMES AND ANN GILLMAN,

The friends with whom he resided, during the above
period, dedicate this tablet.

Under the pressure of a long and most painful disease,
his disposition was unalterably sweet and angelic.

He was an ever-enduring, ever-loving friend,

The gentlest and kindest teacher,

The most engaging home companion.

———

"O framed for calmer times, and nobler hearts!
O studious poet, eloquent for *Truth!*
Philosopher, contemning wealth and death,
Yet docile, childlike, full of life and love:
Here, on this monumental stone, thy friends inscribe thy worth."

———

Reader! for the world, mourn.

A light has passed away from the earth.

But for this pious and exalted Christian, rejoice:

And again I say unto you, rejoice!

Ubi

Thesaurus

Ibi

S. T. C.

[Letters from H. N. Coleridge.]

[1]

10, *Chester Place,* (*Regents' Park,*) *London,*
June 2, 1839.

DEAR SIR: — The Bishop of Vermont having kindly offered to convey a small parcel to you, I gladly avail myself of the opportunity to beg your acceptance of the third and fourth volumes of the Literary Remains of Mr. Coleridge, published by me, and also a copy of a new edition of the Aids to Reflection, in which you will see that I have reprinted your Essay. All Coleridge's works are now printed uniformly, except the Biographia, and sold cheaply; and I hope to add the B. L. to the number, within a twelvemonth.

With great respect, believe me,
dear Sir, yours, very faithfully,
HENRY N. COLERIDGE.

To the Rev. James Marsh.

[2]

April 1, 1840.

MY DEAR SIR: — Pray accept my thanks for both your letters, which were very interesting to me. The principal object of this note, however, is to say that I have never seen the New York edition of the Aids to Reflection, to which you refer. Mr. Pickering's name is usurped in the title page, neither he nor I having any knowledge of the publication; and if it is so used as to induce readers to believe that the edition has any peculiar sanction from us in England, I think it an unfair transaction. Professor McV. I *conjecture* only to be Prof. McVickar. I do not know whether he is the gentleman who used to be known to Mr. Southey, and whose son I met in London about a year ago. Of the merits of the New York edition, or the propriety of the preface, I can of course say nothing in my present ignorance, except that I should not agree with any denial of your having rendered a great service to the cause of sound philosophy as involved in the principles taught by Mr. Coleridge. My uncle was born and bred, and passed all his later life, and died, an affectionate member of the church of England; but the fact of church membership would not in and of itself have influenced one of his conclusions. He was a member of the church, because he believed that he had ascertained by observation and experience that it presented the best form of Christian communion, having regard to primitive precept and practice, social order, and the developement of the individual mind. I am sorry there should be any parties among Christ's disciples; though increasing in strength, they still need union in their warfare.

If you should find a fair opportunity, I should be much gratified with a copy of your reprint of the Aids. I have nothing to send you at present; but am closely getting on, as I find leisure, with an edition of the Biographia Literaria, with notes, biographical and others.

Mr. Green means very shortly to beg your acceptance of a copy of his Hunterian Oration, with notes and appendices, and another Lecture he is publishing in a volume under the title of Vital Dynamics.

Pray excuse this short note, which I write amidst much occupation, wishing you to believe me, my dear sir,

   Yours very faithfully,

      H. N. COLERIDGE.

---

[3]

My Dear Sir: — I trust you will excuse a very few lines in acknowledgment of your last letter. And I wish to mention, that several months ago, I sent to Mr. C. Goodrich a copy of the last edition of the Friend, which, from your silence, I almost fear he cannot have received. I already possess a copy of Dr. McVickar's edition of the Aids. I trust, that you are to be the editor of the new edition of the other works. I am going tomorrow morning

for a ramble on the continent; but hope to get out, soon
after my return, the little volume of which I believe I
spoke to you—The Confessions of an Inquiring Spirit.
You are aware that there are editions of all Mr. Coleridge's
prose works, except the Biographia. With the Friend,
Mr. Green sent you a copy of his Hunterian Oration. I
hope both have been received. Mr. Allen sent me all his
letters, and Dr. McVickar has lately sent me his. The
Editor seems to me totally unfriendly, not to you only, but
to Coleridge.

            Believe me, my dear Sir,
                    Yours very faithfully,
                            H. N. COLERIDGE.

[From Dr. Green.]

King's College, London, Feb. 25, 1839.

MY DEAR SIR :— Interested as I am in all that relates
to the character of my lamented friend Coleridge, and to
the promulgation of those truths which it was the great
aim of his life, even at the sacrifice of his worldly interests, to establish,—I need not say how much gratification
I have received in learning from one, so well qualified as
yourself to give an opinion, that Coleridge's writings are
appreciated, and that with your aid they are forming for
themselves a widening circle of admirers in the United
States.

In reply to your inquiries respecting his works that remain to be published, I beg to acquaint you, that he has
left a considerable number of miscellaneous papers, of the
nature of which you will be enabled to form a judgment
from the three posthumous volumes entitled, " Literary
Remains," which have already appeared. No time will
be lost in putting forth another volume. Much, however,
will still remain for publication, including a variety of essays and detached observations on subjects of theology,

biblical criticism, logic, natural science, &c., in connection with his philosophical views. I dare not, however, promise any finished work, except a short though highly interesting one " On the Inspiration of the Scriptures." And I may add, that, beyond the design of getting these works through the press, and of reprinting those which are out of print, no intention exists at present of publishing an uniform collection of his prose writings.

I presume, however, that your main inquiry relates to the work that was expected to contain the full developement of his system of philosophy; but I regret to say that this, which would have been the crowning labor of his life, was not accomplished; nor can this unfortunate circumstance be a matter of surprise to those who are acquainted with the continual suffering from disease, which embittered the latter part of this truly great man's life. I cannot doubt that the announcement of this desideratum will be no less a disappointment to Coleridge's transatlantic friends than to his admirers in England; but to none will the disappointment prove more grievous than to myself, as the task of supplying the deficiency devolves, by my dear friend's dying request, on my very inadequate powers. I am now, however, seriously at work, in the humble hope of fulfilling this duty, (as far as my means of accomplishing it permit;) and I propose, in the first instance, to give a succinct and comprehensive statement of principles, such as will enable the readers of Coleridge's writings to see the connection of the thoughts under the guiding light of the unity of the ideas from which they flowed. In this attempt to set forth the principles of Mr. Coleridge's system, I am not without the hope of establishing them as the principles of philosophy itself, and of showing that the various schemes which have been framed by the founders of the numerous philosophical schools and sects, are not disparates or contraries, but merely partial views of one great truth, and necessary steps and gradations in the evolution of the human mind in its inherent and necessary desire of philosophical truth. In closing this, I trust that I shall be enabled to rescue

the all-important doctrine of *ideas* from the obloquy and
scorn, which a narrow and barren pseudo-philosophy of
the senses has but too well succeeded in throwing upon a
Method, alone calculated to vitalize and realize human
speculation, and to give power and dignity to the mind.
Nay! I do not despair of reconciling philosophy with religion, and of showing that, whilst philosophy must consent to be her handmaid, religion may derive a reciprocal
benefit, in the proof that religion is reason as the essential
form of inward revelation.   Whether my ability be equal
to the task of giving an outward reality in distinct statement, to Coleridge's high and ennobling speculations, can
be only known to the God of truth, to whom I pray for
light and strength, under the almost overwhelming sense
of the difficulty of doing that which could be adequately
done only by the Author.

I remain, my dear Sir,

Yours, very sincerely,

JOSEPH HENRY GREEN.

To Rev. James Marsh.

[From the same.]

King's College, London, March 5, 1841.

MY DEAR SIR: — When I contrast the date of this letter with that of your welcome communication, I am truly
ashamed of having so long delayed the acknowledgment
of the great pleasure it afforded me, not only on its own
account, but as an earnest (which I trust it is) of our better acquaintance, and of the support which we may mutually give each other, in the establishment of the philosophy
of ideas, of which in the present age Coleridge was unquestionably the reviver and re-originator.   And if the
"Vital Dynamics," with your approbation of which I am
highly flattered, should at all contribute to enlist scientific

men in the cause, and to infuse a more vital philosophy into science, especially physics, I shall derive the high gratification of having been one of the instruments, under Providence, of promulgating the truths of a spiritual philosophy, and of rescuing the pursuits of noble minds from the taint of errors, which I fear are too apt to arise under the dominant influence, hitherto prevalent in physics, of a philosophy, the tendency of which is assuredly to place all reality in sensuous intuition, consequently to withdraw the mind injuriously from supersensuous truths, and in confounding faith with belief, to substitute conjecture, probability, and the subjective condition of the believer's mind, for the proper evidence of the great truths upon which the whole moral life of man is based. We may, indeed, discern an order of Providence in the developement of physical science ; and we can scarcely doubt that it could not have advanced, in connexion with the imperfect nature of the human mind, which sees only in part, except under the condition of a too exclusive attention to the senses, and to the forms of sense, which it mainly owed to Descartes and Gassendi ; whilst we cannot but admit that physical science and natural knowledge are important elements in the cultivation of man, both as it respects the developement of his intellect and the creation of the means and instruments of civilization and of a common participation by the whole race in the blessings granted to any one more favored portion. We have indeed learned a better creed than that derived from a sensuous philosophy, which mistakes means for ends ; and viewing the acquisitions of science in relation to the moral man, of whom the intellect is after all but a fragment, we press onwards to the goal, at which the intellect, with its noblest product, science, is still to be subordinated to the moral will in that moral life of the whole man, head and heart, in which philosophy even must await its final and complete vivification. I fear that you estimate too highly the labors of the English so called natural philosophers, and I should hesitate to ascribe to them generally a higher merit than the talent of generalization ; at all events, the perception

21

of law in the spirit of a true dynamic philosophy has scarcely more than dawned upon some few of my countrymen; and had I not been prompted by a deep sense of the momentous nature of the truths which I have endeavored to inculcate in my oration, I should hardly have ventured with those auditors and readers, to whom it was addressed, to cast my bread upon the waters. Should you think that an advantageous impression might be made by its publication on your side of the water, I pray you to dispose of it as you may see fit; and well convinced I am that a preface from your pen would incalculably aid its effect both there and in this country.

There is, however, one passage in your letter, which has excited an apprehension in my mind that I may have been misunderstood, and that in respect of the relation of God to nature you may be disposed to infer that my doctrines are tainted by the erroneous tendency of Schelling's philosophy to Pantheism; for that such is its tendency, notwithstanding his declaimer, I cannot doubt. Now if there was any one point, on which above all others Coleridge manifested the utmost anxiety, it was that of preventing the possibility of confounding God with nature; and perhaps no better evidence can be offered than the formula, which he was frequently in the habit of repeating: World $-$ God $= 0$: God $-$ world $=$ Reality absolute; the world without God is nothing, God without the world is already, in and of himself, absolute perfection, absolute reality. And this doctrine of genuine Theism he has most nobly vindicated, in its inalienable connection with the doctrine of the Trinity as it is set forth in the Nicene Creed, by establishing as a truth of reason the *Personality* of God; a doctrine which is the very foundation of moral truth, as it is the dominant principle of Coleridge's system, but to which Schelling's philosophy is inadequate; and I do not think that I am asserting too much in saying that its inadequacy to the attainment of the idea is virtually confessed in its utter improgressiveness after a certain period long since passed, and that it is this inadequacy which has probably prevented Schelling's long promised completion of his philosophy in a systematic form.

I send you herewith a small brochure, just published, on a subject which now is agitating the medical profession in this country; and though you can take no part in its particular object, yet I have thought that its general scope and design might not be unacceptable to you, and that it might interest you as a specimen of reasoning by ideas. It will at least show that I am not idle, though drawn off for a time from what I must ever consider as the main business of the remainder of my life,—the exposition, in a systematic form, of the philosophy of my great and excellent teacher.

With my fervent wishes for your welfare, and my sincere prayers for the continuance of your successful labors in the cause of truth,

Believe me, my dear Sir,
Yours ever very sincerely,
JOSEPH HENRY GREEN.

To the Rev. James Marsh.

ERRATUM

There is no portion of the text omitted although
pages numbered from 164 through 187 do not appear.

REMAINS.

24

LETTER TO AN ADVANCED STUDENT.

—

A FRAGMENT.

—

OUTLINES OF A SYSTEMATIC ARRANGEMENT OF THE DE-
PARTMENTS OF KNOWLEDGE, WITH A VIEW TO THEIR
ORGANIC RELATIONS TO EACH OTHER IN A GENERAL SYS-
TEM.

~~~~~~~~~~~~~~~

I PROMISED to comply with your request in regard to a course of study, and though I have so
unreasonably delayed to fulfil my engagement, I
have not forgotten it. What I wished was to furnish such a sketch as, by its distinction and
arrangement of the departments of knowledge,
should enable you to view them in their proper
relations, and so that the preceding should, at
each step, prepare you the better and more adequately to understand the succeeding. After you
left me, instead of completing, as perhaps I should
have done, what I first projected, I was led to aim
at a more enlarged plan, and at exhibiting the
reasons of the method which I adopted. This,
however, I have found to involve questions and
discussions of a nature incompatible with the present purpose, and must content myself with mere-

ly distinguishing and arranging with a view to practical results. The reasons which justify the method adopted, or lead to a better one, I must leave to your own more mature reflections. In many cases, I might, perhaps, have found as many reasons for a different order, as for that which I have adopted; and should I wait to settle all the questions that arise, my promise to you would probably never be performed. The distinctions made, and the objects of knowledge embraced in the different divisions, will be in some more and in some less important, as applied to existing sciences and the present state of our knowledge. I have aimed only to mark in succession, with more or less minuteness, objects of contemplation that seem distinguishable in thought, and deserving, from their connexion and relation, of separate and distinct attention. For the same purpose of avoiding perplexing questions, I have not attempted to group the divisions which I have made under more general heads, but have simply arranged them in an unbroken series.

1. SPACE. By space, as a distinct object of thought, I mean that *in which* all the *outward* objects of sense and sensuous representation are necessarily placed. If we analyze the form under which it presents itself to our thoughts, we must distinguish it into *absolute* and *relative* space. *Absolute space* is that in which all relative spaces and finite determinations of space are *contained*, and which, in the imaginary construction of these,

is always necessarily *pre-supposed* as the condition
of their possibility. It is that in relation to our
outward beholding, which, beyond every excursion
of the imagination, still presents itself as a continuous extension, *comprehending* all forms and limitations, itself *uncomprehended* by any. Again, it
is necessarily pre-supposed in order to the conceivability of *motion*, and to it all actual motion is
ultimately referred, as that *in which* it took place,
while it is itself necessarily conceived as *fixed* and
immovable. It is moreover conceived as a *unity*,
in which all distinguishable and finite spaces are
included *as parts*. It is *one continuous* expansion,
in which there may be *imaginary limitations*, but
no *separation* of parts, and in which all imaginary
divisions are *co-existent* and *unchangeable* in their
relations to each other.

Relative space is any imaginary or real determination of limits in space, conceived as fixed, in the
relation of its parts to each other, but moveable,
in its relation to absolute space. A geometrical
sphere of a given radius, or the orbit of the earth,
is, in itself, the same space, whether at rest or
in motion, and may therefore be conceived as
moving in absolute space. It is to relative space
that all determinations of *place* have reference ;
while with reference to absolute space neither
place nor direction of motion is determinable.
Thus a particular continent has its place on the
earth, the earth and its orbit its place in the solar
system, and this again its place, and perhaps direction of motion, among the fixed stars ; but if

we ask for the place and motion of the material universe in reference to absolute space, the question admits of no possible or conceivable answer.

2. TIME. By time, I mean that to which we ascribe the relations of past, present and future, and in which we represent all events pertaining both to our outward and inward experience as taking place. Events occurring in time we conceive as simultaneous or successive, while the distinguishable portions of time itself are necessarily represented as successive only, in an unbroken, unending series. Time is necessarily pre-supposed, in order to the possible conception of that which occurs in time ; and all distinguishable and finite periods of time are included as parts of one infinite succession. In making the distinction here between relative and absolute, the latter term seems obviously not applicable to time, but the distinction is designated by the word *eternity*. When we represent time as a flowing quantity under the form of distinguishable periods, succeeding each other, we refer it to eternity as the absolute, in which all succession is lost, in the same manner as we refer relative space, conceived as in motion, to absolute space in which it moves, and in which, as the fixed and immovable, its motion is described. That the mind makes such a distinction between time and eternity, any one, it would seem, might be satisfied by the consciousness that we cannot, without obvious incongruity, apply to our idea of God the necessary relations of

time, nor conceive him to be older now, than he was in the beginning of the creation. The same may be said of our ideas of all immutable and absolute truths, as transcending the relations of time. It is necessary here to conceive time, only as the necessary antecedent form and condition of all that is presentable in our experience as taking place, whether in the sphere of the outer senses, or of our inward consciousness. It is, no less than space, necessarily pre-supposed or involved in the conception of local motion, and of all changes in the outer world; and is, moreover, inseparable from the conscious changes, which take place in the agencies and states of our inward being, to which the relations of space do not belong.

Thus space and time are related to whatever else is knowable in our experience, as the necessary *a priori* forms and conditions under which it is presented to our observation. The form in which we present them to ourselves is not learned from experience; but all *experience*, and all *existence* of objects pertaining to our experience, pre-suppose these. We may conceive the removal and non-existence of whatever we represent as existent *in* space and time, but space and time *remain*, and cannot be conceived not to do so.*

3. We have seen that space and time, with

---

* See, on the subjects of space and time, *Kant's Kritik der r. Vernunft, erster Theil. Newton's Principia. Def. 8. Scholium.* and *Kant's Naturwissenschaft.* What they are in themselves, in relation to real being, this is not the place to consider.

the negation of reality existing in them, or *pure*
space and time, are necessary presentations, the
negation of which is impossible. Space expands
itself into a boundless inane ; and time runs on in
endless succession, in which nothing succeeds to
nothing. These so presented, as the intuitions
of pure sense (in distinction from *empirical* sense,
or sense as affected by sensuous phenomena present in space and time) constitute the sphere of
possibility and of those *possible determinations* of
quantity and *figure* which are the object of pure
mathematical science. Whatever may be postu-
lated as possible, and representable to the pure
sense as determinate under the forms and relations of space and time, is properly included as
an object of mathematical intuition. The free
and productive imagination, unrestrained by the
conditions of actual existence and the limits of
experience, here generates and combines for itself all possible and conceivable forms, peopling
the void with its own ideal creations. The law
of spontaneity in the creative imagination itself
is the determinant of its agencies, and the lines,
surfaces, and solids, rectilinear, curvilinear, &c.
of the geometrician are the records and products
of its action. These, in their endless variety, are
the data of the mathematician, and regarded as
fixed and determinate objects of contemplation.
As their *essence* consists in their determinate *form*,
generated by the imagination, and exhibited to the
pure sense, they admit of perfect scientific *insight*
and are the objects of *pure intuitive science.*

We may distinguish here (1st) *geometry*, as the science of pure space, or of delineations in space as the objects of pure sense. Its distinctive character arises from the threefold dimensions of space, and the freedom of the imagination in generating forms in space by the geometrical motion of their boundaries : (2nd) the *science* of *time*, or *chronometry*, the arithmetical numeration of successive distinguishable moments, in a single line of succession, which is the common character of time and of arithmetic. It is, however, obvious, that arithmetic is not limited to time in its application, but extends to quantity universally ; as do also the more general methods of algebra and fluxions : (3rd) the principle of order or syntactical arrangement, having reference to the possible changes which the imagination may make at will in the arrangement of given elements ; the doctrine of permutations and combinations.

It is important to be observed here, in reference to the nature of pure mathematical science generally, and to the place which I have assigned it, that it is strictly *a priori*, and independent of all facts of experience. Even the idea of motion, as an idea, and pertaining to the acts of the imagination, is inseparable from the representation of extension, and the postulates of geometry necessarily involve it. All the constructions of pure mathematics require only space and time, and the free outgoing of the productive imagination. It is thus that the forms of possible existence and action are produced and contemplated in anticipa-

25

tion, as it were, and as the antecedent determi-
nants of the actual in space and time.

It is, again, no less true, and important to be
observed here, that these pure and *a priori* sciences are the necessary antecedent condition of all
our scientific knowledge of the actual phenomena
of nature as given in our experience. They furnish the intelligible principles and forms, under
which the phenomenal forms of nature are contemplated and determined, and by which a scientific
insight is attained into the laws of nature.

It will of course be understood, that I aim at
present to characterize the pure mathematical
sciences only in a very general way, and with a
view to their place and relations in a systematic
arrangement of the different departments of
knowledge. For an enlarged view of their philosophical nature and relations, see *Fries' Mathema-
tische Naturphilosophie, erster Theil*, and his
System der Logik, § 16. *Herschell's Discourse
on Nat. Phil.*, chap. 2.

4. Besides the *a priori* truths of mathematics, certain principles are determinable independently of experience, or at least as necessary principles in regard to the existence, in space and
time, of that which is the possible object of experience and of knowledge for us. These principles have been termed metaphysical principles of
Natural Philosophy. The clearest exposition of
what is here intended as a distinguishable department of knowledge, will be a brief statement of

its general heads as treated by Kant and Fries, the only authors who, so far as I know, have distinctly treated the subject in the form adapted to this connexion. Kant distinguishes, 1st, the principles of Phoronomy, or the necessary laws of motion, as pertaining to that which exists and is moveable in space : 2d, the principles of Dynamics, or of those powers by which matter manifests itself as a space-filling substance, and the necessary conditions of such in order to their possible actuation in space : 3d, the principles of mechanical action, as treated in mechanical philosophy ; and 4th, Phænomenology, or the conditions under which matter, as existing in space, and moving in it, exhibits itself to us.

To these four divisions Fries has added *Stæchiology*, or the principles of affecting the possible modes of aggregation among the smallest parts (στοιχεια) of matter, as in solids, fluids, gases, &c. ; and *Morphology*, or the laws of form necessarily pertaining to that which is extended in space, and their possible determinations.

It is in this treatise, that Kant has controverted, and, as it is generally admitted, confuted the atomic and mechanical systems of Natural Philosphy ; while he has exhibited briefly the principles of the Dynamic theory. The purpose of this is to show, that the phenomena of the material world must ultimately be referred, in our endeavors to form a conception of their grounds, to the agency of *powers*, acting according to fixed and determinate laws. To attain a constituent idea of those

living powers of nature, and an intellectual insight
into the laws of their action, is then the ultimate
purpose of Natural Philosophy. The principles
in question in this division, and exhibited in the
treatises referred to, pertain to the necessary laws
of intelligence, or to the conditions of our knowing, as well as to the conditions of the knowable
in space and time. They consequently imply a
relation between the two, and that the objective
or material is capable of being contemplated under
the intelligible forms or ideas of the subjective intelligence. This relation, however, it is not to
my purpose to consider here ; and the method of
arrangement which I have adopted, requires only
the contemplation of the principles referred to, as
conditions of scientific knowledge in regard to the
world of sense. They are *a priori* and necessary
principles ; yet differ from pure mathematics, in
that they assume the existence of matter as that
which is moveable in space, as that which fills
space, &c., and is the object of a possible knowledge from experience. Assuming this as actual,
they aim to render intelligible the possibility of it,
or what it must be in regard to its properties as a
moveable and space-filling substance, if it be conceivable and knowable at all by us. Thus they
represent matter, not as composed of ultimate
atoms forming perfect solids, and so furnishing
the ground of a mechanical explanation of its
phenomena, but as resolvable into ultimate powers, which belong to all matter as such. Attraction and repulsion, as correlative and counteract-

ing forces, are ultimate constituents of matter, and therefore universal. They are necessary to the conceivability of matter as a space-filling substance ; and nothing higher than these, in the relation of a physical ground, can be conceived as the object of physical science. In transcending these, we transcend nature, and find their ground in the supernatural, which is not the object of science.

In these universal powers of matter, therefore, and the other general laws exhibited in the treatises referred to, I find the point of transition from the pure *a priori* sciences, and the objects of pure sense, to the world of experience, and to those powers and agencies of nature, which manifest themselves in the phenomena of empirical sense.*

5. In passing to those departments of knowledge which immediately concern the objects of our experience, or the actual in space and time, I shall endeavor to direct the attention simply, at each step, to that which may be regarded as the true object of science — I mean the distinguishable powers of nature and their several laws of action. There is, indeed, a necessary distinction to be made here between phenomena and those intelligible agencies which reveal themselves in and through these ; but it is unnecessary for my present

* See on this subject *Kant's Naturwissenschaft*, and his *Gedanken von der wahren Schatzung der lebendigen Kraefte. Vermischte Schriften*, Vol. I. *Fries Math. Naturphilosophie.* 2 ter. *Theil.*, and *Kant's Reine Vernunft.* S. 197—293.

purpose to class the phenomena, as a distinct object of knowledge, and under distinct heads. This will be done sufficiently in designating those powers to which the various classes of phenomena are to be referred, and in their relation to which their only scientific value consists. Thus the phenomena of gravitation are contemplated by the natural philosopher only as indices of that power, and of its law of action; and with the clear intuition of these, as the proper object of intelligence and scientific insight, the phenomena of sense cease to be regarded as having an independent interest. We cannot, indeed, in the existing state of science, understand all the phenomena of the world of sense, and refer them to an intelligible law of action from which they result; but there is yet a striving after and anticipation of the law, and every system of arrangement must have reference to the knowledge already attained.

From the view already taken of those departments of science, which are necessarily antecedent to that of the world of sense and experience, and from the method adopted of distinguishing and arranging the distinguishable powers of nature, as the proper objects of knowledge, the first in order here will naturally be those universal powers, which manifest themselves in space as co-extensive with the material universe, and which have already been mentioned as inseparable from our conception of matter as such. These are *attraction* and *repulsion*, or the universal principle of gravitation, and that inherent power by which any

quantity of matter occupies a given space, or re-
pels and excludes from it other portions of matter.
In any given mass of matter occupying a determinate space, these powers are conceived as being
in equilibrio; and the space filled with a certain
degree of intensity. Hence, without regard to
the superadded agencies, by which different kinds
of matter are distinguished, in the relation of their
parts, as solid, fluid, aeriform, elastic or inelastic,
&c., from the equilibrium of its inherent powers,
as *matter* and a space-filling substance, it remains
at rest in itself, and is only moved from without.
The intensity with which it fills space, and the
energy with which it tends to maintain its existing state of rest or motion, are the basis of its
motive force, without which velocity, however
multiplied, would be a multiplier of zero. These
are the ground of the so-called *vis inertiæ*, and in
connexion with these, the powers above designated, and their laws of action, as applied to all those
phenomena in which masses of matter act upon
each other, either in motion or at rest, are the
proper objects of that wide field of science, embraced in mechanical philosophy in the most extensive sense of that term, at least in its application to the agencies of inorganic nature. I shall
not, however, aim at great precision, or at making
nice distinctions here, in regard to the division of
those sciences, in which the pure mathematics are
applied to inorganic matter, considered as acting
in masses, and as it is acted upon from without.
So long as it is uninfluenced by powers affecting

the inherent form and relation of its parts, the
phenomena which it exhibits in the change of its
outward relations in space, are included in the
general term mechanical ; and so far as concerns
permanent natural agencies, are ultimately referable to those here spoken of. Where other mechanical agencies are exerted, they are still conditioned by these, and the law is still the same,
when once the force and direction of the moving
power are determined. It is unnecessary here to
specify the different kinds of machinery or the
mechanical forces, other than the universal powers
of matter, such as that of steam, &c., since the
general principles of science, which apply to them
as moving powers, are the same. The general
laws of motion, I regard as included under the previous head ; and magnetism, whatever connection
it may have with the powers already named, and
however it may in some respects act mechanically, is now regarded as connected more essentially
with agencies of another kind.

Looking at the subject, then, in a somewhat
different aspect, we contemplate here, as next in
order to the sciences of pure space and time, the
agency of two *living powers,* manifesting themselves to our *outward sense* under the relations of
extension and form *in space,* and having their law
of action determinable by the application of those
pure sciences, which arise from the contemplation
of space and time alone, as objects of pure sense.
Considered in reference to *material substance,* or
matter *in itself* and its properties as a *space-filling*

substance, we may regard them, in the equilibrium of their counteracting forces, as universal, or necessarily pertaining to all matter as such, and, in relation to our *experience*, its *ultimate* constituents. Considered in reference to *bodies* or *determinate masses* of matter, we contemplate them, not as they are united, and neutralize each other in each corpuscle, but as they manifest themselves separately in the action of masses upon each other. It is in this latter relation, that they are the cause of mechanical phenomena, and their laws of action, the object of mechanical science, whether applied to solid, fluid, or gaseous bodies. Here, the masses or portions of matter, whether great or small, in which they become phenomenal, are regarded as acting mechanically and outwardly upon each other, with a motive force resulting from the quantity, velocity, &c. of each mass, considered as a whole, and acting out of itself upon another mass. Thus, in relation to *mechanics*, matter is considered only as it acts *in mass* and *out of itself*, or as composed of parts *extended in space*, and like *those of space itself mutually exclusive of each other*, without reference to the inward being and essential ground of its properties, whereby it thus occupies and acts in space. In its mechanical character and relations, it has *no inward ;* but *outwardness of action and of parts in space* is an essential property, and presupposed in the consideration of attraction and repulsion as mechanical forces. So again, in the application of these as mechanical forces to the different modifications of

26

material masses, under the divisions of solid, fluid
and aeriform, elastic, and unelastic, &c.; these
modifications are assumed according to *given definitions* having reference to their peculiarities of
mechanical action, and not to the inward ground
of these modifications.

On the other hand, when attraction and repulsion are contemplated as united, and counteracting
each other in each corpuscle, they are referred to
the *inward being* of matter, as the universal and
dynamic constituents which pertain to *all matter
as such*, and form the *basis* or antecedent condition of those other powers, whereby different
bodies are modified and distinguished from each
other, and which manifest themselves in these
modifications. In this point of view, they concern
the subjective form of each mass in itself; while,
as mechanical forces, they affect the objective relations of masses to each other in space. Regarded as subjective, or among the inward powers that
reveal themselves in the phenomena of nature,
they are more easily intelligible, and their law of
action is more obvious to our conceptions than any
other. Their agency is manifested to our experience in the spherical form of all bodies, when left
free to the agency of their inherent powers, and
when their parts are so moveable among themselves, as to permit them to obey these laws. It
is important to remark, too, that these powers, as
the constituents of matter, as well as in their
more properly mechanical relations, are conceived
as acting with a determinate relation to space, and

necessarily occupying space, in a manner representable to the pure sense, and determinable, as to its extension and form, by mathematical principles. But the treatises of Kant and Fries already referred to will direct to the right distinctions and limitations here, and I need not dwell longer on this point.

The field of science, embraced in the application of pure mathematics to the agency of mechanical powers, as conditioned by solid, fluid and aeriform bodies, whether in motion or at rest, is of course sufficiently vast, and more cultivated, because more accessible, and the conditions of a scientific knowledge of its phenomena more within our power, than is the case in regard to the more complex agencies of nature. The laws of action that determine the forms and motions of the heavenly bodies, and so of mechanical phenomena under any given conditions, are extremely simple, compared with those from which the simplest forms of organic life result, and it might be expected that science would there gain its first trophies.

I need not refer to authors under this general head, though with a view to its systematic relations I refer again to those mentioned under the last head, and to *Kant's Himmels System* in his *Vermischte Schriften*, vol. 1, s. 283; a part of which, at least, may be read with profit. The French and English works on all parts of this general subject are easily found.

6.   The agencies of nature which seem on the whole next in order for scientific consideration, are those of *Light* and *Heat*.   In their relation to space, and their laws of radiation, reflection and refraction, they have, indeed, a near affinity to those already considered, and their phenomena are equally determinable by pure mathematics.   On this account, they are classed by some with solid, fluid and gaseous bodies, as a fourth division, under the name of radiant matter, and with the science of optics as a division of mechanics.   But whatever may be found true in regard either to the mechanical or chemical relations of these agencies, there seems to be sufficient reason, in the present state of science, and with reference to the present purpose, to contemplate them distinctly and separately and their laws of action as objects of a distinct department of science.   Even though they may be identified with electrical agencies, they yet exhibit their peculiar phenomena governed by distinguishable laws, and these capable of scientific determination.   With reference to our knowledge, and their subjectivity as agencies of material nature, they may be regarded as intermediate between the original and universal powers of attraction and repulsion, and those which are more exclusively exhibited in chemical phenomena.   They are obviously connected with the inward powers by which the distinctive forms of matter are modified, and reveal themselves from within, either as independent and distinguishable powers, or as determinate phenomena of those to

which all properly chemical agencies seem at present likely to be referred.*

7. These powers, which seem to have so extensive and varied an agency in producing the phenomena of nature, are the two polar forces of electricity, the positive and negative, or the acid and alkaline agencies, as they manifest themselves in the electric, galvanic, magnetic, and more properly chemical phenomena. The identity of all these seems to be now admitted ; and if we regard heat and light as products of the same agency, a great apparent anomaly will be removed, and we shall have two correlative living forces, or more properly speaking, *one power*, resolving itself into *two polar forces*, with a tendency to re-union, and producing all these varied phenomena. Regarded in this light, it is the great subjective power, whose agency constitutes the inward life of nature, I mean *inorganic* nature, controlling in its various modes of action the *chemical* affinities and *elementary combinations* of matter, as the powers of attraction and repulsion in their *mechanical* action do the relation of *bodies* to each other.

But although there are no longer supposed to be several distinct powers, from which the phenom-

---

* See on this subject, besides the standard works on Optics and Chemistry, the *Encyclopedia Metropolitana*, article Heat and Light, the *Treatises of Brewster and Young*, and *Oersted's Identité des forces chimiques et electriques*. In this last work, both Heat and Light are exhibited as the products of two correlative powers, which also manifest their agency in all chemical affinities, and, as is afterwards more fully proved by the same author, in the phenomena of magnetism.

ena of electricity, magnetism, and chemical affinity result, but all are referred to the agency of one primordial power varied according to the different relations and circumstances in which it acts, yet these classes of phenomena have still their several peculiarities, and may be, to some extent, separately considered.   *   *   *

8. Next, we may contemplate the dawn of an individualizing and formative power in the crystalization of homogeneous substances, the Bildungskraft of Blumenbach, the power which, without internal and organic action, determines the arrangement of parts by external apposition of pre-existing homogeneous matter, and thereby constructs in each after its kind a specific geometrical form. Read the Introduction to Mohs' Mineralogy.

Then follow the powers of organic life, where, in the relation of the subjective power of life to its correlative object, instead of an *equilibrium* of counteracting forces and consequent *rest*, there is a *predominance* of the *subjective* and a *living process* by which the principle of life *subordinates* its correlatives and *assimilates heterogeneous* elements to the developement of its *own organic form*, and to the attainment of its own *pre-determined end.* This subjective pre-determination of the specific form and of the assimilative and formative process by which its organic structure is unfolded and its proper end realized, is the *Bildungstreib* — Nisus formativus — of Blumenbach, and pertains to each individualized principle of life relatively to its indi-

vidual end. As distinguishable powers in the developement of organic nature, we may consider

(a) *Productivity*, or the simple power of assimilation, nutrition and growth ; the production, in each
individual, of its own form, and the developement of
its organs by subordinating the outward elements
to its use. Here observe, 1st., the unity of the
subjective principle of action ; 2nd, the *immediate*
relation of action and reaction between this and
its outward correlatives ; 3rd, the conditioning of
the actuation of the subjective power by the presence and the correlative nature of the objective ;
yet, 4th, the predominance of the subjective and
the subordination of the objective as means to its
prescribed end. This is the sphere of vegetable
life, and exhibits the dawning of a subjective individualized power, having a unity in itself, and in
its manifold agencies working harmoniously for the
attainment of an end, which end is determined,
not by external agencies, but subjectively, in the
inherent law of working, which predetermines the
form and measure of its outward developement.

(b) *Irritability*, the power of acting upon outward objects, excitable by specific outward stimulants, as in the apathic animalculae of Lamarck,
the nervimotility of Du Trochet, the muscular
fibre, the organic action of different organs, the
heart, lungs, &c., and the nerves of motion in the
animal system generally. Observe here, that in
the animal organism, this power intervenes as it
were between the proper functions of organic life,
assimilation, nutrition, &c., and the outward cor-

relative objects, by which the organic life is to be sustained. In the plant, the organs of nutrition are in immediate contact with the nutritive elements, its subjectivity is comparatively superficial, and its organic apparatus more simple. In the animal there is a higher subjectivity ; the antithetical relation of the subjective principle of life to its correlative objects, by means of which its organic ends are to be attained, is more distinct ; and the conflict is maintained by the aid of an intermediary apparatus of organs, to which the specific character of irritability and of outward organic reaction pertains. I speak here of simple organic irritability and specific reaction, determined by the subjective law of action in the organ where sensibility is still *latent.*

(c) *Sensibility,* a still higher or more central developement of the subjective and a still superadded medium enlarging the sphere of its active relations to a correlative objective. Here is not only a subjective power that *needs* its correlative object as the means of *objectizing* its own *form* and realizing its own *end,* but such a developement of that power as constitutes an *inward finding* (Germanice Empfindung) of its *need,* a *feeling* of its relation to its object, a *sense* of *pain* in the *want* of it and of *satisfaction* in its *attainment.* Simultaneous with this developement of the subjective sense of organic *want* and *craving* of a correlative object, is the developement of the outward organs of sense and the sensuous *presentation* of the outward objects of sense among which the animal is to *seek* its *appropriate* objects and *strive after* the realization of its organic end. When the animal *feels* a *hungering* and *thirsting* after food, the senses direct to the selection and attainment of it in the outer *world of sense*. Where sensibility is thus unfolded, the irritability of the system is of course connected with it, and the muscular organs are excited to act upon their proper objects, through the medium of the inward and outward sensations. Here observe how the nerves of the ganglionic and sympathetic systems connected with the function of nutrition, the nerves of the outward senses, and the nerves of motion are united in a common centre, and give unity and synergy to the whole organism. Remark how in the insect, the organs pertaining to these three distinguishable powers are divided into as many distinct sections, while yet in some form the several powers are present and act each in all and all in each. Observe how, in the progressive developement of powers, the subjectivity of life increases, the sphere of its relations to the outer world is enlarged, its contraposition and conflict with the outward elements become more distinct, and the means of appropriating these for the attainment of its organic end more numerous and complicated. See how, in relation to this end, the irritability and sensibility, the muscular and nervous systems, the sensuous apprehension, the muscular prehension, and the process of digestion with its complex apparatus, are all in order and subordinate to nutrition, while nutrition, on the other hand, serves but

27

to develope these various organs and maintain their several functions. Observe, in a word, how first, the principle of life in all these distinguishable powers and functions is placed in the relation of antithesis to the outward and material elements, how it overcomes and subordinates these, appropriating, transforming and assimilating, so as to make them the bearer of its own form, the plastic material in which it bodies forth and objectizes its own subjective and inward being, seeking as its end the perfect developement of its form, the realization of its own idea. Observe how, secondly, in the relation of the distinguishable powers, organs and functions to each other, we are constrained to admit the apparent paradox that these, throughout the organic system, are reciprocally means and ends, each subservient to all and all to each, and the result of their combined and harmonious action, the full and symmetrical developement and maintenance of the whole organism, in the unity and integrity of all its parts. Observe again, how thirdly, we are constrained, in endeavoring to form a conception of the one principle of life, which thus organizes itself in the harmonious developement of its manifold organs and functions, to represent it to ourselves as a power that, in relation to its organism, is *all in every part*, interpenetrating all its organs in the *totality of its vital energy*, working in all towards the same end, limiting the measure and adapting the form of each of its distinguishable agencies to every other, and thus effecting the *unity of the whole* in the manifoldness of the parts.

REMARKS

THE LEADING POINTS CONNECTED WITH PHYSIOLOGY.

~~~~~~~~~~~~~~~~~

In Physiology, as in all other departments of knowledge, we must distinguish between *phenomena* or appearances and that to which the phenomena are *referred* as their proper *cause*. This distinction we make instinctively and necessarily. We inquire in every case what determines the phenomena to be what they are, and refer them to that which is not itself phenomenal, as their ground.

True, we have given, in the external object of knowledge, no other means of learning what is the *ground* of the phenomena, but the *phenomena* themselves. They are the *condition* of our knowledge; yet knowledge or *science* in its strict sense does not terminate on these, as its *proper object.* There is properly no science of phenomena—But *in* and *through* the phenomena we instinctively seek a knowledge of that which *produces* the phenomena, and whose being and mode of action is revealed, *manifested* to us by these. Phenomena are *fleeting* and *evanescent*, we seek that which is *fixed*

and *unchanging*, as the true and only possible object of unchanging and *scientific* knowledge.

This correlative *object* of science then, is everywhere the *power* or living energy, from the agency
of which the phenomena result, or which is contemplated as the ground of these—or to be more
precise, it is the *law* of its action, as capable of
being discerned in the fleeting phenomena which
it produces, that science seeks to determine; it
being *necessarily* assumed, that each distinguishable power acts *uniformly*, according to a *determinate law* of working.

The question for the scientific naturalist then is
always, *what power*, and acting according to *what
law*, do the phenomena require us to *assume*, as
the abiding ground of the phenomena, and in order
to account for them.   This view, it will be seen,
obviously pre-supposes the most accurate observation and discriminating analysis of the phenomena,
or, as they are called, facts, in every case, as the
necessary condition of our knowledge.   Yet the interest with which this observation is conducted,
depends on the instinctive striving of the mind to
apprehend that which lies beyond the sphere of
sense, and to refer phenomena to an intelligible
and abiding law of action.   How soon, when this
intellectual impulse is not awakened, do the most
novel and striking phenomena cease to interest
and become wearisome to sense !

In entering upon a course of philosophical study,
it is all-important as a ground of right method,
not only that we should bear in mind the true na-

ture and use of facts or phenomena, but in our
contemplation of the powers of nature, as indicated
by them, that we should direct our attention in a
general way, to the relations which these powers
hold to each other. The general remark, to which
the slightest knowledge of physiology bears testimony, and which I have particularly in view, is,
that we discover a progressive developement of
the powers of nature, the higher all along pre-sup-
posing the lower and more universal as the condition of its existence. Thus, for an obvious illustration, the powers of organic life pre-suppose
those of inorganic nature, and the higher powers
in the sphere of organic nature pre-suppose the
lower.

Another general remark nearly connected with
the last is, that, in tracing upward the progressive
powers of nature, and the products of their agency,
we find the more universal taken up, and with the
necessary modifications, included in the more specific, yet so as to be subordinated to its agency.
The universal is present in the specific, but as a
subordinate agency, pre-supposed and necessary,
yet only as means to the more determinate ends
of a higher power. Thus the universal powers of
attraction and repulsion, which belong to all matter, are present, and modify the agency of determinate chemical affinities, and the process of crystallization, while at the same time the law of gravity and its correlative repulsive forces are overcome
by these higher tendencies. So these agencies in
their turn, including also the more universal, are

taken up and made subordinate and subservient to the still higher powers of organic life. Again, in the sphere of physiology itself, we must regard life, organic life, in its lowest form or most general characteristics, as belonging in common and identically to all organized beings, the same in animals as in plants, the same in the blood and in the elementary tissues of the human system, as in the microscopic animalcule. But at every step the higher power, which prescribes the more specific, and so the individualised form and law of action, makes the inferior and more universal the plastic element and material, which it shapes to the upbuilding of its own form, and the attainment of its own higher end.

In looking at the phenomena of material nature, as indicating the distinguishable powers which belong to it, the most obvious are those of *form*. Distinction and determinate arrangement of parts, constituting definiteness of forms in space, express more or less clearly the agency of the powers by which they are produced. At the same time progressive developements of outward form necessarily connect themselves with and assist us in tracing the gradations of living powers already mentioned.

As this consideration of distinguishable and gradually developed forms is a point of great interest in physiology, it may suggest some valuable incentives to reflection if we trace the tendency of inorganic nature and of the more universal powers of matter to manifest themselves in an analogous manner.

We see the great masses of the material universe assume a form nearly spherical. The reason of this and of the variation from a perfect sphere in the tendency to a spheroidal shape, is found in the most universal laws of action pertaining to material masses, and which indeed may be regarded as the necessary and universal constituents of matter — attraction and repulsion — slightly modified by the motions of each particular mass. In other words, we refer the form of the heavenly bodies to the agency primarily of attraction and repulsion, and we can see that such must be the form of a material mass the relation of whose parts was influenced by no other agency. The same law of form, resulting from the agency of the same powers, manifests itself in the soap-bubble and in the globule of mercury or the rain drop. The most simple application of these powers would be where no chemical relations or properties interfere and modify their action, but where the force of repulsion is inversely as the cubes of the distances from the centre, while that of attraction is inversely as the squares. But so far as external form is concerned, the result is the same in all perfectly fluid bodies of whatever density, and so of all masses in which the relation of the parts to each other and to the whole is determined by these powers. In this case then, we can refer the phenomena to the law of action from which they result, and see *a priori* that they must be what they are. We have a scientific insight into the formative power, and contemplate the phenomena as the sensible manifestation of an intelligible law, the form in which the supersensuous and intelligible makes itself visible and tangible. The outward form is *here* and *every where* the visible product and *record* of the power and its law of action.

These powers then, pertaining to matter universally, do not of themselves serve to distinguish one kind of matter in respect to form or otherwise from another, but, unmodified by other powers, would give to all material wholes the same external form. Whatever other powers are superadded therefore to modify the form and relation of parts in a given mass, must pre-suppose the presence of these, and so far as their tendency is diverse in its effect, can become efficient only by overcoming them.

In the process of crystallization, we detect the presence of such a superadded power, manifesting a tendency distinct from that of universal attraction and repulsion, and building up in each kind of mineral substance its *specific form*. While the formative tendency of the powers before spoken of is, like the powers themselves, coextensive with matter and every where the same, we find here diversity of form and of the formative agency, connected apparently with diversity in the chemical and electro-magnetic properties of different minerals. The distinctive characteristics of this power, or formative process, as exhibited in the phenomenal results, form a distinct branch of study, and have acquired a kind of scientific precision. Yet we have not, as in the former case, an idea and scientific insight into the nature of the agency from which the crystalline form results; and the science of mineralogy, therefore, as to its ultimate principles, is still empirical in its character. It is sufficient here merely to direct your attention to a comparison of the phenomena of crystallization as already known to you, with those exhibited in the elementary forms of organic life. Remarks on the general notions of living power and the life of nature.

Observe, that in the formative process in minerals, although the crystal may be regarded as, in a certain sense, an individualization of the specific formative power of a given mineral, yet the phenomena do not indicate that this power has become *subjective* in the crystal, and so works by means of it as its organ. They lead us rather to contemplate it as present with the diffused substance of the mineral in its state of solution, in the same sense in which attraction and repulsion are present to all material substance, and in like manner determining it, when no other agencies obstruct the process, to assume in each mineral a specific crystalline form. Thus in any or all parts of a mineral solution, or influenced by mere extraneous and accidental circumstances, nuclei may be formed, i. e. the individualizing process commenced. This is in fact no true individualizing of the power, but only a manifold exhibition of it in its phenomenal forms. Just as attraction and repulsion manifest their presence in all the drops of a falling shower, so the more specific agency of

28

a higher power is exhibited as diffusively present in the flakes of the falling snow. It acts as it were immediately and outwardly upon the homogeneous crystallizable material, without the intervention of an antecedent seminal principle, as the condition of its action upon the surrounding elements. Thus, when the nucleus is formed, it is not the organic instrument of its own growth; but the same agency which determined the locality and form of a given nucleus, continues to increase it by apposition of successive strata upon the surface.

The crystal has no organs — has an angular and geometric form — is homogeneous in its mass — no internal motion of parts nor included fluids — but is a *fixed solid*.

Here then is the point of transition from mineral to vegetable and animal, from crystalline to organic forms. In the simplest and most elementary form of vegetable or animal existence, whether in the most simply organized plant or animalcule, or in the elementary tissues of more complex forms, the phenomena compel us to assume a subjective power, hypostasized in, and one with, the living form, in which its agency is manifested. The organic form is not a mere fixed product or relic of the agency which produced it, but the outward manifestation of a present living power.

That power, too, in its relation to the organizable elements by which the organic form is to be upbuilt, cannot be regarded as immediately present to them in their local diffusion, but acts upon them only from within outwardly, by means of parts already organized, and through these, as the necessary condition of its outward action. Hence organic forms proceed only from antecedent forms, and cannot be conceived as producible in the order of nature, by any powers pertaining to inorganic matter, and uninfluenced by previous organization.

Again, relatively to the powers of inorganic nature, that of organic formation manifests itself obviously as a higher and controlling power. Without annihilating the mechanical and chemical agencies of the inorganic elements, or even the tendency to crystalline forms, the power of life subordinates all these to the developement of its own specific and individual form. They must be conceived as still present, with all their distinctive tendencies, in the several elements to which they belong, but modified in their action and made the instruments of a higher power, striving, by means of these, for the attainment of its own prescribed end.

In respect to the distinctive phenomena of organic formations, the following particulars may be observed. 1st. In the lowest forms and elementary tissues, we distinguish containing vessels and contained fluids; so that fluids here enter into the organic structure. 2nd. The increase and growth of an organic body is not by external apposition, but by means of elements first received into its vessels, *assimilated*, and made instrumental to a developement from within. 3d. Consequently internal vessels, and the motion of fluids in these,

is the most essential character of organic forms.
4th. By the reception, assimilation, transmission
by vessels, and secretion in the several organs the
nutrition and growth of the whole organism is
effected, and this constitutes the life of plants.

Thus, by means of the assimilative organs, and
the motion of the fluids, the plant has the power
of self-developement and self-conservation, by appropriating and converting into its own organic
form the heterogeneous elements which are the
objective means and condition of its growth. The
relation of subjective and objective is here exhibited in its simplest form. In crystallization we
conceive the crystallizable material, and the tendency to crystallize, as *inseparable* and *coextensive*.
The *material* is *pre-existent*, as a *homogeneous
element*, and merely assumes a crystalline form
without change of its *chemical properties*. While
we distinguish between the power and the material in which it manifests itself, we still do not
conceive it as a *new power supervening*, but as already *present* in the material itself.

In organization, on the other hand, we do not
conceive the organic power as latent in the organizable elements. But this, as an active principle,
exists subjectively only in the seed or germ, the
already organized form, while the correlative object, which is the material on which it acts, is
conceived as merely passive in relation to it, or as
having, *in itself*, no tendency to assume this or
that organic form. It is rather indifferent to all
organic forms, and, relatively to the organific prin-

ciple, the mere plastic material to which it supervenes, and by means of which it developes its own
predetermined form of organization.

Here observe, the *form*, the *specific* and *individual character* of the organism, is *subjectively* pre-
determined, and not *objectively;* in the *unity* of the
living principle, and not by the outward and correlative *material*.   It impresses its own character
on that material, forms out of it, by *assimilation*,
the organic elements of its own growth, and determines the form of its own developement, *according
to its own inward law of being*.   This *inward law*,
pertaining to the *unity* of the *principle of life* in
each organism, and *predetermining* its form of developement, and the end, in the realization of
which its functions terminate, is what I mean by
the *subjective*, while the correlative *objective* is
found in the extraneous and yet heterogeneous,
but plastic and assimilable elements, in which it
seeks, as it were, the *means* to its *ends*, and makes
them the *bearers* of its own living form.

Here again, it must be remarked more directly,
that in order to the *conception* of that which I
have termed subjective, as pre-determining the
organific process, the *relation* of its *agencies to an
end* is an essential point to be considered.   We
see manifold parts and organs, each with its several functions, and with various relations to the
outward elements, but all *working unitedly* towards
one and the *same end*.   It is this relation to *one*
and the *same end*, that gives its *unity* to an organic
system, as a *whole*.   The forms and functions of

the several parts can be *understood* only by their *relation* to the whole; and the *perfection of the whole*, as resulting from the free and perfect developement of all its powers and organs in due proportion and harmony, is *the end*, in reference to which organic action must be contemplated. This end the phenomena constrain us to conceive, as pre-determined by the subjective principle of life, while the objective and correlative elements, on which its transforming power is exerted, are but the plastic material, though the necessary condition, for its attainment. According to the Platonic doctrine, the formative or organific power here is to be conceived as an *idea*, that has at the same time a living, self-realizing energy — as a living law, manifesting itself in the outward forms which it constructs, and constituting their inward life.

This idea of a subjective tendency, or of an end subjectively prescribed in the unity of the vital principle, that end being the perfection of the organism itself as a whole, is that which essentially distinguishes organic from mechanical powers and agencies. In a machine, the controlling idea and power which determines its form, the nature of its materials, and the relations of its parts, is extraneous to the machine, in the mind and skill of the machinist. The end also, which it is designed to effect, is in like manner extraneous, or *out of itself*, and the machine is regarded only as the *means* for the accomplishment of this. On the other hand, that which determines the specific form of an organic system, must be conceived as an actual power, *subjectively present* in the living body, and *building up* by its agency, the form in which it *reveals itself.* In reference to the end for which it works, it builds up its manifold organs in the unity and harmony of their relations, as constituting one organic whole, not, as a machine, for the accomplishment of an *ulterior* end, but for its *own sake.* It is, in short, its *own* end. That which it strives to accomplish as an end, is the perfect realization of the *idea* which constitutes the inward *law* of its being. It is a *self-realizing idea*—an idea working as a living power, and revealing itself outwardly, in the material world of sense, in the organic form which it constructs out of the material elements, which it subordinates to that end.

This train of thought would be incomplete, were it not added, as a truth essentially involved in the idea of an organic system, and manifested by the phenomena which it exhibits, that no particular part, organ, or function, of the system can be conceived as merely a mechanical means in its relation to any other, but *all the several organs and functions have to each other reciprocally the relation of means and ends*; the one living and organific power, in the manifoldness of its distinguishable agencies, thus combining and harmonizing the whole, according to its effectual working in the measure of every part, and making increase of the body, until it attains the full upbuilding and developements of its pre-determined form.

These remarks are general, and apply to all organized bodies. Whether more simple or more complex in the number of their organs and functions, they have the same general characters, in regard to the relation of the parts to each other and to the whole, and of the subjective principle of life to its pre-determined end. The same general relation of subjective and objective also subsists in all cases between the inward principle of life and the correlative elements, which are the outward means and conditions of its actual developement. But in regard to this relation, and the modes and organs by which the subjective, regarded as the unity of life in the entire organism, acts upon, and appropriates its correlative objects, there are connected with the successive gradations in the developement of organic nature, very obvious distinctions. — Only some of the most general need be noticed here.

It was remarked before, that in the organic action of plants, the relation of subjective and objective is exhibited in its simplest form. In this we see the organization adapted to the relative *outward condition* of those elements on which the several organs are to act, *that condition being considered as fixed*, and the plant itself without organs of locomotion. It has no provision for changing either its own place, or the place of those elements which are the conditions of its growth. It simply projects its organs in search, as it were, of its necessary food on the one hand, and of air and light, the other essential conditions of organic life, on the

other. Its root, with its branches and their rootlets, descend, and insinuate themselves into the
soil, while the stem with its branches and leaves
expand upwards, both to act, in the performance of
their appropriate functions, immediately upon the
elements with which they there come in contact.
The transmuting and assimilative functions seem
to be performed by these peripheral organs at the
point of contact between their expanded surfaces
and the outward elements. Here the subjective
and the objective, considered as the power of assimilation and the assimilable element, are in immediate connexion, with no intervening function.
This too, the process of assimilation and growth,
or productivity, by the agency of these organs, is
the whole sphere of vegetable life. The subjectivity, therefore, of the principle of life here, relatively to its corresponding objective, may be said
to be comparatively superficial. This remark will
be better understood and appreciated in the sequel.

If we compare with this the organic relation of
animals to their outward correlatives, we see, as it
were, a greater subjectivity of the principle of life,
greater complexity of organs, and other functions
intervening between the ultimate one of assimilation and the outward objects on which it is to act.
Thus, instead of expanding its absorbent vessels
in contact with their surrounding objects, the animal is provided with an inward cavity, and with
organs for apprehending and depositing within it
the elements on which those organs, which are
29

analagous to the rootlets of the vegetable, are destined to perform their function.

The function of aeration seems to be performed, to some extent in the ascending scale, by the expanded surface, without a more special apparatus. But as we ascend, we find for this function too, special organs, endued with specific irritability, and a power of motion, for the purpose of acting upon the surrounding air. Ascending still farther, we find this, like the other function, provided with an internal cavity, and an apparatus for conveying to it the atmospheric air ; and thus the functions performed by the expanded roots and leaves of the vegetable are here performed by organs wrapped up and secured in the internal cavities of the system, while a complex apparatus, endued with a higher organic power, is provided for preparing and bringing in contact with these now internal organs the material on which they are to act. That which constitutes the objective correlative to the inward power of life, is here, then, instead of being acted upon directly and primarily by those organs which effect a change of their chemical properties, and assimilate them, is first acted upon by a mechanical force, pertaining to an additional set of organs, and resulting from a higher organic power — the irritability of the muscular system. The point of contact, and the primary action and reaction between the organism considered as a whole and the outward elements, is now in the muscular system, and results from the relation between the irritabil-

ity of the muscular organs and their correlative
stimulants in the outer world. Those muscular
organs which act independently of sensation, must
be conceived to have a specific irritability, and to
react immediately and organically to their appropriate stimulants. There is reason to suppose,
that in some grades of organic nature, such irritability alone pertains to the system, sensibility being still latent.

A still higher and the highest form of mere organic developement, considered as the manifestation of a new power, is that of the nervous system,
and the sensibility, which is here superadded to
the irritability of the muscular. Here, too, we
find the complexity of the whole system increased,
the inward principle of life becomes still more subjective, and its primary functions still farther removed from immediate contact with the outward
elements. The muscular organs in turn, instead
of being now acted upon immediately by an outward correlative, are stimulated through the medium of the nervous system, and the organs of sense.
The point of contact between the organism as a
whole, and the outer world, is in its sensibility.
Its muscular powers do not act upon their appropriate correlatives, but on the condition of being
excited and directed by the powers of sense.
Again, the assimilative powers of its digestive and
secretory organs can perform their functions only
as they are supplied with their appropriate materials by the muscular organs which are destined to
that office.

But again, while the inward and more hidden powers and functions of life are dependent for the conditions of their agency upon the more exterior and peripheral organs, with their irritability and sensibility, as the media through which the necessary relations of action and reaction are established between the ultimate subjective principle of life in the system and its correlative objective in the world of sense, it is a proposition no less obvious and important, that the specific susceptibilities of these exterior and as it were intermediate organs and their peculiar relations to the external world are dependent on and predetermined by the inward principle itself. The irritability of the heart and lungs, or their muscular apparatus, for example, and their specific relations to the blood and the atmospheric air as their outward stimulants in general, and so in all their specific modifications, from the white and cold blooded animals with their slight respiration, up to the mammalia and birds, is just that in kind and degree, which the specific nature and wants of the one inward principle of life in the organism determines it to be, or which is necessary for the attainment of its end. So the still more peripheral sensibility of the system and its relation to the external objects of sense, *considered in reference to mere organic existence,* have a like dependence on and are equally predetermined in their susceptibilities and functions, by the one inward principle of life and its specific wants as connected with the outward world of sense. The *mere* creature of sense, in other words, has no sensibility, it is not excitable through the medium of its senses, except by such objects as have a specific relation to the character and organic wants of its inward life.

In a word, the external form and organic excitabilities of the organic system, in its relations with the external elements, must be conceived as subjectively determined in the specific principle of life, yet as correlative to those elements and their inward powers. The specific principle of life, in each organism, strives after the realization of its own ends, in the developement and organic action of precisely those organs, and the agency of those organic powers, which are necessary to the attainment of its end; the outer correlatives in the world of sense, with all their manifold powers and agencies, being pre-supposed as containing the conditions of its outward existence.

In the outer elements, as containing the conditions of its outward existence and developement, the means by which its end is to be realized, the living creature, whether plant or animal, may be said to *seek* and *strive after* the end which the inward law of its being prescribes, by appropriating the necessary surrounding elements as means to that end.

But while we contemplate the organs of muscular action and of sense, with their peculiar functions, as instrumental to the *nutrition* of the system, and so in relation of means to an end, it must not be forgotten, that *all* are *reciprocally* means and ends, and that the function and organs of nutrition, in turn, are instrumental for sustaining all the other organs and functions of the system. In one point of view, we might be led to regard what some have termed the animal sphere, including the irritability and sensibility of the system, as of higher dignity than the so called vegetative sphere, or the nutritive organs and functions, and so the latter as only in order to the former. But it must be considered rather, that in the successive gradations of organic nature, what is termed for the sake of distinction the vegetative system of the animal, does not remain on a level with the organic system of the vegetable, and serve as a basis, on which are built up the higher forms of animal organization. The whole system, regarded in the unity of its vital principle, is higher in the animal than in the vegetable, and in the more perfectly organized animals than in those of simpler organization. With the enlargement and multiplication of its outward relations and the corresponding organs, the subjective principle of life must be regarded as elevated in rank, and every part as partaking of the dignity which belongs to the whole.

Nor can we even with strict propriety distinguish, as some have done, between the so-called functions of nutrition, as *vital* functions, and the other above mentioned, as functions of *relation*. True, in the more highly organized animals these are, as I have said before, the more external and immediate instruments of action upon the objects of the outer world. But in strict propriety, the aliments deposited in the stomach and intestines are still extraneous to the system, in the same sense as the surrounding elements are extraneous to the roots of the vegetable. The subjective assimilative power of the system is still to be exerted upon them, and a relation subsists here between a subjective and its corresponding objective, as well as between the muscular apparatus by which the food is deposited there, and its correlative objects without. In a most important sense, all the organs and functions are vital, and all relative. The system *as a whole* is placed in a relation of action and reaction to the outer world; and the agency of the muscular and sensitive organs, no less than that of the more properly nutritive, terminates in the developement of the one principle of inward life, the realization of the one self-determined end of its whole being. Its most external organs and relations are the necessary condition for calling into action and perfecting the developement of those powers, which are, as it were, more inward, and determine the ultimate tendencies of the system. Thus, while, with the successive gradations of organized being, from the vegetable up to man, its distinguishable powers with their several organs and functions become more and more distinct and individualized in their forms and tendencies, each acquiring by degrees a more fully developed form and individuality of its own, the unity of the whole is still preserved, and the ultimate perfection of the whole organism attained, by the due subordination or proportionateness of each to all and of all to each.

Observe, as another point of some interest, by what successive gradations the organized being, in its relations to external nature as containing the objective conditions of its existence, becomes more and more free, seeks the end which its nature prescribes in a wider sphere, and with increasing power as to the selection and appropriation of means. If we begin with the production of forms in the lower sphere of inorganic nature, we see that a given crystal can be constructed only where the homogeneous integral elements already exist. The principle of life in the vegetable seed, with its assimilative power, can *compose for itself* the materials of its growth, *whenever* the more simple assimilable ingredients are brought within the sphere of its agency.

In the lowest form of animal organization, we find, added to the assimilative functions, an apparatus by which the animal through its own agency *grasps* and *brings in contact* with its assimilative organs, the aliments that would not otherwise be within their reach. At the next step in the ascending scale we find the power of locomotion, by which the animal is enabled to range with more or less freedom in search of its appropriate food, and guided by its senses, to select in a wider and wider sphere of external nature, the means necessary for its organic ends. Yet here we find different species limited as to those means in an endless variety of modes and degrees, by the specific relations both of their assimilative powers and muscular organs to their corresponding objects. Many insects, as the silk worm, are limited in the selection of their food to the leaves of a particular species of plants, or like the honey bee, to the same or nearly resembling fluids secreted by different plants. Some are confined to vegetable, others to animal substances, and all are more or less limited by the outward conditions of climate and the multiplied outward circumstances to which their organization has reference.

In all these respects, the human system is the least limited in the conditions of its existence. It has a greater power of assimilation, and can extract its nourishment from a greater variety of outward elements, or convert them into its proper aliment. The whole sphere of nature is capable of being made, by the agency of his manifold powers, directly or indirectly subservient to his wants, and conducive to the accomplishment of his ends; and the subjective powers of his being, in their full developement, and as the means of this, have the world in all the manifoldness of its powers and agencies as their correlative object.

With these views of the relations subsisting between the subjective powers of the organic system and its correlative objects in the outer world, let us proceed to look more nearly at the subjective principle itself, 1st. in its relation to the material of its organism, 2nd. in that of its distinguishable powers to each other in their successive evolutions, and 3d. in respect to its unity, individuality, and finality or determination to an end, in the successive gradations of organized being:

30

1. The subjective principle of organization, in
its relation to the material elements and the powers which pertain to them as inorganic matter, it
has been already remarked, must be considered as
a higher power, *supervening*, and subordinating
these to its own law of being. Observe farther,
that the conditions of the problem require us to regard it as, in respect to its material, an *interpene-*
trating power. The before inanimate and inorganic matter, when acted upon and interpenetrated
by this, *becomes vital, is*, so long as it constitutes a
part of the living organism, *living matter*, both the
solid and fluid parts of the organism being alike
pervaded by one and the same power. While,
therefore, we distinguish this principle from any
that before pertained to the *unorganized elements*,
it is not to be conceived as extraneous to it *when*
organized. There are no ultimate atoms or mole-
cules, retaining their previous form and character,
by the different *arrangement* and *combination* of
which, as *mechanical* elements, different organic
structures are built up. The *ultimate* parts are
interpenetrated by the power of *life*, no less than
by the power of *gravity*, and, so long as they continue so, have a tendency to assume the organic
form, to manifest the specific irritability, or to convey the peculiar impressions of sense, which pertain to the specific principle of life in each organism. The specific power of life reveals *itself* in a
visible and tangible form, and *constitutes* the essential *character* of the living organ; all inferior powers, being, as it were, taken up into this, and made

the transparent media, through which it manifests itself. Thus, in the eye of the serpent, we cease to regard the mechanical and chemical properties of its visible and tangible parts; and it is not surely the weight, or the chemical agents, as oxygen, hydrogen, &c., which constitute the *organ*. That which we *mean* by the eye of the serpent, and which makes it to be *what it is*, is the inward power, which looks through it, and reveals to our senses the distinctive character of the animal itself. I say *through* it, or *by means* of it, not meaning a *mechanical* instrumentality, separable from the power that uses it, but as being the outward form and living manifestation of the power itself, *correlative* to our senses and percipient faculties, which could apprehend it only under material and sensible forms. The *form* is *instinct* with the *life*, which in its peculiar and impressive power is *felt* and contemplated, as *present in* and *one with* the organ, which *bespeaks* its presence. The same is true of the whole animal, in all that pertains to its outward form and expression, as an object of sense.

Thus the powers of organic nature *enter into*, are *inherent* in, and *identical* with, the material, organic form. This is their mode of existence and of action in the world of sense; and if we intellectually distinguish between the subjective, intelligible principle, as an *idea*, and the extended sensuous form, in which that idea is *realized*, we still recognize them as one and the same object, in its two different relations to sense on the one hand, and to intelligence on the other. The principle of life in the

vegetable seed, or, still farther back, in the powers
which produced the seed, is put forth, attains an
outward existence and developement, in the plant,
which reveals to our senses its specific form, and
all its sensible properties. The living power here
no longer abides in the seed, nor in its antecedent
birth place, the mysterious generative powers of
the parent plant; it is *put forth*, it is *here* in the
plant itself, which it has organized, and in which it
abides as its distinctive and proper essence.

The subjective principle of organic life, therefore, is not a power which, abiding in itself as a
subject, puts forth in the world of sense outward
forms *other than itself*, and having an *objective* relation *to it*. It simply produces and puts forth *itself*, and *loses itself in*, or is *identified with*, the
extended, outward form; in which alone it has an
actual existence. It becomes objectized in the
world of outward forms *through* itself, or by means
of its own organic action, but, in its lower potence,
as mere organic life, in plants and in the vegetable
sphere of animal organization, not *for* itself.

2. But, in the second place, what are the relations of the distinguishable powers of organic life
to each other ? The powers referred to, as distinguishable here, are, 1. Productivity, or the process
of nutrition and growth in the developement of a
specific form; 2. Irritability, whose proper seat
and organ is the muscular fibre; and, 3. Sensibility, which has its organ in the nervous system.

In what has just now been said of the relation

of the subjective power of life to the material form in which it objectizes itself, it must be observed that the remarks apply alike to all the powers of organic life. They all interpenetrate and impart their own character to the material elements and living forms which they animate. But relatively to each other, we may with propriety speak of those forms of organization which are peculiar to the several powers above enumerated, as having successively higher degrees of vitality, and being in the same order more and more removed from the sphere of inorganic nature. Each antecedent power and form of life is in a sense the basis of that which follows, and which is as it were evolved out of it, or makes it the instrument and material by which it objectizes itself. Thus the agency of the productive power of assimilation and organic developement is presupposed as a necessary antecedent to the existence of irritability. This is distinct from the immediate functions of secretion, assimilation and growth, yet cannot exist without these, since its peculiar organs are produced by their agency. Irritability is a higher principle of vitality, a higher form of living action, which realizes itself in nature by means of the lower. In relation to external nature, therefore, it is more subjective, i. e., as a living power, farther removed from those inorganic powers and agencies which are immediately opposed and brought in subjection to the assimilative powers of life; while at the same time, as remarked before, the appropriate action of its organs in the

living system intervenes as it were between the
external objects of nature and the agency of the
organs of nutrition. It is itself opposed, not to
the chemical agencies of inorganic matter, like the
function of assimilation, as its proper correlatives,
but to those powers which oppose a mechanical
resistance to the attainment of the means necessary for organic existence. Its peculiar organs
overcome or remove the mechanical forces necessary to be overcome in order to the prescribed action of the organs of nutrition, and by the functions of locomotion, prehension, mastication, de-
glutition, respiration, circulation, &c., bring the
materials of nutrition into contact with its proper
organs. Where this power manifests itself, therefore, in its higher form of vitality, as in the animal
organization compared with the vegetable, it may
be said to detach and withdraw more distinctly the
organic form to which it pertains, from the sphere
of inorganic powers ; to give to the whole system
a higher character of separate and distinct existence, in the higher developement of its subjective
powers and organs, and in the relation of action
and reaction between these and their correlative
objects in the outer world ; and at the same time,
in its relation to the inferior power of nutrition, to
enfold within its own organs, to protect, and more
effectually to secure, the agency of those functions
by means of which its own existence and agency
are sustained.

PSYCHOLOGY.

CHAPTER I.

THE LIMITS AND METHOD OF PSYCHOLOGICAL INQUIRY.

The term *psychology* (ψυχη, the soul, and λογος, doctrine), according to its etymological import, signifies the science of the soul, or a scientific representation of its several powers ; the phenomena which they exhibit, and the laws of their action.

In its widest extension, as used by some writers, it includes essentially within its sphere all the living powers of human nature. The inducement to give it this extension, arises from contemplating those powers in the unity of that principle of life, of which they are the manifold developement, and which assigns to each its appropriate agency. As it is the *same living spirit*, which manifests itself *outwardly* in the physical organization of the body, and *inwardly* in the phenomena of consciousness, it might seem proper to include the whole under the term psychology, as above defined. Thus all the powers of the soul, as the one principle of life in man, are represented in their proper relations, and connected with the organs, in and through which alone they are manifested to our experience.

This extended view, however, embracing all that pertain to the outward and inward life of man, as a distinct *species* of earthly existence, more properly constitutes the *science of man*, or *anthropology*. As such, it forms a particular branch of that department of natural science, which investigates the phenomena and laws of living nature, or *biology*.

The powers thus manifested in the complex life of man, though referable to one indivisible principle of life, are yet naturally distinguished into two kinds. The one kind constitute the *outward life*, the vegetative organic powers, by which the body is developed, nourished, and sustained ; the other, the *inward life* of the soul, whose phenomena are manifested to our observation only in our inward consciousness.

To investigate the powers of our vegetative, organic life, the assemblage of organs in the living body, their various functions, mutual relations, &c. is the object of *physiology*, or *physical anthropology*.

Psychology, in its limited and proper acceptation, consequently, is confined to the investigation of those phenomena which are exhibited in the inner sense, and concerns itself with those of organic life no farther than they may afford ground of conclusions in regard to its own proper sphere.

The spheres of physiology and psychology, as thus defined, are clearly distinguishable *by the mode in which the facts and phenomena belonging to each are known.* The powers and agencies which manifest themselves in the organic life of the body, in the nourishment, growth and reproduction of its material parts and organs, *are not objects of consciousness,* but of the *outward sense,* under the relations of space, extension, form, motion, &c., of material organs, and the investigation of them is inseparable from the study of anatomy and chemistry.

The phenomena of our inward life, on the other hand, can be known only by *reflection upon our own consciousness, and cannot be exhibited under the relations of space, or explained by reference to the modifications of extension, form and motion in the material organs.*

Though the phenomena which are the objects respectively of physiology and psychology, are easily distinguishable, and known by different modes, they have yet an intimate relation and interdependence, the investigation of which is of great interest, and may be termed comparative anthropology. That mind and body act and react upon each other ; that the powers of life, which determine the form and combination of the bodily organs, are through them connected with those which we find in our consciousness ; and that the agencies of the mind again influence the state and the developement of the material organs, cannot be doubted. Yet we can learn nothing of the form and structure of an organ from the state of consciousness that it serves to awaken in the mind, nor of the nature of feeling, thought, &c., from any examination of the organs of the body.

For a knowledge of psychology, therefore, we must look not to the anatomy of the organs of sense, or of the brain and nerves, however important these may be in the science of man, in a more general sense, but to reflection upon our own consciousness, and a careful observation of the phenomena which are there exhibited. In doing this, the same rules and cautions are to be observed, as in the observation of external nature. To fix the attention, and mark with precision the phenomena presented, to generalize and form conceptions with caution, and avoid hasty conclusions from inadequate premises, are of the same importance here, as in the study of physics, and more difficult.

Simply to observe, to distinguish and arrange the facts of consciousness, as presented in our experience, aiming at nothing more, constitutes *empirical psychology*. To seek for the principles from which those facts may be deduced and explained, and thus to acquire a rational insight into the laws of our inward being, is *rational psychology*, or the metaphysics of our inward nature.

In a system of empirical psychology, it is not of course attempted to establish *a priori* principles ; yet some principles of arrangement must be adopted, and these principles will result from the previous logical and philosophical views of the enquirer. The arrangement of the facts is the application to them of logical principles of method.

In adopting an arrangement with a view to a course of instruction, it is necessary to have regard to the relations of the facts to be observed and systematized, to our consciousness. No true and living knowledge of psychology can be communicated to the scholar, any farther than he is led to observe and recognize the phenomena represented in his own inward experience. Now all the phenomena which properly belong to the subject considered in a general view, are those which belong to all men, and which every man, therefore, capable of the necessary exercise of reflection, may find in himself. Yet some classes of phenomena are more obvious, and more easily to be designated and recognized, than others. For those, therefore, who are commencing the study, it is obviously important to begin with the more obvious, and proceed to the more abstruse and difficult parts of the subject.

We cannot, for this reason, adopt the method pursued by some writers, of commencing with the inward, and as it were central, powers of life in the soul, in order to show in our progress, the relation of the various phenomena to these, as their origin. This view may be taken with advantage by those already accustomed to reflection and familiar with the facts, but would be necessarily unintelligible in the commencement of the study. We must, then, first observe and analyze with care those things which can be most easily designated.

But, in whatever method we pursue the subject,
it will be found attended with difficulties which
do not pertain to the study of external nature.
The natural impulse of the mind carries our attention to the world without, to the objects of the
outer senses. We distinguish, and arrange, and
give names to the objects of the material world,
as matter of necessity, even when not impelled by
the interests of knowledge. But comparatively
few ever turn their attention steadfastly to the observation of what passes in the inner world of their
own consciousness. Those who do so, find the
phenomena here exhibited to their inner sense,
too fleeting to be fixed for the purpose of examination, and too subtle and complicated to be distinctly conceived and classed, so as to be represented by steadfast terms and made communicable
by language.

Hence one of our greatest obstacles to the progress of knowledge here, is the vagueness of the
language relating to the subject, and the difficulty
of one's determining the precise distinction, which
another has intended to mark by a particular
word.

Connected with the difficulties of the language
belonging to this subject, we must bear in mind
the fact so often noticed, that all the terms which
designates facts of our inward consciousness, were
originally metaphorical in this use of them, and in
their literal signification applied to objects of the
outer world. This resulted necessarily from the
process by which language is formed; and beside

the vagueness, which is inseparable from the use of metaphorical terms, has occasioned the introduction of hypotheses and modes of explaining the phenomena of our inward life, which are wholly alien to their nature.

Another consideration of importance here is, that while terms are vague and fluctuating, they lead much more unavoidably to indistinctness and misapprehension in our views of the facts designated by them, than in the study of physical science. Chemists may employ different terms to signify the same substance, and yet perfectly understand each other in regard to it. The substance is or may be before them; and however they may differ in regard to its nature and properties, they are always able at least to know what is the subject of dispute. In psychology, we have no way of designating a fact but by words, or a reference to the outward circumstances in which the fact exists.

Again, it is by no means easy for different writers to come to an agreement, with respect to the technical terms to be employed. The phenomena themselves vary their aspect according to the relations in which they are viewed, and consequently in accordance with the theory which the writer adopts, and with reference to which his technology is formed. Hence the terms cannot be altered and made to coincide, so long as the systems differ. In other words, our *language* here is nearly *inseparable from the theory* which we adopt; and we *cannot speak of facts of our inward consciousness, without betraying by our language,* the *system* by *which we express our views of their* nature and re-lations. Thus, if we use the same words, it is only in a vague and indeterminate sense, or each in a different sense ; and if *we think with precision,* and *reduce our views to a logical and consistent system,* we must have *technical terms corresponding with it,* and *growing out of it.* This arises from the fact, that nothing in our inward life exists sep-arately or separably from the rest. Feeling, thought, will, &c., all co-exist in the same indi-visible state of consciousness, and are the same act under different relations.

Yet the distinction between words and things, between verbal and real definitions, exists here, as well as in regard to other subjects ; and though in the completion of a system, the determination of its technical terms would be essential, it is more important in the commencement of the study to describe the facts in such a manner, as will help to recognize and reflect upon them. When these are clearly apprehended, they must be fixed in the mind, and distinctions marked by the most appro-priate terms which the usage of the language will admit. A technical phraseology, connected with this subject, can hardly to be said to exist to any considerable extent in the English language ; and this fact greatly increases the difficulty of advancing in the knowledge of the subject, but still more of communicating our views to each other.

Yet with all the difficulties which attend the pursuit of this study, the interest and importance of it are such as amply repay the labor which it imposes. As an introduction to logic and metaphysics, a knowledge of psychology is indispensable. It lays open to us, and teaches us to observe and contemplate with ever growing admiration, that inner world of our own consciousness, which, rightly understood, is far more wonderful than all the phenomena of the world without. It reveals to us, in a word, our own being, the power by which we are actuated, and the laws of nature by which we are governed.

Psychology also connects itself intimately with the business of instruction in all its departments; though expectations that are not well grounded in all respects, have sometimes been indulged, respecting the advantages of this sort, which were to be derived from it.

In a more general view of it, we connect it with the history of human cultivation, in the gradual developement of the mind in successive periods, in the history of particular nations, and of the race. Here too, and in the study of the languages of different nations, and at different periods of their progress from a savage and childlike to a refined and cultivated state, we find an interesting application of the knowledge which it gives us of the laws of human thought and feeling, as well as important materials for the enlargement of our knowledge of the science.

In the present course of inquiry, as already remarked, that method of arrangement seems best, which begins with facts most easy to be designated, and recognized in our own experience. In accordance with this purpose, and as best suited to its attainment, the following arrangement will be adopted.

1. A general view of those powers which reveal themselves in our consciousness, their leading divisions and relations.

2. The investigation of the several leading divisions in the order of — 1. The faculties of knowledge, or the speculative powers of the soul. 2. The powers of feeling, the capacities of enjoyment and suffering, or those by virtue of which an interest is awakened on the objects of our knowledge, — and 3. The power of voluntary action.

CHAPTER II.

STATEMENT OF CERTAIN PRELIMINARY FACTS AND DISTINCTIONS.

In the study of empirical psychology, it would seem necessary, as already intimated, in order to consistency, that we abstain from advancing *a priori* principles as the ground of inference, and proceed, as far as may be, in the order of our experience. This method I shall endeavor to pursue as far as possible; though, to a mind accustomed to reflection, the principles which facts of experience necessarily presuppose, will sometimes force themselves upon our notice.

My purpose at first is to state certain general facts, and mark a few general distinctions, which you will see I think to be verified by experience; while some of them may perhaps at the same time be seen to be grounded in a rational necessity.

1. All the knowledge which we have of the soul empirically, is a knowledge of its *conditions* and *relations*, and of its conditional and relative *phenomena*. Experience teaches us nothing of what *must be absolutely* and *unconditionally*, but only what takes place under certain circumstances.

2. We must therefore consider the soul with reference to those conditions and relations in which its phenomena are manifested to us, and observe the phenomena which it exhibits, as the means of learning its nature. This is true of the knowledge which we acquire by experience of all natural objects. The chemist, in order to learn the nature of a substance, observes its general relations to his own senses, and to other substances; and his knowledge of its chemical properties is co-extensive, or rather identical, with his knowledge of the phenomena exhibited by it, in its various relations to and combinations with other substances. Thus the phenomena exhibited by charcoal in its combination with other elements in gun-powder, make an additional item in our knowledge of the nature and properties of charcoal. In this view, it is easy to perceive that our knowledge of its properties, or its possible phenomena, as learned from experience, can be complete only when we have observed it in every possible variety

32

of circumstances in relation to other substances in nature. We can never know that we have learned all.

Note. It will aid us in the use of language, and in understanding what may be said hereafter, if I explain here the senses of the word nature. As I have employed it in the previous sentence, it implies *the sum of all that exists in space and time;* i. e., as extended and continuous, and under the relation of cause and effect, or mutual action and reaction.* In this sense, whatever is a *part of nature* stands in *a necessary relation to every other* part, in *space,* or *time,* or *both.* This is nature considered as phenomenal, and with reference to our power of observation. Considered with reference to the understanding and the laws of its phenomena, we speak of nature as having an inward principle of unity, determining the phenomena by fixed laws. The same distinction is made, when we speak of the nature of a particular substance. In the first sense, it means the sum of the proper-

---

* Action and reaction. Wechselwirking, not the same with cause and effect, but a relation in which two or more things mutually and reciprocally condition and determine each other; as the parts of a machine, or of a body in the mechanical relation of its parts. So the parts of an organic system hold this relation to each other, and all the parts of the material universe reciprocally act and react. A cause, on the other hand, in its highest sense, produces and gives to its product its character as a whole in itself, and in the relation of its parts to each other, without being itself in the relation of reciprocal action with it, or being itself determined by it. Thus the cause and its effect are not parts of one whole. God and the works of creation do not constitute a whole with reciprocity of action, but he produces the universe as a whole in itself, by a free causative act, which goes forth out of himself, and realizes its purpose in the projected reality contemplated as other than the agent.

ties, or possible phenomena, which it exhibits in its relations with other substances ; and in the other, it signifies the inward principle, by virtue of which the phenomena are determined, or their laws given.

3. With these preliminaries, I remark, that the soul, as an object of *possible experience* and *empirical knowledge*, is *included in the sum* of that *which we call nature*, and sustains the consequent relations to the outward world of sense, or whatever exists in space and time. The relations of cause and effect, action and reaction, subsist between the soul and the outward objects of sense. It is capable of being affected by them, and of exhibiting its own corresponding properties. It is by our inward experience, the phenomena exhibited in our consciousness, that we learn how the soul is acted upon, and reacts, in the various circumstances in which we find ourselves placed, and thus acquire a knowledge of its properties.

4. What we learn of the soul, here, is the modes in which it is capable of being affected from without ; the specific susceptibilities, reciptivities of impressions, and powers of reaction, which it manifests. Thus, seeing and hearing, hunger and thirst, are modes in which the soul acts according to its own nature, and to which it is excited by the corresponding outward objects. The life of the plant, though capable of being acted upon from without, and of developing the inward powers of its nature, does not exhibit the powers of which we are conscious.

5. The *susceptibility* of *passive impressions* from without, or the *reciptivity of the soul*, is called the *faculty of sense*, and is the faculty of being excited to action, and to the developement of its own inward powers, by outward stimulants. The specific powers of action, so excited, are necessarily considered as predetermined in the inward principle of life.

In speaking of the determinate relations which subsist between the outward object and the inward susceptibility of being affected in a specific manner, we sometimes represent the outward object as the *cause* of the affection or correlative action of the mind, of which we are conscious, and of this as the *effect*. It is important to observe with precision, in what sense these terms are here used, and what are the precise facts and limitations of our experience in the case. From what has been said, it will be perceived, that the effect of which we are conscious, results from the *specific* relation of *two correlatives*, an *objective* and a *subjective*, the *coincidence* of which is necessary to the result, as known in our consciousness. If *either* were *different* from what it is, the conscious *result* would be *different*. Hence, in regard to the relation of cause and effect, if we say that an outward object is the cause of a result in my consciousness, it is also true, that the *specific excitability* of the powers of the soul, and the *existence* of those powers, are necessary, as a *precondition*, *without which* the outward object could have produced no such effect. Hence, again, we must assume the *relation of ac-*

tion and reaction, instead of cause and effect, as the ground of the phenomena.

I dwell upon this preliminary view of the general relation of the soul to nature, and of the subjective to the objective, because it is important, in order to determine the nature and the direction of our inquiries, and precludes various questions, which have occupied much space in the speculations of former times. Whether we have any innate ideas, or the soul be as a piece of blank paper, or of sealing wax, on which outward objects make an impress, simply, of their own characters or forms, with other questions of the like kind, will hardly be asked by those who have well considered the general relations here exhibited. It will be seen at once, that the phenomena of consciousness which have reference to the world of sense, are determined, not *solely* by *the outward object,* but also by the *specific reaction* of the *subject, according to the inherent laws of its own nature.* Thus, to illustrate the point still more clearly, from a comparison of the agencies of different substances, the diamond, placed among the surrounding agencies of the material world, exhibits only *mechanical* powers of reaction. It reflects, and refracts the light, resists mechanical pressure, &c. A vegetable seed, or plant, not only reacts upon surrounding objects mechanically, but, when acted upon by its appropriate stimulants, *reacts according* to its *own specific law of organization and self-developement.* It unfolds its several organs, with their peculiar functions, and all the phenomena of vegetable *life* and *growth*, according to its *own nature*. Here it stops. It has no reciptivity, no capacity for the impressions of sense; and under no circumstances, by no stimulants, can *feeling, sensibility,* be excited in it. It belongs not to its nature. In the lowest forms of the animal kingdom, we have, in addition to the specific powers and excitabilities of the plant, that of *irritability;* and, if not in the lowest, in the higher forms, that of *sensibility,* the *external perceptions* of sense, *instinct, intelligence,* &c. The point to be remembered here, is, that, in all these cases, the *external objects* and *agencies* are the *same,* so far as the *mere presence* of these objects is concerned, but each reacts according to its own nature, and in the developement and activity of its own inherent powers.

It is not to be inferred here, from the proposition that the soul possesses in itself specific powers, which determine the possible impressions and agencies of which it is capable, that these powers could be unfolded, and called into act, *without the presence of those objects* on which its activities terminate. They belong to the soul, indeed, not as actual, but only as possible, until the presence of their correlative object furnishes the occasion for their developement; just as the power of the magnet becomes actual, only when an object approaches, capable of being attracted by it, and exciting its magnetic power. Though the subjective nature of the soul, as self-determinant, prescribes certain fundamental conditions to all possible excitements from without, through the medium of sense, and determines the formal law of its own possible agencies, yet the relations of sense are necessary to the actual developement and consciousness of its powers. In regard to its reciptivity of impressions through the medium of sense, the soul is conceived as *passive;* or sense is the organ, through which it is acted upon; and the faculties of knowing, desiring, willing, &c., as the inward principles of action, which are not given from without, but require only the phenomena of sense, as the *condition* and occasion of their developement.

In these remarks, I have spoken of the relation of the powers of the soul to the objects of sense, and through the faculty of sense, without reference to the physical organs. Nor from our consciousness alone should we know any thing of the material and organic structure of the organs of sense, as the medium through which the impressions of sense are received.

In speaking of the relation of the soul to the world of sense, I have represented it, as one of action and reaction, the *resulting phenomena* of *which* are *manifested* in our *consciousness.* The objects of sense act upon the mind, and excite to action its inward powers. Here we have a knowledge at the same time, of the outward object, and the inward agency which is excited by it. The *outward object known,* is *extended in space;* the inward *feeling, sensation, desire, thought,* &c., is *not extended in space,* but only *continuous in time.* We cannot conceive those powers and agencies of which we are conscious within ourselves, as occupying space; nor can we conceive any thing as acting upon them and exciting them through the medium of sense, that does not occupy space.

The medium of connexion and the condition of intercourse between these, is the outward life and organization of the body. What this is, as an organic system, we learn, not from our inward consciousness, but, as we do other objects existing in space, by observation and experience. It is only by experience, that we learn the particular connexion of each organ with the intercourse which subsists between the inward life of consciousness and external nature. No consciousness of that which belongs properly to the inner sense, can give us, of itself, any knowledge of the outward form and structure of the organs of the body. In the state of perfect health, the bodily organs are themselves unfelt, and as it were the transparent medium, through which the soul acts and is acted upon.

Yet we recognize the body, each as his own body, and the life of the body, as *his own life.* It belongs to him, as a part of his being, as the *outward form* and *condition* of his *existence in space.* It is the outward man, in and through which the inward powers of the soul express their form and character. It is the necessary mode of our existence *in the world of sense,* without the intervention of which we have no knowledge, either objective or subjective, no *existence in nature*, either in *space* or *time*. It is not merely an *organ*, or material *mechanism*, to be conceived as distinct from our personal self, but *it is our proper self as existent in space*, in the order and under the laws of *nature*. With it are associated all our wants, and all our gratifications, as creatures of this world, and in our relation with the objects of nature. We cannot separate the organic cravings of the body, as hunger, thirst, the want of air, &c., and our wants as self-conscious and personal beings. These, and the higher cravings of our intellectual, moral and spiritual being, are all referred to one indivisible self. *I* hunger, am cold or hot, &c., though these states are at once referred to the body, and used of the inward powers of the soul only in a metaphorical sense. While, therefore, we can draw a clear line of distinction between what belongs to the conscious soul and the outward objects of nature, known to us through the medium of our bodily organs, we cannot so clearly distinguish between the affections of the soul and those of the body, or those which essentially grow out of the physical organization. The early dawn of the inward life of the soul would seem indeed to be, as in brutes, but the life of the body accompanied with consciousness. Thus the pain attending the organic action of the lungs, excited by the first impulse of the air, the feeling of the want of nourishment, and the consequent desire and striving after it, may be supposed to be among the first facts of consciousness, and are essentially connected with the life of the body.

The right view of the relation of the conscious soul to the organic life of the body, seems then to be this. The first principle and organic power of life in the body commences in a lower sphere, in common with the universal powers of life and organization in plants and animals, for a knowledge of which, we must refer to comparative anatomy and comparative physiology. This unfolds itself in the process of fœtal organization and growth, and in the production of the manifold organs of the body with their several functions, antecedent and preparatory to the higher power of consciousness. The organic agencies, thus commenced, continue and carry on their work, in the process of growth and reproduction; themselves in a sphere below our consciousness, but furnishing the ground and nourishment for a higher life, which, having only its basis and the elements of growth in the outward organs and the world of sense, has its principle of unity and self developement in the inner world of consciousness. For as the life of the body begins in an unconscious organization, whose inherent principle, with its whole process of developement, according to the law of its nature, are in unconsciousness, so the principle of our inward life, the life of the soul, has its first dawning, its first actuality, and the whole process of its developement, in consciousness. But that consciousness is awakened, and its materials furnished, by the agencies of our organic life. The organic

cravings of the body awaken the first feelings of
the soul; the first desires are for their gratification
the first direction and use of the outward senses,
and the first acts of the will in the exertion of
muscular power, all have reference to the life of
the body.

Yet in the consciousness of self, and the reference of these affections to self, there is a new
principle of life, it must be remembered, distinct,
from the life of the body, and having its own laws
of action.

CHAPTER III.

ADDITIONAL REMARKS ON THE NATURE AND AIM
OF THE PRESENT INQUIRIES. DISTINCTION OF
THE POWERS OR FACULTIES OF THE SOUL.

In passing from the general relations subsisting between the soul and the objects of the outer
world, to consider it more directly as it is in itself, I wish to make a few additional remarks on
the nature and aim of our inquiries.

The purpose of these studies, then, is nothing
less, than a reflective and rational knowledge of
our own inward being. In strict propriety, we
have no concern with the objects of the outer
world, even the phenomena of our own physical
organization, except as instrumental in bringing

forth into art those powers, and so producing those phenomena, the nature of which is to be learned by reflecting upon our own *inward experience*. The object-matter of our study is that which every one *means*, when he speaks of *himself*. We seek to understand ourselves, by self-inspection.

The possibility of this, and of that self-reflection by which we present to ourselves the agencies of our own being as objects of knowledge, becomes none the less incomprehensible, but rather more and more mysterious, as we reflect upon it. That it is possible, we know from the fact of its reality ; and it is by the exercise of this power, that all self-knowledge is to be attained. We place our own being, as it were, before us, and subject it to our own scrutiny, observe its phenomena, and determine the laws by which they are regulated. These phenomena, as they appear to our conscious observation, are fleeting and changeable, varying with each successive moment, yet all referred to the same ground of being, and recognized as modifications of the same self.

This then, is the form of that inward experience, by which we advance in a knowledge of ourselves. In relation to all that exists as reality, we think of its *existence* as *independent* of its *being known*, and equally real, whether known or not. So in relation to our own being, we may distinguish between the reality existing, the powers at work in us and the laws of their agency, as *objects of knowledge*, and the reflex act, by which

they are *known.* The one seems to us independent of the other.   It is by reflective thought, by
making ourselves reflectingly conscious of what
we do, and feel, and think, that we gain experience, such as will advance our self knowledge.
The first state or relation of our *being,* as distinguished from our conscious *reflection upon it,* is as
it were the direct and immediate going forth of
the powers of life, seeking their own ends according to their inherent laws of action ; just as in those
organized beings to whose powers of life and action no consciousness supervenes.   The other
state or relation of *knowing* supervenes as it were,
finds and recognizes the powers and agencies of
our being as already given, as antecedent to and
independent of our knowledge.

Yet the conscious self recognizes these powers
and agencies thus given, as *its* proper attributes.
It is *I* that know, and feel, and desire, and will,
and at the same time reflect upon these modes of
being and acting as *mine.*   I refer them to *self;*
to my own being, as their proper ground or cause ;
to one identical self, as the subject in the *unity
of which* are included all those attributes, or rather
as the one cause of all those agencies, of which I
am conscious.   The subjective self, however, considered in this relation, is not the *immediate* object of intuition and experience, but is *inferred* as
the *cause* of those effects which are immediately
known in our consciousness.   It is not myself, in
the *constituent principle* of my being, but the *suc-*

cessive and *empirical acts*, or states, which form
the momentary conditioning of my being.

The one identical principle of self, as thus inferred, is conceived as the inherent principle of
life, having the same relation to the powers of the
soul, which the principle of organic life has to the
organs and functions of the body. In all the manifoldness of its operations, it is still the *same principle*, pervading and giving life to all. It is the
same self, that feels, and thinks, and wills, that
sees and hears, fears and hopes, and in its essential being, prescribes the possible forms of its
agencies. We represent its several modes of action as *distinguishable powers*, to which the corresponding phenomena are severally referred; yet
we conceive these powers and modes of action, as
*predetermined in the unity of the one living prin-
ciple*. In other words, we conceive a *unity* and
spontaneity of action in that to which we refer as
the first principle of our inward life.

Since at *each moment* of existence only a *particular condition* or modification of our powers is
manifest in our consciousness, we think of self as
embracing not only that momentary form of being,
but also that essential principle, and those powers
of possible manifestation, to which the momentary
states are referred, and which are conceived as
permanent in the subject.

The spontaneity of the principle of life consists
in its *inherent tendency* to unfold its powers according to the *inward law of its own being*, and work
towards the attainment of *an end* to which it is

determined, not by *mechanical* force from *without*, but in its own *nature* and *constituent idea*. The soul, like every other living power, is thus determined, and puts forth spontaneously its *own powers* for its *own ends*; though it requires the outward conditions before spoken of, in order to the actuation of its powers, and the realization of its ends.

The *passive feeling* of that *want* of the *necessary conditions* of self-developement which exhibits the soul in its negative relation as a capacity to be filled, whose supply or corresponding positive is to be sought for out of itself, and which is the inseparable accompaniment, or rather inherent form, of conscious existence in the *feeling of self*, may be conceived as the *common ground* necessarily implied in *all particular states* and modifications of consciousness. So too all the specific powers and actuations of our inward being are inseparable from, and only conceivable as proceeding from, the one principle which we call self, as the manifold forms in which its being is manifested.

This primary feeling of self, in one view, may be considered a *passive* state, as we cannot conceive of its arising, but in conjunction with an impression from without, or, as a state of being affected; and every such state must be a *particular state*, or a specific determination of self. But then we have seen, that the same feeling rises in conjunction with *every* specific determination of consciousness, and must, therefore, be in itself universal. It involves, too, the developement of a power, distinctive in its character, and not belonging to the lower orders of the animate creation. It is, therefore, a specific activity of the soul, awakened, perhaps, from without, but an essential form of its being, and having the same relation of *antecedency* to all particular modifications of self, which space has to all the possible determinations of form in space, as the *ground of their possibility.* Though we may not be distinctly conscious of this, we in fact involve it, whenever we use *I* as the subject of a proposition. If I say, *I am cold*, the universal *I am* is involved; and so, in the application of every particular predication to the subject *I.* So much for the general idea of self, and its relation to the specific powers and agencies which are unfolded to our consciousness.

What, then, are these powers, and the most general distinctions among them?

Though the feeling of self is a necessary accompaniment of all particular states of consciousness, whether active or passive, yet we have no such intuition of its nature, as to be able to determine, *a priori*, the powers and agencies of which it is capable, or the possible effects of which it is to be the cause. These, we can learn only by *experience;* and it is only by the process of abstraction, applied to the *phenomena of experience*, that we distinguish what we call the several powers, or faculties, of the soul. The mode of distinguishing them, or of classing the phenomena, has not, indeed, been uniform. Without stopping at present to give an account of different methods, or their several merits, I shall state briefly that which seems to me the most satisfactory.

1.   In the first place, then, we may distinguish the *powers* of *knowledge*, or the *cognitive faculties*. Whether these should be placed first in order, seems to admit of some reasonable doubt; but it will be most convenient to treat of them first; and unless we aim at a metaphysical deduction of all the powers of the soul from a first principle, it is not a question of primary importance. There are, however, very good grounds for placing these before the others, since in the presence of an object to our *cognitive* powers, nothing else is necessarily implied as *antecedent* to it; while any other agency of the mind, of which it is the object, presupposes a recognition of it as present. We experience the cognitive agency of the soul in the first act of consciousness, and can conceive a being endued with a conscious *knowledge* of objects, or capable of *representing* them to itself, without the feeling of any *interest* in them, and incapable of *acting* upon them. The human mind, indeed, has sometimes been treated as if it consisted essentially in the power of knowing, or of representing to itself the objects of knowledge. Practically considered, however, we may perhaps regard the power of representing the objects of knowledge to ourselves, as only an instrumental agency, subservient to the developement of other powers, and the attainment of other ends, than those which *terminate* in knowledge merely. We cannot at least separate the exercise of this pow-

34

er from those principles of our being which give a practical interest to knowledge, without leaving knowledge itself unsubstantial and lifeless.

2. In connexion with the inward feeling of self before treated of, there arises in us a consciousness of the *state* or *condition* of self. Every such state or condition has a relation to the inherent nature and tendencies of our being, in the spontaneous direction and agency of its powers, as determined in the essential law of our inward life. *Certain conditions* are necessary to the developement of the powers of life, and to our being in that state which the law of our nature requires in order to our *well-being*. Thus a feeling or consciousness of our present state is a feeling either of *want* or of *satisfaction* in relation to the demands of our nature. From the sense of want, as of hunger, arises a *desire* for those objects which our nature *craves* for the attainment of the *ends* to which it is spontaneously directed ; and hence we have an *interest* in those objects. In the gratification of a specific *desire*, excited in us by the attainment of its correlative *object*, we find *pleasure*, and *pain* in the want of it; as we feel also *aversion* to that which obstructs the gratification of our desires. Thus our *wants*, our *propensities*, our *desires* and *aversions*, as the ground and occasion of the *interest* which we feel in the objects of knowledge, of our *hopes* and *fears*, our *pains* and *pleasures*, form the second division of the powers of the mind. From the connexion which they have with the wants and the develope-

ment of the organic system, and their analogy to the system of nutrition in the powers of organic life, they are often distinguished as the *heart*, or the source of life and action in our inward being.

3. As we can conceive a perception or presentation of an object without any feeling of desire or aversion directed towards it, so we can conceive the additional awakening of these feelings without any power to act either for obtaining or avoiding it. Thus we can conceive a plant endued with a consciousness of its wants, and with a knowledge and desire of the objects necessary to satisfy them, without any power to act in relation to the means of supply. Again, we can conceive such a relation between a living being and the outward objects by which its organic wants are to be supplied, as that the action and reaction shall be immediate, and uncontrolled by any other than a physical force. This seems to be the case with pure instinct, where the presence of the outward object and the feeling of want produce a living action directed to its attainment, of the same nature with the spontaneous contraction of the muscles in breathing, where the stimulus of the air and the reaction of the organs is independent of thought or volition. The only difference between this purely organic action and simple instinct, seems to be, that the action and reaction in the latter requires the intervention of sense, as a representative or cognitive power, through which the outward object excites the action of the powers necessary for its attainment.

To make still another distinction, we may conceive a power working in an orderly manner towards the accomplishment of a particular end, without any distinct conception or consciousness of the end to which its labors are tending. This is exemplified in the formative power by which all organic forms are developed; in the instinctive working of the bee in building its comb; of the bird in building its nest, &c. In these cases, the inward impulse to outward action prescribes the law of action, and determines the result by the same law of nature and necessity in the agency which works in the insect, for the forming of its wing, and by means of it as its instrument, for the building of its comb or nest.

But we are conscious in ourselves and experience in our working a higher power than any of these. We have not only a perception and knowledge of the objects which correspond to our wants and a desire to appropriate them, but also a power to act for the attainment of the ends which our wants and desires prescribe. We have not only a power to work towards the attainment of an end, but also the power to conceive beforehand, to deliberate and resolve upon the end to be attained and the means of its attainment. When the presence of the object has excited the desire for its attainment, the action does not follow by an organic or mechanical law of action, but we have power to determine freely whether we will gratify the desire or not. This seems to me a fair statement of the power of the will, as we recognize it in our experience. It is not necessary here to solve all the difficulties connected with the philosophical doctrine of an absolute freedom of will. I will merely say, however, that it is not implied in the doctrine of a free will, that it acts independently of the understanding and the desires and propensities of the heart, or that its determinations are without grounds; but only that the grounds of its determinations are in the character of the will itself. We have power to make ourselves conscious of the inward impulses and the outward excitements which stand in the relation of action and reaction to each other; and instead of being carried along as passive spectators of an agency beyond the control of the conscious self, we feel that we are able to interfere by our own act, to judge of the influences that work upon us and of the propensities of which we are conscious, to approve or disapprove of that which the law of our nature is working in us, and either to resist its tendencies or deliberately to make it our own work. This power of deliberate resolve is what is meant by the will, as distinguished from the heart or the seat of the desires; and that power of thought and intelligence which is thus directed by the will for the attainment of its own ends or the determination of its own resolves, is the power of voluntary thought and self-control. It is the *understanding*, as connected with the faculties of knowledge, and distinguished from those which are involuntary or spontaneous in their agency,

It is this power of voluntary self-inspection and self control, which places man above nature, even his own nature, and constitutes him a free and responsible agent, and the deliberate resolves of his will, made, that is, in the exercise of his understanding, his own acts. The brute is incapable of conscious and deliberative resolve ; and what it does is therefore the product of the power of nature working in it, and cannot be imputed to it as its own work.

In this power of self-control is involved not only a control over our outward acts in the use of our muscular powers, but also a power of modifying and directing the phenomena of our inward being and the agencies of which we are conscious, with a view to the accomplishment of our own deliberate purposes. Thus all that belongs to our nature is in a certain sense placed under our own control, and we have the power of self-developement, of voluntary self-cultivation, in bringing what pertains to our nature under subjection to laws which we ourselves impose, and with a view to ends which we have ourselves chosen.

The principles which predominate in the will in doing this, constitute the character of the will, and of the man as a free and responsible agent.

The relation between the conscious soul and the world of sense, I have remarked, is one of action and reaction. The inward powers of the soul can be actuated, only as they have a correlative which excites them to action, and on which their agency terminates. Again, it was said, they can neither act nor react, but according to that inherent form of being, or law of action, which constitutes the inward nature of the soul.

The same is obviously true of the principles of organic life; and the growth of the body till it attains its perfect form and stature, is but the developement of powers necessarily implied and presupposed in the first incipient process of its organization. These powers, too, stand in the same general relation to the objects and powers of nature. The inward principle of life can be unfolded only by means of those external elements which have a correlation to its specific wants and agencies. If we look now at the process which takes place here in the developement of the organic system with reference to time, we know that from the necessity of the case it must be, at least in part, antecedent to sensibility and consciousness, and in that respect analogous to the life of a plant. We know too by our daily experience, that the mere powers of organic or vegetative life may exist and act in their full vigor without consciousness, as in sound sleep. In these cases, neither the inward wants and activities of the organic system, nor its relations to nature, are matter of consciousness or knowledge; and the question is, how, to these states of the organic system and the agencies which take place between it and the surrounding objects and powers of nature, sensibility and consciousness supervene.

In answer to this, we can only state the fact, and some of the conditions in regard to the state of the organic system and the arrangement and connexions of the nerves, which observation and experiment have shown to be necessary to it. Why it is that in a particular state of the organs of nutrition, and with the necessary connexions of the nervous ganglia belonging to them, I should feel the affection of hunger, or thirst, or nausea, or any other affection, whether pleasurable or painful, we cannot tell, nor conceive any resemblance between the state of the material organ as its phenomena are exhibited to our outward senses, and the feeling of hunger. We do, however, know the relation of hunger to the organic wants of the system; and this feeling is the inward form in which those wants are made known to the being itself, in order to their being supplied. It expresses, under the form of consciousness, a relation between the organic life and the objects of nature necessary to unfold and sustain it. It reveals itself in our consciousness, and is felt as a want, as a striving of our physical nature after its appropriate objects in the world of sense; or rather, perhaps, the organic state is accompanied by a conscious affection, which excites a desire and striving after the means of its gratification.

Here we must distinguish between the relation which subsists between the organic life and its means of developement, or its correlatives in the material world, and our feeling of that relation, or the phenomena of consciousness which arise from it. We can conceive the relation to subsist, and a consequent action and reaction to take place, as in plants, and in many of the involuntary agencies of our organic system, which do take place, independently of our sensibility or consciousness.

When consciousness does not exist, as in the spontaneous agencies of the system, the relation between the organic wants and the outward objects to which they are related, is immediate, and independent of voluntary action. Where a sense or consciousness is awakened in connexion with the organic wants of the system, we find a muscular apparatus, supplied with nerves from the centre of consciousness, which that sensibility excites us to call into action, for the accomplishment of the ends which the organic wants require.

But I have spoken only of that sensibility which is immediately connected with the wants of the system; and we have reason to suppose that this is the first of which we are conscious, and that which primarily gives us an interest in the objects of sense without us. The obscure feeling of want impels the infant to seek the means of supply, and here the muscles and the organs of sense, properly so called, are put in requisition, and are ready furnished as instruments by which the cravings of nature are to be supplied.

But not only are the organs ready for use; the correlative objects in nature also are at hand, and that action and reaction which in some cases we have seen to be immediate, is here accompanied with the developement of the higher power of sensibility, and conscious pleasure or pain.

I have presented the subject again in this view, in order to point out distinctly the relation of the

35

organic wants of the system to our consciousness and to the developement of the inward powers of the soul, and also their relation to the outward muscular organization of the organs of sense.

I shall not give an anatomical account of these organs, but proceed at once to what belongs more strictly to the subject.

~~~~~~~~~~~~~~~~~~

CHAPTER IV.

COGNITIVE FACULTIES. CONSCIOUSNESS AND SELF-CONSCIOUSNESS.

In entering upon a more particular consideration of the powers of knowing, I wish to direct your attention to a distinction which is fundamental in relation to the whole subject of self-knowledge.

All the powers of our inward being, it was said, like those of our organic life, require in order to their activity — to their being put forth in act — the excitement of their correlative object. As the power of the magnet cannot be put forth, unless excited by the presence of a correlative power, or agency in the iron, so no power of the soul can become active, or be in act, but with a corresponding relation to an object by which it is excited, and on which its action terminates. Conceive then, the law of action and reaction, in regard to the powers of knowing, to be the same as in our òrganic powers and in the magnet, and the reaction resulting from excitement to be equally *immediate;* and let us apply the comparison which is here suggested.

When the power of the magnet is excited by the presence of iron, its agency is immediate and inseparable from the notion of its existence in the magnet. When the fibres of a muscle are irritated by nervous or galvanic influence — that is, acted upon according to the nature of their specific excitability — they immediately react, and the reagency is exhibited in the contraction of the muscle. Here, however, let it be observed, that the organic reaction of a living and organic power is not, like mere mechanical reaction, to be measured by the force of the excitement according to any mechanical law. But the point to be noticed here is, that the reaction is of a specific nature, and is *immediate*, determined by, and flowing from the nature of the organ.

In like manner, it is the function of a part at least of the nervous system to feel. The nerves are organs of sensation, and when acted upon — affected either by the state of their organs, with which they are connected, or by an agency from without, they react according to their specific nature, or law of action; and this reagency of the nervous organ manifests itself, not in motion under the relations of space like the muscle, but in the *sensation* of pain or pleasure, of sweet or bitter, &c., according to the specific function of the nervous organ affected. The reaction here, observe, is *immediate* as before, and its specific form is manifested not in space, not outwardly, but in time, and inwardly in the mind.   In these cases, so far as the action and reaction is simply organic, i. e., pertaining to the state of the organ, the one is limited and determined by the other.   The feeling of pain ceases with the exciting cause ; the sense of sweetness, with the action of its exciting cause upon the nerves of taste.   So with all the affections of sense, so far as they are *immediate* and arise from the immediate and organic reaction of the nervous organs of sense.   Sensation is the form of immediate and organic reaction of the nerves of sense, and ceases with the influence which excites it.

But though sensation is thus, in its strict sense, limited to the present state of the organ of sense, it properly belongs not to the body, but to the mind, and is·the result of the most immediate co-incidence of an objective with a subjective agency in the nervous system,. as the organ or necessary condition of such action and reaction.   Now sensation is inseparable from intuition, as the form of immediate knowledge, since it is a finding of a determinate affection ; and in this therefore, we have the first awakening of the faculties of knowledge, in their immediate reaction, as excited through the nerves of sense.

The point then, on which I wish to fix your attention here, is, the distinction between immediate knowledge, or immediate consciousness, and reflective self-knowledge.   According to the common use of the word consciousness, it is inseparable from sensation, since a sensation of which we are not conscious, is no sensation. Yet there is no difficulty in conceiving a capability of sensation, when the reaction should be in every sense limited by the exciting cause, should cease with it, and leave no further trace of its existence. May we not conceive the same of a form of conscious knowledge therefore? i. e., of a consciousness fleeting like the successive changes in the state of the organs; a finding of fleeting affections and phenomena of sense, that is at the same moment a losing; a self, that at each successive instant is wholly absorbed in present feelings and impulses, with no power to loose the chain that thus binds it to the present and the real. Does it alter the case, whether that which thus absorbs the consciousness, be a feeling of organic pain or pleasure, or the presence to the outward senses of objects exciting desires, or even of images of those objects to the inner sense? All the self-knowledge arising from such a consciousness, would be a successive knowledge of present states; and if the images of the past were represented in the consciousness, it would be without the power of comparison, or of thinking of them as belonging to the past, or of distinguishing between the real, and the possible or imaginary. It would not be indeed a self-knowledge at all, or awaken a consciousness of self, as distinct from the present state of consciousness, or from the object of knowledge.

But the consciousness which is the instrument of self-knowledge, is a higher form of consciousness, and necessarily involves the idea of self, as distinct from the object. Conscious knowledge, in the proper and philosophical use of the term *conscious*, always implies this distinction, and the reference of successive states of consciousness to self as the permanent ground of its existence. Here is not only the immediate reaction of that power which belongs to sense, and is coextensive with the affection of the organ, and specifically distinct in each several organ; but there is awakened a higher power, which stands in the same relation to the immediate phenomena of sense in general, as the powers of sense do to their several correlatives. I mean, that the conscious self is excited by every state of sensuous affection, and reacts according to its own higher law of action. Whatever is present in the sense is its correlative.

This higher consciousness is therefore simple, and does not admit of being distinguished into parts, either like or unlike. It cannot therefore be described, but can be known only by being possessed. The immediate affections of sense, and the immediate consciousness of these, as I have been speaking of it, is one thing when we hear, another when we see, &c.; but that of which I am now speaking, the consciousness of self, is always the same, and identical with itself. It is the same *I* that is conscious of the various affections of sense, both of the outer senses, as of hearing, seeing, &c., and of the inner sense. In this sense

of the term consciousness, there are not several
kinds of consciousness, but several and various
kinds of objects present to one and the same consciousness.

This consciousness then may be considered as a
sort of inward eye, whose objects are the successive and manifold modifications of our immediate
and primary consciousness; or rather, the immediate and primary affections and agencies of our
being, as manifested under the forms of sense.
As such, it is the organ of self-knowledge, and
under the control of the will. Its most essential
characteristic, as distinguished from that presence
of objects which is immediate in the sense, is its
subordination to the will, in regard both to its intensity and the extension of its view.

Its character will be understood from a reference to the ordinary use of language in regard to
self-consciousness, and the degrees of clearness
or obscurity in our consciousness of our own powers and their agencies. I am at no time distinctly
conscious of all the knowledge which I possess,
or of the various powers of thought and feeling
which yet belong to me, even though I may never
have been distinctly conscious of their agency. So
too I may not be distinctly conscious of exercising
all the powers of thought which are active at a
given moment; and to become conscious of them,
must employ a vigorous effort of attention. So
even in regard to the outer senses. A harmony of
sounds or a combination of colors, blending together, produce an effect on my senses, while yet

I do not consciously distinguish or make myself distinctly conscious of them. I feel the combined effect, but can become distinctly conscious of what was present to the sense, only by a voluntary effort of consciousness. Thus, too, I see in the face of an individual that which enables me to distinguish him at once from all other individuals, but am unconscious what it is in the immediate phenomena of sense that is thus distinctive. By representing the phenomena and directing my attention to them, I may become conscious of that which I saw before but unconsciously. So when an extensive prospect lies before me, regaling the senses with sounds and odors, as well as form and color, the whole is continuously present to the sense, and cannot become more so by any voluntary effort on my part; but I can render myself more distinctly conscious of a particular fragrance in the air, or the music of a particular bird, or the beauty of an individual object of sight, by a voluntary effort of attention directed to what was already an object of sense and of immediate sensuous intuition. The same may be said of the phenomena of the inner sense. The mind may be absorbed in a reverie, either occupied with the images of the past, or involuntarily shaping some picture of the future, with fluctuating emotions of regret or hope and fear; and we may in a moment arrest the spontaneous succession, and fix our thought at will upon any one of the phenomena that fill the horizon of the inner sense, make ourselves conscious of the agencies that we find in play, and the objects about which they are employed.

That attention by which a particular object present to the sense, is rendered more distinct in our consciousness, may be excited by an involuntary interest awakened by it; or it may be voluntarily exerted, and admits of degrees of intensity. When feeble, we know little of what is present to the sense; when intense, we distinguish with rapidity and clearness the distinguishable in the sensuous impression or intuition. The consciousness thus excited may embrace many objects lying within the horizon of sense, or may be limited to a single object or a mathematical point. Whatever is present in the agencies of the soul, and capable of affecting the sense, may by an effort of will be made an object of consciousness; some with less, others with greater facility. There are many agencies going on in the mind of all men from day to day, and within the reach of distinct consciousness, of which yet most men never become conscious. But we cannot become distinctly conscious of those agencies of our being which are not phenomenal in the sense, or do not affect either the outward or inward sense. That which is present in the sense, constitutes the material of reflective consciousness; and nothing can be in our conscious thought that was not before in the sense.

It is by the excitement of the power of self-consciousness — of the reflective *I* — directed to the phenomena of our own inward life, that we

gradually attain self-knowledge. This, either excited by an involuntary interest or determined by
the will, brings into the clear light of conscious
self-knowledge the obscure agencies of our being.
The control and direction of this is the ground and
condition of all mental discipline and cultivation.
Without it, the activity of the mind is dissipated
and lost without purpose or method; and by it we
take, as it were, the powers which nature has giv-
en us, and the materials of knowledge furnished
in the data of sense, under our own control, and
direct them to the accomplishment of preconceived ends. The power of the will and of the
understanding over the direction of our attention
and consciousness, is the innermost power by
which man holds the control of himself, and with
a spiritual or supernatural efficiency, transcends and
regulates the movements of his own nature. This
wakeful and intelligent consciousness inwardly distinguishes what the man is and does; wherein he
is free; and for what he is responsible. It raises
the man above the sphere of obscure organic feelings and impulses, and brings the inward agencies
of his being into the clear light of knowledge, and
under his own self-control.

The rude and uncultivated man lives absorbed
in the world without, and knows nothing of himself but the relation of his wants to the external
objects of sense. The awakening of reflective
self-consciousness lays open to his view the processes and the character of his own being, and

renders it possible for him to apply to them the conscious law of moral obligation.

But here it may be necessary to repeat more distinctly, that this higher and reflective consciousness can have for its object matter, only that which is present in the sensuous and momentary consciousness before described. When I look upon a strange face, though I do not become at once distinctly conscious of what it is that distinguishes it, and must become so by an effort of attention, yet no effort can make me conscious of any thing there, not already contained in the sensuous intuition. The immediate intuition of the outward object may cease, and the sensuous image recur to me and be the repeated object of study ; but I can bring nothing out of it, nor find any thing in it, that was not *given* in the original impression. Thus reflective consciousness brings and gives nothing to the object of consciousness ; but only notices, marks, distinguishes what was given in that primary consciousness, which was coextensive in every respect with the impression of sense.

So it is in regard to self-knowledge, or the reflective self-consciousness of the powers and operations of my own inward being. I can become conscious of, and study reflectively, only that which is present and *given* for my observation in what is generally termed the inner sense, or in that which has the same relation to my inward being which the outer senses have to the external world. I am *sensible* of the successive states of my own feelings, as pleasant or painful ; of hope and fear ;

of the activities of thought, desire and will; and it is only that of which I am *sensible*, that I make an object of conscious attention. The sense, here, as in the agency of the outer senses, does not indeed know, but furnishes all the materials of knowledge. When I look into my own inward being, I *find* there certain phenomena in the horizon of the inner sense; just as when I look abroad in space, I find phenomena there which are given independently of my will, and may be attended to or not. *That presence then of the phenomena of my inward being by which they become possible objects of attention and distinct consciousness*, is what I mean by the *inner sense*. The powers and agencies of my being which do not affect the inner sense, or are not presentable under the forms of sense as a something given and *appearing*, cannot become an object of consciousness. From the phenomena which are manifested, we may infer the existence and reality of such an agency; but we can never be conscious of it.

Consciousness, then, in its proper sense, begins with the distinguishing of self from that which is other than self; and is increased in the increasing habit of reflection upon those agencies which have their origin in our own being. It would have its completion, if such were possible for us, in the simultaneous intuition of all the powers of living action which belong to us, in the unity of their origin; so that our being and our knowing should be identical.

To take a very general review, then, of the steps by which we arrive at self-consciousness, we may begin with the power of life. In the vegetable, we have simply the productive power, or growth; a continuous going forth of living power producing its outward organic form; a continuous striving after the realization of the specific idea *in space.*

Now suppose the plant, in striving after its specific end, of which it has no knowledge, to be influenced by sensibility, a feeling of pain, which restrains it in one direction, and of pleasure, which allures it in another; that when the ascending shoot meets with an obstruction, there is a sensation awakened that impels it to vary its direction, and seek the end for which it is striving in a new course. This may be conceived without supposing in the plant any notion of the end, or of self as the agent seeking that end.

Again, suppose the power of life, in seeking its own developement, to require and be furnished with the apparatus of animal organization, and capable of apprehending and appropriating by its outward organs, the objects around it, to its own purposes. Suppose it to be impelled by inward desire, and guided by outward senses, in appropriating the surrounding objects necessary to its specific ends. Suppose it to be repelled from one object by a sense of pain, and attracted to another by a sense of pleasure, and by the senses as organs of perception, to distinguish the objects of desire and aversion, so as to seek the one and avoid the other. May we not conceive its powers of knowledge as limited to this, and perfectly sub-

ordinate to the wants of its nature, as instrumental
for their supply, and directed solely to the discrimination of those outward objects which are necessary to this end. Such powers, with the keenest
sagacity in detecting the objects of desire and skill
in the adaptation of means to ends for their attainment, are clearly distinguishable from the power
to reflect upon those subjective wants and desires
which impel us to action, and give us an interest in
the objects of knowledge, and upon the power of
knowing itself.

Thus to reflect and distinguish consciously between the subject *I*, as feeling, desiring, willing
and knowing, and the object of desire or knowledge, and to refer the successive states of consciousness to self as its acts or affections, is the
dawn of self-consciousness, and an attribute of
personal existence. The power of self-conscious
reflexion, by which I pronounce the word *I*, and
recognize a thought, or an act, as *my* thought or
my act, involves the highest form and mystery of
existence, the completed developement of the series of natural powers, and is the dawn of spiritual existence.

CHAPTER V.

THE POWERS OF SENSATION.

We proceed, then, to apply the power of self-
conscious reflexion, which stands in the same rela-

tion to all that is knowable, in the agencies of our being, to an examination of the powers of knowledge, as co-ordinate in the arrangement before given, with those of desire and will.

In treating of the powers of knowledge, we distinguish,

First, that of immediate or sensuous intuition ;

Second, that of thought, or mediate cognition.

The distinction between these will appear more fully, when we come to the consideration of the second, or the faculty of thought. For the present, it is sufficient to say of sensuous intuition in general, that I understand by it that power of presentation, whose objects are immediately present in their individual reality, as distinguished from those general conceptions which belong to the faculty of thought.

The power of immediate sensuous intuition may be distinguished again, into 1, that of the outer, and 2, that of the inner sense.

1. The outer sense, or that power by which we become acquainted with the external world of sense as distinguished from our own inward being, has its several distinct organs in the structure of the human body. These organs are the media, and furnish the conditions, of our intercourse with the world of sense, and of our knowledge of its existence and properties. Our possible knowledge of it by experience, is limited and conditioned by the modes of knowing which pertain to these several organs. Whether in the nature of things, other forms of sense revealing to us other proper-

ties of the objects of sense are possible, is more than we can determine.

It will be of use to distinguish in the functions of the outer sense generally, the two relations of *subjective* and *objective*. The subjective relation of a conscious affection of sense, is that affection considered with reference to the subject as a modification of its state of being, and may be distinguished in its connexion with the feelings of pleasure and pain, as agreeable or disagreeable. An affection, or a conscious *presentation*, thus referred to the subject, is a *sensation*.

The same considered in its external relation to an immediate and individual *object* of sense, is an *intuition;* and this term is used not only with reference to the organ of sight, but to all the senses.

With this distinction, it may be observed, that in comparing the affections of the different organs of sense, or the presentations peculiar to them, we find in some a predominance of the subjective, or the sensation, in others of the objective, or the intuition of the outward object. Whatever consciously affects the organic system, may be considered as affecting the sense, and in this use of the term, the whole body is an organ of sense, since by the universal diffusion of the nerves, the whole seems capable of being so excited as to awaken conscious sensations. The sensations connected with the ordinary functions of life, as hunger and thirst, and the pleasure arising from the satisfaction of the appetites, the general sense of health,

or sickness, of elastic vigor or the langor of fatigue, all belong to the body as an organ of sense,
and connecting our conscious being with a world
of sense. We may distinguish here also, various
peculiar affections of the nerves generally, diffused
over the surface of the body, or particular parts of
it, as those produced by tickling or by rubbing the
skin, and the general sensations of cold and
warmth. In all these, it is obvious the subjective
affection is almost exclusively recognized; though
in all cases of a conscious affection of sense, in
which we feel ourselves passively acted upon, a
change produced in our state of being without a
conscious agency on our part to originate it, we
refer it more or less distinctly to a cause other
than self, and out of self.

From these vital sensations or subjective affections of the organs, terminating in the subject,
there is a gradual transition to those which are
almost wholly objective; and we may state it as a
general law, *that the more distinct the subjective
sensation, the less distinct is the objective intuition,
and inversely.*

In enumerating the powers of sensation, and the
modes in which we are capable of being sensuously
affected through the organs of the body and by
means of the nervous system, we should perhaps
consider the diffusive power of conscious sensation
which is common to all parts of the body, as the
common basis of the more specific affections, and
coextensive with the diffusion of animal life. By
virtue of this, every portion of the organic system

37

is capable of conveying to the mind a sensation of pain or pleasure ; and the sum of such sensations, united in the common consciousness, makes up at each moment the state and condition of our organic existence, as pleasurable or painful. In this, we embrace the inward functions of life, the feeling of health and sickness, as well as the immediate affections of the external nervous tissues. I repeat again, that all such bodily sensations, though, as sensations, subjective in the sense above defined, and giving no distinct intuition of an object, are yet *referred by the mind, to a cause out of the mind*, and gradually, with the progress of experience, to distinct organs and localities in space.

Above the sphere, as it were, of this universal sense, or as a higher developement and specification of it, we enumerate the so called five senses of touch, taste, smell, hearing, and sight.

Of these five senses, that of *touch* is in some respects more nearly allied than the others to the general sensibility of the system. It extends in some degree to all parts of the surface, since the skin is every where more or less sensible to the touch, and enables us to distinguish some of the properties of objects brought in contact with it. Even below the surface indeed, in the opening of a wound, we can distinguish the temperature and perhaps some of the other properties of bodies inserted into it.

Yet, however, this sense is more distinctly developed in its peculiar organs, the ends of the fingers. By the more full developement of the nerves of sense at these points, the delicate texture of the skin by which they are protected, and the support and fixture which the nails give when we press our fingers upon an object, we attain by these organs, a distinctness in the impression and corresponding perception of this sense, which is not given by any other part of the body, and probably does not belong to any other animal. The ends of the toes also have, in some instances of a loss of the hands, been found capable of nearly equal delicacy and precision in their sense of touch, and the end of the tongue is often used for the same purpose.

These organs, in common with the general surface of the body, are sensible to cold and heat, though from their general exposure, less so to the changes of temperature in the atmosphere than parts of the body which are less exposed. We however use them when we wish to examine the temperature of a body with more accuracy, as an external object of perception, and a property of the body. Of the nature of caloric, as taught by chemistry, and the laws of its action, or of any thing concerning it, but as a sensible property of bodies, the organs of touch give us no perception.

The perceptions peculiar to the sense of touch, are those of properties belonging to the surface of bodies, as rough and smooth, moist and dry ; and to this sense, aided by the muscular movement of the hands and the intuition of the relations of space, those also, pertaining to the figures and solidity of bodies, as even and uneven, round and

angular, hard and soft, elastic and unelastic, &c.
In all cases, the organs of touch must be in
contact with the object, in order to give us a perception of its properties.

The sense of *taste* has its distinct and peculiar
organ, to which, as in all the senses but that of
touch, its power of sensation and perception is exclusively confined. This organ is the tongue and
palate, which are furnished with a peculiar nerve
of taste, distinct from the general nerves of sense.
Here too, the object must be in contact with the
organ, in order to awaken the sensation of taste,
and must moreover be dissolved in the fluids of the
mouth.

In the affections of this sense, the subjective sensation predominates, and the attention is ordinarily
excited by and directed to the sensation, rather
than the object of sense. Of itself indeed, the sense
of taste gives us no aid in representing to ourselves
the outward form and the mathematical or mechanical properties of bodies ; and the knowledge
which it gives us, is confined wholly to their
chemical properties, such as acid and alkaline,
sweet and bitter, mild and corrosive. These,
however, we perceive by this sense as properties
of external objects, as distinctly as we do the
properties which come under the cognizance of the
other senses.

This sense is peculiarly and immediately connected with the organic wants of the body, and
the functions of nutrition. As such, its sensations
are nearly allied to those connected with the gen-

eral functions of organic life, in health and sickness; and as an organ of knowledge, it is easily and often vitiated by the general state of the organic system of nutrition.

In its relation to the feelings of pleasure and pain, the sense of taste is peculiarly important, as compared with the other senses; and it seems to be capable of higher cultivation as an instrument of pleasure in man, than in any other animal, in regard to the variety and to the exquisiteness of its affections. We eat and drink, not merely to satisfy our organic wants and still the cravings of appetite, but for the specific pleasures which it affords. By this circumstance, again, we are led to employ it with more effect in distinguishing those properties in bodies which stand in correspondence with the specific excitabilities of this sense.

To the sense of *smell* may be applied also many of the remarks which have been made respecting that of taste. Like that, it is intimately connected with the functions of organic life; and there is a like predominance of the subjective in its affections. Its sensations, too, can be excited only in its proper organ, and by the influence of the exciting cause upon the peculiar nerves of this sense diffused over the expanded membranes of the nose. Its affections are unlimited in variety, like those of taste; but in its relation to life, and to the feelings of pleasure and pain, its more ordinary function is rather to warn and protect us against that which is offensive and injurious, than to serve as a means of enjoyment.

Of external objects it gives us no distinct knowledge, except of their power to excite the sensations of which we are conscious; and the properties in bodies to which this power is referred, are in most cases distinguished only by referring them to the objects to which they belong, as the odor of the rose, of musk, &c. These properties of bodies are not perceived, or the sensations excited, as in the senses before mentioned, by the contact of the object with the organ, but by means of a diffused influence of the body upon the atmosphere, or of effluent particles which reach the organ of sense.

In regard to the degree of excitability, and of the correlative perceptive power of this sense, though not perhaps in the multiplicity and variety of its affections, we seem to be placed behind many species of the inferior animals.

The sense of *hearing* has for its organ the outer and the inner ear; and the external cause of its sensations is the vibrations of the atmosphere produced by the vibratory motion of elastic bodies. These vibrations are conveyed by the outer ear to the complex mechanism of the inner ear, through which they affect the nerve peculiar to this sense.

The subjective affections of the sense of hearing are not referred as readily to the organ of sense, as in those before described. Its subjective relation is no less affecting with reference to the feelings of pleasure and pain which it excites; but those feelings are less organic, and seem to belong more immediately to the inward life of the soul. We are pleased or pained by sounds; but the

pleasures and pains are not like those of taste or
touch, felt as sensations in the organ. It is only
when the concussions of the atmosphere are extremely violent, or the sounds discordant, that we
feel a local affection of the organ ; and persons
seem often in doubt whether both or only one ear
is at all sensible to sound.

The general expression for the objective perceptions of this sense is, *sound*. We hear sounds,
and nothing but sounds, as the organic nerve can
react to outward impressions in no other mode. It
is not necessary that impressions should be conveyed to the nerve in the way above mentioned in
order to the sense of sound, since a vibration communicated through the bones of the cranium so as
to reach the nerve, is known to produce the sensation.

Sounds are perceived and clearly recognized as
objective, but without experience cannot be referred to the outward cause ; nor can any outward
representation of it be made from the affections of
the sense of hearing alone. It is by experience,
and the observations of the other senses, we first
learn to distinguish the sounding body, and the vibrations in it and communicated by it to the atmosphere, which are the conditions of sensation.
We do not, therefore, perceive sounds immediately
as properties of bodies, as we do the properties
perceived by touch and taste, nor as having form
and permanence in the outer world of sense ;
though by experience we learn to refer it to the
proper cause, and to judge of its direction and distance.

But though we do not give to the perceptions of this sense, shape and coloring in the outward relations of space, and they seem to have but a fleeting existence in time, yet they establish a relation between man and nature, more affecting and more exciting to the powers of our inward being than any other sense. Sounds have for our feelings a significance, as if the heart of nature was speaking to our hearts, and gave us an insight into the inward life powers of the natural objects by which we are surrounded. Hence the effect upon our feelings, produced by the roar of the tempest, the rolling of thunder, and the soothing murmur of the rivulet; or the cries of animals, and the singing of birds. But the peculiar world of sound is the product of man's own spirit, in music and language, by which, in a more distinct and intelligible form, mind holds intercourse with mind, and heart with heart.

The distinctions of sound most general and important, as perceived in the affections of sense, are, confused and tumultuous sounds, in which the vibrations of the air cannot be referred to any intelligible law; and tones, either musical or articulate.

Of the sense of *sight*, both as to the mechanism of its organ, the eye, and as to the outward conditions of its sensations, we know more in some respects than of the other senses. By this, however, it is only to be understood that there is more in the organ, in its relation to the outward conditions of sight, that is intelligible on mechanical principles, and more in the agency of light, the outward medium of vision, the laws of which can be scientifically known, than in the affections of the other senses. Why it is, that, under these mechanical conditions, rays of light, falling upon the retina of the eye, produce the phenomena of vision, we cannot explain, and only know it by experience.

The organ, we know, is so constructed upon optical principles, that rays of light, coming from an outward object, are refracted by the chrystalline lens, so as to form an inverted image of the object upon the corresponding portion of the retina of both eyes; that the retina, an expansion of the optic nerve upon the back side of the interior surface of the eye-ball, is connected by the optic nerve with the substance of the brain; and that these conditions are necessary to our seeing the object.

Why it is, that we see objects single with two eyes, and erect, while the image upon the retina is inverted, are questions that seem to suppose the images to be objects of vision, as if there were another eye behind them; otherwise, there would be the same reason for inquiring why we hear but one sound with two organs of hearing. It is a matter of some interest to observe the circumstances in which we do see objects double, and the influence of the understanding in correcting the irregularities, in this respect, of the organic action.

It is a more important point, to distinguish what is the peculiar power and agency of this sense, and its subjective and objective relations. These are

essentially the same as in the other senses, so far
as this: that there is a peculiar subjective power
of sensibility, and a peculiar objective agency as
its proper correlative; and the product of these,
in the relation of counteracting forces, is the specific sensation belonging to this sense. That specific sensation is color. If, then, it be asked,
whether color is subjective or objective; whether
it is an affection of self or a property in bodies;
the answer is, that the affection of color, as a conscious affection of the sense, is a product, having
two factors; the specific sensibility of the optic
nerve, and the rays of light coming in contact
with it upon the retina of the eye. This is the
point of union of two distinct and counteracting
forces, the product of which is the sensation of
color; and the product has no actual existence,
but so long as the two powers are in act, and under these conditions and relations. Now, if we
look for the sensation of color in the excited action
of the nerve, as if this needed only to be wakened
in order to produce the sensation of color, we shall
find, in the agency of the organ and its nerve, nothing resembling color. So, if we investigate the
laws of light, and the properties of luminous bodies, and fully understand the science of optics, with
the chemical agencies of light, all of which, except its peculiar relation to the optic nerve, may
be understood by one born blind, we shall find
here nothing in the least resembling the conscious
affection of color, or that could by possibility give
us any knowledge of color. The affection is not

only not knowable, but does not exist, except in and during the *actual* counteragency of these *two polar forces*, the *product* of which is the *matter* of my *immediate* consciousness.

It is a peculiarity of this sense, that we are more conscious of the waking state and activity of the subjective power of the organ, in the absence of the objective condition necessary to its proper sensations, than in the other senses. The optic nerve is perhaps always excited in our waking moments; or at least, we are often conscious of an effort to see, where no rays of light meet the eye; and we therefore speak of seeing blackness or darkness, though in truth there is in that case no sensation of seeing, but only a conscious striving after the objective condition necessary to sight.

As the subjective cause of the sensation of seeing is voluntarily put forth, and the organ directed at will towards different points, we naturally see colors in the direction of the organ. While the organ is fixed, we can direct the attention to different points around that to which the axis of the organ is directed, and thus acquire the notion of an extension of the color to the distinct points, and so over an extended surface, from all points of which the external agency, which is one of the factors of the sensation, proceeds.

By the immediate and proper function of this sense, then, we have the sensation of color; and by this, connected with the power of voluntarily changing the direction of the organ and the con-

scious attention of the mind, we represent the
color as diffused over the surface of bodies.

The affections of this sense vary in intensity or
quantity with the degrees of light, from zero to
the highest point of illumination; and in quality,
from blackness to whiteness, and through the modifications of the several colors of the spectrum.
The study of these properly belongs to optics, and
need not be dwelt upon here.

In regard to the immediate intuitions of the sense
of sight, it may be said farther, in proof that they
are not simply intuitions of things in themselves,
considered as lying passively before us, but products of two factors, as before described, that they
are not the same for different persons, nor for the
same person at all times.   Instances are named of
persons who can make no other distinction of color
but black and white, with their varying degrees of
intensity; of others who distinguish all the colors
of the spectrum but blue.   It is, moreover, as true
of the perceptions of color as of the affections of
any other sense, that we can never determine
whether they are alike in different persons.

The same is true of the apparent magnitude of
objects as immediate objects of intuition.   If you
ask how large the moon appears to my eye, I can
answer only by comparing it with some other intuition.   If I say, as large as an eighteen inch
globe, the question recurs, at what distance the
globe is supposed to be placed; and so we come
to the angle subtended by the object.   But this
angle does not determine the apparent magnitude

absolutely, since the distance of the object is not given in the immediate intuition, and different persons represent the moon as at different distances, and the same person at different times. We see an object, then, under a determinate angle simply; and its apparent magnitude will vary from a minute point to a magnitude indefinitely great, according to the distance at which I represent it; and sight alone does not determine the distance.

Still it does not appear to me true, as sometimes represented, that extension is not given at all in the immediate intuition of this sense. Both the impression upon the retina and the corresponding presentation of the outward object have extension, since neither is a mathematical point. Distinct points are given, and diversities of color, side by side in the same presentation; and, as before remarked, the presentation remaining unchanged, the attention may be directed successively to these several points and colors in a way that seems to me necessarily to involve the distinctions of place, as given in the sensuous presentation, in the same sense as the color itself is given; i. e., so that it needs only attention, to be conscious of it. It is the essential characteristic of space, and of objects existing in space, as known to the sense, that every part is out of, or extraneous to, every other part; and this is certainly given in the immediate presentations of the sense of sight. This is still more obvious, if we suppose the eye to move so as to change the direction of its axis, or the objects present to it to be moved at an angle with

the axis; either of which would exhibit the phenomena of motion, which is inseparable from the
representation of space.

~~~~~~~~~~~~~~

CHAPTER VI.

DISTINCTION BETWEEN EMPIRICAL AND PURE OR
MATHEMATICAL INTUITIONS OF SENSE; AND BE-
TWEEN WHAT BELONGS TO SENSE AND WHAT
BELONGS TO THE HIGHER POWERS OF UNDER-
STANDING AND REASON.

Still, the distinctive and peculiar presentations
of the sense of sight are colors; and we can only
say, that space, as an object of pure sense, and its
relations and forms, as objects of the understanding and imagination, are more obviously suggested
by the phenomena of this than by those of the
other senses.

It is equally true of all the senses, that their affections give us an immediate and intuitive perception of an objective reality of a something distinguishable from self, and independent of our own
voluntary agency; of something other than self,
and out of self.   How the mind is first awakened
to a consciousness of this sense or perception of
outness, and so of space, we cannot tell.   But we
can see that the representation of space, consciously or unconsciously, is necessary, *a priori*, or

as a necessary prerequisite, to all outward experience, and all knowledge through the intuitions of the outer senses. We cannot conceive or represent to ourselves the possible existence of any thing as the object of the senses above enumerated, under any form that is not extended, and that does not presuppose the antecedency of space as that in which it exists.

Thus too, we represent what takes place or is presented to our senses in our experience, as occurring in time and under the relations of time, as coexistent or successive, and we cannot do otherwise. The knowledge of time, like that of space, is necessarily *a priori*, as the antecedent condition of our experience and knowledge of that which is in time.

Again, space and time being once presented to our consciousness, we cannot again divest ourselves of this form of consciousness. We cannot conceive the negative of space and time. They are immediate and necessary intuitions, including all other possible intuitions of sense, and being the necessary ground of possibility for all others. Time is inseparable from consciousness. The affections which in our consciousness we refer to self, are successive. The conscious self, as present in the successive states of consciousness, and continuously the same, is the necessary condition of our representation of time as successive.

Though the intuitions of space and time may be excited in our consciousness, by occasion of our experience or perception of something in space

and time, they are still therefore in their proper
origin antecedent to, and the *a priori* ground of,
all experience, and predetermine the conditions of
our knowledge.   They are implicitly contained as
the ground form of whatever is known in our experience, — space in our outward, and time in both
our outward and inward experience.   Thus we
may abstract from our perception of any thing
known, all those properties which affect us with
the sense of reality in the phenomena of touch,
taste, smell, &c., but its ground form as extended
in space, or continuous in time, or both, still remains and cannot be abstracted.

Thus we have an intuition of space and time,
independently of any thing existing in space and
time, and this is what is meant by *pure sense*.

The intuition of objects existing in space and
time, in those immediate affections of sense which
are peculiar to the several organs of sense, as
warmth, color, sound, &c., is distinguished from
the former as *empirical* sense.

Here, if we would distinguish accurately between that which belongs to sense, in our immediate intuitions, and that which belongs to the
higher powers of understanding and reason, several observations are necessary.

1.   An essential character of what pertains to
sense is its manifoldness, and the mutual exclusiveness of its parts.   In the intuitions both of
pure and of empirical sense, every part is out of
and excludes every other part.   In the objects of
pure sense, time and space, the parts are alike ;

but in the intuitions of empirical sense, there is an infinite manifoldness in quality, as well as quantity. Not only are the affections of the different senses unlike and exclusive of each other, but there is an infinite manifoldness in the quantity and quality of the affections and intuitions of the same sense. This is illustrated by the distinguishableness of that which affects the sense in the tones of voice, to such an extent, that the blind man learns to distinguish persons without limit, by this alone.

2. The sense takes cognizance only of the present and the individual, in the objects of empirical intuition, in distinction from that which is absent either in time or space, and from that which is general or universal. Thus the affections of sense are essentially transitional, and in a perpetual flux. The difficulty of understanding this, arises from our confounding what strictly pertains to the senses, with what results from the agency of other powers. I find myself at the present moment affected by a determinate impression of the sense of sight. I see what I have learned to call a piece of white paper. If I remove the paper, the sense is no longer affected by it. The image of it, which I may represent to the inner sense of the imagination, is then present to the inner sense *as an image*, which, by the exercise of another power, I refer to an absent object, and a past impression, of which it is the present representative. A reference of that which is present in the sensuous consciousness to the past and

39

future, or to the absent in space, does not pertain
to the faculty of sense, but to the understanding.
The empirical sense is limited to the present and
the actual, as a passive receptivity of impressions;
and we can find in our consciousness of these, only
what is given in the passive affections. Again, to
illustrate the individuality of sensuous intuitions,
as opposed to general conceptions; suppose yourself looking at an object which you call a tree.
Now the word tree will serve to express an indefinite number of intuitions, no one of which is identical with that which you now see. The word
tree, expresses a general conception, and does not
serve to represent the present intuition. If you
can designate it more particularly as an oak tree,
your term is still general; and when you have exhausted the powers of language, in seeking adequately to express what belongs to the sensuous
intuition and distinguish it from other sensuous
intuitions, there will still remain an infinity of
particulars which belong to its individuality as an
immediate object of sense, which may be thought
of as distinguishable by thought, but which we
have not yet attended to and designated by the
faculty of thought, and by language. The distinguishable in the immediate intuitions of sense is
thus the inexhaustible material of thought, in itself
infinitely manifold, and infinitely diversified. Each
present intuition of each of the senses, is distinguishable as an intuition of sense from every intuition of the other senses, and from every other intuition of the same sense, as other than these, and

having its own distinctive individuality, and its own reality.

3. Unity, therefore, and the principles by which the manifold in the intuitions of sense is combined together and represented as one, and by which the individual is referred to the general, do not belong to the faculty of sense. So far as space and time are, properly speaking, objects of sense, as implicitly contained in the intuitions of empirical sense, they are presented only as a manifoldness of parts, mutually exclusive, without a principle of union. Suppose I look upon an extended landscape, and see its parts as coexisting in space. For the immediate intuition of sense, there are as many distinguishable parts as there are points, each given in its position as related to the eye and to the other points in the sphere of vision, given also in its determinate qualities of form and color; and what I wish to say here, is, that the faculty of sense furnishes no principle of unity, by which these manifold phenomena are presented and thought of as one, or as parts of one whole. So with relation to time. The affections of sense, considered as successive, are represented in our consciousness as a point in motion; and each successive moment excludes from the sphere of immediate sensuous intuition, that which was present in the previous moment.

4. That which belongs to the faculty of sense, as the passive receptivity of impressions, in its strict limitations, is to be distinguished, both from that which we perceive as *necessary*, (the contrary

of which is seen to be impossible,) and from that
which depends on *the will*. In an affection and
intuition of sense, as when I open my eyes upon a
window, I find myself conditioned, my conscious
state modified in a precise and determinate manner, and have a precise and determinate intuition
of a sensuous object. Its apparent extension,
form, color, multiplicity and relation of parts, &c.,
as present in my intuition, are wholly independent
of my own will. They are there before me; and
when I open my eyes, I see them, whether I will
or not, with just these precise and determinate
limitations of quantity or quality, neither more nor
less; and no effort of thought or will can make them
different as sensuous phenomena, from what I see
them to be. I seem to myself to be the passive
recipient of impressions; to have the state of my
consciousness affected by that over which I have
no control. It presents itself, therefore, as an independent reality, of which I have the highest possible certainty. My intuition contains the unequivocal assertion of its reality in all its particulars.
Again, my affection or intuition changes perhaps,
with each successive moment, with the variation
of the intensity or the direction of the light, or
from other causes, and this too, independently of
my voluntary agency. And thus, though I see
and assert the *reality* of the phenomena here, and
the *existence* of that which is present to the sense
as independent of self, and so objective, I do not
see or assert its necessity, or the impossibility of
its being otherwise than it is at any given moment,

or of its entire nonexistence.   This is the character of all that is known empirically, or by means of the empirical sense.

5.   There is then, a wide difference between the functions of sense as an organ of empirical knowledge, in our immediate and merely sensuous intuitions of the manifold in space and time, and that which we have called pure sense, as an intuition of the *a priori* and necessary ground of experience, under the forms of space and time.   In the former, we experience a fact, and our knowledge is *assertory*.   In the latter, we have an intuition of necessary truth, and our knowledge is *apodictic;* I affirm not merely the fact that *it is now* so and so, but that it *must of necessity* be so, *now* and *at all times*.

Again, in time and space, or what are called the intuitions of pure sense, we extend our view beyond all the limits of experience, and represent them as infinite.   We moreover combine the manifold intuitions of empirical sense, under the forms of time and space, and represent them as included and as composing *one universe*.

Whence then come the ideas of necessity, of infinity, and of unity, in these representations?

Strictly speaking, only the *qualities* of objects corresponding to the distinctive perceptivity of the several senses, and empirically known as realities in space and time, are the objects of sensuous intuition; and the *a priori* ground of the possibility of experience in the presentations of space and time, with the ideas of infinity and unity, belong to the *reason*.

Each of our senses has its distinct and peculiar objects in nature. The sense of sight perceives colors; that of hearing, sounds; that of smell, odors; each so different in kind from all the rest, that if one sense be wanting, its immediate and proper objects can never be known by the separate or combined agency of all the rest. There is nothing in the perceptions of one to suggest, or in any way to connect with it, those of another. The principle of unity, therefore, must be referred to the unity of our reason. It is by the developement of this, that we represent to ourselves *space*, which to the empirical sense is but an infinite manifoldness, or an infinite multiplicity of points, each extraneous to all the others, as being yet *one space*, of which all particular spaces *are parts*, and which therefore comprehends infinite manifoldness in unity.

It is by the same principle of unity in reason, that we combine all the manifold variety of phenomena presented to the several senses in space, as belonging to and parts of one world, included in space. Neither of these is perceived by the empirical sense; but this mode of representing them originates in the mind with the *dawn of reason*, and we think of it as a *necessary* mode. It is not founded in experience, but is *a priori*. If we strive to represent the matter otherwise, we fail to do so, because the mind still assumes a higher unity in which all are included. Such is the spontaneous utterance of reason, the moment we are capable of rational insight, and take a rational

view of the objects of knowledge. The same remarks apply to our representation of time, and of
the sequence of events in time. We represent
time as one continuous succession of like parts,
and cannot think of it as broken and severed into
two or more. So of nature, as including the whole
series of events in time. We represent it as an
unbroken series; and if we seek to do otherwise,
our imaginations spontaneously fill up the interval
and connect the one with the other, as necessarily
parts of the same unity.

If now we consider our representations of a
limited and individual object in space and time,
we shall find the process to be of a like kind. It
includes three things clearly distinguishable.

1. The intuitions of empirical sense, in the
sensible qualities of the object. These are manifold, and as immediate phenomena of sense, are
wholly dissimilar and disconnected. Sound has
no affinity to color, nor hardness to the affections
of smell.

2. The intuition of space and time, in which
these qualities are represented as existing objectively each for itself.

3. The union and comprehension of these separate qualities, the immediate objects of the several senses, in a limited and determinate form and
figure in space and time.

Of the two first, nothing more need be said at
present. By what process of the mind we come
to represent sensible qualities under the determinate relations of figure and position in space and

of duration in time, as in the third particular, needs further inquiry.

Here it is important to observe the distinction between the immediate perception of the *qualities* of an object, which express its *relations to the percipient* as susceptible of being specifically affected by them, and the representation of its *quantity*, as determined by its *extension and mathematical form* and relations in space.

Our perceptions of *qualities* generally give us, in the affections of the outer senses, a knowledge of reality, existing out of self and in space; and, moreover, excite the spontaneous powers of the mind, not only to the contemplation of the unity, the several dimensions and the boundlessness of space, but also to the construction of mathematical forms in space, each having its unity given to it by the mind itself. Now this power of the mind, thus freely and independently of the control of the empirical sense, to construct forms in space, is called the *productive imagination.** No-

---

* The simplest and most obvious import of the word imagination is that which is suggested by its etymology. An image is the sensuous *form* and *representation* of an object, without the substance; as a shadow, a picture, the colored image of an object reflected in a mirror, or formed by a lens. These are external to the mind; and, as well as the objects which they represent, belong to the outer sense. The word image is also used to designate those representations of outward objects which are presented to the inner sense; as, when I call to mind an absent friend, I have his image present to my inner sense. Rather, that which is so presented to my inner sense, when the abstract object is called to mind, is called an image; and the power of presenting and making use of such images is the imagination in the most obvious sense. Now such images are presented in the ordinary remembrance of an object formerly known. An image is also presented in the casual succession of images, under the law of spontaneous association.

thing is plainer than that this power can, independently of experience, produce mathematical forms and constructions without limit, in the exercise of its own activity, with only the postulates that are given in the immediate apprehension of space.

This is an important point; and the *mathematical intuition of forms and their relations in space* is properly the common ground of all our knowledge of distinct outward objects, and of our ability to understand each other in regard to the identity, the quantity and quality of objects. The mathematical intuitions of pure sense and the productive imagination enable us to give to the manifold empirical phenomena of an object, a synthetical unity, by representing them as combined under a determinate figure in space.

Here the mathematical *form*, as the construction of the productive imagination, and the object of pure sense, becomes the *fixed and determinate limitation* of the *qualities* which are referred to the object as an object of empirical sense. We can represent the qualities as varying in number and degree; but the figure and position in space, as an object of pure sense, cannot be abstracted; but remains as the fixed ground of reference and comparison. The imagination, in representing the figure of an object, and its relations and boundaries, is excited, indeed, and guided, to some extent, by the empirical affections of the senses of touch and sight; but we can acquire distinct knowledge only by reflexion upon the empirical phenomena, in their relations to possible forms con-

40

templated as objects of pure sense. It is by its
freedom from the domination of the present and
the actual in the immediate affections of empirical
sense, and its activity in the construction and contemplation of the possible, that it furnishes the
antecedent ground for such reflexion, for the comparison of the empirical with the mathematical;
of the fleeting and indeterminate with the fixed
and determinate ; and thus enables us to represent
the actual under mathematical forms. Thus the
spontaneous agency of the imagination and the
intuitions of empirical sense furnish the form and
matter of our knowledge of objects; and it is by
observation and reflection, that our knowledge is
rendered distinct.

Here it is to be observed, that only the *qualities*
are immediate in the intuitions of empirical sense,
and that in them there is no principle of unity.

Again, in the intuitions of pure sense, as belonging to the passive sense alone, there is no
unity, but infinite manifoldness.

The representation of unity, the contemplation
of the *manifold* as *one*, is *an act* of the mind itself, grasping its object, and comprehending the
many in a unity of consciousness.

This representation of unity, or the power of
comprehending many as one, belongs to the original form of the understanding, and is the subjective condition of knowing. The mere presentation of the manifold in the intuitions of empirical
sense, is not knowledge ; but the material of a possible knowledge, or that which *may be known*.

The understanding *apprehends* and takes cognizance of it, according to its own inherent forms
and powers of apprehension and of knowledge.

The distinction of the subjective from the objective, of the self from the not self, in the primary act of self-consciousness, it has been already
remarked, is the activity of the awakened power
of thought. So the reference of that which is
given in an immediate intuition of sense to self as
one, or to an object considered as one, is an act of
the understanding. The doing this is the uniting
of the manifold in a unity of consciousness; and
this is the form under which the understanding
takes cognizance of that which is presented as the
material of knowledge. An object of knowledge
for the understanding is that in which the manifold qualities of a sensuous intuition are combined
in a unity of consciousness. We represent various distinct qualities, as extension, hardness,
sweetness, whiteness, &c., as united in one and
the same *object*. Each of these, as immediately
affecting the sense, and contemplated as an objective reality existing in space, I represent as having
its reality, and as being *substantiated*, in a *subject*
other than self and out of self, and therefore in
space. Now I say, the understanding, in combining these in a unity of consciousness, and at the
same time giving them outwardness in space, refers *many qualities* to *one* and the *same subject* in
one and the *same space*. But this other *subject*
represented in space is the *object* of the understanding; and what is represented as an *object in*

space, is of course extended and constructible by the imagination under the mathematical form, and determinations of pure sense as a figure; and thus the empirical qualities of an object are presented as united in a form representable in space.

<hr>

CHAPTER VII.

CONTINUATION OF THE SAME SUBJECT. THE IN-NER SENSE AND ITS OBJECTS.

The principal aim here is, to distinguish clearly between what is *given* in the immediate affections of *sense* as the passive *receptivity* of the mind, and what pertains to the higher power which takes *cognizance* of what is thus *given*. In the former, we have the material or *object-matter* of *possible* knowledge, as *manifold* as our susceptibility of impressions under all the forms and affections of sense ; in the latter, that *agency* of the mind which is excited by and directed to this, *apprehending*, *knowing it*, &c. Now to this higher agency there necessarily belongs a unity, inseparable from the unity of consciousness as expressed in the form, *I think, I know*. In the self, as knowing, there is no representation of manifoldness, but a simple unity. The manifold, as given in the intuitions of sense, I combine in one consciousness, or refer to self as one percipient. This is the necessary form

of thought and of conscious knowledge.   That
which is given as the material of thought and of
knowledge, is an *intuition*, and *antecedent* to the act
of knowing, by which the manifold of the intuition is synthetically combined in a unity of conscious perception.   The act by which I represent
the manifold in a unity, is an *act of spontaneity*,
originating in the cognitive power, and does not
belong to the sense.   We can represent nothing
in the immediate intuitions of sense as synthetically combined, without having first combined it
together by our own act.   Whether we are conscious of it or not, the representation of the union
of many distinguishable qualities in one object
does not come from the objects; is not *given* in
the affections of sense; but proceeds from the understanding itself.   It is not meant to say that the
object is *not* one, and that the synthesis is not real;
but only that its unity is not among the qualities
given in the affections of sense.   Nor indeed is
the unity and connexion of parts here intended,
such as we learn by experience to exist in an organized body, or by any particular bond of union
in the object itself; but that which the understanding spontaneously gives to whatever is presented, and must give, in order to bring it within
its apprehension and make it an object of knowledge.   Thus we think of the sum of all outward
existences as *one universe*; of the objects within
the sphere of our vision as *one prospect, one landscape*, &c.; and contemplate the particular objects
embraced as *parts* of one *whole*.   That we cannot

do otherwise does not prove that the unity is given
in the intuitions of sense; but only that we do so
by an act of *spontaneity*, and not an act of *choice*.
The power of perception or apprehension, when
excited by that which is present to the sense, acts
spontaneously and independently of the will, as to
the mode of *apprehending* it; just as the sense,
when affected from without, acts spontaneously in
the intuition of that which belongs to sense.   The
intuition of the *manifold* in the immediate affections of sense, is the spontaneous agency of
the faculty of *sense*; the *apprehension* of what
is given in the intuition in a *unity* of *consciousness*, is the spontaneous act of the *understanding*,
according to its own inherent laws of action.
Neither the intuition of sense, nor the perception
of the understanding, is under the direction of the
will as it regards the laws of their agency.   The
agency of both is thus far immediate upon the
presence of its object, and inseparable from it, and
therefore, as it were, organic and antecedent to
voluntary reflection.   We can only, in regard to
these agencies, reflect and make ourselves distinctly
conscious of *what* we have done, *after* we have
done it.   Thus, in this case, we are not conscious
of the *synthesis* of the distinguishable qualities of
an object as our *own act;* but the subsequent analysis which we make of the object as apprehended
by the understanding, proves an antecedent synthesis, and we distinguish by analysis, only what
we had combined in the synthesis.   Here observe,
that all the qualities so combined, are given in the

intuition ; and it is only the synthesis or *putting together* of these in what the understanding presents to itself as *one object*, that originates in the act of the understanding ; and all that analysis can do again, is to dissolve the unity, and distinguish the original qualities given in the intuition. The *union* of many in one is not properly an *additional particular*, to be enumerated with the several particulars so united. Nor does the representation of unity arise from a perceived connexion of the several parts or particulars, but that of connexion rather from the antecedent unity. It must therefore be sought for in that agency of the understanding, which, from its own subjective nature, must be the same for all the objects of its apprehension, and independent of any ground of the representation in the nature of the objects so apprehended.

Here it may be necessary, in order to avoid misconception, to mark more clearly another distinction ; that, I mean, between the subjective and the objective unity of our perception.

By the subjective unity of a perception, it is meant to express the identity of the conscious perceiving, as directed to the several distinguishable particulars in an object. It is the same self and the same agency, that apprehends the several qualities of an object as coexisting in space, or as successive in time. The thought, that all the several particulars given in an intuition belong to *me*, constitutes the subjective unity of a perception. It combines the manifold in the affections of sense in one act of self-consciousness, and I represent them all as *my* affections. There is an identity of the conscious percipient in all ; otherwise, self would be as manifold as the qualities of the objects of sense of which I am conscious.

The objective unity of a perception, on the other hand, is the representation of the immediate qualities perceived in an intuition, not as having an identity of relation to me, but as having a mutual relation and connexion with each other as qualities of one object. Again, in its objective unity, an object of perception has its determinate position and direction in space, and stands in *relation to other objects*. It is necessarily represented under the mathematical forms and relations of pure sense, and has its extension, figure, &c., determined for the percipient by the constructive agency of the imagination. As such, and so determined, it becomes a distinct object of the understanding, as distinguished from sense, and an object of perception as distinguished from intuition. The intuition is the immediate presentation of the manifold in the affections of sense ; the perception is the presentation of the many as *one objective* thing, combining manifoldness in unity.

The same remarks which have been made respecting our apprehension of that which we present to ourselves as existing in space, will apply, for the most part, to our apprehension of objects as existing in time. Whatever is present, either to the outer or to the inner sense, is necessarily represented as existing in time, or as having duration ; and the same distinction between pure and empirical sense manifests itself, as in regard to existence in space. The same distinction holds also between the manifoldness of what affects the empirical sense and the unity of consciousness under which it is apprehended by the understanding. The successive moments, and therein distinguishable parts of duration in time, are apprehended as combined to make up one time; or those within given limits, as one period of time, one day, and one hour, &c.; and thus an object is apprehended (abstractly from its qualities, which affect the several senses empirically), as having *extension, figure* and *duration, mathematically determinable in space and time;* and an *objective unity,* combining *in one object a manifoldness of parts and properties analytically distinguishable from each other.*

2. The term *inner sense,* as distinguished from the outer senses already treated of, properly designates the *immediate consciousness* of the states and agencies of our own inward being. As I have an immediate intuition of the qualities of outward objects, as color, hardness, &c., which I refer to a ground of being out of 'self, so I have an *immediate intuition* of affections and agencies, which I refer *to self, as their proper ground and source;* such as the feeling of pleasure and pain, desiring, willing, and the activities of thought.

It is not, however, to be understood, that we mean by this language to indicate a specific sense, having its distinct organ, like the several external senses. It is meant only that the states and agencies of our inward life are immediately present to

41

our consciousness, as the passive material of
knowledge, and so apprehensible to the understanding ; in the same way as the immediate affections and intuitions of the outer senses are apprehensible. When we direct the attention of the
understanding to what is passing in our own being,
we find the objects of attention presented for observation in a form which has all the characteristics (in its relation to the apprehensive faculty)
which were before enumerated as pertaining to
sense. As present in our immediate consciousness,
or in the inner sense, they are manifold, immediate and individual, present and actual, as the material of knowledge, and distinguishable from that
agency of the reflective understanding which takes
cognizance of them. They are presented, not as
extended and objective in space, admitting of construction by figure, and so picturable to the outer
sense, but as continuous in time, and capable of
being designated and reproduced in our consciousness.

An essential difference here between what pertains to the affections of the outer and what we
speak of as the inner sense, is, that while the objects affecting the outer senses exist independently
of our agency, and require only that the senses be
directed to them, and the attention excited, in
order to be perceived, those that belong to the
inner sense are our own agencies, and *exist* only
so long as the mind is in act, or actually affected,
conditioned in the manner which we wish to observe. When the feeling of pleasure or pain, or

the act of desiring, willing, thinking, &c., has ceased, it no longer exists as an object of the inner sense; and how can we have a sensuous intuition of that which has no existence, or a perception of that of which we have no intuition?

It is only, therefore, by reproducing and bringing again into the conscious presence of the inner sense, our past states of consciousness, by the activity of our own minds, that they can become possible objects of attention and observation. This is done either spontaneously by the law of association, or voluntarily by the control of the will over the faculty of thought.

Thus, whatever I have once been conscious of as a state of my own inward being, may be reproduced in my consciousness; and whatever has such a connexion with my inward being as to be potentially reproducible in my consciousness by the activity of my own reproductive and representative faculty, may be said to belong to the inner sense, and to be a part of the internal world; as whatever exists in space, so as to be potentially an object of outward intuition, belongs to the outer sense, and to the external world of sense.

It will be seen from this view, that we include among the objects of the inner sense those *agencies* of the soul which have for *their object* the outer world of sense. Thus I present to myself an absent object of sight, a house, a tree, &c., whether in a dream, a reverie, or by a voluntary act of thought; and I picture it as outward, in space, with all its surrounding accompaniments.

Here the agency itself has or may have an outward object perceptible to the external senses.
But that which is now actually present to the
mind is not the outward object itself, nor is it present to the outer sense, but a representative image
of it only, the work of the reproductive imagination; and this image, which exists only so long as
the imagination presents it, belongs only to the inner sense or the inward consciousness. It has no
reality out of the mind; and as an object of the
inner sense, is a sensuous image or representative
of an outward object, having the same relation to
the inner sense which the object itself has to the
outer sense. As an act of the reproductive imagination, it has the same reality for the inner sense
that the object itself has for the outer sense. Thus
all the reproduced images of the outer world, considered as representative acts of the imagination,
in dreams, &c., and reflected upon by the understanding, are presented to its apprehension as sensuous and present in the inner sense.

The same remarks of course apply to all the
agencies and states of the mind, in doing and suffering, in thought, desire, and will. Considered
as objects of the reflective understanding, they are
presented for its apprehension in that immediate
consciousness of the inward phenomena of our own
being which is termed the inner sense.

The inward life and activities of the soul are
subjected to our observation and conscious notice.
I not only feel pleasure and pain, joy and sorrow,
love and hate, desire and will, think, imagine, &c.,

but can make all these agencies themselves the objects of the reflective understanding; can apprehend and fix my attention upon them as objects of study and of knowledge. Their presentation in the *inner sense* or immediate consciousness is the beginning and primary condition of self-knowledge, as the presence of the material world to the *outer sense* is the condition of our knowledge of that.

But the point of most importance, here, is to distinguish clearly between what pertains to sense, or is sensuous, and the proper agencies and products of thought, or of the understanding as the faculty of thought. Whatever is presented as immediate and individual in our consciousness for the attention and apprehension of the understanding, and so as the object matter of its cognitive agency, belongs as such to the sense; while that which is derived from it, by comparison, abstraction, &c., in the form of general conceptions, belongs to the understanding, as the product of its agency employed upon the immediate intuitions of sense. Following this distinction, not only the original intuitions, whether of the outer or of the inner sense, but the re-presentation of these in their manifoldness by the agency of the imagination or representative faculty, is also sensuous; and such a re-presentation is not a conception, but an image of sense merely; and the mere reproduced sensuous image, like the original intuition, is not knowledge, but only the material of a possible knowledge.

It may be remarked here, that the objects of the inner sense are embraced in the general form of self-consciousness, or are recognized as existing *in self;* as the objects of the outer senses are referred to a ground out of self, and recognized as existing in space. This consciousness of self, as the ground and *presuppositum* of those phenomena which I refer to self, is termed *pure* and *a priori self-consciousness,* as the necessary *a priori* ground of our knowledge of the particular modifications of self, as the intuition of space is the necessary antecedent ground of our representation of objects as existing in space. The conscious *I am* is necessarily involved as an antecedent in every qualified determination of consciousness which makes known to me *how* and *what* I am. To this, too, pertains that representation of self, or the conscious *I,* by which all my individual and successive feelings, desires, thoughts, &c., are presented and combined as the activities of one and the same individual. What are the possible modifications and agencies of that self of which we are conscious, can be known only by experience in the progressive developement of its powers, and by making ourselves conscious of those agencies as manifested in the inner sense. Here they may be more or less distinctly manifested, or our power of attending to and apprehending the phenomena there presented may be greater or less, according to age and habits of thought, or to the general discipline and power of the understanding.

In general, it may be said, the phenomena presented to the inner sense, like those of the outer world, are in a state of perpetual flux, varying with every fluctuation of the powers of our inward life, and the numberless influences which serve to repress or to excite them. To most men, too, it is an unknown world, as their observation and their thoughts are directed exclusively to the world without; and it is only by careful discipline of the understanding, and great precision in the use of it acquired by philosophical reflection, and a critical discrimination of terms, that we can seize upon and trace the phenomena of our inward being.

CHAPTER VIII.

MEMORY AND POWER OF ASSOCIATION.

Thus far, in treating of the powers of knowledge, we have considered only those agencies by which we have an *immediate* perception of a *present* object, as *existent* in time and space. The distinctive characteristic of these is, that they are accompanied with a *sense of reality,* and an irresistible conviction of the actual present existence of the object perceived, as it is perceived, and independent of the act of perception. The immediate affections of sense in these agencies are passive and involuntary; and what is given in the sense is apprehended by the understanding, as determined so and so in all its modifications of quantity, quality and relation, and existing at this precise time and place.

We proceed now to the consideration of other agencies and other modes in which the mind presents to itself the objects of its attention. In these, the mind is more or less freed from the immediate and absolute domination of sense and the law of outward necessity; and they form a sort of transition from the passive determination of sense to the freedom of voluntary thought. These, according to the common use of language, may be designated, in their general character, as the memory, the power of association, and the fancy or imagination. But without attempting at present to use these terms with precision, either as they are or as they should be employed, I shall aim merely to point out the more important distinctions in things, as they are verified in our own consciousness.

1. The power of simple *sensuous re-presentation* of a past intuition of sense, or, in general, of a past state of consciousness.

When, by those agencies which have been already treated of, we have had an immediate perception of the objects of knowledge, either in the presentation of the outer or of the inner sense as present to the sense, we can afterwards *re-present* and contemplate them as *past* and *absent.* If, in travelling, I pass a house upon the road, and observe it, have a distinct perception of it, my mind can afterwards, when the object is now distant or no longer in existence, re-present the house and make it again the object of attention.

But observe, that in this *simple representation,* the present agency of the mind is determined by the past consciousness. It is merely, as it were, a recurrence of a past state of consciousness, not now as actual, indeed, but as representative, yet limited and determined in all its particulars by the actual past. The mind exercises no freedom of construction, but presents to itself the past and absent object *as it was,* with all its attendant circumstances of time, place, &c. In regard to its object, the mind is equally passive as in the immediate perception of the house when present to the outer sense. That which is now present to the mind is the simple counterpart or the representative image of that which was before present. Such a re-presentation of a past consciousness may be called either *simple memory,* or referred to the *re-productive imagination.* In its relation to our powers of knowledge, it may be considered as the reserved copy of an actual experience, reserved in the mind, and capable of being re-presented as an object of attention, and as containing the sensuous material of knowledge for the understanding; and the more perfectly it re-presents the actual past, i. e., the more entirely the present act of the mind as representative is passively determined by the past as real, the more perfectly does it subserve the purposes of the understanding.

42

2. But again, the mind can present to itself a *modified* image of the past, or a part only of a past object without the remainder. This is done involuntarily, in the imperfect and indistinct representations which we make of our past experience. Thus, in the illustration above given, I may represent the house without being able to fix the time and place in which I observed it; or I may recall these and have but an indistinct image of the form, color, size, &c., of the house itself. Here is an involuntary modification of the original consciousness. The present image, as representative, only partially represents the past and real, or presents it with the *abstraction* of more or less of that which belonged to the original. Here we have the distinction of *remembering* and *forgetting*, and our ability or inability to re-present a past object of perception; and the degree of clearness and perfection with which I am able to represent it, depends upon various circumstances, both in the original activity of the mind in the perception, and in its present agency. In the progress of our experience, the mind becomes stored with the images of the past, forming for each individual a world of his own, in which he expatiates, or the parts of which rise and fall, as it were, present themselves clearly and adequately, or vaguely and imperfectly, in the horizon of his present consciousness, and supply him with the materials of thought and knowledge. An important point to be observed here is, that in the modified and partially abstracted images of the past, the mind is already to

some extent freed from the domination of the *immediate* impressions of sense.

3. The images which the mind has thus formed, which had their origin in, and were representative of, immediate and individual objects of sense, *become* wholly *freed* from the order in time and place, and from the connexion with each other which they had as strictly representative of past reality; and are spontaneously recombined in a different order in time and place, and in new combinations with each other. Thus if, after passing one house upon the road, I pass another of different size, form, color, &c., I may afterwards re-present the latter as antecedent in my experience to the former, and combine in the representative image the color of one with the figure and situation of the other; or their qualities, without regard to time and place, may be transferred and recombined with each other, and with the qualities of other objects without limit. In a word, the combinations of distinguishable particulars, as presented in our actual experience, are dissolvable in the inward agencies of the mind, and the particulars reproducible under new arrangements and combinations without limit, as we experience in our dreams and our waking reveries, and witness in the effects of delirium, &c.

4. In the new arrangements and combinations which take place in the spontaneous reproduction of these sensuous images, we trace the operation of certain principles by which they are determined, and which constitute what is called the *law of association*.

The substance of this law in general, as the law of spontaneous association, is, that images or partial images of past states of consciousness have a tendency, when present in our consciousness, to recall others by relations subsisting among themselves, and independently of voluntary effort. Thus, in our dreams, and whenever the spontaneous activity of the mind is left free from the control of the will and the interference of voluntary thought, we find one image calls up another, and a continuous succession of phenomena float before the inner sense. These, indeed, are not composed wholly of images of the outer sense; but whatever has preexisted in our consciousness may be represented and affect the present succession. Not only so; the present state of feeling, as cheerful or melancholy, may have its influence in determining the character of the associated imagery; and this again may have a reciprocal influence upon the tone of the mind itself.

The most general principle, in regard to the tendency of one object to recall another, is, that whatever affections have once coexisted in our consciousness, as parts of one total impression or state of consciousness, acquire thereby a tendency mutually to reproduce each other. Thus, if, while observing the house upon the road, I was conversing with a fellow traveller, not only all the outward circumstances would tend each to recall, when re-presented to the mind, all the others, but the subjects of our conversation, and the images which that brought before the mind, would become associated with the house, and tend to recall it. A single word, or tone, or momentary feeling, if afterwards heard, or felt, or represented, may serve to bring the whole scene or any particular part of it again before the mind.

Subordinate to this general principle, (1.) one image will tend more or less strongly to recall another, in proportion to the strength of the original impressions, and of the connexion which was formed between them as parts of one total impression. Thus, if two objects of novel and peculiar interest are present and occupy my mind, as two distinguished persons, for example, at the same time or in immediate succession, one will thereby acquire a tendency always to recall the other. (2.) This tendency will depend upon the relation of the present state and tone and occupation of my mind to the object to be associated, and a particular image will excite this or that other image of objects originally forming parts of the same total impression, according as one or the other is most consonant to its present state. When cheerful, the same image would suggest a different train of associated images from what it would when melancholy. (3.) The principle of similarity in the original affections of consciousness has an influence upon the succession of the train of representations. Affections of one sense tend rather to recall each other, than the affections of another sense; sounds suggest other sounds, colors other colors, &c. In general, the nearer the affinity of representations to each other, the greater is

their tendency, other things being equal, to associate each other.

We may enumerate, in addition to these, the
principle of order, of contrast, &c., but it is more
important to remark that all the agencies of the
mind are connected together as manifestations of
one inward life; and the excitement of one power
has a tendency in a greater or less degree to excite every other. The present feelings influence
the associations of the past; and whether in a mu-
sing mood or in a dream, this or that particular
train of imagery, this or that incident in our past
history, this or that picture of life originally formed
in the mind by the chance medley of a dream or a
novel, shall be now brought back to our consciousness, depends upon contingencies that can be reduced to no general rule.

The clearness and vividness with which we represent past intuitions and states of consciousness
depend upon several circumstances; as, (1.) the
force and distinctness of the original impression;
(2.) the fitness of the occasion to reproduce in all
its parts what constituted the original state of consciousness; and, (3.) the present vigor of the mind
and activity of the reproductive imagination itself;
(4.) state of health and affections of the organic
system.

In general, if one part of a total and complex
impression of sense, as one distinct object in a
landscape, awakens a strong interest and produces
a vivid impression, the remainder will produce but
a feeble one; or if a variety of strong impressions

are produced at the same time, they tend to confuse each other; and these different effects will be obvious in the subsequent representations.

It is only by the power of association, or the tendency of a present consciousness to reproduce former experiences, that the accumulated stores of past observation and experience are treasured up in our minds; and in this way, as we have reason to suppose, all the materials of each one's past history are so linked together as to be capable of being represented to our consciousness. If so, then nothing is in such a sense forgotten as to be wholly lost from our minds; and we often find that what at one time we could not recall by any effort of recollection, will at another, without an effort, and by the spontaneous power of association, be brought clearly and vividly to mind.

In common language, however, we are said to have *forgotten* a thing, when we cannot recall it by the voluntary effort of the understanding in directing the train of associations.

On the other hand, the *power of memory*, more strictly defined, is the faculty of re-presenting to the mind what has been before present to it, with the consciousness that it has been so. We may distinguish, here, the case in which we merely are conscious that what is now present has been before present, and that in which we refer it to its original connexions in time and place.

From the law of association, also, in part, arises the formation of habits, and the anticipation of the future. When the same process in which

either the agencies of the mind alone, or those of
the mind and body together are concerned, has
been often repeated, each antecedent act excites
and reproduces its consequent by *immediate and
spontaneous association*, without an effort of thought
or of will.   So, in regard to the future, when we
have seen phenomena often succeed each other in
a certain order, the occurrence of the antecedent
awakens the representation of the consequent in
the same relation of time, i. e., as yet future.   By
this passive or rather spontaneous association with
the present of that which is yet future, even the
brutes have the power of foresight.

Thus far, I have spoken of the law of association as a principle of spontaneity; and of memory
and imagination chiefly as dependent on this, and
spontaneously reproducing the past in our consciousness.   In this form, merely, they exhibit
only the uncultivated and rude nature of man, as
it is common to him with the brutes.   Left to this
alone, he would be wholly the creature of circumstances, directed by sensuous impulses, over which
he could have no power of control.

But, practically speaking, the will and the understanding in every one, with the first dawn of
conscious intelligence, controls and modifies, in a
greater or less degree, the law of spontaneous association.   It was before remarked, that, even in
the spontaneous agencies of the mind, the order
and combinations presented in our actual experience are dissolved, and new arrangements and
combinations produced.

I proceed now to remark, that the association of
objects presented to us can be influenced by the
will, and that we can, by voluntary efforts of the
understanding, determine the order and the connexion of that which is treasured up in our memories.   Thus, among the particulars presented in a
total impression to the outer senses, or at the same
time present to the inner sense, we can at will fix
the attention upon an individual or upon any portion of the whole, abstract it from the rest, and
connect it or associate it by voluntary thought with
whatever else we are able to bring before our consciousness.   If our attention, for example, be fixed
upon a ship, as part of a scene presented either to
the outer or to the inner sense, we can think of it
in its relation to science or art, or in its relation to
natural scenery, and determine its associations accordingly, in its relation to our former stores of
knowledge.   In this way, I determine, in a greater
or less degree, by my own voluntary effort, my
subsequent ability to remember it, and the associations by means of which I shall be able to recall
it.   It is by this higher power of thought, directed
to the objects present in the horizon of our consciousness, that we are able to choose and limit
the objects that shall occupy our minds; shut out
intruding associations; and thus pursue a fixed
purpose, and give a predetermined method to the
succession of associated thought and imagery.
Thus the spontaneous agencies of the mind are
gradually brought under methodical arrangement,
determined by the prevailing habits of thought;

43

and even our dreams give proof of the mode in which our waking hours are employed, and of the degree in which our minds are disciplined and cultivated.

The influence of the power of attention, both in fixing particular states of consciousness or particular objects in our memories, and in rendering our associations methodical, is of the highest importance. The power to select, among the numberless objects present to our consciousness, that which is suited to a preconceived purpose, with the exclusion of the rest; to retain it against the force of the natural current of spontaneous association; is that which renders us capable of self-cultivation and self-control. By this, we are able to rise above the law of mere brute nature, and direct the agencies of our minds to the accomplishment of purposes which reason prescribes.

The voluntary activity of the mind is no less distinguished above its spontaneous agencies, in what we have called the productive imagination. In its spontaneous agencies, it was remarked that it often produced new combinations among the images of the past, as in our dreams, etc. But these are rather the product of nature working in us, than our own work. They are the results, revealed in our consciousness, of powers which lie beyond the reach of our immediate and voluntary control, no less than the organic agencies of the nervous and arterial systems.

But the imagination, in its higher functions, is the power by which we are able voluntarily to present to ourselves images, constructed and combined otherwise than they are given to us in our experience. If my mind were absolutely limited by my actual experience, and I could only *re-present* the actual past, then a series of objects, seen to exist in only one order and mode of combination, could not be presented by the mind to itself in any other mode. The objects a, b, c, if known in our experience only in the order of succession in which they are given, would always be represented in the same order; and there could arise in the mind no occasion for the distinction between the *actual* and the *possible*. But we know not only that the spontaneous law of association may represent them in a different order, but that we can arrange and combine them, in the images which we present to ourselves at will, without regard to the order in which they were known in our experience, and thus make ourselves conscious of the distinction between the *actual* and the *possible*.

Thus the imagination is not at all limited in its agencies, by the forms and combinations of the real world of our experience; but those images which are first furnished by the intuitions of sense, we can, by an exertion of voluntary power, shape and combine together, and present to the inner sense in an endless variety of forms. We can represent an individual object, like the sun for example, as multiplied or enlarged, and think of the sky as filled with a thousand suns. When we see an object of a red color, we can represent to ourselves that color as extended to other objects, and spread over all that surrounds us. So we can represent the qualities of an object, as abstracted one after another, till the whole disappears, and is represented as non-existent.

In all its creations, however, the imagination is limited in regard to the materials of its workmanship to that which is given in the intuitions of pure and empirical sense. However free the play of imagery in fictitious representations may be, the imagination, under the control of the will, can only contribute the form and method in which the materials already given are combined together. Hence the man born blind can combine in the creations of his imagination no representations of color, nor the deaf of sounds. Thus all the materials are from the empirical sense ; the form and principle of combination in space and time, from the mind itself.

A distinction of great importance is made here, between the mere aggregations of forms and imagery, and that agency of the imagination in which the imagery is strictly subordinated to the expression of a pre-conceived idea. The former agency is distinguished by some as the fancy, the other as the imagination, in its proper sense. It is the office of the former to collect and call up as it were the images of the inner sense, as the materials by which the creative ideas of the imagination are to be expressed or realized.

The power to distinguish the possible from the actual, and to present to ourselves a scene or combination of circumstances, as possible, differing from and better than the real, is the ground of hope, and the exciting cause of all effort to improve our condition. It is the guide of the understanding, as it were, in presenting beforehand the objects not yet existing, which the understanding contrives the means of attaining.

It is this power, also, that constructs those figures which are the necessary objects of the understanding, in seeking after general truths, as the basis of its conceptions. We abstract from the individual images of sense their distinctive characters, and present a general outline that applies to several individual objects in common. When we use a general term, as man, house, tree, &c., we bring before our mind a sensuous representation of it, that serves to designate the meaning of the word, without including the characters which distinguish individuals of the species named from each other. Or rather, perhaps, the imagination enlightens the understanding here, by presenting varying forms, or differing individual images of the class, each of which includes the characters combined in the general conception, with the consciousness of the distinction between the conception and the individualized image. This will be best exemplified by reference to the construction of geometrical forms, all which are the work of the productive imagination. When we represent to ourselves the meaning of the word triangle, ellipse, &c., it is by constructing figures, each of which includes the characters combined in the definition, with the consciousness that they are only inclusive of the conception, while the individual peculiarities of each are unessential.*

Again, the activity of the imagination is necessary to invention, in the useful as well as in the fine arts; since whatever is to be realized, must first be presented by the imagination as a possible construction.

~~~~~~~~~~~~

CHAPTER IX.

RECAPITULATION.

Before proceeding to treat more particularly of the understanding as the power of voluntary thought, let us review very briefly what has been

* A scheme, as constituting the identity of a conception in different minds, and the ultimate ground of community in language, can exist only in the common method, or rule of representation, by which the imagination is directed in producing images of objects included under a general term. An individual object can be subsumed under a general conception, only as it has in it that which is identical in kind with the conception itself; i. e., as it is generated, in the mode of conscious representation, by the same method, by the same rule of generation in the productive imagination.

Different minds are brought to a mutual understanding of terms, as designating a determinate agency in consciousness as common to them all. Thus the images which A and B present to themselves, when the word triangle is used, are not identical, and may be widely diverse. How then, since they represent the word, each by the image in his own mind, does it mean for them the same thing? It does so, only as they are able to determine a method in the productive agency of the imagination, by which the image is constructed, and in the identity of the method is found the basis of intelligibility in the use of the word.

said of the powers of knowledge. I wish to do so, chiefly, for the purpose of bringing together into one view the leading *distinctions* which have been made, and stating, more technically perhaps, the *terms* by which I shall usually designate them.

1. In speaking of the powers of knowledge, we mean those agencies of the mind whose function it is to know, or by whose activity we present to our consciousness, under some form, that which pertains to our knowing, as distinguished from designing and willing.

2. To know is a verb active, and necessarily implies a something known. Every exercise of the powers of knowledge, therefore, involves the distinction of *an act*, and an *object* on which that act terminates.

3. That on which a specific act terminates, as its specific correlative, is its *immediate* object. The object, according to its etymology and the sense here given it, is that which lies opposite or over against the agent.

In order to render more obvious the distinction of immediate in our knowing, I must anticipate, in a word, an account of that which is mediate, as contrasted with it. When I have formed a previous conception, no matter by what method, and by means of that, as applied to the objects around me, call this object of sense a triangle, that an apple, &c., my knowledge that the one is a triangle and the other an apple, is through the *medium* of the conceptions previously formed and present in the understanding; and this knowledge is, there-

fore, *mediate*. Now the *intuition* of *that to which
the conception is applied* is antecedent to and independent of the act by which we determine *what* it
is, as coming under this or that *determining* conception.

4. That faculty by which we present to ourselves, or become conscious of the presence of,
that in our knowledge which is thus antecedent to
the determining of *what* it is, of that which is
knowable in distinction from the act of knowing,
is the faculty of *sense*.

In this strict employment of terms, therefore,
the sense does not know, but is the organ by which
we present to ourselves the material of knowledge.
It is the receptive faculty, the *vis receptiva* of the
mind; and that which is present in the sense is a
something *given*, of which the sense is the passive
recipient.

5. The act of receiving, here, however, in what
is denominated the passive reciptivity of the sense,
is, nevertheless, an act, and supposes a specific
power of action. To be receptive of the impressions of color, sound, &c., implies a specific susceptibility, not belonging to inanimate things. In
every conscious affection of sense, therefore, there
is a present determination of the passive susceptibility of impressions, as in the affections of red-
ness, sweetness, hardness, &c.

6. In these determinations of our consciousness, we have the most immediate and original
union or coincidence of the *self* with the *not self*;
of the subjective and the objective; and distin-

guish, in the same state of consciousness, the acts of seeing, feeling, hearing, &c., from the immediate correlatives of these in the qualities seen, felt, heard, &c.

In these immediate and passive affections of our consciousness ; in these agencies of the *vis receptiva*, in which we thus distinguish the conscious *seeing, tasting*, &c., from a somewhat *seen, tasted*, &c., consists the feeling which we have of *existence* of something *real* and *actual*. In every such state of consciousness, there is an affirmation, a certainty of the reality, not only of the acts of seeing, &c., but of the somewhat seen, inseparable from the consciousness itself.

7. That in our immediate affections of sense, which we are conscious of as our own act, we refer to self, as the abiding ground of its reality ; and that which we are conscious of as present to the sense, but not as originating in our own agency, we refer to a ground of reality out of self. That out of self, to which we thus refer what is immediately present in our consciousness, is an object of perception ; and the affections of sense which we refer to it are its qualities, and express the relations between the object and our susceptibility of impressions, or the modes in which it is presentable to our minds.

8.   Again, whatever is a possible object of knowledge for us, must be, in some mode, presentable in our consciousness, as the condition of its being known.   Now the various forms and impressions of sense, are the modes of presentation

44.

in which whatever is existent in time and space can alone manifest itself to us and become apprehensible as an object of knowledge.

9.   All our powers of knowledge are originally excited and called into conscious action by the affections and excitements of sense; and all the original materials of our knowledge are given in the immediate consciousness of sensuous affections, either of the outer or of the inner sense, and are presented as existing under the forms and relations of space and time, or, in regard to the objects of the inner sense, of time alone. This proposition must be understood as limited to knowledge founded in experience.

10.   In the immediate intuition of an object, as existent in space and time, the following particulars are distinguishable :

(1.) Those qualities of which we have an immediate consciousness in the empirical affections of sense, and our knowledge of which, as objective realities, is, both in kind and degree, determined by that which is present in our immediate consciousness. That agency of the several powers of sense by which we become conscious of these qualities, is *immediate empirical intuition;* and in the strict limitation of the term, each sense renders us conscious only of its specific correlative in the qualities of the object; the sight, of colors; the hearing, of sounds, &c.

(2.) The *intuition* of *space and time*, as distinguishable from the empirical qualities represented as *existent in space in time*, and the necessary *a priori* ground and condition of that representation. This intuition is the agency of *pure sense*, as distinguished from *empirical*; and, as belonging to the sense merely, is the presentation of the unlimited manifoldness and mutual exclusiveness of parts as coexistent in space and successive in time, without unity or form.

(3.) The representation of *a unity and mutual relation of parts* to each other in space and time, and in the object represented as existent in space and time. The unity and relation here spoken of, are the necessary form under which the understanding apprehends the manifoldness of that which is present in the affections of sense, in order to make it an object of knowledge. The various qualities presented to our consciousness by the empirical intuitions of sense, are referred to one ground of reality, existing objectively in space. Thus it is apprehended by the *spontaneous agency* of the *understanding*, as *one thing* with *manifoldness of properties*.

(4.) There is in the perception of an object, as existent outwardly in space, also, a necessary excitement and activity of the imagination as a power of construction. The object, in its relation to space and time, is represented as having *figure*, mathematical form and relations in space, and duration in time. Strictly speaking, the manifoldness of an object is apprehended in a unity of consciousness, perhaps only by means of the unity of its mathematical figure as constructed by the imagination. This may be termed the *original and a priori unity of perception*, as grounded in the necessary form of the understanding and the unity of consciousness, and independent of the particular form and relation of parts in the object apprehended.

11.   As objects in space and out of self are presented to our consciousness in the immediate affections of the outer senses, so what belongs to our own agencies and the subjective states of our inward being, is present to our consciousness as the possible object of knowledge, in what is termed the *inner sense*, or the *immediate empirical self-consciousness*.

12.   What has been once consciously presented to the sense in our experience as actual, or as an object of immediate intuition, can, afterwards, and when absent, be *re-presented* in an *imaginary intuition*, or presented in an *image of sense* which is distinguished from the *real intuition* as *representative* only.   The simple re-presentation of an object in an image of sense, is referred to the agency of the *reproductive imagination*.

13.   Such a reproduced image, with a conscious reference of it to a past experience, or with a consciousness that it has been before present to the mind, is *memory*.   The voluntary reproduction of an image of the past by means of the law of association, is *recollection*.

14.   The *law of association*, considered distinctively from the agencies of the understanding, is the tendency which the phenomena of our consciousness have, *spontaneously*, to recall each other.

It is exhibited in its most simple form, in the re-
calling of past experiences in the order and arrangement as to time and place which belonged to
the original impressions, as in ·simple memory.
But any objects which have been present in our
consciousness, as parts of a total impression, acquire thereby the power·each to recall the other.

15. By the voluntary effort of attention, we
can abstract and associate particular objects in a
total impression, with reference to the purposes of
the understanding, and gradually subordinate the
spontaneous agencies of the reproductive imagination to the methods of the understanding, as the
power of voluntary thought.

16. The *reproductive imagination* is the power
of presenting imaginary intuitions of past states
of consciousness, or images representative of past
intuitions, in an order determined by associations
previously formed among the objects or agencies
represented, whether those associations have been
formed spontaneously or voluntarily.

17. The voluntary employment of the reproductive imagination, in calling up images of past
states of consciousness and of absent objects, is
the *fancy;* and the relation which those images
have, when thus called up by the free play of the
imagination, and not subordinated to a pre-conceived end, is a merely *fanciful* relation.

18. The conscious presenting to the mind of
an antecedent idea or purpose, and the subordination of the images of sense to the intelligible developement and manifestation of that idea or pur-

pose, by so shaping and associating them as to give them the form and position which the purpose requires, is the *productive imagination*. The most simple exercise of this, is in the production or construction of geometrical ideas and forms in space. These, for the pure sense, are purely ideal and imaginary constructions; as, when I think of a line or a circle, my imagination produces it, constructs it as an object for the pure sense. I represent it to the empirical sense, when I draw it with chalk upon a black-board, determining the direction of my hand by reference to the ideal construction presented by the imagination under the form of pure sense. Here that which is presented to the empirical sense has no use or meaning, but as it serves to awaken and fix in the minds of others, the mathematical idea of which it is but an imperfect image. So of the images of sense made use of by the poet, to express the ideas which give character and unity to his representations. They are only the plastic matter to which the imagination gives form, or which it uses as the subordinate material in the production and realization of its own ideal creations. The idea, the form here which determines the shape and relation of parts in the combined unity of the whole, and in comparison with which the images employed as the material of its construction are matter of indifference, is the production of the creative imagination. This is the higher and peculiar power of imagination, as distinguished from the power of merely representing, whether spontaneously or voluntarily, images of past states of consciousness.

19. It should be added, that under the law of association are connected together, not only images of past objects and states of consciousness, but all the powers and activities of our inward life ; so that the excitement of one awakens the activity of another, according to the principles of association by which their agencies are connected. Thus, an image of sense excites a feeling of pleasure or pain ; and that, an act of will ; that, a conception ; that, another image of sense, &c.

20. It is of comparatively little importance, in a practical point of view, to particularize and distinguish the relations by which the spontaneous associations of our minds are determined. These associations, under the law of spontaneity alone, belong to our mere irrational nature ; have no inherent unity nor rational tendency, but are varied by all the accidental influences to which the susceptibilities both of the outer and the inner sense are subjected.

21. An involuntary interest or predominant passion, exerted and continuing its influence, may direct and fix the attention so as to determine the associations and form habits of mind ; but unless brought under the control of the self-determining power of thought, and directed to rationally prescribed ends, it is still but the dominion of nature, working in us, and subjecting us to its law, as creatures of sense.

22. All rational, systematic discipline and
cultivation of mind, consists in the acquired dominion of the power of voluntary thought over the
mere natural and spontaneous law of association.
In proportion as the mind is cultivated, the principles of a higher order and of logical relation are
introduced, and influence the associations by
which images are re-produced in our consciousness, and manifest themselves in the wildest play
of fancy and even in our dreams.   It is the proper
aim of self-cultivation thus to bring all the treasures of memory, all the stores of fancy, and all the
agencies of the mind, under subjection to laws of
method, prescribed and realized by the power of
the reflex understanding, and with reference to
those ultimate ends which reason and conscience
prescribe.

Thus the spontaneous association of the phenomena presented in our consciousness among
themselves, and the influence of voluntary attention and thought, are the two fundamental principles which determine the connexion aud succession of all that pertains to the inner world of our
consciousness.   The former is properly distinguished as the law of *association*, the latter as *reflexion;* and they are, in a certain sense, opposed
to each other, since the exercise of reflexion dissolves the connexions which subsist under the law
of association, and forms new connexions, and new
sequences of thought and imagery.   Thus, by the
voluntary and repeated contemplation of objects
under any determinate order of arrangement, we

acquire the power of always re-calling them in the same order.   On this principle, we can voluntarily form associations according to the relations of cause and effect, of genus and species, of resemblance and contrast, or by any other law of method which the understanding may determine, and which is best adapted to the particular purpose in view.

The power of reflection over the law of association, is best shown in the formation of habits. Here we often see that a series of thoughts or images, of mental acts or muscular motions, which at first were connected with conscious and laborious efforts of attention and reflection at every step, as in learning to read or speak a language, come, by repeated exercise, to follow each other without effort ; and the perfect triumph of reflection here is exhibited, when that which the understanding has prescribed and introduced by reflection, and for a self-proposed end, comes to be performed by the law of spontaneous association. We thus give law to the agencies of our own minds, and the law which we impose becomes a second nature.   It is not only true, as it seems to me, that we are not *conscious* of an effort of reflection in the performance of that which has become properly a habit, or is fully established in our associations, but that there is no longer an act of reflection necessary.   The acts follow each other by the law of spontaneous association, each antecedent exciting and producing its consequent in the series ; subject, however, to the control of the understanding, in regard to the purpose to which such agencies are, for the time being, directed.

This power to subordinate the associative power to the pre-determined purposes of the rationalized understanding, forms a striking distinction between man and the brutes ; and the degree in which it is actually so subordinated in the individual mind, marks the degree of its rudeness and of its cultivation, of its weakness and of its strength.   The man of sound and cultivated mind subjects all the activities of his mind to his own chosen purposes ; the uncultivated or powerless mind is the sport of associated images and impulses, over which he has no control.

CHAPTER X.

PECULIAR FUNCTION OF THE UNDERSTANDING.

The agencies of the productive imagination and of the understanding are alike under the control of the will, and alike control the associations of fancy, and subject them to their own law ; but for different ends, and in different ways.   The imagination combines images, giving them, as far as may be, at the same time, vividness of form and coloring, while it shapes them either to the more fanciful display of its own energies and the production of mere amusement, or subjects them to the more rigid requisitions of a higher law of reason, in the production of the *beautiful* and *sublime*. The understanding, on the other hand, abstracts from the individualized images of empirical sense their generic characters and forms, and combines them according to their logical relations and in rigid subordination to the requirements of truth, or to the attainment of its own pre-determined ends.

The understanding, as the faculty of reflection, by the voluntary control over the re-productive imagination, in recalling for the purposes of reflection past states of consciousness, and by directing its attention to the phenomena presented to the inner sense, aims at a rational self-knowledge. The immediate intuitions of the inner sense are but momentary and fleeting states of our inward life manifested to our consciousness. Rational self-knowledge requires an insight into the laws of those agencies of our inward being whose sensuous phenomena are exhibited to the inner sense. For the attainment of this, the agencies must be voluntarily re-excited, the phenomena reproduced and often contemplated; and to do this, requires not only the power of directing the attention inwardly to the agencies of our own minds, but the energies of thought.

The power of doing this, of voluntarily re-exciting and contemplating, as by an inward eye, the agencies of our own inward being, is the faculty of thought, the understanding in its strict and proper sense. It is thus, too, the faculty of self-knowledge, a higher consciousness, to which the mere empirical consciousness of the affections of the inner sense is subordinate. It is by this repetition of our immediate consciousness, and the direction of our understanding to the re-presentations thus consciously recognized in the inner sense, that we are able to rise above mere sensuous intuition, and attain *knowledge*.

It was before remarked, that our immediate sensuous intuitions are not properly a knowledge of their objects, but only contain the material of knowledge. It is the function of the understanding *to know what* is presented in our intuitions. When the senses are first directed to a novel object, they have at the first moment an intuition of its qualities as an immediate object of sense ; and scarcely any thing is gained in the clearness of the immediate sensuous intuition by its continuance or repetition. As an object of sense, it may be clearly and fully before me at once. Yet every one is conscious that the instinctive desire of knowledge is not satisfied with this, and that indeed it is not knowledge. Higher powers than those of sense are awakened, and we instinctively inquire WHAT *it is*. We seek to interpret to ourselves the phenomena presented to our sense, and make that which is already an object of intuition for the sense, an object of knowledge for the understanding. We repeat our attention, perhaps, to an outward object, in order to be able to present a more clear and perfect image to the inner sense ; but the ability to present such an image, though a step towards it, is not yet a knowledge of the object which it represents. It is not an act or product of the understanding, but remains in the sphere of sense.

But though neither the immediate intuitions of the outer and the inner sense, nor the sensuous images of these presented to the inner sense, constitute a knowledge of their objects, yet they contain all the *materials* of our knowledge of them. In these immediate intuitions of sense, the objects of knowledge have imparted, as it were, to our minds, all that our minds can receive. We have presented them in our consciousness, in the only mode in which we can take immediate cognizance of them; and in the images of sense, we have reserved and can represent to our minds all the characteristics of the original intuition which are necessary for the purposes of the understanding. Here, too, observe, that in the images thus represented, though sensuous in their form, there is not only a partial abstraction of the individuality and manifoldness which belonged to the original intuition, but, as representable images, they have become a possession of the mind itself, partaking of its character, and no longer dependent upon the condition or continued existence of that which they represent.

It is the materials thus treasured up, and reproducible in the inner sense, or, rather, the states of consciousness here represented, on which the energies of thought are employed, and from which the knowledge of the understanding is derived.

The attainment of this knowledge, moreover, is, properly speaking, self-knowledge. Our immediate knowledge of the objects of sense is comprised in the intuitions of sense; and the exercise of thought is directed to the consideration and understanding of what is contained in those intuitions. The aim of reflection is thus to know our own knowing; to understand the intelligible form of that which is present in our immediate consciousness. The energies of thought, of reflection, cannot go beyond this. The understanding has no insight into the object of knowledge, aside from what is given in the conscious affection of sense. It can only know what is already given in the intuitions of sense, and the re-presented images of these; that is, what is already the possession of the mind in a sensuous form. But its aim is, to render us distinctly conscious of that in our immediate experiences, of which we were not before conscious; by considering, reflecting, comparing, distinguishing, &c., to bring out and mark with distinct consciousness what was already present and *contained* in our immediate sensuous presentations, but was not *noticed*. Thus the sensuous presentation to the inner sense, of the room which we employ for a chapel, contains all the materials which we have or can have for a knowledge of it. But this may be present to our minds without our noticing the likeness or unlikeness of its parts, or any of those relations, the consciousness of which constitutes, in fact, our knowledge of it. To make ourselves distinctly conscious that

the windows on the opposite sides, in this image
of the room, are equal in number, but different in
form; to compare their size; to notice their relative position, the character and size of the panes
of glass, as compared with those in other windows;
and so of whatever is distinctly knowable in the
object presented as the mathematical figure of the
room; the geometrical figures formed by its diago-
nal or other lines, &c., is the province of thought.
However full and perfect the sensuous representation may be, without such thought, we *know* nothing about the object. It is plain, too, that
thought adds nothing but its own activity; and that
in the sensuous image we had presented to ourselves, had already possessed the mind of, all that
can be known by the most mature reflection,
whether referable to the external object or to the
spontaneous agency of the mind itself. If, therefore, the presenting of the sensuous image be a
knowing of the object represented, the purpose of
reflection is, as before observed, only to repeat
consciously and thoughtfully to ourselves, what we
already know; to re-cognize our former knowing;
to reconsider our former doing; in a word, to
bring distinctly before the eye of our reflective
self-consciousness, what was already a part of self,
as an agency of the mind, and permanently representable to the inner sense.

Observe, that all which is given in the case supposed, of the re-presented image of the room, as
the material of reflection, is determined by the law
of spontaneity, as distinguished from voluntary

agency. We have recalled the image of the room to mind, perhaps, voluntarily; but all that the image contains is independent of our will. Its unity as an object of consciousness, its figure and relations in space, and all that belongs to the affections of empirical sense in the image represented, its connexion with other objects, near or distant, and its being included as a part in the unity of nature, &c., the mode in which we present it in all these respects, is determined, I say, by the law of spontaneity. But whether *I reflect and reconsider what* I have thus presented, and *how* I have presented it, its *distinguishable qualities* and *relations*, depends upon my will. The exercise of the faculty of thought, in other words, is voluntary.

But again, though I may think or not think, as I will, yet, if I think at all, this agency, too, has its law of spontaneity. I can think, only according to the inherent and necessary laws of the understanding, as the faculty of thought.

CHAPTER XI.

GENERAL CONCEPTION OF REASON, AND ITS RELATION TO THE UNDERSTANDING.

That which I have now spoken of as the *spontaneous* agencies of our conscious being, in distinction from the *voluntary*, is, in *one sense of the term*, the manifestation of the power and law of *reason*. But I have before spoken of these spontaneous agencies in the empirical affections of sense, and the sequences of the spontaneous law of association, as being a mere *irrational nature* in our minds ; as nature working in us, rather than our own work; and probably the same in the higher order of brutes, as in man.

These two statements are apparently contradictory, yet both true. Considered as *reason*, the power thus actuated and manifesting itself to our reflection, is not *our* reason, yet a power working in us according to a *rational law*. In its immediate relation to the understanding and will, that is, to the personal self and self-consciousness, it is the *law of our nature*, given to us, and working in us, as the organific power of life works in the organization and growth of a plant, or of our bodily systems, independently of our own personal contrivance or purpose. Yet, considered in itself, and as the subjective law of action in our minds, so far as the mode and form of that agency is spontaneous, (and, in regard to our wills, *necessary*, not acquired by experience, but *a priori*, i. e., determined by its own inherent principle, antecedently to experience,) it is a *rational agency*. It is the actuation in us, of that universal power which is the real ground and actual determinant of all living action, and one with the power and life of nature. We recognize it as reason, only so far as we make ourselves conscious of it in the opera-

46

tions of our minds, as a necessary law of action.
Thus, when, by the excitement of the outer
senses, I am led to represent to myself an object
existing outwardly in space, thence to the intuition of pure space, of the unity and infinite extension of space, the possibility of producing a line
in the same direction *ad infinitum*, and to see the
necessity of what is so presented to my consciousness, I recognize the power thus called into action
and consciously exerted, as the spontaneous agency of reason, acting according to its own law, and
determining, for our understanding, the modes and
conditions of all our knowledge. When, in the
example before made use of, I represent the room
in its form and relations, *as I do*, including all that
is knowable in it, as an object of reflexion, it is
plain that my will has no power to present it otherwise. The whole is fixed and determined by
the spontaneity of reason and a law of necessity,
which I cannot contradict without placing my understanding in contradiction to reason. A difficulty arises, here, from our habit of considering
the mind as simply passive, in regard to the presence of the immediate objects of sense. Yet a
moment's reflection, only, is necessary to make
ourselves conscious, that in the presentation of
these to our distinct consciousness, the mind is active; excited to action, perhaps, from without;
but when excited, acting according to its own law.
What its agency is, and the law of its action, we
learn, as before observed, by the voluntary exercise of the faculty of thought.

So of the law of thought itself; we learn what it is, by making the operation of the mind, when we think, itself the object of reflective thought. And this is the purpose of logic ; to ascertain and exhibit in the abstract, the necessary laws of thought. Now that which is necessary and *a priori*, in the agency of this power, or the inherent ground why I think so and so, and cannot think otherwise, as to the mode of my proceeding, in the agency of thought, is the law of reason. Thus, in reflecting upon what is presented as the object of knowledge, I think of it under the relation of *subject* and *predicate*, or *substance* and *attributes*, the *thing in itself* and its *qualities*, of *unity* and *multeity*, &c. And that which prescribes these necessary laws of thought, is the *pure reason*, by its own *spontaneity*, independent of and antecedent to any determination of the will, or purpose of the understanding, itself considered as the instrument of the will. We can only, by voluntarily directing the exercise of thought upon its own mode of proceeding, make ourselves conscious of these laws; of what we do, and how we do it, when engaged in the employment of the understanding.

But a very interesting and important example of what I mean by the spontaneity of reason, and of the relation of its agencies to that of the reflex understanding, is found in the mathematical intuition of pure sense. This has already been referred to incidentally ; but the nature of mathematical intuition, as distinguished from the faculty of thought, is deserving of more particular attention on its own account, as well as to exemplify the point now in question.

In *mathematical intuition*, we are immediately conscious of an agency which we recognize as *necessary*; independent of *experience*, and antecedent to *reflection*. If we refer again to the image which we present to ourselves of the chapel, we find that we have presented it in a determinate mathematical form, in its relation to space. If we reflect farther upon what we have done in this act of presentation, we become conscious that we have presented a mathematical figure limited on all sides by a something affecting our senses of sight, touch, &c. ; but that this mathematical figure in space is independent of those material boundaries, and still remains fixed, as a distinct and permanent object of *pure sense*, when that which affects the *empirical sense* is abstracted from the image. The figure itself we cannot abstract. We may cease to think of it, but when we do think, we represent it as still there, and always of necessity there, with the same mathematical determinations of form.

Again, on further reflection, I find that I have given this mathematical figure, in its construction, certain *determinate properties*, of which I can make myself distinctly conscious. I have represented it as *longer* in one direction than the other. I see that I have made itsoppos ite sides *parallel*, each of its sides a *rectangle*, and the whole figure *rectangular* and *six sided*; that in this six sided figure, two of the sides are placed *horizontally* and four *perpendicularly*. If I reflect still farther, I am conscious that I have represented each of these sides as bounded by four *mathematical straight lines*, meeting in mathematical *points*, at four right *angles*, and the opposite sides *parallel* and *equal*. I see that a line drawn diagonally through this four-sided figure, divides it into two *triangles;* that in these triangles, two sides and the included angle of the one, are equal to the corresponding parts in the other ; that they are necessarily equal, and the three angles of each equal to two right angles.

Again, if I look farther at the parallel lines, I see that they are so related to each other, that if produced indefinitely, they will never meet; and that they cannot enclose a space.

In addition to this, I become conscious by reflection, that certain properties, which I find in this figure and its several parts, belong not only to this particular figure, in this particular place, but necessarily to all six sided rectangular figures, rectangles, triangles, straight lines, &c. Thus in contemplating the properties of these straight lines, I may become conscious that *no two* straight lines can include a space ; that not only in these but *in all possible triangles*, the three interior angles are equal to two right angles ; and *that it cannot be otherwise.* So, too, in looking at the relations of the sides and angles of a triangle, I see them to be such, that in all *possible constructions* of it, it will be either *right-angled, obtuse-angled* or *acute-angled;* that any two sides will be *greater* than the third side, &c. The same remarks may be extended to all the constructions and demonstrations of pure mathematics.

The important point of distinction to be noticed
here is, that these solid and plain figures, lines
and angles, together with the properties enumerated, and whatever else the geometrician may distinguish and demonstrate as their properties, are produced and presented to the inner sense by a power
whose agency is antecedent to reflection, which
makes them *what* they are, and *gives* to them the
properties which we discover and demonstrate.
By attention and reflection I *add nothing*, but only
become *distinctly conscious* of what was *given* and
unalterably *determined* in the *original construction*. In the mathematical construction, I *had
made* the lines parallel, &c. ; and to think of them
pre-supposes them already made.   Now that *antecedent agency* which determined the form of these
constructions and assigned them their properties,
was a *spontaneous* agency of that power which I
have denominated *reason*. No matter what was
the occasion or the excitement which called it into
action ; I recognise its agency in the geometrical
constructions, whose properties I contemplate. In
these I trace the law of construction, and the
working of a power which is its *own law* ; which,
in its developement, in its spontaneous goings
forth, is not, like the affections of sense, determined
from without, but by its own inward principles of
action and by its spontaneous agency, gives form
and law to that which it produces.

Now it is the peculiar advantage of geometry,
as a means of illustration here, that we can more
readily make ourselves conscious of the immediate

agency of that power which works in us, and the products of whose agency we contemplate in all the objects of our knowledge. The spontaneity of the organic power of life in the functions of nutrition and the nerves of motion, are wholly beyond the reach of our consciousness. In the functions of the higher power of the organic system in the affections of sense, we seem to ourselves simply passive, and are not conscious of that agency which yet we know to be necessary on the part of the subject as organic reaction, in order to sensation. So the presenting of the manifold outward affections of sense, in any case, under a unity of consciousness ; we may convince ourselves, by reflection upon that of which we are conscious, that it is an act of our own minds, originating in the essential unity of consciousness and the spontaneity of our own reason, but we are not immediately conscious of it. It is a matter of inference, not of direct self-consciousness. But of the construction of geometrical ideas in space, we may make ourselves directly and immediately conscious. We have a direct and immediate intuition of the constituent law of geometrical construction, and see the necessary and unconditional truth of geometrical propositions. * * *

ON THE WILL,

AS

THE SPIRITUAL PRINCIPLE IN MAN.

[IN A LETTER TO A FRIEND.]

Burlington, Jan. 1, 1836.

MY DEAR SIR,—I have read over your friend's
manuscript on the free-will, repeatedly, with a
view to comply with your request ; but was always
at a loss where to begin, and how best to make
intelligible, to you and to him, the bearings of my
views upon those which the piece contains. I regard it as expressing some fundamental distinctions, and as implying a deep insight into the
mysteries of the human spirit; but—shall I say
it—the ideas seem to me not fully wrought out
and clearly reduced to the unity of a system.
The distinction which he exhibits between liberty and freedom, though I could not adopt those
terms to express it, or perhaps follow him in his

details, I understand to be the same which the old divines make, and which you will find, as I recollect, in one of Cudworth's sermons, (not the one re-published by Henry.) The man who has what the manuscript terms liberty, is sin's free-man, (Jer. Taylor's *free only to sin*,) and the one who has freedom, in the sense of the manuscript, is *God's* free man. Not that Cudworth's statement includes all that the distinction here made is intended to convey : I speak only of two kinds of freedom, essentially different from each other, as there taught. But in following the manuscript in detail, I should be obliged to go into long explanations on every point, and give, after all, but a partial view of what I regard as the truth, because taken from a position that admits only of a partial view. I shall, perhaps, therefore, answer the wishes of your friend better, if I present a brief outline of my own views, and leave him to compare them in the aspects which they present relatively to each other and to their own ground principles. I do not pretend to give the views which I shall express as original, nor are they directly copied from any one or more authors. I give them, too, only in a hasty and imperfect outline, with the familiarity and informality of a letter, to one who needs but a hint in order to think out for himself that to which it tends, or which it intends.

I shall proceed, then, without farther preface or apology, to endeavor to fix a few points in a series of developements, the contemplation of which seems to me to lead to the most intelligible view of that which is distinctively *spiritual*, and of the relation of *our finite spirits to nature* on the one hand, and to *the* spirit, as their own proper element, on the other. I must not be understood as attempting to give more than hints, and these such as I would not venture to express, where I did not presume that they would be, at least, kindly interpreted. Nor can I now undertake to give all the links in the chain by which the elementary powers of nature are connected with the highest, and with the supernatural. I speak, as you will perceive, of *powers*, and shall assume, at the outset, the truth of the dynamic theory, which seeks the *reality* of all the objects of our knowledge in living powers, knowable to us only in the law of their action, as they manifest themselves in their phenomenal relations and aspects.

1. Let us begin, then, with the elementary and universal powers which manifest themselves in the material world. Here we find each distinguishable power *conceivable* only in its actual and immediate relation to its proper correlative or counteracting power; so related, that each presupposes the other, in order to, or as the condition of, its possible actuation. Take, for example, the Kantian construction of the conception of matter, *as such*. The universal and necessary constituents of matter, as matter, are, attraction and repulsion, each the measure and determinant of the other, and the resulting equilibrium, the basis, as it were, of the material world. Now, extend this view, and see

how the same conditions apply to those superadded powers which it is the business of the chemist to investigate ; and how, throughout inorganic nature, whatever is fixed and determined, is found, so far as analysis has extended, to result from the synthesis of counteracting powers, and remains fixed so long as those powers remain in equilibrio. Apply it, also, to electricity and magnetism, and observe, that, throughout the sphere of inorganic powers, the equilibrium of specific correlative and counteracting forces results in a state of rest and apparent inaction ; but with a product that is the abiding witness of their abiding and living energy.

Now the point to be observed, here, is, that these distinct powers are, (1.) conceivable only as relative, each to another, which is necessarily presupposed in order to its actual manifestation in nature ; and this being mutual, necessarily again leads to the assumption of a higher and antecedent unity, which is, therefore, *supernatural;* and, (2.) are terminated and fixed in their agency, each, immediately, by its correlative, producing, as the result of their counterbalanced energies, the world of death, or of what we term dead and inorganic matter.

2. Observe the dawn of the individualizing power, in the formation of crystals, where each specific product of the elementary powers of nature separates itself from all that is heterogeneous, becomes attractive of its own kind, and, with a semblance of organic life, builds up, each after the law of its kind, its geometric forms. Here, too,

but a moment's reflection is necessary, to see that
we are compelled to regard the power which is
determinant of the form to be assumed, by a salt,
e. g., held in solution, as one that is universally
present, or all in every part ; since the perfect
form of the crystal is presupposed and predetermined in the first step of the process, and every
particle assumes the position necessary to realize
the antecedent idea. But though we have, here,
the manifestation of a formative power, yet it is
limited, in its agency, to the building of geometrical forms, by mere apposition, out of elements of
the same kind, with no assimilative energy, and
terminates in the production of fixed and lifeless
forms. There is yet no organific and living process.

3. In the principles of organic life, even in
their lowest potence, we have a power which manifests itself as paramount to the elementary powers
of nature, and subordinates them, and their inorganic products, to the accomplishment of its ends.
We find, here, an energy that dissolves and trans-
mutes, assimilates to its own nature and appropriates to its own uses, the heterogeneous elements
subjected to its agency. It cannot be conceived
as springing out of inorganic nature, as merely a
higher potence ; or as being the proper product of
its elementary powers. (For, how can death produce life ? How can powers, which have neu-
tralized, and whose only agency is, as correlatives,
to neutralize, each other, and which, so long as
their equilibrium is undisturbed from without, re-

main forever at rest, give birth to a higher and in some sense antagonist principle?) The power of life, then, does not come from beneath, out of the inferior elements, but from above. Yet it presupposes the existence of those elements, as the condition of its own manifestation, and comes to them as to its own, enters and takes possession, and out of them builds up its manifold and wondrous forms. With the power of life, it imparts to the assimilated elements a formative and organific tendency, and, in its infinite diversifications, propagates and diffuses its specific forms, each after its kind.

Here, then, we have the powers of life and of living nature, I mean of organic life and organic nature, educing, from the inferior elements, the visible and tangible material required for the developement of their organism, but conferring upon these elements their own living forms. But I must not forget the purpose for which these perhaps apparently irrelevant matters are introduced.

4. Leaving, then, the relation of the organic life of nature to the inferior elements, for the present, what are the distinctive characters and higher developements, which may help us to understand the supernatural life of the spirit? Observe, first, the continuity and self-productivity of the organic life of nature. The assimilative and plastic energies, co-working in each principle of organic nature, tend, with limitless repetition, to reproduce their own form, whether individual or specific. Thus, the principle of life in the seed of an apple,

for example, produces and realizes its own individual form, and, with continuous productivity,
multiplies that form, with a distinct repetition, in
each bud, with its attendant leaf; and, whether by
the continuous growth of the same stock, or by
buds and scions transferred to others, propagates
itself without limit. Here, too, in the highest
perfection of the individualized power and form in
the developement of the flower and fruit, we see
the higher specific principle of life resolving itself
into its polar forces, in order, by their reunion, to
reproduce the kind, and so in endless succession.
Observe, here, more closely, how absolutely transitional are these successive individualizations;
how each bud, in the very process of growth, does
but pass into other individuals, and lose itself in
the moment of becoming; while the specific principle, again, here, as throughout nature, manifests
itself only in the production of new individualizations.

Observe, secondly, how, in the animal organization, the assimilative and plastic powers, in their
productive agency, effect, not, as in plants, a
succession of transitional forms, with no true circulation of the productive power, and no self-
affirmation in any, but a continuous reproduction
of the same individual form and organism. Here
we find a more complex organization, and the
assimilative and plastic powers, with their proper
organs, clothed with those of the systems of irritability and sensibility, by which their relations to
the outer world are determined, and the specific

ends of each organic nature attained. But it is an important point to observe, thirdly, how, in every organic being, every organ and function must necessarily be conceived as reciprocally a means and an end, a cause and an effect, in relation to the others; and how the manifoldness of the parts is combined and harmonized in the unity of the whole; how the one principle of life in the entire organism, as the all in every part, seeks the realization of its own predetermined end in the full development of its essential form; and how, even in the productive and organific agencies of nature, the self-seeking principle is manifested; and with it, in a lower form, the principle of self-determination: for, fifthly, while in every gradation of the powers of life, the inward principle unfolds and manifests itself only under the condition of being excited from without by that which corresponds with its wants, and furnishes the means of its assimilative agency; yet the specific mode of its action is determined by its own inherent law; and no change of outward circumstances can determine it to any other action, or mode of development, than that which is predetermined in its own nature, or antecedent idea. The outward circumstances of soil, exposure, &c., may modify the accidents of outward growth, size, color, &c., of an oak, but no possible outward circumstances can make an acorn produce any other tree than an oak. The inward principle of life is here self-determined, and not determinable from without. So, as to the self-seeking tendency, each vegetable principle of

life strives, by the assimilation and subjugation of
the inferior powers of inorganic nature, after the
realization of its own predetermined end, in the
development of its outward form : and what are
the appetites or appetences of animal nature, but
the striving of the inward principle of life to attain
(by means of those corresponding objects, which,
being presented through the medium of sense,
stimulate the appetites and excite the irritability
of the system) the ends which that nature prescribes. Thus, according to the universal law of
organic nature, each individual principle of life
seeks the realization and perpetuation of its own
form, the attainment of its own end, as the law of
its nature. Observe here, too, that as the power
of organic life generally, while it does not spring
out of the inferior elements, yet presupposes their
existence, so in every gradation of organic nature,
each subjective excitability presupposes its specific
exciting cause, without which it has but a potential reality, and can never have an actual existence
in nature.

The relation of the subjective powers of life
here, to surrounding nature, as the corresponding
objective, and the action and reaction necessary
to the development of the subjective, while yet the
agency of the subjective, as to the law of its action, as well as its ultimate end, is self-determined,
and must be conceived as antecedent to the objective, and having an independent origin, are points
fundamentally important.

6. With the dawn of sensibility and consciousness in its lowest form, we find the inward
tendencies and seekings of the principle of life, revealing itself as a craving after that which the
ends of our organic nature prescribe. In its simplest modification, may we not conceive it as analagous to the productive agency in vegetable life ;
a self-finding, but at the same moment a self-losing power ; continuously transitional and fleeting,
momentarily and continuously directing the organic agencies, but with no power to retain or reproduce the consciousness of the momently past, and
therefore without the consciousness of time ?
In this form, it connects itself with the relation of
the subjective to the objective in their reciprocal
action and reaction, but only as a medium through
which the other agencies of the system are excited
and the ends of nature secured. In regard to these
agencies, moreover, and the relation of the subjective wants to their outward correlatives, in the highest human consciousness, we find them determined
according to a law of nature ; each inward appetency seeking its correlative object, and the organic
affections of pleasure and pain arising according as
the organic wants and tendencies are satisfied or
repressed. Suppose such a consciousness to go
along with the agency of the organic powers, and
let us trace its different gradations. Observe, 1st,
the immediate action and reaction of the subjective
and the objective in the vegetative sphere ; 2dly,
the intermediate agency of the organs of sense
and of the muscular system, by which the relations

48

of the subjective principle of life to surrounding
nature are enlarged, and its appropriate objects
brought within its reach at a distance in space ;
and, 3dly, the superadded powers of instinctive
intelligence, or the adaptive faculty, enlarging still
farther the powers of devising and employing the
means for the attainment of the specific ends,
which the individual nature prescribes ;—and we
may still regard all this as the action and reaction
of the subjective and the objective, according to a
fixed law of nature, or of cause and effect ; and
the subject to be still lost to itself and absorbed in
the pursuit of its correlative objects, and of those
ends which the law of its nature prescribes ; pursuing now this and now that object, this or that
end, according to the accidental relation subsisting
between its present wants and the objects that are
within the sphere of its organic action.

7. Now let us suppose, superadded to these
powers, a higher consciousness, by which we can
reflect upon, and represent to ourselves, these inward propensities of our individual nature and their
various relations of action and reaction to their
outward correlatives ;—that we have thus a perfect
knowledge of our nature, and are distinctly conscious of its agencies and its states, as pleasurable
or painful ; that we see them as it were passing
before us, but passing by an unchangeable law of
nature, over which we have no control. This,
too, is certainly conceivable. But suppose again,
that in addition to a perfect knowledge of our nature and its various appetites and agencies, with

their correlative objects in the world of sense, we
have the power of reflecting upon the pleasure and
pain which attends this or that particular agency ;
of comparing one with another ; of bringing in the
consideration of time ; of subordinating the present
to the future, the less to the greater, and instead
of blindly following present impulses, seeking with
prudent foresight the highest sum of that which
our nature prescribes as its proper end. Should
we not still be within the sphere of our individual
nature, and limited to the ends of that nature ; and
can that which, by such a process, grows out of
nature, be conceived capable of rising above it and
seeking any ulterior or higher end? However
great the power of intelligence, according to such
a supposition its highest result must be to harmon-
ise the various tendencies of natural appetites or
propensities, and give unity and consistency to
their agencies, so as most effectually to attain the
end already prescribed by the antecedent law of
nature, as self-determined and self-seeking. The
resultant would be absolutely determined by the
law of nature, and would be a mere nature ; therefore not a will, not spiritual. To prevent misapprehension, too, I should say that no such self-
consciousness as that represented above, properly
belongs to a mere nature ; and that the subjective
wants and propensities of a nature are not necessarily limited to mere organic wants, but may embrace whatever subjective properties or excitabilities can belong to an individual self-seeking principle, having their correlative objects, with the

relation of action and reaction between them, according to the universal law of nature.

8. With this imperfect sketch of the inward impulses of living natures, let us look for a moment more connectedly at the possible relations of consciousness to these agencies of the principle of life. The inorganic powers of nature, as we have seen, are properly in a state of activity only so long as their equilibrium is disturbed, and immediately restore themselves to a state of rest. In the lowest principles of life, in the vegetable, there is a continuity of living action, but with no true circulatory agency, no fixed point and centre of action, remaining the same with itself and affirming itself, —but a continuous transition of the living energy into other and still other outward forms, so that even a momentary self-finding is inconceivable, since there is no true self, and the powers of life, e. g., that exist in union in one joint of a grape vine, as they send forth their productive agency, do not revert for the reproduction and perpetuation of the same individualised power from which they proceed, but proceed still outwardly, and reunite in the production of another joint or individualised germ. In the animal organization and organic action, on the other hand, there is a true circulation or returning into itself, and a continuous self-reproduction of the organic system, a self-circling and self-centering of the living functions, which may possibly render in some sense representable to us (it can certainly do no more than that) the idea of a self-finding power,

or the lowest form of consciousness, in the sensibility to pleasurable and painful states of the organic system. Suppose the sphere of sense enlarged, so as to include a sensibility to all those relations which subsist, according to the law of nature, between the subjective excitabilities and their outward correlatives, so that the sense is a medium of action and reaction between these; and we have exhausted the sphere of sense as a function of the organic system. The form of consciousness, here, as merely sensuous, must be conceived as transitional, and, as before remarked, a perpetual self-losing, without the conscious relation of time, with no conscious recognition of the present as identical with the past, and with an absorption of the self in the objects towards which its subjective powers are directed.

Let the involuntary reproduction of sensuous images, and the spontaneous law of association, both of which pertain to the sphere of sense, be superadded, and may we not consider this as expressing the highest form of a mere sensuous nature, as we find it in the brutes, and as Protagoras in Plato's Theætetus, and as Hume, have represented human nature? There is, and can be, in such a nature, no true self-consciousness, and no true will; even as there can be, in nature, nothing above or over against nature.

9. It was said, above, that the power of organic life could not have its origin from, or spring out of, inorganic nature; since powers in equilibrio cannot produce a higher power, subordinating them

to its agency. So, here, it is equally manifest that the will and the power of personal self-consciousness, the spiritual principle in man, cannot come out of the powers of his natural life, *but cometh from above.* That self-affirmed and self-conscious *I*, which unites in itself the personal will and the free self-directed faculty of thought, and which places itself over against nature, even the individual's own nature, and contemplates its agencies, does not, I say, spring out of that nature; but is a higher birth, a principle of higher and spiritual energy, and having its proper relations to a world of spirit. It enters into the life of nature, in some sense, as the power of organic life enters into the lower sphere of inorganic matter. In its own essence, and in its proper right, it is supernatural, and paramount to all the powers of nature. But it has its birth in, though not properly from, an individual nature, and we may now look more nearly at the relation of the spiritual to the natural in our own being.

10. The principle of natural life in us, as in all organic beings, is self-seeking, and strives after the highest realization of self, as its ultimate end. If we suppose a power of intelligence included in the organism of nature, as remarked in No. 7, no matter how great, it will only be subservient to the ends of nature, and cannot conceivably seek after an ulterior and higher end. But here we have a power of will and intelligence, that, potentially, and in their true idea, are above nature, and have their proper ends above those of nature. But

it has, also, its true source and ground of being in
the supernatural, or that which is above the man's
individual nature and the agencies of his individual
life. Observe, then, how the finite will and understanding, or reflective faculty, constituting the
man in the man, the supernatural, enter into, become absorbed in, and, in the determination of ultimate ends, limited by, the self-seeking principle
of nature. The understanding, reflecting and reproducing, in its own abstract forms, the fleeting
experiences of the life of nature, its wants and its
tendencies, seeks, in the false and notional unity
which, by reflection, it forms out of these, its own
centre and principle of action; seduces the will
into the pursuit of the ends thus determined ; and
thus the spiritual principle is brought into bondage
to the life of nature. It has formed to itself a
false centre, out of the mere notional reflexes of
sensuous experience, by which its inward principle and its ultimate end are determined. It has
thus become a self-will, not governed by the spiritual law, but by a principle originating in itself,
and bringing it into subjection to the law of sin,
the self-seeking principle of the mere individual
nature. Observe, it has not become a nature,
which is, by the law of necessity, self-seeking; but
is still a spiritual principle, and, of right, subject to
the law of the spirit. In 'this fallen state, it is
still self-determined, since it is not determined
from without, but by an inward principle, which
no outward circumstances can change. Inasmuch,
too, as that principle of self-will is the ultimate

principle, and a selfish end the ultimate end which it strives after, nothing can be a motive of action to it, which is not subordinate to that principle and end. It cannot rise to the pursuit of a higher end and the obedience of a higher law, for it cannot rise above itself, its inward principle, and, being in bondage to a law of nature, obey a law above nature. It is in view of this, that the Apostle exclaimed, in the name of fallen and enslaved humanity, ' O, wretched man that I am! who shall deliver me,' &c. Neither the finite understanding, unenlightened from above, can rightly apprehend, nor the finite self-will, unaided and unempowered from above, effectively pursue, the objects and ends which are truly spiritual.

11. What then is the relation of the will, as spiritual, to that which prescribes its true and rightful end ? The ultimate fact of consciousness, here, is the sense of responsibility to a law above nature, prescribing, unconditionally and absolutely, ends paramount to those which the self-will, as the law of nature, prescribes. This fact alone is enough to establish the principle, that the will is, in itself, essentially supernatural, having its true correlatives, not in the sphere of nature and the world of sense, but in those objects that are spiritual. The life of nature has its proper correlatives, by which its powers are excited and evolved in the world of sense. The principle of natural life has in itself only the antecedent form, and has only a potential reality, till it receives from surrounding nature those assimilable elements, by which its

powers are excited, and manifest their living form
in the actual world of nature. So the spiritual
principle may be said to have only a potential reality, or, as it enters into the life of nature, a false
and delusive show of reality, until, awakened from
above by its own spiritual correlatives, (spiritual
truths, or those words that are spirit and life, in a
word, revelation of spiritual things), it receives
the engrafted word, and is empowered to rise
above the thraldom of nature.

Here, however, it may be said with propriety,
in regard to the analogy referred to, that the world
of sense, in its relation to the spiritual, is analogous to the inferior and assimilable elements in
their relation to the principle of organic life as
furnishing the material of duty, and the sphere of
action into which the higher spiritual principle of
life is to carry and realize its own inherent form,
and, while it embodies itself in those outward
agencies which belong to the world of sense, confer upon them the higher form of its own spiritual
law of action and of being. But here again is the
important distinction, that while the development
and perfection of its organic form is the true self-
determined end of the principle of organic life, it
is aimed at *unconsciously*, and even the appetites
of the animal, which it seeks to gratify with their
proper objects, are unconsciously subservient to
this end of the principle of life : but the principle
of spiritual life is a *self-conscious* principle, and
must consciously intend and strive after its proper
end. The immediate appetency of the plant is for

49

the elements of earth and air, which may be assimilated to its organic life ; the immediate appetite
of the brute is for the outward object of sense by
which the appetite is stimulated, and in the attainment of that its action terminates; it is by a
power not their own, unconsciously working in
them, that this agency becomes subservient to the
development of their beautiful and magnificent
forms ; and what *they are* thus unconsciously,
it is *our* duty to *become* by our own act, presenting
to ourselves the end which the law of spiritual life
prescribes to us, as our end and purpose.

12.   What then is the law of spiritual life, and
the end which that law prescribes ?   I answer, in
a word, the law of conscience ; or the absolute and
unconditional prescripts of reason, as the law of
conscience.   It is in this, that we are placed in
immediate and conscious relation to that higher
spiritual world, to which our spirits of right belong, and with which they ought to hold habitual
communion.

That which thus presents itself to us as a commanding and authoritative law of duty, claiming our
unconditional obedience, and prescribing to us an
end paramount to the ends of nature, is not to be
regarded as a product of the discursive understanding, even joined with the natural and moral affections ; but a higher power, and a spiritual presence,
the same in kind with our spirits, and by its presence, always, so far as we receive it, enlightening
our understandings and empowering our wills.   In
a word, it is the revelation in us of that higher

spiritual power, or Being, shall I say, from whom our spirits had their birth, and in whom we live and move and have our being.

The immediate presence of that power to our spiritual consciousness, is the only true ground of our conviction of the reality of any thing spiritual; and it is only by wholly denying and forfeiting our spiritual prerogative, that we can lose that conviction.

13. The true end of our being, as presented by the spiritual law, is the realization, practically, in our own being, of that perfect idea which the law itself presupposes, and of which Christ was the glorious manifestation. To be holy, as God is holy, is the unconditional requisition of the law of our spiritual being. In the renewed and regenerated soul, a hungering and thirsting after righteousness is the conscious actuation of the principle of spiritual life, striving after its appropriate object, and seeking to clothe itself with the perfect righteousness of Christ, in whom shone the fulness of divine perfection. But I must not enter also into theological mysteries, and will only add something more of the symbols of nature, by which light seems to me to be cast on spiritual things.

14. The law of nature, it was said, throughout the sphere of organic life, is the law of self-production and self-seeking. Every principle of life strives after the realization of its own predetermined idea, and in its proper agency subordinates whatever means its agency embraces to its own individual ends. But we see also that nature,

or rather the supernatural, in and through the individual nature, provides also for the interest and propagation of the kind ; i. e., makes the individual subservient to ends paramount to its individual ends. In many of the plants and of the insect tribes, the individual perishes in the reproduction of its kind. So too in the higher animals we see instincts implanted, which impel them to hazard, and even to sacrifice, their individual lives for the preservation of their offspring.

How obviously is the purpose of nature here paramount to the welfare of the individual ; and how does the specific principle of life take precedence, and manifest itself, as of higher authority than the individual self-seeking principle. Yet the individual acts by impulses which are imparted to it as an individual, and is unconscious of the presence of a higher law, even while obeying it. So in that relation of sex, by which the multiplication of the species is secured, the individual may seek his own selfish gratifications, while nature has in it a higher purpose. Here, too, as in so many other cases, we are compelled to refer those agencies which appear in nature, as two correlative polar forces, to a higher specific unity, which has, therefore, its reality in the supernatural. Here is then a higher law, manifesting itself, asserting and securing its claims to the accomplishment of ends, in and through the individual, which are paramount to the ends which that individual, obeying the law of his nature, prescribes to himself.

It is the law of the kind, seeking the interests of the kind, having its origin in a ground higher than the individual nature, and seeking ends paramount to its ends. Suppose that law to rise into distinct consciousness, as a law to which our selfish ends ought to be subordinated ; and what will it be but the law$ of conscience, which commands us to do to all men as we would have them do to us ; i. e., to seek the good of our kind. It is the universal law, the law of the kind, revealing itself in the individual consciousness, and for all men the same identical law of the universal reason. As an illustration, too, of the tendency of the narrow, self-seeking principle, see how often all that is implanted, even in the instincts of human nature, for the interests of the kind, is subordinated as the means of base self-gratification, and the welfare of children sacrificed to the self-indulgence of the parent.

15. It is only by freeing the spiritual principle from the limitations of that narrow and individual end which the individual nature prescribes, and placing it under that spiritual law which is congenial to its own essence, that it can be truly free. When brought into the liberty with which the Spirit of God clothes it, it freely strives after those noble and glorious ends which reason and the Spirit of God prescribe. But as the wheat must be cast into the earth and die before it can bring forth fruit, and as the insect must sacrifice its individual life in order to the multiplication of its kind, so the individual self-will in man must be slain, must

deny itself, and yield up its inmost principle of life, before that higher spiritual principle can practically manifest itself, which is rich in the fruits of the spirit, and which, as a seminal principle of living energy, multiplies the products of its power.

I will just add here—See how near, according to the above way of looking at the objects of knowledge, every thing in nature is placed to its spiritual ground, and how the higher spiritual consciousness in man finds itself in immediate intercourse with the spiritual world; rather, in the immediate presence of God.

ON THE RELATION OF MAN'S

PERSONAL EXISTENCE AND IMMORTALITY

TO

THE UNDERSTANDING AND THE REASON.

[IN A LETTER TO A FRIEND.]

~~~~~~~~~~~~~~~~~~

Burlington, Dec 4, 1837.

MY DEAR SIR, — I began an answer to your
letter soon after receiving it, and wrote over more
than a sheet like this, with a view to show the
proper shape in which it seemed to me the question of immortality should be placed, relatively to
the understanding and the reason. However, I
was not satisfied with what I had written, and
other duties have prevented my taking it up again.
But it seems to me, in a word, that the understanding and reason cannot properly be placed in
antithesis to each other, in respect to this point, as
in the conversation which you reported. That
form of instinctive intelligence in the brute which
most nearly approximates the human understanding, but is not enlightened by reason, (and so is but

the highest power of a sensuous nature, in its relation to a world of sense,) is, indeed, to be supposed equally perishable with the organic form. But the understanding in man is differenced from the corresponding power in the brute, by its union with the spiritual, the supernatural, the universal reason. Now, though we may intellectually distinguish, here, and speak of the understanding in distinction from reason, yet, in its proper character as the human understanding, it can no more be separated from the reason, on the one hand, than it can form the faculty of sense, on the other. Disjoined from and unempowered by the reason, as that which potentiates it for the apprehension of the universal and the supersensuous, the "faculty judging according to sense" would cease to be an understanding, and become identical with intelligence in the brute. It has before it, indeed, as the material of thought, as the correlative objective on which its agency terminates, the phenomena of sense; but it has behind it, as it were, as that in which it is grounded, and from which it receives the inward life of its life, and which constitutes its true and very being, the universal life of reason. Now its union with reason is such, even in the unenlightened and unsanctified mind, that we properly term it a rational understanding. If we term it the discursive faculty, in distinction from reason as contemplative, still the purpose of its discursions is to reduce or bring back the manifoldness of sense to the unity of reason, and not to lose itself in the bewilderments of sense. If we

compare it to Ezekiel's wheels, as that which
runs to and fro in the world of sense, we must say,
not only that it bears up the living creature, or
manifests the living truths of reason in their relation to sense, but the spirit of the living creature
is in the wheels also. It is the potential indwelling of the universal life and light of reason, that
makes it an understanding. Now we may, indeed,
comparatively speaking, be blind to the apprehension of rational truth, and lose ourselves in the
fleeting and shadowy phantoms of sense; but we
can no more absolutely exclude the generalific and
substantiating power of reason from our intellect,
than we can inward freedom and responsibility
from our will.

In reference to the question proposed, indeed, it
seems to me that the understanding and will are
inseparable, so that we cannot conceive the finite
understanding without the personal will, nor the
will without the understanding; and that the unity
of these constitutes the principle of individuality
in each man. If so, then you would of course
say, that in its constituent idea as the correlative of its ultimate end, it is essentially immortal;
or that the form of intelligence and will which
constitutes the proper being of humanity in each
individual, is so preconformed to, and so partakes
of, the universal and spiritual, as to be, in its own
right, placed in antithesis to the ever-becoming and
continuously evanescent phenomena of nature, and
to have a principle that is abiding, and one with
itself. We must, I think, identify this principle

50

with the understanding and will, if we identify it with the individual at all, as such; since the reason, as contra-distinguished from the understanding, is universal, so that there is but one reason, the same in all.

Some have held, you know, that the individual soul is not in fact immortal in its own proper essence, but only becomes so by regeneration, receiving by this the principle of a higher life, without which it is a mere perishable product of the life of nature. But it seems to me, that this contradicts philosophy no less than revelation. The idea of man as being in a fallen state, and in bondage to nature, according to the Christian system, implies, at least, that humanity, in its original and rational idea, is of supernatural essence; and the consciousness which every man has of an obligation to obey a law above nature and absolute in its requirements, teaches the same truth. Hence, though the understanding may turn itself to the world of sense, and be self-blinded to the light of reason, and the will swerve from the perfect law of conscience, in obedience to the lusts of the flesh, yet the one no more ceases to be an understanding, than the other ceases to be a will. Reason is still the true and proper light of the understanding, as conscience is the proper law of the will.

When we speak of the understanding as the reflex faculty by which we repeat to ourselves the experiences of sense, and which has the phenomena of sense as its proper correlative objects, we must still be careful not to conceive it as being produced out of our sensuous nature. As the intelligentical principle in the self-conscious individual *I*, it has, indeed, its birth in nature, and has the powers and experiences of the man's individual nature as its correlative objective, and as the condition and means of its developement. But it has its true origin from a far other source, and "cometh from above." The developement of the faculty of self-conscious reflection and of a consciously responsible will, is a birth of the spiritual, of a power specifically above nature, individualizing itself in each personal subject, and rightfully claiming a dominion over the agencies and tendencies of nature. It brings its own law of being, and that which prescribes its true and proper end, from its own higher sources. The law thus received, and the end thus prescribed, are themselves above the law which nature obeys, and the end which nature strives after. That we turn from the inward light of truth to lose ourselves in an abandonment to the outer world of sense, is a debasement of the understanding, no less than a perversion of the will, and is a fall of our proper humanity from its own proper sphere into the sphere of nature. That principle of intelligence which we call understanding, in other words, has for its proper end the attainment of rational truth ; or it is its proper end to become rational, in the sense that the conditions and limitations which pertain to its knowledge as the "faculty judging according to sense," shall be re-

moved by the attainment of absolute or strictly
rational intuitions. Thus all the conditional phenomena of gravitation, are subsumed in the law of
gravity. It is the end of the understanding, therefore, to lose itself in the reason, as it is of the
human will to lose itself in the absolute law of the
divine will, the natural in the spiritual, the conditional in the absolute, the finite in the infinite. It
has its birth in nature, and the world of sense is
the material which it assimilates to its own higher
form as the means of its growth ; but it seeks an
end, and can rest only in the attainment of an end,
that is beyond and above the ends of nature. All
this, as it seems to me, must be predicated of the
understanding, no less than of the will ; and of
both, as constituting the one principle of individuality in the man. The understanding, in this case,
no more ceases to be the individual understanding,
as the condition of reflection and individual self-
consciousness, than the will ceases to be an individual will, as the condition of personal responsibility ; i. e. neither the finite understanding nor
the finite will is to be conceived as so swallowed
up and absorbed into the universal, as to cease to
be a distinct individualized principle of personal
existence.

Thus, on the whole, you will see that I regard
the understanding, like the will, not as pertaining
to the man's nature, but as that higher power of
knowledge, by virtue of which he is able to take
cognizance of that nature, and make it the object
of thought and knowledge. It therefore pertains

to the supernatural and spiritual, and is inseparable from the individuality of our personal being. I am aware that what I have said is not all very perspicuous, and that I have, especially in the last long paragraph, made transitions which it may be difficult to follow. Still, I know not that I should better it, without writing a system, so as to place all the parts in their proper relation to the whole, and thus show where the understanding belongs.

DISCOURSE.

~~~~~~~~~~

AND HEREIN DO I EXERCISE MYSELF TO HAVE AL-
WAYS A CONSCIENCE VOID OF OFFENCE TOWARD
GOD AND TOWARD MAN.—Acts xxiv. 16.

God has not left us, like the brutes that perish,
to the dominion of sense, and the blind impulses
of nature. He has not formed us to follow implicitly and without reflection the onward current
of our inclinations, unconscious of the principles
that actuate us, and regarding only the outward
objects of desire. When he had distributed to the
other portions of his animate creation their several
powers, each after its kind, he created man in his
own image, and breathed into him the breath of a
higher and more mysterious life. He endued him
with those principles of spiritual and personal
being, by which he is far exalted, not only in
power and dominion, but in his essential character
and worth, above the beasts of the field and the
fowls of the air. He has not only given him a
more comprehensive intelligence in respect to the
world of sense, than belongs to brute and irrational
natures, but has imparted the principles of a higher

knowledge, and opened his vision upon the objects of the spiritual world. He has made him capable of emancipating his thoughts from the imperfect and ever-changing present, and rising to the contemplation of the perfect, the infinite, the unchangeable, and the eternal. He has given him, as an essential and constituent principle of his being, the power of distinguishing between right and wrong, between good and evil, and as necessarily connected with this, of recognizing a law of moral rectitude,—a law that takes cognizance of actions and events, not in their outward relations and consequences, but in regard to the motives and principles in which they originated. He gave him the power of self-reflection and self-consciousness; the power of looking inward upon the workings of his own spirit, and trying it by principles of truth and duty. To these he superadded a power still more mysterious,—that faculty of free will, which is the condition of moral responsibility, and of all essential distinctions between moral good and evil. From the conscious possession of this power, indeed, and its possible opposition to a perfect and holy law, results not the knowledge only, but the very possibility of that which alone is truly and essentially evil. From the connexion of the will with the inward and conscious recognition of such a law, and with that power of self-inspection which enables us to compare it with the requirements of the law, it results that we and all men are personal and responsible agents; that we are responsible for the moving and originating princi-

ples, which give their character to all our actions ;
that it is possible for us to incur, and that we do
incur, that evil, which should be the object of our
deepest abhorrence.

Here, then, we find a point in the character of
man of the deepest interest, if rightly understood ;
that we are made capable of knowing and experi-
encing the difference between moral or rather spiritual good and evil, and that we have a conscience.
Let us inquire, therefore, what is the nature and
office of that power which St. Paul speaks of in
the text, what does it require of us, and by what
peculiar sanctions are its requisitions enforced.

The remarks already made by way of introduction, are designed in part to indicate the general
principles necessary to a full examination of these
questions. At present, however, we can consider
the nature of conscience only so far as to explain
its peculiar character and necessary conditions, as
the practical law of our actions. Something of
this kind, and not a little also of reflection and
accurate discrimination, seem unavoidable, if we
would understand the essential nature and vindicate the reality of that which is in fact for us the
ground and substance of all reality. Let me refer
every one, then, to his own conscious experience
and reflection, for the interpretation and truth of
the following statements. When we notice the
actions of our fellow-men in the intercourse of
society, we are conscious of marking a striking
diversity in those actions, and in the feelings which
they awaken in our own minds. While we look

upon one with approbation, as a praiseworthy act, another is contemplated with abhorrence, as a deed of darkness. Again, we are conscious that these diverse sentiments in our minds have regard, not to the possible or actual *consequences* of the deed contemplated, as advantageous or otherwise, but to the moving principle in the agent. The same action, followed by the same outward results, is seen to be good or bad, according to the character of the principle in which it had its origin. The man who supplies the necessities of a poor neighbor, performs an act, the effects of which he cannot predict. It may raise up that neighbor from obscurity or the grave, and make him a blessing to his country, or it may preserve him for deeds of murder and treason. Is the benefactor the proper object of praise or blame for these consequences of his act? Certainly, no farther than they were previously contemplated and designed in connexion with the act itself. If he bestowed his charity in the simplicity of his heart, with no other view than to obey the law of love, who will not pronounce him worthy of blessing? But if he bestowed it with the selfish and wicked purpose of making his neighbor the corrupt tool and pander of his own vices, who does not see and feel that, whether he obtain his purpose or not, he has already incurred the guilt and the curse? We cannot indeed know the motive of another in such cases—for no man knoweth the things of a man, save the spirit of man, which is in him; but the judgment which we nevertheless pass upon the

51

act, always proceeds upon *the assumed and imputed character of the motive.* How is it, then, when the act contemplated is our own act? Here we can look beyond the outward circumstances and consequences, and, instead of inferring the motive and purpose from the outward act, we have an immediate and intuitive knowledge of that which constitutes its essential character as a moral act, in the originating principle itself. At least, such and so wonderful is the constitution of our being, that, unlike the inferior orders of creation, we have, together with the power, a conscious obligation thus to know ourselves, and, while we act, to turn our thoughts inward upon the spiritual source from which our actions spring. Are not the sentiments of which we are conscious when we do this, precisely the same as in the former case, except that now the feeling has immediate reference to self, and becomes self-approbation or self-reproach? Indeed, the sentiments with which we look upon the conduct of others, must necessarily have arisen primarily from our ascribing to them the same actuating principles, and the same grounds of responsibility, of which we have acquired a knowledge in our own inward experience. For *in ourselves only,* and by reflecting upon our own consciousness, can we know the essential distinction between the *principles* of good and evil, and the true grounds of praise or blame-worthiness. It is with this distinction, as we find it in the motives and principles of our own conduct, therefore, that we are chiefly concerned ; and we shall have gained one step towards our object when it is added, that conscience is the *power which, in the bosom of every man, bears testimony to the character of his actions, as good or evil,* as directed to right or wrong ends, and thus decides for him the question of his innocence or guilt. It is an indwelling and ever-present power. It is capable of witnessing, and, if we give heed to it as we ought, does witness and record, the character of every act and purpose ; and we may thus have always within us the testimony of our consciences to our good or evil deeds.

But here the question will be suggested, how is this power exercised ? Before the character of our doings can be recorded, it must have been determined and made known. How, then, and by what law are our actions judged ? What is the authority of conscience for the testimony which it bears ? To these questions it may be answered, in accordance with the language of St. Paul, that all men have present in their own consciousness a living and abiding law of moral rectitude, which in its faithful application determines the character of every deed and thought. This inward law, self-consciously applied to the motives and purposes of our actions, is the ground of conscience. It may with propriety be called the law of conscience. It is, indeed, combined with the office of conscience already described, properly denominated the conscience itself. Thus in the text the apostle seems to mean, that he always aimed to do that which conscience or the law of conscience required of him. Taken in this more comprehensive sense, then, conscience is an indwelling and inalienable law of duty, manifesting itself to the soul of every rational being, and prescribing the ultimate ends at which he is to aim. It is, moreover, an absolute and unconditional law, since no change of condition can alter the ends which it prescribes. What it commands and what it forbids, it commands and forbids, therefore, imperatively and without appeal. The law, observe, is applied directly and simply to the motive * and controlling purpose of our actions, as related to the ultimate ends at which we aim, and hereby every man knows for himself, and in his own consciousness, whether his deeds are good or evil, whether he obeys or violates his convictions of duty, whether he is aiming at ends which the law of conscience approves, or at those which it condemns. Obviously no man can innocently do that which he believes wrong. No man can conscientiously violate his conscience. The supposition is self-contradictory and absurd.

If now it be inquired, what relation, then, has conscience, in this use of the term, to the law and will of God, the answer is, it is one and the same thing. God has revealed his law in the consciences of all men. Those who have not the written law, are a law unto themselves, and show

---

* By motive, I mean not motive in the common acceptation, but the moving principle in the agent; the subjective character, by virtue of which the outward object becomes a motive to good or evil. In this sense the ultimate motive force is always in the will of the agent.

the work of the law written in their hearts. The Jews had, as the apostle tells us, the form of knowledge and of truth, that is, the form and lineaments of truth, distinctly manifested in their written law; but still, as he clearly teaches us, the same truth, the same knowledge of good and evil, which is written in the hearts of all men. The truth of God is without contradiction. The law of God is a universal law, one and the same for all men, and directing all to the same ultimate end. Is he the God of the Jews only? Is he not also of the Gentiles? The consciences of all men judge them daily, and all men will be judged at the last day, by the same immutable and eternal law of God.

It may be objected here, that the consciences of men have not the same law, inasmuch as they differ in their conscientious views of the same act. One believeth that he may eat all things; another, who is weak, eateth herbs; and no man may make the law of his conscience the standard for the conscience of another. For who art thou, that judgest another man's servant? But though it would lead us too far from the present purpose to make all the distinctions necessary for entirely removing this objection, it may be sufficient for the present to remark that the diversity of men's judgments in such cases results in fact not from a diversity in the law of their consciences, as prescribing ultimate ends, but from a difference in their conceptions of the act to which it is applied, considered as a means to the end. These differ as men's

understandings and judgments differ. All that is
necessary to convince us that a man may honestly
differ from us in a case of conscience, then, is the
possibility of his having a different view of the circumstances of the case and its relation to ultimate
ends. We always take it for granted, that if he
have the same view of it,—that is, if it 'be the
same moral act in his apprehension as in ours, and
if he judge honestly, his judgment will coincide
with our own conscientious decision. In other
words, we always assume practically the truth of
the doctrine, that all men have the same law of
conscience, and that the same ultimate end is consciously prescribed to all.

Again, it has already been remarked, that the
law of God, so revealed in the consciences of all,
is absolute and without repeal. It should be
added, by way of explanation, that its rectitude
and its claims to our obedience must not, consequently, be resolved into any other principle distinct from the law itself. We may, indeed, resolve
its obligations into the authority of the Divine law ;
but this is simply to recognize what has already
been said, that it is identical with that law in its
authority and in its requisitions. Considering it
in this light, we may not inquire why God, either
through the conscience or by his word, has given
us such a law, rather than a different one. We
mistake the nature of conscience, and of the law
of God, if we seek to comprehend the grounds of
their authority, or to find reasons for obeying them.
They involve their own grounds, and carry their

justifying reasons with them. They are themselves but manifestations of the supreme and infinite self-revealing reason and will of God — not
an arbitrary dictation of mere absolute will, but
the will of a holy God, acting from the necessity
of his own divine perfections, declaring, and enforcing in all hearts, the dictates of infinite wisdom and goodness. The *law* is holy, and the *commandment* holy, and just, and good. Our inner
man, our conscience, approves them as such, not
because this or that reason can be assigned to justify them, but for what they are in themselves; not
with reference to their consequences, but in their
essential character. They are good, because God
and our consciences approve them; and they are
thus approved, because they are good — good in
themselves and for their own sake. God, as revealed in the manifestations of his holy and perfect will, is himself the highest, the ultimate good,
of all rational beings. We cannot go beyond that
which is ultimate. We cannot assign a reason for
that which is itself the perfection of reason, nor
conceive as referable to any other ground of its desirableness, that which is itself an absolute good,
and the satisfying portion of the rational soul.
Whatever, then, the perfect law of God requires
us to do or to be, is in itself good, and desirable
for its own sake. To do and to be that which our
consciences and the law of God command us to do
and to be, is absolutely and unconditionally right
and good for every rational soul; to do and to be

other than they require of us, is unconditionally wrong and evil.

But to render this view of conscience perfectly intelligible, in relation to that good and evil which are its specific objects, it is essential to observe, farther, that the law of conscience presupposes a responsible will.   It concerns only those acts which we feel to be our own acts.   It passes sentence upon the *determinations of our own free will, and those only.*   For these we are, and know ourselves to be, responsible; and it is only in the *consciousness of this freedom, that any act becomes our own act.*   Without this, the act and the agent cease to have a moral character, and *conscience and responsibility are words without meaning.*   The good and evil to which conscience relates, are not physical good or evil, or actions considered relatively to their physical or natural consequences, as beneficial or otherwise.   The good which conscience commands, and the evil which it forbids, are moral and spiritual.   It *regards actions in their spiritual source.*   It takes cognizance of the relations of a *free will to the perfect and unconditional law of God.*   To be conformed to that law, is good; to be unconformed, is evil.   Any other good may be to us the occasion of rejoicing, but not of self-approbation, and of that peace of God, which passeth understanding.   Any other evil may be matter of regret, but not of remorse.   It is only guilt, the conscious violation of a law which conscience approves, it is only this inward spiritual evil, that fills the soul with horror, and makes us know and feel what is indeed essentially evil. This is the evil, for which we are and know ourselves to be responsible. It is the self-conscious freedom of a personal will, therefore, that renders possible the sense of amenability to an absolute law. Of that sense, and of the consequent obligations of conscience, we cannot divest ourselves. The abiding law of conscience, and its claims to the obedience of the will, are inalienable. It is the most inward and essential principle of our rational being. It is that by which we are most nearly and consciously connected with Him, in whom we live, and move, and have our being. It is the voice of that abiding and living truth, which reveals itself inwardly to all men, and is more than man. It is that essential truth in our spiritual consciousness, which, however it may be suppressed for a time, and held in unrighteousness, no sophistry of the human understanding can wholly pervert; and which will, sooner or later, vindicate itself by the light of eternity and the power of Omnipotence. It is the still small voice of God, his guiding and warning voice, revealing, in the sanctuary of our souls, the truths of eternity, reproving us for our sins, recalling us from our wanderings, and saying unceasingly, this, *this* is the way; walk ye in it.

But in proceeding to examine what are some of the requirements of conscience, it should be remarked more directly, that none can be more obvious, or more necessarily involved in its very nature, than this: *that we always consult it, and, with*

52

simplicity of heart, listen to its dictates. To live and act inconsiderately, to yield to a reckless levity of mind, or to suffer ourselves to float onward as we are borne by the current of the world, is of itself a violation of our most solemn duty, and a forfeiture of our prerogative, as responsible beings, capable of the obligations of conscience. We are bound, at all times, and know ourselves to be so, as rational beings, to act rationally, and with a conscious reference to our responsibility. We are bound to bring forth into the clear daylight of our consciousness, the secret, and, to the eyes of others, inscrutable motives, of all our actions. We violate the obligations of conscience, we break their bands asunder, and cast away their cords from us, if we refuse, or neglect, distinctly to recognize the law of conscience, and apply it to every principle and purpose of our hearts. *To act ignorantly and in the dark, with respect to the motives that govern us, is of itself to act wrong.* The duty of serious and conscientious reflection is a fundamental duty, in the neglect of which no other can be performed aright. To neglect this, and to act with a view only to the gratification of our appetites and passions, to make the opinions and customs of the world the rule of our conduct, is to turn our backs upon the light, and to involve ourselves in moral darkness. We cannot, by so doing, escape from our responsibility. It reaches to every thought; and for every idle word we shall give account in the day of judgment. We are bound to be always in earnest. Conscience re-

quires us to examine our hearts, to take heed to
our ways, to walk circumspectly, not as fools, but
as wise. It requires us to reverence every conscious feeling of obligation, as that which constitutes the highest capacity and excellency of our
being, as a revelation of the law of God in our
hearts. To be without conscience, is to be no
longer men; is to be estranged from our true being; to be without God in the world. *The conscious recognition of responsibility to the law of
conscience, is, in a word, an essential principle of
our personal being.* To lose this, is to lose ourselves, to become the abandoned slaves of circumstances, to betray the trust which God has committed to us, and to lose our souls.

But again, the obedience which conscience requires, is *spiritual obedience.* It has been already
observed, that the law of conscience takes cognizance of motives and principles; and that the good
and evil with which it is concerned, are spiritual
good and evil. But this may need, perhaps, farther illustration. By true spiritual obedience, then,
is to be understood the obedience of that which is
spiritual in man; the obedience of his personal will.
But the question returns again, what is meant by
the obedience of the will? To answer this, let
me ask, then, Is the man properly subject to the
law, and truly conformed to it, when, from some
inward principle distinct from the law and from
the love of it, he yields a constrained obedience to
its requirements? Conscience requires us, for example, to speak the truth, and to deal uprightly.

We obey, that is, we perform the outward and visible acts which obedience involves; but the principle which impels us to do so, is a regard to the good opinion of our neighbors, a regard to our worldly interests; or perhaps the fear of future punishment; that is, for a selfish end, and under a slavish condition. Is this such an obedience as will satisfy the demands of the law? Certainly not. We know that the law is spiritual; and however studiously we may conform our outward actions to its requirements, however cautiously we may bring our words and thoughts into conformity with them, so long as we do it from the constraint of a wrong motive, from a self-seeking and separative principle, and for a wrong end, so long we fail of spiritual obedience, and come short of the glory of God. Conscience requires that we obey the law, not from some foreign consideration, not for the sake of some other good, but *for its own sake, and because conformity to it is itself the highest good*. It requires us to love truth, to love righteousness, to love the Lord our God, for their own sake, and with all our hearts. Can a love to God which requires the compulsion of fear, or the stimulant of an expected reward, then, be such as he will accept? No; by no means. The principle of that spiritual obedience which the law of conscience requires, must be found in an inward conformity of the will itself, of its ultimate and controlling motive, to the living word and spirit of God. It requires that the law itself, in its living power and controlling energy, should become the inward principle and motive of all our actions; that the will should act, *not by constraint, but freely, spontaneously, in accordance with a holy and perfect law of rectitude*, the law itself working in us by its own exceeding lawfulness. The inward power and spirit of holiness, so actuating and quickening us, is the law of the spirit of life. Without this, our best obedience is but an obedience to the law of works, a lifeless, spiritless obedience; and the commandment, which was ordained unto life, we shall find, with the Apostle, to be unto death. The word of God is quick, (that is, a living word,) and powerful, and sharper than any two-edged sword, piercing even to the dividing asunder of the soul and spirit, and of the joints and marrow, and is a discerner of the *thoughts* and *intents* of the *heart*. In a word, though the conscience is not sufficient of itself to produce that spiritual obedience, which, in fallen beings, in beings that are carnal and sold under sin, needs for its accomplishment the life-giving influences of the divine Spirit, it is yet abundantly sufficient to teach all men the deficiency of any other obedience, and thus to reveal to them their sinfulness and alienation from the life of God. It is sufficient to convince all men, when aroused from the lethargy of sin and led to reflect upon its' requirements, that their hearts are not right with God; that there is a law in the members, warring against the law of the mind, and bringing them into captivity to the law of sin. That holy law which is written in the heart of every man, is adequate to

accuse and to condemn; to convince him that
there is in him, by his birth in Adam, a root of bitterness, a principle of evil, that vitiates all his actions; that there is a principle of action in his
will, an originating source and fountain of evil in
the very heart of his being, which will not endure
the searching eye of God; which does not come to
the light, lest its deeds should be reproved. So
long as such a principle remains, the conscience
cannot be void of offence, or be at peace with God.
The claims of conscience can never be satisfied
with any thing less than an entire surrender of the
will itself.   They cannot be satisfied, till the inward and evil principle, which seeks an end distinct from that which the law of God proposes, is
eradicated, and our will becomes one with the
divine will.   Thus the law is our schoolmaster, to
bring us to Christ; to convince us of the inefficacy
of any obedience that flows from a will unconformed, in its essential principle, to the will of
God; and our need of that renewing and life-giving spirit, which Christ came to impart; to teach
us, that no obedience but the *obedience of faith*,
that no law but the law of the spirit of life in
Christ Jesus, as the inward and controlling power
in our hearts, can prepare us to stand before God
in peace.

Time will only permit us to make a single remark further in regard to the requisitions of conscience; and this is, that conscience requires us
necessarily *to admit the truth and reality of all that
is essential to the rational vindication of its own*

truth, and of the authority which it claims. To
illustrate this, let us suppose that a man professes
to have convinced himself of the truth of the doctrines of materialism or fatalism,—of the doctrine,
for example, that, though we seem to act freely,
yet in fact all our actions are necessitated by a
power out of ourselves, such, and acting in such a
manner, as to render the idea of responsibility contradictory and absurd; such, in short, as to resolve
our agency into a mere instrumental and mechanical agency. Would not this, if truly believed
and practically applied, necessarily subvert the
authority of conscience, make its claims a solemn
mockery, and place the feeling of remorse on a
level with the horrors of a feverish dream? *Can,
then, a doctrine thus subversive of the reality of
conscience itself, when seen to be so, be believed or
confided in without a violation of conscience?*
Does not conscience command us to believe that
we act freely, in such a sense as to render the
feeling of responsibility a well-grounded and rational feeling? Can we in fact so believe a doctrine that would seem to free us from the obligations of conscience, as not to feel in the commission of crime the horrors of remorse? Go, ask the
experience of the murderer. Let his heart be
entrenched in the strong holds of unbelief; let him
have been persuaded that heaven and hell are visions of the fancy, and death an eternal sleep; or
that he acted only as the instrument of a blind and
necessitating fate. Will this serve to cheat the
conscience of its claims, and will it lay aside its

terrors? By no means. Conscience is too deeply seated to be thus removed from its steadfastness.
No arts of self-delusion, and no subtilty of false
philosophy, can strip it of its authority, or disarm
it of its power. When awakened by the grosser
violations of its law, it reasserts and enforces its
authority, with a power before which all the delusions of misbelief are as the spider's web. " Remorse is the implicit creed of the guilty." It is
on this ground, and from a principle of power thus
inalienable in the very heart of our being, that we
are commanded, as by the voice of a holy and
omnipotent legislator, to ascribe reality and actual
existence to all those ideas which are necessary
to the authority of conscience itself; to the ideas
of the soul, of free-will, of immortality, and of
God. We are not left, in a point so essential to
the obligations of conscience itself, to derive our
knowledge or our faith from the influences of education, or the uncertain speculations of our own
understandings. This is a faith which no man
can learn from another, but which every man may
and must find in himself. The righteousness
which is of faith speaketh on this wise :—Say not
in thine heart, who shall ascend into heaven, or
who shall descend into the deep. The word is
nigh thee, in thy mouth, and in thy heart. It is
an all-powerful and convincing word; and he that
hearkens not to the still small voice of its admonitions and warnings, he that is contentious and
does not confide in its truth, but trusts in unrighteousness and unbelief, shall hear its denunciations

of indignation and wrath, in a voice which he cannot mistake. Confide, then, with humility and submission of spirit, in that indwelling and ever-present power, which claims over you an authority you cannot question, and enforces it with sanctions you cannot escape.

But let us proceed to inquire more particularly, for a moment, what are the peculiar sanctions by which the requisitions of conscience are enforced. What are the immediate, the known, and conscious results of obeying or of violating the convictions of our duty? For the truth and reality of such sanctions, observe, we depend not upon outward evidence, or the arguments of a speculative reason. We may appeal to your own experience, to your own consciousness. What does their testimony import, then, with regard to the question before us? Have you ever found occasion, let me ask, to regret that you obeyed in any instance the voice of conscience; or was the consciousness of having done your duty ever attended by the strange and mysterious feeling of remorse? Even when, by obeying your convictions of right, you have failed of some worldly advantage, which a worse man would have secured, though you might regret the loss, have you regretted the act that occasioned it? Has not rather the conviction of having sacrificed interest to duty been to you a matter of inward joy and triumph? Supposing your experience to have been such as, according to human observation, would be strongly calculated to shake your faith; supposing your honesty has exposed you to

53

oppression and injustice, while your unjust and unprincipled oppressor has been permitted in the providence of God to prosper in his wickedness; does not a moment's reflection awaken a consciousness of moral worth, in view of your conduct, which you would not exchange for all the worldly advantages which prosperous wickedness could ever obtain? This, notwithstanding the influence of a worldly spirit in blinding our minds to the superior nature of moral good, is yet the conscious experience of every man who has knowingly and intentionally sacrificed an outward advantage to preserve the inward purity of his conscience. And if such be the case in regard to partial acts of self-denial; if, when you obey a particular requirement at the expense of some worldly good, you are conscious of a corresponding peace of mind, have you not reason from your own experience to anticipate increasing happiness from increasing holiness? Ask those who have made the greatest progress in subjugating themselves to the law of conscience. Ask those who have surrendered themselves in the integrity of their whole being; those who have not only denied this and that passion and appetite, but the inward and ultimate principle of self-will; who have received the law of holiness into their hearts in the love of it; ask them of their experience, and they will tell you of that peace of God, which passeth all understanding. Great peace have they that love thy law, says the Psalmist, and nothing shall offend them. But what, on the other hand, has been your expe-

rience, when you have knowingly violated the
obligations of duty ? Have you been conscious of
the same peace of mind, and found the same inward satisfaction in reflecting upon your conduct ?
Have you delighted in this case to bring your
actions to the light; to recall again and again the
motives by which you were actuated ; to make
them manifest to the inward eye of your consciousness, and compare them with your known
duty ? No, it may safely and confidently be
answered for every individual of our sinful race ;
the conscious violation of the law of duty is attended rather by feelings of disquiet, and an inward
shrinking from that light of conscience, which
would more clearly expose the character of our
doings. Every one that doeth evil, hateth the
light, neither cometh to the light, lest his deeds
should be reproved. However prosperous and
successful in its outward results may be the commission of evil deeds, the inward accompaniments
are a fearful withdrawing of the soul from communion with itself, a conscious feeling of self-
distrust, and misgiving, and dread. The heart is
no longer steadfast and self-assured ; and in place
of that cheerful confidence which belongs to the
heart conscious of its own integrity, we find a
slavish fear, a *sense of alienation* from that holy
law which urges its claims upon us, and a *dislike
to retain God in our knowledge.* Even when
given up to a reprobate mind, there is still an abiding conviction *that all is not right ;* an indistinct,
perhaps, yet fearful looking for of judgment. It

needs but a moment's reflection to remind every
one that this must be and is the case, even in our
best estate, and when at the height of worldly
prosperity and enjoyment, so long as the heart is
unreconciled to God. So long as men offend wilfully against the law of conscience, they love darkness rather than light ; and could they always shun
the light of truth, could they forever escape the
knowledge of themselves, could they truly and forever cast off from them the binding power of a
holy and unchangeable law, could they cease to
be men, and take their place with the brutes, they
might then follow blindly their own chosen way,
and perish with the brutes. But though we may
act like the brutes, we cannot escape the responsibilities of men. We cannot always, even in this
life, escape, in the commission of sin, such a
knowledge of our own hearts, as will not only
make us feel that all is not right there, but will
convince us that all is wrong, and overwhelm us
with the sense of shame and remorse. In those
moments of reflection, which will sometimes take
by surprise the most reckless and the most reprobate, the stifled sense of responsibility is awakened, and a calm and dreadful eye is upon them,
which seems to search the very secrets of their
hearts. They are made to know and feel that
there is a power within them which they cannot
always suppress, and that there is no darkness nor
shadow of death where the workers of iniquity
may hide themselves. Nor may our consciences
be for a moment quieted in sin by the delusive

notion, that such feelings are the result of education, and that our sense of guilt and remorse will
prove groundless. Nor let it be supposed that the
anticipations of good and evil which accompany
the consciousness of uprightness and of sin, rest
merely on the evidence of authority, or of past experience. It is characteristic of those sanctions
which are immediately connected with the requirements of conscience, that they are essentially
involved in the existence, in the heart, of those
principles which it commands or prohibits; and
the present consciousness of evil, of essential evil,
in our moral and spiritual being, involves as it
were the future in the present. The anticipation
of future evil is in this case inseparable from the
consciousness of present guilt in the soul of the
guilty. Does the fearful looking for of judgment
and fiery indignation, before which the soul of the
wretched criminal stands aghast, proceed merely
from its past experience of the temporal consequences of sin; or from the fear of that which the
evidence and authority of a *written* revelation alone
have impressed upon his mind? Why, then, may
not one creed counteract the effect of another, and
infidelity save him from the pangs of remorse?
No! conscience is its own evidence, and its rewards are sure. The faith which the good man
feels, with the cheerful enjoyment of a good conscience which lightens his path, is itself the substance of the things hoped for, the evidence of the
things not seen. His holiness and his happiness
are inherently and indissolubly connected together.

And on the other hand, the sense of guilt, and shame, and remorse, are the inseparable accompaniments of sin, and have the same relation to future misery, which true faith and conscious peace of mind have to future glory. They are the incipient gnawings of that worm that never dies; the kindling flashes of that fire that will never be quenched.

DISCOURSE.

NECESSARY RELATION OF OUR REAL PURPOSES TO THEIR LEGITIMATE RESULTS UNDER THE DIVINE GOVERNMENT.

FOR THERE IS NOTHING COVERED, THAT SHALL NOT BE REVEALED; NEITHER HID, THAT SHALL NOT BE KNOWN. THEREFORE, WHATSOEVER YE HAVE SPOKEN IN DARKNESS, SHALL BE HEARD IN THE LIGHT; AND THAT WHICH YE HAVE SPOKEN IN THE EAR IN CLOSETS, SHALL BE PROCLAIMED UPON THE HOUSE-TOPS.—LUKE xii. 2, 3.

These words of our Saviour were uttered in connexion with a warning, addressed to his disciples, against the hypocrisy of the Pharisees. In their immediate application, they were intended as a dissuasive from that conscious purpose of concealing selfish and corrupt principles under the show of respect for the law of God, by which the Pharisees were distinguished. They enforce the

conclusion, that the evil designs and vicious practices of the hypocrite, however carefully cloaked
under the outward garb of virtue and religion, will
one day be brought to light, and stripped of their
disguises.   But considered in themselves, and
apart from the more immediate purpose for which
they were introduced, they may be taken in a more
extensive sense, and as expressing a general truth,
well worthy of our consideration.   They may be
regarded as exhibiting the necessary relations of the
apparent to the real, and of the responsible acts
and purposes of men to their legitimate results
under the natural and moral government of God;
and so, as containing matter of grave importance
as applied to the formation of our whole characters, and to all our habits and principles of action.
In this more general view of the import of the
text, I propose to illustrate and apply it in the
present discourse.   I shall consider it, in other
words, as warning us to shun not only conscious
hypocrisy in its grosser forms, but whatever in human character and conduct involves a discrepancy
between what we are and what we would seem to
be in the eyes of our fellow men and before the
Searcher of hearts.

In doing so, it may render the practical import
of our Saviour's declaration more obvious, if we
contemplate briefly the general character of mankind in this respect, and the extent and ground of
the danger to which we are exposed.   This is of
itself a topic of deep interest; and the evil to be
considered might seem to connect itself with the

essential conditions of our existence as free and
intelligent beings. The power so to reflect upon
ourselves as consciously to distinguish our thoughts
and purposes as such, from the mind in which they
originate, to express and hold them forth to others
either as ours or as not ours, is not the less mysterious, that we are so familiar with the fact of its
existence. How much more strange, then, would
that process of reflection seem to be, by which we
distinguish our purposes as they are cherished in
our own minds, from the outward forms by which
they are naturally exhibited to our fellow men,
and designedly hold forth such as are not our own,
or that which represents them other than they are!
It implies not only, indeed, that self-reference by
which we recognize our own distinct and individual existence, but a farther reflection, by which we
distinguish ourselves as we are inwardly for the
eye of consciousness, from what we are outwardly
for the observation of others. Thus it is only by
that faculty of thought which enables us to distinguish what exists in thought alone, from that
which has outward and visible existence, and by
that power of arbitrary will by which we can intentionally represent as actual what we have but
conceived as possible, that we can be guilty of the
fault against which we are warned by the language
of the text. Nor is the principle of action by
which we are prompted to the commission of it,
less deep and universal. So soon as we begin to
act our part among our fellow beings, and to be
conscious of the relations which we hold to them

as co-workers in the world, we find the opinions which they entertain of us and of our purposes are intimately connected with our self-interest, and affect the accomplishment of our designs. Hence no worldly possession is more eagerly sought for or more universally coveted, as holding the relation of means to ends, than the favorable opinion of the community in which we dwell. On this ground, therefore, men act not more habitually with a reference to their pecuniary interests, than from a regard to the impressions which their language and conduct will produce upon the minds of others, and the reputation which they wish to maintain in view of their fellow men. Thus we come to live habitually in the eye of the world; to consider not so much whether an opinion be true or a purpose right in itself, as how it will appear to a certain class of men, or to the world at large, and affect our character and interest by these outward relations. We come to consider as things perfectly distinct from each other, what is true inwardly, and what appears outwardly; what we are in ourselves in the light of our own consciousness, and what must be conceived of us by others in order to the accomplishment of our ends and the maintenance of our rank and character in the world. While we are and more or less distinctly know ourselves to be one thing, we carry before us and hold out to others quite another thing, as that by which we would be known and judged. How much, too, of that which men prize and contend for, under the name of character and reputation, pertains to this other and counterfeit self, rather than to what they really are! How many, for example, have felt themselves constrained to expose their lives in defence of an assumed character for honor and courage in the esteem of the world, when their consciences told them that, instead of being in reality what is thus contended for, they were but cowardly knaves, with no character worthy of being defended! So general is the habit in civilized communities, of thus acting with reference to what will be thought of us by others, either from motives of self-interest, or from an unconscious respect for that universal law which we recognize in the moral judgments of our fellow men, as well as in our own consciences, that to act with entire simplicity, and show forth, with perfect freedom from the restraint and artifice which such reference imposes, our inward feelings and purposes, and to appear in our language and conduct simply and truly what we are, is ever regarded as betraying extreme inexperience, and an utter ignorance of the world. It may justly be considered, indeed, as indicating, in respect to the individual, one of the two extremes: either that he yet knows nothing of himself or the world, and so acts unconsciously of the relations in which he is placed, or that he knows and has conquered both himself and the world. So universally do our narrow understandings and the seductions of self-interest lead us to disguise ourselves and our real thoughts and feelings, and to act in an assumed character in the theatre of the world. The evil

links itself with the primal sin of our fallen nature, by which we are brought in bondage to the
world; and in this sense we may say that we all
partake of that leaven of the Pharisees, which is
hypocrisy. As opposed to this character, so inseparable from the worldly mind, conscience and the
precepts of the Gospel require us to aim at perfect
unity and simplicity of character; first, to be truly
and in our inward feelings and principles what we
ought, and then fearlessly and confidingly to make
our language and conduct the undisguised expression of what we are. Thus only can we act
freely, and possess a true confidence in ourselves,
when the character which we sustain really in the
light of our own consciousness, is the only character we have to maintain, and the same with that
which we would hold up before the world; when
we have no secret and hidden purposes which we
fear to have exposed, no mere outward show of
character and worth, the falsehood and hollowness
of which we dread to have discovered.

To this extent, then, and to our characters as
viewed under these relations, we may apply the
declaration of the text as a ground of action ; as
a motive to guard ourselves from all duplicity and
falsehood in the relation of what we are inwardly
to what we would seem to be, and to strive after
that unity of both in truth and rectitude, which
approves itself in the eye of Him who sees through
all disguises, and by whom we shall be judged according to our real worth.   In illustrating and applying the declaration of the text with this view,

we may consider, in the first place, the necessary tendency of all our responsible acts and principles of action, however we may disguise them, to manifest themselves in their consequences, and become at length known in their proper results. Under this head, I propose to refer only to what may with propriety be termed the natural consequences of our moral habits and principles, considered as revealing outwardly, in the world of experience, the inward source from which they spring. And here the general principle taught by the language of our Saviour, and confirmed by observation, is the same which we find to be true in regard to the powers and agencies of the natural world. Every tree is known by its own fruit. As in nature, every power and every principle of living action has its distinctive character and produces its appropriate fruits, so in the moral world there is the same unvarying relation between our principles of action and the consequences which flow from them. It is not meant, however, it should be observed, to speak here of the moral and spiritual influences which act upon our minds to form right principles, and to renew the will, but of the relation of our principles and purposes, whatever they are, to the outward product of their agency, by which their existence and character are known in our experience. Nor is it intended to assert that in the world of sense, and within the ordinary limits of human observation and experience, we can always determine with certainty, every principle and purpose of a man, from his outward actions and their consequences. Yet, in respect to such as have become actual and are in progress toward the attainment of their end, the limitation arises rather from our want of observation and skill, than from the absence of indications by which they might be known. As the most obscure and hidden powers of nature cannot act without producing distinguishable results according to fixed and invariable laws, so the human will can act outwardly, and put forth a power for the attainment of any end, only by an agency combined with that of nature, and in conformity with its laws. It cannot attain ends without means; and in the world of sense, either that in which the powers of nature manifest themselves to our outward senses, or that which reveals to us the agencies of our own nature, all its means are comprised. By these it must work, if it would make its purposes effectual; and thus expose its every act in a sphere in which it can no longer control the results that spring out of it. Thus, although an evil purpose, or any given state of mind, may perhaps exist for the agent himself with no outward effect by which it could be known to others, the slightest movement in the adaptation of means to a proposed end, though but the excitement of our own natural affections, betrays it to the tell-tale world, and no power or craft of ours can ever recall it. That sphere of nature in which we find ourselves, in which we can freely put forth the energies of our free will, and which is in some sense subjected to our control as the instrument of a higher

power, is itself intensely filled with living energies, in which every impulse is propagated and
manifests itself in thousand-fold variety of form.
In the relation which, as free and responsible beings, we hold to the goings on of nature, we may,
indeed, impart a new impulse, and begin a new
series of changes within its sphere, designed for
the attainment of our self-proposed ends; but
when the impulse has once been given, we can
neither assign its limits, nor with knowledge less
than infinite, determine the modes in which its
character and effects will be made manifest.
This it is, in part at least, which makes it so fearful a thing to act as responsible beings, and to put
forth the energy of a *free will* for any other than a
wise and hallowed end. Here, too, we find one of
the causes why the mind of the yet concealed
criminal is never fully at ease in regard to the
secrecy of his crime. He finds, too late, that he
cannot hedge up the consequences of what he has
done. It shows its effects in a thousand ways
which he had not foreseen. It produces a tumult
in his own passions, which he had not anticipated,
and cannot control; and, in defiance of his efforts,
reveals itself in the tones of his voice, in the expression of his eye, and in his whole demeanor. These,
too, are among its natural consequences, by which
it proclaims itself to the world, and that which
was hidden, is brought to light. How often has
the general and perhaps too abstract principle
here stated, been exemplified, not only in the history of atrocious crime, but of those more common

vices, which, for the sake of their reputation in the world, men practise in secret, and would have no eye see, or thought conceive! Wholly ignorant and unconscious of the outward and sensible effects which have resulted from their vicious indulgence, they go on, perhaps, believing their secret to be hidden from every human eye, and that it has not yet been spoken even to the ear in closets, when the practised eye has long since marked its infallible signature, and when it is already proclaimed upon the house-tops. How often do men, in utter ignorance that they are doing so, detail to their physician, for example, the unquestionable proofs of secret vice, which is undermining their constitution, and betraying itself in its effects upon their health, their social habits, and in a thousand other forms, of which they are wholly unconscious! Thus in all our agencies, as connected with the laws and the phenomena of nature, we have to do with a world that keeps no secrets, and where our very efforts to conceal what we have done, are necessarily among the means of proclaiming it. Every act and every purpose to which we give effect, is scored upon the tablet of our history, and no art can efface it. Its character and influence become inwoven in the web of our destiny, and no human power or skill can remove them. Every fault committed, and every duty neglected, records itself in its effects upon the character and condition of the man; and though neither himself nor his fellow man may now be able to read the record, it is yet there, and as enduring as his own existence.

Thus far I have spoken of the relation of our principles and purposes to the world of sense, as revealing them to others as well as to our own observation, wherever there is experience, and skill to mark their effects. But in the second place it may be observed, as coming within the general scope of the subject, that even where evil designs and secret practices chance not to betray the guilty, or are not known to do so, and involve him in the *outward* consequences of guilt, they yet stand revealed in the light of his own conscience, and have the sentence of the law proclaimed against them. The outward world of *sense* is not the only world in and for which man exists, nor that in which he most truly has his being. Nor is the light of the sun, and that which renders outward and material forms visible to the bodily eye, the only light in which our deeds reveal themselves. We only deceive ourselves, when, in the belief that our sinful purposes and deeds are cloaked and concealed from the eye of sense and kept in the secret chambers of our own souls, we suppose that there is therefore no light thrown upon them, and that they are shrouded in utter darkness. That inner world of consciousness has also its light, which, to the guilty soul, sometimes becomes more intense in its power of revealing what was before hidden from his sight, than the effulgence of a thousand suns. It can bring out from the obscurity of the past, from the hidden depths of long-forgotten crime, and expose and compel him to see and remember, what he would give worlds to

55

forget. How many, in this conscious exposure of their guilt by the power of inward truth, and under the withering and blighting influence of its soul-searching light, have felt their outward exposure to the world as nothing in the comparison, and have freely confessed their crimes! And though we may, for a longer or shorter period, avoid reflection, and so the distinct consciousness of the evil of our doings, yet from the very necessity of the case it will at length find us out. Just so far as we thus deal falsely with ourselves and play the hypocrite with our own consciences as well as with the world, we are nourishing a viper to sting our souls ; we are, in the strong language of revelation, treasuring up wrath against the day of wrath. There have been many arts of memory devised ; but there is, and can be, especially here, in regard to the records of conscience, and as against the revealing power of its inward light, no art of forgetting. We must stand forth as we are in our true character, with all our deeds and all our purposes emblazoned and on imperishable tablets. And who is there so pure, and with a conscience so void of offence, as not sometimes to be painfully reminded of this inward power, and made to dread what it may yet have in reserve for him ? When we blush at the apparently casual remembrance of a long-forgotten impropriety of conduct, even if we do not writhe in the awakened consciousness of past guilt, we have a proof that the whole articulated series of our past history *may* again come before us with all its guilt and shame. It bears testimony, that for us there is no guarantee of inward peace, so long as our souls are defiled with sin; and that however hidden from the view of the world and from our own present consciousness, it will one day be proclaimed in our ears, and reveal itself in all its turpitude, more clearly than by the light of the sun.

But this leads me to remark, in the third place, that the declaration of our Saviour in the text may be considered also as having reference to the revelation of the great and final day. Then we are taught that the secrets of all hearts shall be revealed, and every one shall be judged according to his deeds. Though we live now concealed from the eye of the world, and to a great extent in a state of self-ignorance and self-oblivion, yet in that day of the Lord's coming he will both bring to light the hidden things of darkness, and will make manifest the counsels of the hearts. Though we should not take in their literal sense the bold and sublime representations that are given in the volume of revelation respecting the transactions of that day, every man's conscience bears testimony that the grand point which it sets forth for our apprehension and belief is a most solemn reality. All the stores of visible magnificence and of terror for the guilty are here exhausted, in expressing to our minds a great moral and spiritual truth. To the mind fully awakened to a consciousness of spiritual realities as known in our inward spiritual enjoyments or sufferings, they may appear, perhaps, as figurative representations, yet of a truth

not the less real. And how indeed could spiritual
truths of that kind be expressed to the understandings of a sensual world otherwise, than under the
forms and by the images of sense? How could
remorse of conscience be more forcibly or truly
expressed, than by that agony which properly
designates the writhing and wrestling of the body?
Thus the whole picture which is given us of that
day, of the Judge coming in the clouds, surrounded
by his retinue of angels and seated upon the
throne of judgment, of the archangel and the trump
of God, of the rising and assembling of the countless nations of the dead, of the opening of that
book of remembrance in which every idle word
and every secret thought has been recorded, and
of the passing of a final sentence according to
what is then revealed, by which the everlasting
doom of each is decided; all this finds, I say, a
solemn echo in the conscience of every man, which
assures him that the substance, the meaning of
what is thus represented, is true, at least for him,
and that he must abide the coming of that day.
What a fearful sense of reality, moreover, is given
to these representations by the facts in our experience before referred to, in which we find the
long-forgotten past again, and with startling vividness, called up to our remembrance! The common observation, too, that in extreme old age the
scenes and occurrences of youth, which had been
buried in oblivion during the whole period of active life, are recalled almost in their original brightness, as well as similar facts connected with certain

affections of the nervous system, might lead us, aside from revelation, to believe that nothing which has ever been within the sphere of our consciousness, much less any responsible act or any plague spot of sin and guilt, can ever be so obliterated as not to be capable of reproduction with all its attendant train of sorrow and remorse. Here, then, in the facts of our *own experience*, in the convictions of our own *consciences*, and in the solemn declarations of the word of God, we have the assurance that there is nothing covered that shall not be revealed, neither hid that shall not be known and come abroad. We have the assurance that God cannot be mocked, and that we cannot always deceive either ourselves or the world ; that our characters, be they what they may, will at length appear in their true light, and all discrepancy between the inward truth and reality and the outward appearance will be taken away. Let us beware, then, in all its forms, of that leaven of the Pharisees, which is hypocrisy, and in simplicity and godly sincerity, not with worldly wisdom, but by the grace of God, have our conversation in the world. Especially does this subject address itself to the young, to those who are not yet hackneyed in the artifices and politic disguises of a corrupt and evil world. The farther you go in that direction, the farther are you removed from the simplicity of the gospel and hardened against the power of divine truth ; and it is only by resolving to be in all things what truth and conscience command, and then with a free and ingenuous spirit to show forth in word and deed what you are, that you can be truly at peace with conscience or with God.

And let us all, in the consciousness and with the humble but free confession of the many secret sins which in the great book of remembrance are recorded against us, flee to Christ as our only Saviour from sin and condemnation. Let us rejoice that, in that most glorious work of divine wisdom and mercy which the Son of God has accomplished, provision is made for our deliverance, so that by the efficacy of his blood, both the power and pollution of sin may be removed from us. Would that we might all flee to this as our refuge, lest at the coming of that day when our sins shall be arrayed against us, and we shall be compelled to stand forth exposed in that light of eternity which reveals all our hidden corruption, we call upon the mountains and rocks to fall on us and hide us from the face of him that sitteth on the throne, and from the wrath of the Lamb.

THREE DISCOURSES

ON THE NATURE, GROUND AND ORIGIN OF SIN.

~~~~~~~~~~~~

DISCOURSE I.

IF WE SAY THAT WE HAVE NO SIN, WE DECEIVE OUR-
SELVES, AND THE TRUTH IS NOT IN US.—1 John i. 8.

This declaration of the inspired Apostle has obviously a primary reference to those whom he recognizes as his fellow disciples. He is addressing
them affectionately as his children, and holding
forth to them the grand truths and messages of
revelation, that they may more fully participate
with him in the divine light and life which they
impart. But though enlightened by the knowledge of God, and walking in the light which shines
from heaven, he yet does not represent them as in
themselves perfect, or wholly freed from the con-
tamination of evil. In saying that the blood of
Christ cleanseth us from all sin, he cannot be un-

derstood, consistently with his other declarations,
as meaning that our hearts are made so pure and
holy as no longer to need the exercise of pardon-
ing grace. For he immediately adds, with reference to the same persons, in the language of the
text, If we say that we have no sin, we deceive
ourselves, and the truth is not in us. It is not
those, indeed, who partake most largely of the redemption that is in Christ, and are most illuminated by the truth of God as revealed in their own
consciousness, who are liable to think of themselves as without sin. Though they may be, as
compared with those who know nothing of themselves, eminently good men, and gaining daily con-
quests over their yet unsubdued and evil propensities, yet such at the same time is the increasing
brightness of that divine light which shines within
them, and their deeper sense of the extent and
strictness of that law which reaches to the thoughts
and intents of the heart, that they become more
self-abased as they become more holy. It is only
because men reflect so little upon what they ought
to be, and contemplate so little that absolute truth
and righteousness, that unapproachable purity and
holiness, which ought to be ever before our minds,
that any can find reason for self-gratulation in a
consciousness of what they are. I have heard of
thee, says the ancient patriarch, by the hearing of
the ear, but now mine eye seeth thee; wherefore
I abhor myself, and repent in dust and ashes.
Such has been the experience of the most eminently godlike and holy men in every age. The

light of divine truth, practically revealed in the
consciences of men, dissipates all self-flattering
delusions, by exposing in their true character the
motives and principles which govern them. To
conceive ourselves free from sin, therefore, only
shows that we are ignorant of our own hearts, and
estranged from the knowledge of God. It is of
itself a proof, according to the strong and decisive
expression of the Apostle, that we deceive ourselves, and that the truth is not in us. If, then,
such be the fact in regard to those whom the Apostle addresses as his children and his fellow disciples, we may safely extend his declaration to those
who are less enlightened, and so apply it to the
whole family of man. It is true of all men, that
in proportion as they have a practical knowledge
of their own hearts, as manifested by the light of
truth, and tried by the law of righteousness, they
are constrained to humble themselves in the sight
of God. Before human tribunals, indeed, in comparing ourselves among ourselves, and in reference
to the conventional rights and duties of civil society, we may stand upon our integrity, and lay
claim, perhaps, to virtuous and upright intentions.
But when we consider what is demanded by that
law which is holy and spiritual, and place ourselves before Him who searcheth the heart, we
can only say, God be merciful to us sinners. We
may discourse, too, of the exalted rank and dignity allotted us among the creatures of this lower
world, and with good reason render thanks to God
for the high destiny to which we were formed in

the divine purpose. But when we look into ourselves, and inquire what have been our purposes,
and whether we have designedly and steadfastly
cooperated for the attainment of our true and proper ends, we are constrained to confess again, that
we find evidence only of blind folly and perverseness. In its proper sense, therefore, as used by
the Apostle, and pertaining to the character of man
in its relation to the law and will of God, sin is
imputed to all men. The text may be considered
as strongly asserting the same doctrine which is
contained in the conclusion of the Apostle Paul,
that all have sinned, and come short of the glory of
God. Nor is this the mere assertion of a few iso-
lated passages of scripture, but its truth is necessarily implied in the whole system and in all the
peculiar doctrines of Christianity. Such is its relation to the gospel, and such the grounds of our
conviction of its truth, that, without regarding the
diversities of individual character, or any knowledge we may have of the conduct of particular
men, we are authorized to address the terms of
salvation to all men, as partakers of the same bondage to sin, and in need of the same redemption
from its power. We are authorized to say of all
who may have the boldness to plead exemption
from the charge, that they are ignorant of their
own hearts, are the victims of a miserable self-
delusion, and estranged from the light of truth.

Such is the most general view of the relation of
man, as a moral and accountable being, to the holy
law and character of God. It is, consequently, a

matter in which we have all the same personal concern, and is the ground of our common interest in that gospel which is proclaimed alike to all. Let us proceed to inquire, then, more particularly, and with a deep sense of its practical relation to our own souls, what is the true import of the doctrine. The subject is so important in all its bearings, so fundamental in its relation to the essential truths of the gospel, and withal so exposed to injurious misapprehension, that we have at least abundant reason to urge the inquiry, and to give to it our most serious thoughts. In prosecuting the discussion, I shall aim, in the first place, to determine the essential character of sin as a fact of individual experience, and as known within the sphere of every man's consciousness; in the second place, to point out, as clearly as the nature of the case will admit, its ground and origin in respect to the distinguishable powers of our own being, and so the conditions of its universality; and in the third place, notice some of the practical conclusions which follow from the views thus presented.

In contemplating the character of sin, then, as a fact of experience interpreted by the light of our own consciousness, and independent of speculative theories, we are compelled to regard it *as truly and unconditionally evil.* It is evil in itself, and independently of all relations, in the sense that no conceivable circumstances or relations could convert it into good. It is thus clearly distinguished from mere physical evil, as it is termed, and whose character, as such, depends upon outward relations. Whatever may be the accompaniments or consequences of sin, it is still the occasion of self-reproach and remorse as evil. The severest and most painful evils of an outward and physical nature, we know, may be the means and the necessary condition of our highest and best good. We may thus have occasion to rejoice in afflictions, to give thanks to God for sickness, for bonds and imprisonment, and even for death itself. But can we ever have occasion, or could we ever dare, to render him our thanks that we have been guilty of sin? Even when we believe that our sinful intentions have been overruled, and made instrumental for the accomplishment of desirable ends, do our intentions, as moral acts, appear any the less evil? Such a belief, whether well grounded or not, can never in the least alleviate the sentence of condemnation, which conscience passes upon the commission of sin. Even if we charge God foolishly, and suppose that our transgressions were designed by him, in the order of his government, for the accomplishment of his purposes, we cannot thereby diminish the sense of our guilt and of the inherent evil of sin. We cannot, indeed, by any speculative notions of what sin, and acts originating in a sinful purpose, are, relatively to what is beyond the sphere of our consciousnesss, such as their outward consequences, or the overruling purpose of God, change their character, as they are in themselves, and in their immediate relation to our own consciences. We ourselves know what they are, as opposed to our sense of duty, and contrary to that holy law which is revealed in the conscience of every man. Without a reference to that law, indeed, we cannot interpret and understand the essential nature of sin as here represented. Whosoever committeth sin, says the apostle John, transgresseth also the law; for sin is the transgression of the law. If the law, then, were other than it is, the nature of sin would also be changed. It is because that law reveals and affirms itself in our consciousness as an ultimate and unconditional law of rectitude, as in itself essentially and absolutely good, that we find the transgression of it to be always evil. The law to which the apostle refers, is no mere arbitrary law, nor is it simply a rule of action prescribing the appropriate means for the attainment of a given end. It is rather the necessary law of the supreme reason itself, unchangeable as the being of God. It is inseparable from our idea of God as the supreme good, and prescribes for all rational beings, not immediately rules of outward conduct, but ends, the rightful and ultimate ends, at which they are bound to aim. As such, and as revealed more or less clearly, according to the heed we give to it, in our consciences, it takes cognizance and determines the character of our purposes, and of the ends which we propose to ourselves. To transgress the requirements of this law, and to aim at ends opposed to those which it prescribes as absolutely good, is sin; is that evil and bitter thing which the soul of the transgressor recognizes in the oppressive sense of guilt and remorse. To misconceive and misrepresent the law of conscience, therefore, and to derogate from its character and claims, as an ultimate and absolute law of duty and right, is to change the character of sin. Were it possible, indeed, by the delusive misconceptions of philosophy falsely so called, to produce a practical conviction that the law of conscience is but the product of our own understandings, deduced from the facts of experience, and that whether thus or otherwise determined, it is but a rule of conduct, prescribed as the means to the attainment of an end, it would at the same time destroy our practical conviction of sin, and this would indeed cease to be for us that evil which we now know it to be. Sin, as a transgression of the law, then, is directly opposed and contrary to that which we recognize as in itself right and good. When we do that which the law of conscience forbids, or neglect and refuse to purpose and do that which it requires, we place ourselves in direct contrariety to that which is good; and no extraneous circumstances or relations can change the character of our conduct, or make it otherwise than evil.

What it is for us, observe, it is and can only be, as seen in the light of our own consciences, and by the law of God. It is here alone that we can know it in its true character; and the more distinctly we bring our purposes into that light and to the tribunal of that law, the more clearly will they be revealed to us as good or evil. If we choose to

walk in darkness, and will not come to the light
lest our deeds should be reproved, that of itself
proves that we are doers of evil.   Let us beware
then, how we deceive ourselves in regard to the
nature of sin, and the essential character of that
root of bitterness which we find within us.   Let
us beware how we seek to alleviate our sense of
guilt and ill-desert in the commission of it, by
turning away from the light of truth and the law
of righteousness, and trying it by our own uncertain speculations.   Let us never forget that it is
the transgression of a holy law, contrary to the absolute and supreme good ; an evil which conscience
condemns and God abhors, and which can stir up
in our own undying souls, the never-ceasing horrors of remorse.

But again, we may remark under this head, as
an essential character of sin, and known as such by
the light of every man's consciousness, *that it is an
evil for which we are directly and solely responsible.* This is practically and inseparably involved
in the simple sense of guilt and self-condemnation.
This feeling in regard to our conduct necessarily
implies the assumption, that what we condemn was
truly our own act, and performed under the condition of a just responsibility for the deed.   It is incompatible with any such sense of guilt, to refer
our conduct to whatever cause we may conceive,
out of ourselves, as efficiently producing it.   In
condemning ourselves for it, we impute it to our
own causative agency, and recognize it as truly
and properly our own.   Conscience tells us not

only that we have transgressed the law of righteousness, but that we ought not to have done so,
and are personally accountable for the evil. We
cannot escape this conviction, without misrepresenting and falsifying the unequivocal testimony of our
own consciousness. Practically, indeed, we cannot wholly divest ourselves of the sense of responsibility for our evil purposes and deeds, by any
speculative notions which we may form in respect
to the nature of our moral agency. But were
such an effect possible, it must necessarily be produced by every system which refers our moral
principles and acts to the agency of any cause or
motive out of ourselves. Whatever divests us of
our free-agency in the eminent sense of that term,
according to which our moral purposes and acts
have their true and proper origin in our own being,
divests us, at the same time, of all real accountability, and makes the sense of guilt contradictory
and delusive. Sin, in that case, at once, and of
necessity, ceases to be the evil thing which we
took it to be in the simplicity of our conscientious
convictions. It becomes, instead of a positive evil,
originating in ourselves, and opposed to God, only
the means to an end ; and of course derives its
character from the end and purpose which it serves.
By the same process too, we must cease to be the
true causes of our actions, or in any proper sense
responsible for them, since we move but as we are
moved, and are but the passive instruments of a
higher and controlling power. Thus the true
character of sin, as truly and in itself evil, can be

interpreted and understood only by the assumption
of a free and responsible will. The existence of
this is no less necessary than the law of conscience as already referred to, if we would not
contradict our own consciousness, and put a lie in
the place of that which our inmost souls affirm to
be the truth of God. The testimony of our consciousness, and our inward sense of responsibility
for every act and purpose which conscience condemns, is, or should be, the ultimate ground of our
conclusions. No speculative argument, drawn
from other grounds of reasoning, can supersede the
immediate convictions of practical truth in our
moral being. However we may imagine ourselves
irresponsible, or infer from a course of reasoning,
however plausible and well-intended, that our
minds are swayed and our purposes controlled by
the force of motives acting from without as a
necessary cause, a fully awakened conscience
breaks through all such sophistries, and tells the
guilty soul in terms which it cannot deny, that the
evil is from within; that out of his own heart
originated and came forth the guilty purpose, and
all that which conscience condemns as sin. No
matter what may have been the outward motive
or occasion; *it was still by virtue of the evil heart
within, that it had the power to become a motive,*
and prompt the thief to his midnight plunder, or
the murderer to the assassination of his victim.
But though we cannot so deceive ourselves here
that conscience will not resume its power and enforce the practical conviction of our responsibility,

57

yet we may, and it is to be feared too often do, weaken the authority of conscience over us, and endeavor to quiet our minds in sin, by trusting in our own speculations. Those who are resolved on following their own chosen way, will ever be ready to invent or adopt any theory which may seem to shift off the responsibility from themselves, and help them to practise a lie to their own consciences. With such, it is but a hollow device, a refuge of lies, which is liable at any moment to be swept away, and they are at last taken in their own craftiness. But may not the sense of responsibility and consequent guilt be weakened in young and more ingenuous minds, by theories which turn away their thoughts from the direct testimony of their own consciousness and the verdict of their own conscience, and teach them to determine on some other grounds, the moral character of their doings? Yet, however we may deceive ourselves, or permit others to deceive us, conscience will at length vindicate its claims, and we shall find ourselves held responsible for every deed done in the body, for every purpose of our hearts, and for every idle word. Whatever may be the moral character of these, good or evil, they derive it from our own responsible agency, and must be answered for as our own purpose and deed.

Once more, it must be remarked here, as pertaining to the character of sin, and not fully anticipated in the previous remarks, that as the evil for which we are strictly responsible, and to which

the verdict of conscience relates, it is neither the
consequences of our actions, nor properly the outward acts themselves, but the inward principle and
purpose from which they spring.   Thus it is obviously not by experience of the outward effects of
a course of conduct, that we learn whether it is
right or wrong in the view of conscience.   However beneficial the consequences of our conduct
may seem to be, yet if we meant it for evil, we
are none the less guilty of sin.   Whether beneficial
or otherwise, moreover, the consequences of our
actions and our purposes, as they pass into outward
act, are placed at once beyond our power of control ; and except as they were intended by us, are
no more ours than any other events connected
with them in the world of sense.   *They have, in
themselves, no moral, but only an outward and physical character.*   They may be beneficial or injurious ; but apart from the character of the purpose
in which they originated, are neither right nor
wrong — the object neither of praise nor blame.
The same may be said of the mere outward act, as
distinguished from its more remote consequences
on the one hand, and the originating purpose on
the other.   Apart from the purpose of a responsible being, it is not a moral act, and can have no
moral character.   It can be imputed only on the
assumption of a purpose in which it originated,
and from this alone it derives a moral character.
Thus the killing of a man becomes murder, only
on the imputation of a malice prepense.   Let me
add, too, as the plain doctrine of our Saviour, that

if we cherish the malicious purpose, and need only
the outward occasion to carry it into effect, we are
already guilty of murder in the view of conscience
and of God. No such distinction can be maintained, therefore, though so often attempted, as that
which would make an act right in itself, but wrong
relatively to the agent. Considered apart from the
agent, it is neither right nor wrong. We have no
concern with it in regard to a supposed moral
character, except as it is contemplated in a living
union with our own moral being, and grounded in
our own purposes and inward principles, as good
or evil.

On the other hand, when we look away from the
outward and circumstantial, and seek the character
of our deeds in their inward origin, we learn what
is the true import of moral distinctions. We there
view our actions in their proper and only moral
grounds. We there bring into the light of distinct
consciousness, that which is truly our own and dependent upon no outward conditions ; our purposes,
our inclinations, our inward principles of action.
We need but little reflection upon what we find
there, to see that, so far from needing the results
of outward experience in order to determine what
is right or wrong, the moral question and the
grounds of its decision are necessarily antecedent
to all experience of external and actual results.
We have but to reflect upon an action as possible,
upon a purpose as merely conceived and determined upon, though never yet carried into effect
by ourselves or others, and while we have yet per-

formed no outward act for giving it effect, and its moral character is already known. The consequences, immediate or more remote, may or may not prove what I anticipate and intend; *the sole question for me is, what do I intend, and from what motive?* It is the coincidence of my intentions with that law which prescribes imperatively and without appeal what I ought to intend, for which I am responsible. As right or wrong, our acts, our purposes, our principles, have a character equally decided in the moment of their first conception and adoption in our minds, as when all their consequences are known by experience. It is obviously, too, our duty to consider and know what is the character of our purposes, as they manifest themselves to us in the secrets of our own bosoms, and while yet no human eye has the means of knowing what they are. Nor do these assertions go at all beyond the decisions of common reason and moral feeling, in regard to the moral character of man. Every one knows and admits, that an individual may be a very bad man or a very good one, though from disease or otherwise unable to do the smallest act, to utter a word, or to move a finger, for carrying into effect the thoughts of his heart. He may be full of malice, and murder, and blasphemy, and inwardly goaded by the reproaches of his conscience, or he may be wholly intent upon those purposes which God and his own conscience approve. Neither his good nor his ill desert, in such cases, would be the less from his inability to act and show outwardly what he is. *The will is imputed for the deed.* Thus it is not strictly what a man does, since that may not depend upon himself, but what he would do, that determines his moral worth. It is not his outward acts, but his inward principles of action ; not what he is, in so far as that depends on external circumstances and the accidents of birth or fortune, of health or sickness, but what he is in himself, that constitutes his true character in the sight of God.

And here we may notice a farther distinction, of no small importance in respect to our views of sin, between our particular resolves, or our purposes as they are relative to the circumstances in which we are placed, and the higher principle within us by which they are determined. These have, thus far, been referred to as belonging alike to the inner man. We distinguish both from mere outward acts, and ascribe to both a moral character of good or evil. It is obvious, indeed, that our immediate conscious purposes or resolves, and the higher principle by which they are determined, come equally under the cognizance of that law of conscience which prescribes the ultimate ends at which we ought to aim. Yet our immediate and daily purposes may be said to have a more superficial and contingent character. Though not produced by the outward circumstances in which we act, as their proper cause, they have a necessary relation to these, and must vary with them. They have their true origin from some higher principle in our own minds, which practically determines the end and constitutes the inward and proper motive or

moving cause of our actions.   As to their essential
moral character, they would be the same in whatever change of condition and consequent variation
of outward form, so long as they spring from the
same principle and aim at the same end.   They
are the varying devices and inventions of the understanding, as applied to the outward sphere in
which we are placed, and striving to realize a prescribed end by appropriate means.   Thus, the man
who is actuated by a principle of ambition, and is
devoted to the attainment of political distinction,
will shape his more immediate and conscious purposes in subordination to that principle, and with
a reference to its proper end.   Yet, according to
outward circumstances and the judgments of his
understanding as applied to these, he might practice the arts of the demagogue as a candidate for
popular favor; might become a crouching syco-
phant at the footstool of power; or in reliance
upon superior physical force, boldly usurp the reins
of sovereignty.   While the immediate purposes
and corresponding outward acts, here, would vary
according to outward relations, their essential character would remain the same.   It is determined as
good or evil, not by what is conditional and accidental, but by the relation of the higher principle
inherent in all the acts and purpose of the ambitious man, as such, to the law of conscience.

With these distinctions in view, then, it is obvious that we can neither refer to outward occasions
and circumstances, as determining at all the moral
character of our actions, nor limit our responsibil-

ity and the application of moral distinctions to those immediate and more conscious purposes, which are necessarily relative to the outward and circumstantial. We are *responsible also* for the *higher principle*, as working in us, and shaping our ends for good or evil, in conformity or in opposition to the law of righteousness. The votary of a lawless ambition is responsible not merely for the particular wrong which he purposes and commits, as incidental to the end aimed at, but for the wrong principle itself. This necessarily follows from the positions which have been already asserted, upon the ground of our moral consciousness. Whatever principle of action manifests itself within us as directing and controlling our purposes, in opposition to that law which prescribes the ultimate and absolute ends at which we ought to aim, we recognize as wrong, and *impute to ourselves* as sin for which we are responsible. Nor can we feel our responsibility or our guilt the less, that we find such wrong principles of action *deeply seated* in our minds, and exposing us to *deceive ourselves* in respect to our character as sinners. The fact that our own evil principles have acquired an entire control over us, and have blinded our minds to all right views of what we ought to be, cannot be plead in extenuation of our guilt. Experience, indeed, shows that the deeper and more radical the principle of action which gives its character to our purposes may be, the more we are *absorbed* in devising means and in executing subordinate purposes for accomplishing the end which it prescribes, the less conscious we become of its presence and its power. Look, for example, at the man of business, with his whole mind occupied and all his thoughts engrossed, or as we say with propriety, *absorbed* in the accumulation of wealth. His ordinary consciousness extends only to the immediate purposes and occupations of the day. Of the deeper principle which characterizes these, and of the ulterior end to which they are directed by its influence, as something distinctive, and as having a moral character of good or evil, he is, perhaps, for the time, wholly unconscious. Yet, at the same time, it will be obvious to the enlightened and comprehensive observer, that the whole character of the man is distinctly marked by the pervading and controlling influence of the principle in question. To his view, it will betray itself by innumerable and infallible tokens, while the subject himself is unaware that he has given any indication of his character, or of the principle by which he is governed. He unconsciously assumes that all men are actuated by the same principle and pursue the same end with himself. His conscious being, his thoughts, his purposes, his interests, are so limited and encompassed within the sphere which it prescribes, and so determined by the character which it imposes, that he can no longer place himself without the compass of its influence and contemplate it as it is, in the pure light of truth. On the contrary, he sees all other things through the colored medium which, as an artificial

58

atmosphere, it throws around him. To his view, the objects of nature in all their beauty and glory, the powers of intelligence, as unfolded and enriched by education and science and art, and even the higher excellencies of moral worth, have no character and no interest, but in relation to the purposes of gain. He sees in them only the more or less appropriate and efficient means and instruments for accomplishing the ends which the essential principle of his own character prescribes. He can discover in the occupations and pursuits of other men only well or ill chosen means to the same end which he is pursuing, and is wholly blind, not only to the desirableness, but to the possibility of proposing any other. Shall we say, then, that such an one is excusable for his blindness and insensibility ? Is it not rather sufficient to say, as a plain and obvious truth, that he ought not to be thus blind and insensible, thus unconscious of the law and obligations of duty, and heedless of his higher destiny as a rational and moral being ? Will not his own conscience reproach him, whenever he is awakened to a sense of its admonitions, for the domestic and social duties which he has been led to neglect, as well as for the wrongs which he has committed, in his blind obedience to a principle and his eager pursuit of an end which, in the supremacy thus acquired by them, are not in accordance with the law of righteousness ?

But if we are responsible for such a principle, even when ordinarily unconscious of its character, and condemn ourselves for our blind ambition or devotion to wealth, as well as for the more immediate and distinctly conscious purposes which have their origin in these, will the case be altered in regard to our responsibility, if we find these principles embraced as but *accidental modifications* in one *still deeper and more universal?* It is obvious that different men, actuated by the same principle of ambition, will, according to their outward circumstances, employ different means and form different subordinate purposes. To these alone, as diverse from each other, their ordinary consciousness is limited. Yet if we suppose them to reflect and bring into the distinct view of their minds the controlling principle which alike governs them, they will find it the same and having the same relation to the common law of conscience in all. Should more earnest reflection and the clearer light of divine truth, then, convince us that such principles of action as ordinarily distinguish men from each other, ambition, devotion to wealth, the love of pleasure, and all those which diversify the surface of human society, are but the comparatively outward forms and phases of one and the same principle, present in each of them and imparting its character to all, we may still find, in regard to that, also, the same sense of responsibility, and recognize its relation to the law of conscience as good or evil. Though, by the supposition, not within the sphere of our common consciousness, like the immediate and particular purposes of to-day, and farther removed from it even than the several principles by which different men and classes of men are distinguished from each other, yet, when awakened to a deeper knowledge of ourselves, and made conscious of its presence, either immediately or in its effects, we may be constrained to feel, not only that we are responsible for its character, but are justly chargeable with it as evil, in the view of conscience and of God. And this is what I understand by sin as a principle of action, and what the universal experience of men, whenever they have reflected enough to understand distinctly the principles which actuate them, proves to be the truth in respect to the character of man. The import of it is, that there is an ultimate principle of action common to all men, and therefore deeper than those by which they are distinguished from each other. It teaches that this principle, common to all, imparts its character to the more specific and more immediately conscious principles and purposes of each, by determining in every individual the *ultimate end* at which he aims, as *including* and *modifying all subordinate and limited ends*. It imports, moreover, that the principle thus *universal* in respect to the race, and thus *comprehensive* in respect to the agencies of the individual, when brought into distinct consciousness by the clear light of truth, and tried by the law of righteousness, is found to be a wrong principle, and imputed to himself, by every man, as one for which he *feels and knows himself responsible.*

In view of these distinctions and illustrations, then, we cannot but recognize the importance and the practical nature of the position which they are intended to explain ; that it is not the consequences of our acts, nor strictly our outward acts, as such, but the inward purpose and the still deeper principles of action in which that purpose originates, that we distinguish as morally right or wrong. It turns away our attention from the outward and accidental, in our relations and in our conduct, to the abiding fountains of good or evil in our own minds. It points us to a knowledge of ourselves, of the secret workings of our hearts, and of the ultimate ends for which we are striving, as alone enabling us to determine what is our character in the light of truth. But especially does it bring to notice the fact, so important in its practical applications, that our sense of sin, of that inward moral evil for which we find ourselves responsible, is *not limited to our immediate and distinctly conscious purposes*, but extends to the secret and yet *unconscious principle* from which they spring. According to the view presented, it is not necessary that we should have reflected and made ourselves fully conscious of the principles from which our actions flow, in their relation to the law of righteousness, in order to their being justly *imputed to us as evil*. Those principles, obviously, do not become evil by being known merely, *but were evil before they were known*, and while we yet acted in *blind* subjection to their power. When awakened to a serious examination of our charac-

ter and conduct, and when, by opening our minds
to the light of divine truth, we become more deeply conscious of the inward sources in which our
daily purposes have their origin, we find principles
of action of which we were not before conscious,
but which our own *consciences bear witness, ought
not to be there, and condemn as evil.*   It is enough
that we find them there as principles of action in
our *personal being*, and opposed to the law revealed in our consciences.   *We necessarily impute
them to ourselves, as our own principles, and their
contrariety to truth and righteousness as our own
sin.*   No matter how blind we may hitherto have
been to the true character of the inward principles
which determine our purposes and ends; so soon
as they are brought into the light and distinctly
seen to prescribe other ends than those which God
has ordained, we recognize them as evil, and ourselves as guilty in his sight.   A principle of lawless ambition is not the less blameworthy, that we
are so wholly subjected to its influence and absorbed in the pursuit of ambitious ends, as to be unconscious of the claims of duty, and heedless of
the wrongs which we commit.   A corrupt and
*engrossing selfishness, under whatever decent exte-
rior, is still evil and unholy, though we may remain
ignorant* of its all pervading and all-comprehending power in our hearts.   We cannot shun responsibility by abiding in darkness.   We cannot escape
the consequences of the evil principles which lurk
within us, by remaining in ignorance of what they
are.   It is enough for us, that we ought not to be

ignorant of ourselves, but to walk in the clear light of our own consciousness and to keep consciences void of offence. *It is the very purpose and effect of divine truth, and of the holy law of God, to make known to us our true character, to bring to light the hidden things of darkness, and to make manifest the counsels of the heart.* What these determine concerning us when faithfully applied to the inward principles in which our actions originate, *that we are in very truth.* The evil which they bring to light is the sin about which we are discoursing, and for which we must answer at the bar of God. If, by their verdict, as revealed within us and testified by our own consciences, we are convicted of transgression and sin, not only for our avowed purposes, but for every inward principle that is found at variance with the true law and purpose of our being, we must abide by their decision, whatever speculative objections we may find against it.

What is meant here and explained by the previous illustrations is the simple fact, that we do find such principles within us, and that when found, though we may never have been conscious of them before, we do condemn ourselves on that account as sinners. The existence of such principles of action in our minds, or rather of a universal principle common to all men, and found in all to be contrary to the law of conscience, is what is asserted by the doctrine of original sin. It is the principle in which, as the ultimate ground in us, in distinction from more superficial principles or purposes, our actions truly originate. It is that, too, in which they have their origin, as distinguished from all causes out of ourselves, and by virtue of which we are *really and truly the authors* of our own acts in respect to their moral character and the ends to which they are determined. We find evil originating in our own hearts, or we originate that which is evil. *In acting out of an originant principle thus prescribing an end diverse from that which the divine law prescribes, we transgress the law, and* IMPUTE *it to* OURSELVES AS SIN. *It is in this sense that we should understand the import of the term, when* SIN *is charged upon all men, or the whole race of man represented as guilty in the sight of God.* It is not that all have committed distinct and conscious crimes, or overt acts of known and wilful transgression ; but that all, when awakened to a true sense of their own characters, as tried by the law of holiness, will find a *principle* of action *not in harmony with it.* It is in respect to this deep and radical principle of action that we are most liable to deceive ourselves, and most need the light of divine truth to reveal to us the secrets of our hearts. If any deny the existence of such a principle, as by nature working in them and determining the ends at which they aim, we may say, in the language of the Apostle, they deceive themselves, and the truth is not in them.

I have thus endeavored, as was proposed in the first general division of the subject, to determine what is the essential character of sin as a fact of individual experience, and capable of being known within the sphere of our personal consciousness. I have aimed simply to set forth and illustrate that which every man, who will earnestly look into himself and examine the deeper principles of his conduct, may verify by its proper evidence. Nor is it possible to determine on any other grounds of knowledge, either what is the true import of the language of revelation in regard to moral distinctions, or what is our character as responsible beings and as transgressors of a moral law. Such, then, on the only evidence which the nature of the case admits, is the essential character of sin, and our individual character as sinners. These are, as it were, the facts of the case, to which all our speculative views must conform. We cannot find relief from the sense of guilt in a speculative notion that it is an evil only in appearance, but really and in itself the necessary means to a good end, and therefore good. The witness within tells us it is an evil and bitter thing, the *adversary and opposite of all good*. We cannot cast off our personal responsibility, and the attendant sense of remorse in the commission of sin, by the delusive doctrine that we are but the passive instruments for working out the designs of an overruling power. Conscience charges the evil upon us as its authors, and we know that we must abide its decision. Nor can we find a refuge for our pride, or alleviate the humiliating and upbraiding sense of our character and condition as sinners, by regarding the sin with which we are chargeable, as an

59

outward and merely incidental affection. We can
neither attach the imputation to our acts considered in their outward relations and consequences,
nor limit it to that which is merely relative and
accidental or variable in our conscious intentions
and purposes. We are constrained to take it home
to ourselves with all its guilt and shame, and with
all its forms and degrees of culpability, as grounded
in the inmost principles of action which pertain to
our personal being. We are necessitated, by the
testimony of our own experience and the verdict
of our own consciences, to confess that sin, as we
find it in ourselves, is no superficial evil, to be
subdued and eradicated by a few slight efforts and
good resolutions, which we have always the power
to employ, but grounded in a principle which, by
its influence, is present in and modifies all our
responsible agencies, with reference to the ultimate end to which they are determined. We
recognize it as a deep and radical evil, affecting
our essential characters as accountable beings, and
constituting us sinners in the sight of God.

If such, then, be the truth on this great subject,
it cannot be denied that it is truth of a practical
character, and deeply concerns us all. Have we
faithfully examined our hearts and tried our inward
principles of action by the light of truth, to see
whether, in relation to ourselves, these things are
so? Have we resolved in all earnestness to know
the truth concerning ourselves; or have we chosen
to walk in the dim twilight of uncertainty, to
leave the most important of all questions undeter-

mined, lest we might be constrained to forego our purposes and renounce the principles on which we act? Let us not deceive ourselves with the notion that our own ignorance will excuse us in this matter. If we know not that we are sinners, or have but an obscure and doubtful sense of our guilt, it is because we have not liked to retain God in our knowledge. It is because we have chosen darkness rather than light, and have wilfully closed our ears to the whispered admonitions of conscience. The fact that we thus deceive ourselves, and that the truth is not in us, makes not our course less contrary to the law of righteousness, but prevents our fleeing for deliverance to Him who alone can save us from the power of sin. Though we have not aggravated our guilt and braved the terrors of the Most High by distinctly and consciously resolving that we will not obey his law, and that the purposes of our own evil will shall be our portion, yet our consciences convict us of sin so long as we neglect to choose Him for our portion, and to yield all our powers to His service. Let us then go to Him with confession of our sins, and implore the aids of His grace, that we may henceforth walk in the light, as He is in the light. With that sense of our unworthiness and ill-desert which cannot be separated from the indwelling of the word and truth of God in our minds, let us look to the Lord Jesus Christ and his righteousness, as that alone by which we can be saved from the pollution of sin and from its condemning power. For God so loved the world that he gave his only begotten Son, that whosoever believeth in him should not perish, but have everlasting life.

~~~~~~~~~~~~~~~~~~

DISCOURSE II.

With these views of the nature of sin, as we find it in our experience, we may proceed to consider the second general division of the subject. In this it was proposed to point out, as clearly as the inherent difficulty of the case will permit us to do, the ground and origin of sin in respect to the distinguishable powers of our own being, and so, the conditions of its universality. We are here obviously concerned with questions of a different nature from those which have occupied us in the former part of the discourse. Instead of simply exhibiting, as it was there intended to do, the nature of evil as every one may find it in his immediate experience and consciousness, we are now to determine that concerning it of which we are *not immediately* conscious. The inquiry, therefore, becomes more speculative in its character, and belongs, indeed, to that vexed sphere of immemorial controversy, which I should not, I confess, except under strict limitations, deem entirely appropriate to the services of the sanctuary. It is only in the hope of arriving at practical results, and of removing difficulties in regard to moral and religious truth which speculative minds are sure to meet, and by which the most ingenuous are often stumbled, that I venture to make such an inquiry a part of our religious service. Yet observe, it is not the *origin of evil*, on the broad ground of speculation upon which that subject is often discussed, with which we are concerned, but the origin of sin in our own personal being. Whatever moral evil may have existed out of our minds and antecedent to our existence, that is not now the subject of inquiry; but what can we determine of its origin in ourselves, as that for which we are individually responsible, but which is yet common to all? What do the practical principles already established on the ground of our common consciousness, necessitate us to admit in respect to the inquiry now before us? For we cannot too carefully bear in mind what was stated under a previous head of discourse, that no *merely speculative conclusions* can supersede the immediate convictions of *practical truth* in our moral being. In seeking to determine the origin of sin in those agencies of which we are not immediately and distinctly conscious, therefore, we are strictly limited by the conditions which our conscious knowledge of the essential nature of sin imposes upon us. Nothing can be received as true, which contradicts our consciousness in this matter; and it is strictly, indeed, by means of that which we find in our conscious experience, as already exhibited, that we can alone determine the truth and reality of what is affirmed in relation to this part of our subject.

Thus our views of the origin of sin in our personal being can have no authority and no reality for us, except as they are necessarily involved in the facts of our consciousness and the testimony of our conscience, as awakened and illuminated by the power of divine truth. If they are such as to involve the inference, that sin is not what we have already found it to be, on the highest ground of evidence, they must be rejected as false. It is for this reason, that I have endeavored first to show what sin is in its essential characteristics, as a fact of inward experience; and no speculation in regard to its origin must be allowed to change, or at all to modify, our sense of its evil nature, the conviction of our responsibility for it, or of its deep seated malignity, as grounded in our own personal being. Under these limitations, and with a view indeed to guard these practical convictions from being weakened by speculative objections drawn from the same source, we may be safe at least, if not in attempting to explain the origin of sin, yet in making the distinctions necessary to guard us from practical error, and to show the nature of the mystery which the question involves.

The view then, which I shall aim to illustrate, as in accordance with these conditions, and involving what is most important in reference to a right understanding of the subject, is, *that sin has its origin in the* WILL, *or in that which is spiritual in man, and is a* PRINCIPLE *of action in this, contrary to the law and will of God.* This proposition, rightly understood, may be said to contain

the whole truth, so far as we are practically concerned with it ; and at the same time is so clearly
involved in our conscious experience of the character of sin, (so far as our consciousness extends),
as to be admitted by all. Yet it is liable to such
misapprehensions, both from false notions of the
will, and from superficial views of the nature of
sin as originating in it, as to render necessary an
extended illustration of its import. We cannot
rightfully apprehend it and leave our practical convictions unassailed, without some just views of the
will, as the distinguishing prerogative of our personal being, and of its relation both to the law of
our inferior nature on the one hand, and to its own
law of truth and righteousness on the other.
These are the points in which the subject connects
itself with the essential truths of the Gospel, as
well as with the facts of our inward experience ;
and with the elucidation of these I shall chiefly
occupy your attention.

In referring to the will, then, as that in which
sin has its origin, it is intended to designate, not a
mere faculty of choice, subordinate to a controlling principle, and directed by the understanding
and the senses in the selection of means for the
attainment of ends. It means, rather, that highest and constituent principle of our personal being, that power of self-determination, whereby
we are raised above the creatures of sense, and
are said to be formed in the image of God. It
is that power of free agency, by virtue of which
we are capable of the obligations of law and

reason, and which determines, in each man, not the mere choice of means for prescribed ends, but the *ends themselves*, and the *ultimate* ends at which he aims. As such, instead of being guided and controlled by the understanding, it has this and all our other powers as subordinate instruments for attaining the ends which it prescribes. It is that in which most truly centres all that essentially characterizes the individual man in respect to his moral being, and by virtue of which we denominate him a good or a bad man. It is that supernatural power, by which we hold affinity with the spiritual world, and are capable of being made partakers of the divine nature, or, by its perversion and consequent reprobation, of falling to the opposite extreme of Satanic hostility to God, and to all goodness. As a spiritual power, it is essential to the very idea of it that it is self-determined, or have in itself the ultimate principle of its moral determinations. Nor does this sufficiently distinguish it, without adding also, that, as a responsible will, it is inseparable from the idea of conscience, or the self-conscious recognition of a *law* by which it ought to be governed, as prescribing its *true* and *rightful end*. It is in the power of this spiritual prerogative and self-conscious freedom of moral action, that we are raised above the blind necessity of mere natural agents, and have, as a matter of right and duty, the world of sense, with all the powers and faculties and creatures of sense, in a sphere below our proper being, and subjected to our control.

Without the idea of such a power, placing us in a sphere of action above the control of that law by which all mere natural powers are governed, and by virtue of which our principles of action and the ends which we pursue are conceived as our own and self-originated, these principles and ends can be neither right nor wrong, and the requisitions of conscience are an absurdity and delusion. This supernatural power, in its inseparable and self-conscious relation to the light of truth and the law of duty, is that which constitutes our essential being as personal agents. It is most nearly synonymous with what we mean by the pronoun *I*, when we speak of ourselves as individuals, and as personally responsible for our actions. It is the man himself, in his highest character and distinguishing prerogative. It is the ultimate subject of all that is predicable of him as a man, and in the consciousness of which he thinks and speaks of his material body, with all its marvellous powers, as something extraneous to himself and subordinated to his control. Thus, in saying that sin has its origin in the will, we mean that it originates, or has its true beginning, in the man himself, in that indivisible and spiritual or self-determined unity of living action, which is most truly and properly himself, in distinction from the subject appetites and propensities of his nature, and from the functions of the understanding and the faculty of choice, considered as merely adaptive and instrumental agencies, by which he works towards the attainment of his end. It is, in this view of it, therefore, *a spiritual evil, not strictly chargeable upon our natural powers and affections as such, but to be imputed to the personal will,* as its *ultimate ground* and only *proper cause.* This distinction is a fundamental one, and cannot be too much reflected upon, if we would understand the grounds and just limits of our responsibility, and refer to their proper source those higher principles of action by which our essential character is determined. Nor is the distinction a novel or unusual one. It is contained in all languages, and constantly implied in the ordinary intercourse of men. We practically assume it in all our moral judgments, and never indeed impute either moral good or evil, except where we conceive the agency of a will or self-controlling power, as distinguished from mere natural causes. No one holds the brute morally responsible, or charges it with sin and guilt, however noxious and hateful its nature may be to us, simply because we ascribe to it no power above its nature. It has no *personal* being, and the law of its nature is the only law of which it is capable. We cherish, indeed, the innocent lamb, and destroy the ravenous wolf; but for the same reason that in a still lower sphere of nature, we cultivate those plants that are useful or pleasing, while we banish from our gardens the noxious and offensive. In respect to the moral law, they are upon the same level, and alike below its sphere. Whatever may be the specific nature of the animal, its determinate relations to the objects of sense, its appetites and instincts, so long as there is no power whereby it is conceived capable of controlling these and making them the means to a higher end, the obligations of duty and the imputation of blame are felt to be heterogeneous and absurd. In obeying their appetites, they are controlled by the same necessity, and are alike irresponsible with the current of a river in obeying the law of gravity. I have dwelt upon this, for the purpose of characterizing the mode of action which pertains to the powers of nature universally, as distinguished from a responsible will. Now man also has his natural powers, more various, more complicated and perfect, than any other creature of this lower world ; and as he came from the forming hand of God, pronounced, like all his other works, to be good. As a creature of sense, he has a necessary relation to the world of sense. The powers of animal life in man, as in all other animals, have their proper law of action, and require, as the condition of their natural agency, their corresponding objects in the world for which they are formed. The specific functions of sense and sensation, the appetites and instincts of nature, are grounded in the necessary relation of our natural life to its outward means of subsistence. This relation, both in respect to the race and the individual, is wholly and obviously independent of any conceivable agency on our part ; and the affections, the impulses and instinctive propensities of which we are individually conscious, as immediately resulting from this, pertain to the necessity of nature. Thus, we cannot avoid the sensations of hunger and thirst, nor the natural impulse to action which they produce. These, with whatever else pertains to our nature as a distinct species among the creatures of the world, or to its peculiar modifications in the individual man, are determined by the Author of our being, and controlled by laws of action in nature and providence, which make them what they are. For what is thus constituted and determined, independently of any personal agency of our own, we cannot conceive ourselves responsible, nor impute it to ourselves as either good or bad. We have the best authority, if that were necessary, for saying that it is not because the individual himself or his parents have sinned, that a man is born blind; and on the same obvious ground, we may say it is no matter of personal responsibility on our part, that we are born with a phlegmatic or a sanguine temperament, with mild and gentle or naturally excitable and violent affections, with great or small natural endowments of any kind. These, irrespective of the control of a higher or supernatural power, and the ends to which by its agency they are made subservient, have no moral character; and we cannot, therefore, impute sin to them as its proper cause. It is thus, again, because we recognize in ourselves a power distinct from all that pertains to the agencies of our sensual nature, by which we are capable of rising above these, and of exercising a self-control, that the sense of moral accountability and the very distinction of right and wrong become possible for us. It is only for that in our character and conduct which has its ground and origin in this higher power, that we are responsible. However sin, therefore, may be connected with the exercise of our natural powers and the indulgence of our natural propensities, it must be borne in mind, that it pertains to them, not by virtue of what they are in themselves simply, but only as they derive a character from the free will to whose ends they are made subservient.

Here, then, in the fundamental distinction between the necessary and blind agencies of our natural powers, and that free intelligence and will by which we become capable of responsible action and of moral good and evil, we find some of the conditions necessary for determining what is the origin of sin. We cannot do otherwise than refer it to that higher power, by virtue of which alone we can be conceived capable of sin. What, then, let us inquire in the next place, is the form of evil by which the will transgresses the law of God; and what is its relation to the agencies of our nature? What is the true import of the doctrine, that we are by nature the children of wrath, and in bondage to a law in our members which is opposed to the law of the spirit? The view which I shall present, as answering these questions consistently with what has already been said, is, that the free will, or the spiritual principle in each man, instead of putting forth its powers in conformity with the spiritual and universal law of truth and righteousness, and seeking the ends which that law prescribes, determines itself to the pursuit of ends

limited by the conditions of the man's individual
nature, and so becomes a natural self-will, receiving the law of nature as its law and inward principle of action. The fact here asserted is, that
each and all of us seek in the experiences of
sense and within the limitations which our own
sensuous *natures* prescribe, the self-proposed and
ultimate ends of our *personal* being. Instead of
finding in the sphere of sense and in the subject
powers of nature merely that which, by the essential conditions of our existence in a world of sense,
we must find the outward objects and materials on
which to exercise the agency of our higher intelligence and will, and making these subservient to
our true end and the law of our spiritual being;
every man, I say, seeks within the limitations of
his individual experience and sensual nature the
end also to which his purposes are directed. Thus,
to illustrate these distinctions by a familiar example, the natural wants and appetites, both of the
brute and of the man, excite to the attainment of
their proper food, and in both a sensual pleasure is
experienced in its reception. But while the agency of the brute here is limited and controlled simply by the natural appetite, so that it seeks food
only as its nature craves and the sense of hunger
prompts, the man, in the exercise of a power which
does not pertain to the brute, can and does, even
in the absence of the natural appetite, seek a repetition of the pleasure as a self-proposed end.
Again, while the natural appetite of hunger is limited by the wants of his organic system, and ceases

when that want is satisfied, the desire of sensual pleasure, as arising from the gratification of the appetite and the pursuit of it as a self-proposed end, is without limit, and partakes of the infinity of that higher power in which it originates.

It is plain here, moreover, that in the pursuit of such pleasure as an end, the powers and agencies of his nature, as known in his conscious experiences, become the subordinate instruments of the will for the attainment of an end distinguishable from the ends of nature itself.   Thus, as we well know, the epicure artificially stimulates his appetites, and abuses the powers of his nature, perverting them from their proper end, in order to that more prolonged and intense gratification which is his own purpose and end.   This end, therefore, as distinguishable from the ends of nature, and pursued at its cost, or capable of being so, is one which we propose to ourselves ; or in reference to which we act, only in the exercise of that reflex understanding and free will whereby we become capable of responsible action ; yet, in the case supposed, is sought within the sphere determined and limited by a particular appetite of our sensual nature.   We freely seek, in this case, an end of our own, and one for which we are responsible, yet inseparable from a sensual appetite and limited by its condition.   Nor is it conceivable, that while we limit our understandings and wills, in the determination of an end, to the conscious experiences pertaining to this appetite, we can get beyond its sphere, or pursue any higher end.   We can only vary the forms and increase the degree of pleasure within the limits which the nature of that appetite prescribes.

Suppose, then, that instead of limiting ourselves to the experiences connected with a single appetite, we have the whole compass of our sensual nature, and of the world of sense, as the sphere in which we seek the determination of our personal ends and purposes; and we are still bound, each by the conditions of his individual experience. The highest result of thought and reflection, so directed for the determination of our purposes, can be but the pursuit and attainment of the highest end within the limitations of our individual and common nature, and can *never transcend these.* Thus, if we were to imagine brutes of different species, and of different grades in the scale of existence, to be endued with the power of reflection and voluntary action, and each to limit its reflection and the determination of its purposes to the sphere of its own sensual experience and specific nature, the silk-worm and the tiger would necessarily pursue different ends, as their natures are different. It would, in each case, be an end determined under the conditions which the nature of the animal imposes; the one within wider limits, and in some sense of a higher kind than the other; but in both, a conditional end, and subjected to the law of a specific nature. So of ourselves, though the highest in the scale of nature. So long as we seek our personal ends in the sphere of our nature and in the world of sense, they are still conditional ends, and in the will of every man are determined under limitations which his nature imposes. The ends which each man proposes to himself under these conditions, will consequently differ from those of every other man, as his individual nature and experience differ. The ends thus determined, observe, are obviously not identical with the end and purpose of nature as such, nor grounded in nature as the active principle by which we purpose and pursue them ; but have their ground and origin in the understanding and will. Yet while the will, in every man, seeks its ends under the conditions supposed, it is necessarily a conditional will, and every man must pursue his individual ends as limited by the law of his nature. A will then, which, in the determination of its ends, thus limits itself to the sphere and conditions of an individual nature, is a self-will, and in bondage to nature. It can never, under these conditions, rise above nature in respect to the ends which it pursues, nor aim at any thing above and beyond the sphere of self-interest, as prescribed by the nature of the individual man. *Now, if we conceive the will to be thus determined to seek its ends in the sphere of sense, by a necessary law of cause and effect,* it no longer answers the *idea of a will, or spiritual power,* but becomes a mere link in the *agencies of nature.* It must be conceived as self-determined and self-limited ; and we thus come back to the statement of the ultimate fact at which I have been aiming, and which, I trust, will be better understood from these illustrations, that the will, or

61

spiritual power in each man, and so in all the individuals of our race, determines itself to the pursuit
of ends limited by the conditions of an individual
and sensual nature. *The spiritual thus brings it*
self in bondage to the natural, and man becomes a
FALLEN *being.* In respect to the ends which he
pursues, and the corresponding principle in the
will by which he governs his conduct, he has fallen from his true sphere, as a free and rational
being, formed in the image of God, into the sphere
of nature and the world of sense. He has turned
away from the light of truth and the law of righteousness, which prescribe his true end as a personal being, and turned himself, with all the powers of his free intelligence and will, to the seductive shows by which we permit the senses to
beguile us.

I have thus aimed to exhibit what I conceive to
be the ultimate fact which can be made intelligible
to our minds, in respect to the relation of the spiritual to the natural and of the universal to the
individual in man, as a fallen and sinful being. We
cannot go farther, and inquire for a cause of the
fact, consistently with that idea of the fact itself,
which reason and conscience require us to assume.
It must be referred to the free-will of the man, as
its ultimate ground and only proper cause, or we
cannot impute it to him as sin. But here again,
we have the unalterable testimony of our consciences, that it is sin, and that, in obeying the conditional law of our sensuous nature, we transgress
the absolute and rightful law of our personal being.

With the earliest dawn of conscious existence
and of reason, we have a sense of obligation, and
hear the whispers of that still small voice, which,
listened to and understood, commands us to break
the bonds of a sensual nature, and to bring all its
powers and agencies into subjection to a higher
law and subservience to a higher end. These convictions, again, necessarily involve the idea exhibited in the account of the creation and fall of man,
that in his original destiny, and in respect to that
image of God in which he was created, he was, in
his essential character and highest prerogative as
man, a spiritual being, in such a sense that the absolute and universal law of truth and righteousness, or the law of the spiritual world, was his
law, and that which prescribed his true and proper
end; that in obeying the law and placing himself
under the conditions of a nature, therefore, he is
in a fallen state, and subject to an alien law, from
the bondage of which he needs to be redeemed.
Hence the deliverance of man from the thraldom
of sin, or the limitations of his natural self-will,
must be conceived as a redemption from slavery,
and a restoration to his primitive state of freedom
in obeying the essential law of his own spiritual
being. The conscientious convictions, I say, of
every man who reflects, in respect to what he ought
to be, compared with what he is, are such as to
awaken the idea of a fallen condition corresponding with that which I have represented, and what
I understand as contained in the language of revelation. This condition, too, as we have seen, is

not a fault of nature, and is given neither by creation nor inheritance; and though common to all, must yet be imputed to each, as having its ground in the determination of his own will, or in that which is his most true and proper self. It is a condition of the will, for which every man knows himself to be responsible, and for which every man has in himself the sense of guilt and the sentence of condemnation. It is nothing less than a fall and alienation of the man himself from that state in which, according to the divine idea of humanity, he was destined to hold free and spiritual communion with God, walking in the light as he is in the light, and freely conforming to the perfect law of righteousness; and is a subjugation of himself, in his highest spiritual prerogative, to the narrow conditions and enslaving law of a sensual nature. This is that state of spiritual bondage in which, by nature, we all find ourselves; and this we recognize as our misery and our guilt. We find, in the heart of our personal being, a principle and law of action which prescribes other ends than the law of conscience prescribes. Instead of obeying the truth in the spirit, and with free and rejoicing hearts putting forth the fulness of our strength in the pursuit of all that is true and holy and godlike, as we ought to do, we are enslaved to the law of our self-interest, and strive to subordinate all things to our individual ends. Instead of subordinating the powers and propensities of our inferior nature to the higher law of our spiritual being, thus assigning to them their appropriate sphere, and clothing them, as we ought, with a supernatural dignity and glory, we rather carry disorder and confusion into the sphere of nature itself. We strive to force its powers and capacities beyond their prescribed limits, and to impart to them that infinity which alone can satisfy the wants of our personal being. We bring, as it were, our spiritual powers into the sphere of a finite nature, and then seek to make it the instrument for satiating our infinite desires. We strive with capricious folly and madness to stimulate and task the powers of a corporeal and perishable nature, and to accumulate the means of sensual enjoyment, till they shall satisfy the infinite and endless cravings of that which only the infinite God and the absolute good can ever fill.

Thus I have endeavored, as was proposed in the second division of the subject, to show the ground and origin of sin in respect to the distinguishable powers of our being, and the conditions of its universality. I have presented a view which seems to me perfectly compatible with what was before said of the nature of sin, as determined in our practical convictions, and in accordance with all that is taught or implied in the word of God respecting the nature and origin of sin. I have endeavored to show, that in all its length and breadth and depth and height, as an evil principle in the heart of our personal being, it is one which we and we alone have originated, and for which we are individually responsible. The view presented renders it apparent that this form of evil, which as an ultimate and original principle is common to all men, is such a determination of the will or spiritual power to the conditions, and such a subjection of it to the law, of an individual nature in each man, as constitutes a corruption and debasement of the will, limits it to the ends which that nature prescribes, and renders it in its inward and ultimate principle, a will of nature, or a self-will. As such, it is opposed to that universal and absolute law of God to which it ought to be subject, and which requires the subordination of conditional and selfish ends and interests to those moral and spiritual ends which have an inherent and absolute worth, and an equal interest for all. In making the ends prescribed by his individual nature his ultimate aim, therefore, each man swerves from his own true end, which can be attained only in the subjugation of the individual to the universal, and of the finite to the infinite; of himself, therefore, as an individual, to the prescriptions of the absolute reason, or rather to that Being of beings, in whom we no longer contemplate an individual as co-ordinate with other individual existences, but the reality of the absolute and universal in a personal form. In making ourselves, then, and our own interest the end to which we subordinate all other interests, we put ourselves in the place of God. We strive to distinguish and exalt the conditional and individual above the absolute and universal, and worship the creature more than the Creator, who is over all, God blessed forever. And such in each of us is the nature, the origin, and the infinite evil and sinfulness of sin. Let us, then, not deceive ourselves with any vain efforts to believe that we are not sinners, or that the sinful principle which we find in ourselves is not a ground of personal blameworthiness and the just displeasure of a righteous God. Let us rather listen to the testimony of our consciences, and with a full conviction and confession of our exceeding sinfulness as transgressors of his holy law and rebels against his rightful authority, implore the bestowment of his grace, and of the redemption that is in Christ Jesus.

DISCOURSE III.

The views thus presented of the nature and origin of sin, as we find it in our personal being, though apparently abstract and speculative in their general character, are yet inseparably connected with all that is most important in respect to our practical duties. True, it may be said, and few would say it with more emphasis than I am disposed to do, that in addressing moral and religious truth to the consciences of men, we may safely assume all that just and wise speculation can teach and prove in respect to the character of man as a sinner. This is, for the most part, undoubtedly, the course pursued by the original preachers of divine truth. Such, too, is the course ordinarily most appropriate for him who would awaken the consciences of men, and lead them to repentance. It might, perhaps, be always and exclusively proper, were there no false opinions prevalent among speculative men, by which their minds are closed against the right apprehension of practical truth, and their consciences made inaccessible to its power. It is when the force of truth, as applied to the conscience, is weakened and turned aside by the influence of partial and false systems of speculation, that it becomes necessary in addressing the consciences of men, to meet the cavils of objectors, to remove the obstacles which error has raised against the influence of the truth, and to vindicate the authority of conscience itself.

The more subtle the objections by which men shield their consciences, and the deeper the sources from which they are drawn, the more difficult, but at the same time the more necessary, does it become to expose their fallacy and guard our practical convictions from their influence. In doing this, the most abstruse and subtle distinctions are sometimes indispensable and infinitely momentous, in order to the vindication of practical truth. No where, obviously, can they be more so, than in what concerns the grounds of our moral responsibility and the immediate relations of our personal will to nature and to God. It would be difficult, perhaps, to over-estimate the mischiefs which have resulted both to morals and religion from false speculative views on these points, applied to practice both by moralists and by the preachers of the gospel. How often must the enlightened christian rejoice that there is a depth and power in the conscience and in the practical convictions of men, which no speculative error of the understanding can wholly destroy, when he hears arguments used and sees means employed, which, if it were possible, instead of promoting, as they are designed to do, would subvert both morality and religion! In looking, then, at the practical relations of the views which I have presented, as was proposed in the third division of the subject, I remark, in the first place, that if I have guarded my language as I intended to do, there will be found in it nothing that tends in any way to weaken our sense of personal responsibility, or to alleviate our convictions of sin and guilt as transgressors of the law of God. In speaking of the origin of sin, I have limited myself to sin as we find it in ourselves, and as it is a principle of action in our personal will; and I trust the views presented and the illustrations employed will rather strengthen than contradict the testimony of an awakened conscience. But their relation to the immediate convictions of our moral being is so far given in connection with the views themselves, that we need not dwell upon it more at large.

I proceed, then, to observe, in the second place, as a matter of great practical moment in the application of these views, that if they be correct, the distinction between motives of self-interest and the obligations of duty cannot be too strongly marked, in seeking to promote the interests whether of morality or religion. In how many systems, and those too which have been taught in the higher schools of learning, has this distinction been virtually if not explicitly denied! How often has the violation of duty and conscience been represented as arising merely from want of a prudent foresight and a miscalculation of our own self-interest! Nay, is not conscience itself, in the systems most generally prevalent, resolved into a mere product of the sensualized understanding, and regarded as comprising the rules by which we are to be guided in the pursuit of happiness, as the supreme object of desire? Not only from the theories of moralists, but too often from the language of the pulpit also, it would be supposed that an enlightened self-interest was the highest, and indeed the only principle of action, by which it is possible for a wise man to be governed; and that the only difference between the good and the bad man is, that the one understands his interest better than the other. Yet, if there be any ground of truth in the views which I have advanced, the pursuit of self-interest as an ultimate end is in direct conflict with the law of conscience, and the very root and principle of evil in our personal being is the determination of the will to the attainment of our individual ends, as distinguished from those which conscience commands us to pursue.

So long as our own happiness is the supreme object of desire and the controlling motive of action, there can surely be no *essential* difference of character in the sight of God, whether we seek it with careless impetuosity, or with cautious and far-sighted prudence, in this world or a future one; or even whether it be by obeying or violating the prescriptions of a divine law, so far as both are possible from the same motive and inward principle of action.   If self-interest, as a principle of action, and in its relation to the law of duty, be what I have represented it, then out of this there can spring no true obedience to the divine law. The highest that it can produce is what St. Paul designates as the works of the law, or a mere outward form of obedience, without a right spiritual principle within.   It is consequently not true spiritual obedience, and is not accounted righteous in the sight of God.   The first step, therefore, of man, as a fallen being and in bondage to the evil principle, the very beginning of right action, is *repentance*, or a turning away of the mind and will from the ends of self-interest, and a turning to God, as in himself the supreme object of desire. There must of necessity be an absolute denial of self, not the subordination merely of a less interest to a greater, or of a present to a future; but an entire subordination of the individual and natural will, and of all particular ends, to the will of God and the ends prescribed by the universal law. This, conscience commands, in its every admonition of duty; and this is the law of duty, as distinguished from the instinct of nature and the law of the natural will.   This, too, is the repentance and self-denial which alone will satisfy the dictates of an awakened conscience and the conditions either of the law or of the gospel. To effect this, by awakening in the minds of men a distinct consciousness of their relations as responsible beings, of what they are as sinners, and of what they ought to be, by strengthening the convictions of duty, and as far as human agency can do so, empowering the conscience, is the true and legitimate purpose of all moral and religious truth, addressed to men as sinners and in need of repentance. What, then, in relation to this end, must be the proper effect of that instruction, which, instead of enforcing truly the conviction, that in seeking our own interest as the supreme end, we have grievously sinned and done evil in the sight of God, under whatever form and by whatever means we have pursued it, teaches that it is only conditionally wrong, and that our guilt is but an error of judgment in respect to the right means of attaining the desired end? What is this, in effect, but to resolve duty into the cautious and prudent pursuit of happiness, and all sin into a want of prudence, or a mistake of judgment?

Again let me ask, what must be the effect of that predominance, which we so often witness in the instructions and exhortations of the pulpit, of appeals to motives of self-interest, over that simple exhibition of divine truth, which is fitted to awaken a consciousness of sin, and of the obligation to be holy? True, our Saviour and his apostles sometimes address themselves to the interests, the hopes and fears of men; nor can any one doubt, that to arouse men from the lethargy and false security of sin, it is necessary and proper. But as the highest motive by which the good man should be governed, and as a principle of action on which the awakened sinner can safely rest, it is authorized neither by conscience nor the word of God. Is there not reason to fear that the character and purpose of the gospel, and of the christian system, are exposed to grievous misapprehension, from a too exclusive reference to the natural desire of happiness, in enforcing their instructions? Some of us, at least, have met with men of strong minds and not wholly regardless of truth and duty, who have been alienated from the doctrines and duties of christianity by being led to misconceive it, as a system which appealed only to mercenary motives, to the fears of punishment, and hopes of reward in a future life. Such men see and know, that these are not the true and highest grounds of moral action, and so will maintain that they have a better system, and are governed by higher motives than the preachers of the gospel urge upon their hearers. So much occasion, too, is sometimes given, unhappily for men, who, instead of studying the gospel as they ought, receive their impressions of it from what they hear, to fall into this fatal error, that one might be tempted to wish, according to a fable of one of the Christian fathers, for the annihilation of both heaven and hell, in order that men might serve God from pure love, without fear of punishment or hope of reward. The true end and purpose of the gospel, in regard to the moral condition of man, unquestionably is to subdue and eradicate the self-seeking principle of our natural will, as essentially evil, and contrary to the law of the Spirit, by the power of divine truth, and the aids of that spirit which accompanies and abides in the truth, to impart a higher and spiritual principle of obedience to the divine law, and thus to restore in us the ruins of the fall. But we obviously cannot hope, from any conceivable relation of the means to the end, to accomplish this by addressing to others, or by considering ourselves, excitements to action, which appeal to, and so call into exercise, the principle itself which we aim to subdue. To urge upon one, that he must deny himself for the sake of himself, and his own interest, in any strict and absolute sense, is either to expose him to self-delusion, or to perplex him with contradiction and absurdity. But to teach us that we must truly deny ourselves, must suppress every motive of self-interest, and subordinate all individual ends to the higher ends of truth and righteousness, must esteem our lives but for the truth's sake, and our most chosen ends only for righteousness sake ; that we must love our neighbor as ourselves, and God above all, is to second the admonitions of conscience, and co-operate with the word and Spirit of God. Again, if we persuade men, that they must obey the law of God in order to attain happiness, and so make holiness of life only the means to an end, we are involved in a like contradiction, and preclude the true idea of holiness as itself an absolute end, and desirable for its own sake. Nor is it more rational, according

to these views, to urge the love and worship of
God merely as a being able and disposed to promote the happiness of his creatures.   We obviously regard him and his agency in that view only in
the relation of means to an end, and our love and
worship properly terminate upon the ultimate end,
of which he is but the instrument.   But if, while
we humble and abase ourselves in the dust, and
lose sight of all inferior ends, we fill our souls
with the contemplation of God, as including in
himself all absolute good, if we reverence his wisdom, if we adorn his holiness, if we are penetrat-
ed and overawed by a sense of his omnipresent
power, as pervading and sustaining all life and all
being, if we love and worship him as in himself
all glorious and worthy of love and adoration, and
look to him as not only the first cause, but the
last end, not only of whom and through whom,
but to and for whom are all things, we may learn
more justly to appreciate the pursuit of happiness,
and its relation as a motive to the attainment of
our true end. We may learn what it is truly to forsake ourselves, to come forth from the narrowness
of our self-will, and with christian liberty to obey
God in spirit and in truth.   This we can never do,
so long as we practically confound the requisitions
of the divine law with the dictates of self-interest,
and measure our obedience by our views of its
profit.   It is only when the self-will is crucified
with Christ, that the free spirit of man can go
forth unshackled, and become fruitful in all good
works.   It is only when that slavish bond of self-

interest is broken, that the man can delight in and
without restraint pursue every good end, doing in-
differently whatsoever things are true and lovely
and of good report.

But I proceed to remark in the third place, that
from the views which I have presented of the nature and origin of sin and of our character and
condition as sinners, we are able to understand our
need of redemption from the power of evil, and to
see that Christianity is a system adapted to our
need. Sin and redemption, the fallen state of man,
and that system by which, in the wisdom and love
of God, his restoration is to be effected, have a
necessary relation to each other. The deeper and
truer, then, our knowledge of sin may be, the better can we understand and appreciate the character
of Christ and his gospel. Our views of Christianity, indeed, must be, and always are, conformed
more or less fully, according to the extent and con-
sequentness of our reflection upon their relation
to each other, to our views of the natural condition
and character of man. If we regard ourselves as
not truly sinners, alienated in our personal being
from God and our true end, not so fallen and lost
as to need a divine power to redeem and save us
from spiritual death, but only ignorant and impru-
dent, needing but instruction and warning to
secure the attainment of our true end, and capable
of being educated into a life of holiness, then we
shall of course regard Christ as but a teacher, sent
to point out to us the way of duty and happiness, and his gospel but a volume of instructions,

which we are of ourselves fully competent to observe. It could be for us, in that case, only a system or collection of truths and admonitions, not essentially differing in kind from the various systems of ancient wisdom, in which the highest good, and the way of attaining it, are professedly taught. It might, indeed, be better than these, but would still differ only in degree ; and Christ, instead of being a manifestation of God and the divine humanity, a realization of the highest idea of reason under the forms of sense, is but an individual man, and to be classed as one of the ancient sages. With those superficial views of the nature of sin, and of man as a sinner, which amount to a denial of the doctrine of original sin and of the fall of man, I say, Christ and the gospel of the grace of God can rationally be understood in no higher sense. Whatever perplexities we may find in explaining its language on these assumptions, whatever apparent mysteries and strange pretensions to a supernatural and divine character there may be in Christ, and in those words which he tells us are spirit and life, we must resolve them into metaphor and eastern hyperbole, or give up the whole as an unintelligible enigma.

But on the other hand, if we are indeed sinners, and if sin be an evil of such depth and malignity, and having such a relation to our spiritual being, as has been represented in the former parts of this discourse, then, again, we are prepared to apprehend the character of Christ, the meaning and power of his words, and to appreciate Christianity,

63

as a system in all its parts and relations, in a far
different manner.   The whole then acquires a
depth and fulness of meaning and intelligibility of
relation, which of itself is a strong presumptive
evidence that those views of our native character
and condition are essentially true, and such as
were acted upon by Him who knew what was in
man.   It was not, indeed, the peculiar and appropriate purpose of the gospel to teach at large the
doctrine of man's fallen condition as a sinner,
since this is adequately revealed in the conscience
of every man who is in earnest to know his own
character, and was taught both in schools of philosophy and in the more popular mythologies, as
well as in the Old Testament, before the coming
of Christ.   It was, therefore, assumed, and must
be regarded as the antecedent ground and condition to which Christianity was adapted, and without an assumption of which it must remain unintelligible.   In order, then, to a right interpretation
of the system, and a right understanding of it as a
system, we must necessarily inquire what was assumed, and on what assumption is it possible to
understand its meaning.   What I mean to say,
then, is, that the views presented in the former
parts of this discourse, not only have their own
proper grounds of evidence, but that, when applied to the Christian system, they mutually
explain and confirm each other ; and that we are
thus prepared rightly to estimate the work of redemption.   On this ground, and with this view,
we cannot too often or too deeply meditate upon

our lost condition, the extent and malignity of the
evil, the depth and hopelessness of the ruin, from
which, in the boundless love of God, his Son came
to redeem us.   We cannot be too cautious to admit the whole truth on the one hand, in order to a
just appreciation of the whole truth on the other.
If, then, we are in ourselves estranged from the
law of God, and in our personal being wholly in
bondage to sin, in the sense represented, we can
understand what our Saviour means, when he tells
us the Son of Man is come to save that which was
lost.   If we are not only poor and miserable in
ourselves, but guilty of rebellion against God and
opposition to a holy law, and therefore under a
just condemnation, exposed to the righteous pen-
alty which we have incurred, we may apprehend,
in some measure, how God commendeth his love
toward us, in that, while we were yet sinners,
Christ died for us.   Again, if we so feel the evil
of sin, as a principle affecting the essential character of our spiritual being and bringing us in bondage to the law in our members, as to realize the
necessity of a higher principle than belongs to our
enslaved natural will, in order to overcome and
subdue its malignant power, we are prepared to
receive the doctrine, that we must be born again,
and to hail, with joy and thanksgiving, the proffered aids of that spiritual power which is in
Christ and in the Spirit of all grace, to deliver us
from the dominion of death, and restore us to spiritual life.   According to the depth of insight with
which we contemplate the apostasy of our whole

race from God, and the import of the language
which represents the world as lying in wickedness,
so will be, in like manner, the degree of justness
with which we appreciate the ministry of reconciliation, and the doctrine that God was in Christ
reconciling the world unto himself. Thus at all
points one thing is over against another, and all
the provisions of the gospel have a meaning and
an application which we can fully apprehend only
when we look deeply and steadfastly into our own
hearts, and become conscious of our spiritual mal-
adies and our perishing wants. An adequate
knowledge of ourselves and of our spiritual character and relations is thus the necessary condition
of our knowing what Christ is, as the Saviour of
sinners, and of our rightly interpreting all that in
the volume of revelation, which has reference to
our inward experience, and to that which is spiritual in us.

Nor, in reference to our personal estimation of
the need of Christ and the infinite worth and importance of what he has done and is ever ready
and willing to do for us, will mere speculative
views of the nature and origin of sin suffice. It
must become, for each of us, a matter of personal
concern. So long as it remains in the head, it can
only remove the speculative obstacles to the practical admission of the truth. We must take it
home to our hearts. We must practically and
deeply realize that we, even we ourselves, are
guilty and exceeding sinful in the sight of a just
and holy God. We must not only feel that we are

in danger, and our eternal happiness at stake, but that we are ill-deserving, transgressors of the law of God, and exposed to the righteous judgment, not only of our own consciences, but of Him who is of purer eyes than to behold iniquity. This, for the fully awakened conscience, unquestionably is the point of practical moment and of highest concern. Before the tribunal of conscience, it is not a question of self-interest, of safety or danger in respect to present or future enjoyment, but a question of desert; not primarily how we can be saved from suffering, but how we can be saved from the inward reality and the oppressive sense of sin and guilt. How can man be just with God, and become holy and acceptable in his sight?

It is in this state of mind, with these questions pressing themselves home upon our hearts, and giving us no rest till we find an answer, that we can know the meaning of the gospel. It is when we are overwhelmed with a consciousness of our guilt, of the exceeding sinfulness of transgressing a holy law, and of worshipping the creature more than the Creator, of serving ourselves instead of the adorable God, that we can feel the power of those words of our Saviour, Come unto me, ye that labor and are heavy laden, and I will give you rest. It is from the evil and burthen of sin, that Christ came to deliver us; for he was sent not to call the righteous, but sinners to repentance.

DISCOURSE.

THE TRUE GROUND, IN MAN'S CHARACTER, AND CONDITION, OF HIS NEED OF CHRIST.

IN THE LAST DAY, THAT GREAT DAY OF THE FEAST, JESUS STOOD AND CRIED, SAYING, IF ANY MAN THIRST, LET HIM COME UNTO ME, AND DRINK.— JOHN vii. 37.

The circumstances in which these words of our Saviour were uttered, are briefly indicated in the text. He seems to have seized upon a favorable occasion which offered itself, as he often did upon other incidents of a worldly nature, to give greater significance and effect to the spiritual instruction which his words conveyed. Could their full import have been understood, and its relation to themselves appreciated, by the thronging multitudes around him, how unheeded would have been the pomp of their festival, and how would all ears have listened to the words of him who spake as never man spake! The occasion here referred to was connected with the feast of tabernacles; and, even to our minds, perhaps, may serve to present in stronger relief the character which Christ assumed, and the import of the proclamation which he made. The festival, in its general character, even as instituted by Moses, was one of great national interest. In the pomp of its ceremonial, and in the multitude of those who in after times went up to participate in its numerous sacrifices and to pay their vows unto the Lord, it was the greatest and most celebrated of all the national anniversaries of the Jews. Designed to commemorate their long and painful sojourn in the wilderness, where, hungry and thirsty, their soul fainted in them, it was at the same time connected with the autumnal harvests, and was a season of thanksgiving to Him who had delivered them out of their distresses, and was now crowning the year with his goodness. As they looked upon the crowded tabernacles, or temporary coverings, under which they were required to seek shelter during the period of its celebration, their minds were carried back to those tents which had been pitched upon the waste and barren desert, where they wandered in a solitary way, and found no city to dwell in. But these, again, were now but an occasion for national joy and thanksgiving, by their contrast with that great city of habitation to which the good providence of God had conducted them, and with those surrounding palaces in which God,was known for a refuge.

Especially was it matter of rejoicing, that they now pitched their tents in the precincts of their national temple. This was the bond of union, and the common centre of attraction for the whole people ; and hither, at this season of national thanksgiving, they came up from their cities and villages, whether near or more remote, to contemplate its outward magnificence, and to worship before the holy place of the tabernacle of the Most High. It was thus, that at each anniversary, its courts were thronged with rejoicing multitudes, and the solemn rites of the occasion performed with that fervor of national enthusiasm, which they could not but inspire. To these rites, as instituted by Moses, we are told that in these latter times many additions had been made. Especially was the eighth day, here called the great day of the feast, which was at the same time the last in the festive solemnities of the year, crowded with many pompous ceremonies, and celebrated with peculiar splendor. It was a day of universal jubilee among the assembled people ; and so greatly was it distinguished, that the Jewish writers were accustomed to say, " He had no conception of a jubilee, who had not witnessed these festive scenes."

Among the additional observances practised in these times, the most remarkable was that of carrying water in a golden phial from the fountain of Siloa, and pouring it upon the altar. This is supposed by many to have been suggested by the pro-

phetic language of Isaiah, and to have been adopted with reference to the expected blessings of the
Messiah's kingdom. It was at least regarded as a
sacred symbol, and carried with circumstances of
excessive joy, with sound of trumpets and shouted
hallelujahs, while the priests sang in chorus the
words of the prophet, " With joy shall ye draw
water from the wells of salvation." It was probably, we are told, with reference to this interesting rite, and amidst these multitudes, dazzled with
the imposing splendor of outward ceremonials and
intoxicated with sounds of joy, that Jesus presented himself, and addressed the people as related in
the text. And who *is* he, and what is his message,
who, upon the threshold of that temple, and upon
such an occasion, claims attention to himself and
his words? We see him in the calm dignity and
commanding power of a higher consciousness, but
with no outward marks of distinction, standing
there, and calling away the attention of the multitude from the sacred waters of Siloa, and from all
their outward occasions of national festivity, to
himself as the paramount object of regard. He
proclaims himself as being, both for them and for
all men, the true fountain of the water of life. If
any man thirst, let him come to me, and drink.
He that cometh to me shall never hunger, and he
that believeth on me shall never thirst.

What, then, let us inquire, is the true import of
a declaration, which, by the circumstances in
which it was made, so loudly claims our regard ;
and on what grounds, in respect to its author and

64

to the individuals of our race, can the declaration be justified to our understandings and our hearts?

In answering these questions, I shall endeavor, first, to explain the import of the figurative language in which it is expressed; 2ndly, to show what it is in the character and condition of man, which is the ground of the relation to Christ implied in the text; and, 3rdly, to exhibit the character of Christ, as corresponding to that relation, and in reference to our spiritual wants.

1. In the first place, then, we are to inquire what is the literal sense of the figurative language of the text. Such language is, indeed, of very frequent occurrence, and may seem too obvious to need explanation. From the circumstances in which it was used, however, and in reference to the views which I propose to take of it, I shall venture to regard it in two senses, nearly connected, indeed, yet distinguishable from each other, and worthy of distinct attention.

According to the first and more obvious of the senses to which I refer, the terms of the expression are used, as hunger and its corresponding gratification often are in like circumstances, for any conscious desire in relation to its appropriate object. As employed by our Saviour here and elsewhere, they must be understood to refer to a conscious desire for those spiritual blessings which were but symbolically represented in the festival rites of the occasion, but which he claimed the power to impart. To those engaged with fervent enthusiasm in the solemnities of their national

worship, the meaning of his declaration was, if any
man truly and earnestly desires the spiritual reality, which is here exhibited but in types and shadows, let him come unto me, and satisfy the desires
of his soul with substantial good. Ye who look
and long for those waters from the wells of salvation, turn away from the symbolical waters of
Siloa, and come unto me. In me will you find
the spiritual blessings which you seek ; and whosoever drinketh the water that I shall give him, it
shall be in him a well of water, springing up into
everlasting life.

Similar to this language of our Saviour in its
figurative character, is that invitation of the prophet Isaiah : Ho, every one that thirsteth, come ye
to the waters ; and that expression of intense desire in the Psalmist, in which he exclaims, My soul
thirsteth for God, for the living God : when shall
I come and appear before God ? How blessed, in
their relation to him, are all those who find in themselves this conscious and outbreaking desire for
the spiritual treasures that are in Christ, and that
he is so ready to impart ! Blessed are they that
hunger and thirst after righteousness, for they
shall be filled.

But according to the other and less obvious
meaning which I ascribe to the declaration in the
text, it is understood to refer to that inward need,
which, though he may be unconscious of it, the
soul of every man has of Christ and of the spiritual blessings which he proffers for our acceptance.
In this more extended metaphorical sense, the same

language is often applied, not only to the unconscious need of beings capable of conscious desire,
but also to the lower orders of organic existence,
and even to inanimate objects in relation to what
may be necessary for the attainment of their supposed end. Thus every creature may be said to
thirst for and to seek after its appropriate good,
and that which is necessary to the attainment of
its prescribed end, though unconscious, and consequently undesirous of that to which it holds such
a relation. In this sense our Saviour may be understood as saying that the inward necessities of
every human soul place it in this relation to himself. Such is the proper end towards which it is
borne by the original law of its spiritual being, and
such are the conditions of its attainment, that it
stands in need of Christ, and must come to him
for the supply of its spiritual wants. In other
words, Christ here proffers himself as the good
which the spirit of man needs ; and the intensity of
that need he expresses by thirst, the most unap-
peasable of our natural organic cravings, the most
indispensable of our bodily wants. Whatever
else we may do without, according to the sense of
our Saviour's language, we cannot do without him.
He is that for our souls, and the inmost necessities of our spiritual being, which water is for the
body when fainting and perishing for thirst. The
invitation of our Saviour, therefore, is to every
man to come unto him for the supply of his spiritual necessities ; for that without which he can

never attain the true and proper end of his being, but must remain restless and unblest forever.

2. But let us proceed to inquire more particularly, in the second place, what it is in the inward character and condition of man, which is the ground of this relation to Christ. To this it might be answered in a word, that it is found in that higher capacity for the reception of spiritual good, which, however unconscious he may be of it, pertains to the soul of every man, and which no inferior or worldly objects can ever fill. To render this fully intelligible, however, in its distinctive character, and in the actual condition of man, farther consideration may be necessary.

In a general way, then, what is here said of the soul of man may be illustrated, by referring it to that universal law to which all finite and creaturely existences are subjected ; that, namely, of dependence and insufficiency in themselves for the accomplishment of their proper end. All need and require, as the indispensable condition of their existence, a good out of themselves, which they may be said, according to their several powers, to seek after, and which in turn is suited to their wants. Look, for example, at that beginning of the ways of God, the mysterious life of the vegetable world. See how it puts forth in boundless luxuriance its ever-varying forms. With what pervading power it forces its way through all the apparent obstacles of inorganic nature, clothing the rocks with its verdure, and diffusing its fragrance over the burning sands of the desert. But

on the rock and in the desert God has provided it
with the means of its subsistence, with the materials of its growth, and endued it with the powers by which it seeks out and appropriates them
to its use. While it clothes the earth with beauty, and sends upwards its expanding foliage,
breathing healthful influences into the surrounding air, and paying homage to the sun, it must be
remembered that in and by these it lives ; that it
receives from the earth and air and sun the elements of which all the substance of its growth is
composed, its form of beauty or of stateliness, the
verdure of its leaves and the fragrance of its
flowers. It is God who has thus fitted them for
each other, and who so clothes the grass, which
to-day is, and to-morrow is cast into the oven.

We may carry the same principle upward
through the whole range of living nature ; and
while we are compelled to refer to a specific power of life within, we are under an equal necessity
of looking to the specific provision for the developement of each successive power in the world
without. Thus, while the inferior life of the plant
finds the material of its existence and the conditions necessary to the proper ends of its being in
the inorganic elements, it is itself, in turn, the outward condition of life and growth to the various
orders of animal creation. These, as they go
forth in countless myriads upon the face of the
earth, as they pass through the paths of the seas, or
fly in the open firmament of heaven, seek, each
after its kind, an appropriate good in the world

around them, and receive their supply from the same all-bountiful Giver. He causeth grass to grow for cattle, and herb for the service of man. These all wait upon Thee, that thou mayest give them their meat in due season. That thou givest them, they gather; thou openest thine hand, they are filled with good. Thou hidest thy face, they are troubled; thou takest away their breath, they die, and return to their dust.

Thus far, the relation of man to external nature, as the necessary outward condition of his existence, is obviously the same with that of the inferior orders of creation. As to the powers of his organic life, he stands related to all the elements. The earth and sky, the illuminating and warming rays of the sun, the vital air, the manifold products of vegetable and of animal life, the world, in all its fulness and variety, are the sphere and contain the outward conditions of his animal existence. These, the Giver of all good has placed around him, and among these he must, by the conditions of his existence as a creature of this world, and in the exercise of his physical powers, seek the means necessary to his sensual life. Without these he cannot live. With all his superior powers of life, and the wonder-working energies of his complicated organs, he needs that which they cannot give; he hungers for a morsel of bread, and thirsts for a drop of water. *These* he *must* have, or his eyes will start from their sockets in the consuming rage of hunger and thirst. He that feedeth the fowls of the air, must feed *him* also.

But has man no higher powers than those which
belong to him in common with the brute ; and is
he connected with nothing out of himself, as the
necessary condition of their developement, other
than that on which his physical existence depends ?
This is one point for which I wished to prepare the
way by the illustrations already adduced ; namely,
from what is so undeniable in regard to the powers
of vegetable and animal life, to render more pre-
sumable and evident the truth of the same principle in respect to whatever higher powers and capacities we may possess. If there be that within
us which is nobler than the instincts of organic
life, and strives for the attainment of a higher end,
it is yet equally dependent upon that which is provided without, as the condition on which alone
that end can be attained. Nor can those higher
wants be satisfied and that higher end secured by
means of the *same* outward objects and conditions
which suffice for the brute and for our own mere
animal nature. Strictly speaking, it is only in respect to those powers of life which man possesses
in common with the vegetable and brute creation,
those concerned in the growth and perfection of
his bodily organs, that he is immediately related to
the inferior objects around him, as before described.
It needs but a moment's reflection to see that he
has powers of action and capacities of enjoyment
which cannot find in these the means and conditions of their growth, but must be excited and
nourished by that which has a specific relation to
their higher wants. For in the midst of material

nature, and surrounded by a ceaseless exuberance
and variety of that which supplies the mere wants
of the body, what is man without men? Will he
or can he become truly a man, without that human
intercourse, and the presence of those more than
merely sensible objects, which properly awaken
and call forth the distinguishing powers of humanity? Will he hold intellectual converse, and discourse of truth and right, with the senseless plant
or the speechless brute? Will the human, the social and moral affections of his soul find adequate
excitement in the beauty of flowers, in the subdued or even impassioned look with which the
forms and aspects of brute natures address his eye,
or the tones with which their thousand voices fill
his ear? Will he indeed find awakened in himself those moral affections and charities which
raise him above the brute, and pour them forth, as
from an inward fountain, while, in the wide world
around him, there is no human heart that answers
to his? To these questions, reason, analogy, and
experience, so far as it is possible to have its testimony, answer, No. In these circumstances, man
would himself remain, as to the actual developement and exercise of those higher powers which
characterize him as a social and intelligent and
moral being, little more than a speechless brute.
However his bodily hunger and thirst might be
satisfied, and his corporeal organs attain their full
developement and symmetry of form, his soul's
need would be unprovided for. There would be
a hungering and thirsting for some unknown and

65

unexperienced good. His higher powers and tendencies would fail of their appropriate objects and
ends, and show their existence only in obscure and
ineffectual longings for that which the surrounding
world could not supply.

The human soul, then, in respect to those powers of intelligence and those moral and social affections which are manifested in the relations of
society, has its appropriate sphere of existence,
and finds the conditions of its growth and well-
being in the intercourse of mind with mind and
heart with heart. It neither finds its proper nourishment, nor attains its proper end, without something above and beyond that which feeds the body.
As its own peculiar powers and affections are
higher and more inward than the life of the body,
so it seeks in the world around it for that which
has also a higher life and a kindred heart. It *loves*
only that which can *return* its love. It opens the
deep fountain of its joy and sorrow, the sacred
source of smiles and tears, only to that kindred
power whose presence it recognizes in the expression of a *human* eye, and in the tones of a *human*
voice. It speaks, it utters forth a thought, a word,
out of its inner world of thought, only to that
which has also its inner world, and understands,
and utters back, a word. This it is, and this
alone, which can call forth, and feed with food convenient for it, the inner soul, the mind and heart
of man. This is the provision which it needs, and
which again it must have, as the condition of its
moral and intellectual life, of its truly becoming a

human soul. And here, too, who will not recognize the wisdom and goodness of the same all-
wise and bountiful Giver, in the rich supply for
these wants also, which, without our agency or
care, we find thrown around us. From the very
dawn of our existence, we are compassed about by
his care. As he supplies the wants of the body,
so he satisfieth the longing soul, and filleth the
hungry soul with goodness.

The world which our souls need, is the world
in which we live and move from infancy to age.
Look at the infant upon its mother's bosom. Does
it seek there for the food which nourishes its body,
believing as it were, with at least an implied and
undoubting faith, that He who gave it life has
made provision for its wants? With the same
earnest seeking, and a like urgent need, does its
eye search for that which is necessary to the higher ends of its being, to the powers and capacities,
the dawning affections and sympathies of a human
soul. And lo! this too it has found already there,
and beaming upon it in the look of a mother's love.
There, in alternate smiles and tears, and in those
tones which come from the heart and reach the
heart, it has found the provision which it needs.
It has found that which awakens and cherishes
the inward attributes of humanity. Thus, by all
the expressions of human kindness, the corresponding affections are awakened and cultivated. How
soon, too, is the faculty of thought and of speech
excited and nourished by the sounds of our mother
tongue, and the mind brought into communion

with other minds! This stage in the developement of our powers once gained, the wants and purposes of the heart converted into thoughts, and thoughts into words, how rapidly are those wants multiplied, and how eagerly do we seek in the world around us for the objects which they require! These we find, according to our need, from childhood to youth, and from youth to manhood, in the intercourse of kindred minds; in the sentiments, the passions and purposes which are manifested around us and nourish our own. By all that environs us in the sphere of humanity, the various institutions of civilized society, the conflict of interests and passions in which we are involved from day to day, and especially by the treasures of thought in the language which we inherit, the powers of our own inward being are called forth and their wants supplied. By these, as the outward means and conditions, we, too, come to the conscious possession and enjoyment of all that pertains to the social and intellectual life of man. We, too, become prepared to exhibit the character and to act the part of men, in the duties and responsibilities of human life.

Thus the individual man is the nursling of humanity. As the life of his body is nourished in the lap of nature, and seeks its proper food in the material elements around it, so the soul is embosomed in the human world, which a never-failing and all-comprehending Providence has made ready and suited to its foreseen necessities. In this it lives and grows, breathing the atmosphere of hu-

man affections, and feeding on human thoughts.
And how should our souls glow with special gratitude to God, that we have had our birth in a world
so richly fraught with provisions for the supply of
all their need! Above and around us, in the records of the past, in the interests and movements
of the present, and in the hopes and fears awakened by the impending future, we have enough to
call forth all our energies. The manifold examples of great and good men in all the departments
of human action, are held forth to our view, and
shed down their influences upon us as stars in the
constellations of the firmament. We inhale an
atmosphere of domestic and social affections, invigorated by the free institutions of our fathers,
and still retaining something at least of the higher
and healthier tone which it received from their
Christian spirit. We inherit and may feed upon
the accumulated treasures of ancient wisdom, and
we have the language of Shakspeare and Milton
for our mother tongue.

By these illustrations, which may seem, I am
aware, unnecessarily prolonged, I have endeavored
to render intelligible what was stated as a universal law, and to furnish at least the means of better
understanding its application in the case before us.
In the last example, especially, which for this reason has been exhibited so much at length, I have
aimed to advance the main purpose of the argument, by showing that we are endued with powers
of action, of enjoyment and suffering, which,
though they have their adequate objects and may

attain their proper end in this world, are yet unde-
niably of a higher nature than those of our mere
sensual life, and require, as the outward condition
of attaining that end, objects in like manner above
the proper sphere of sense.   For the powers
there exhibited, as constituting the true life of
man in the relations of human society, pertain not
to the outward life of the body, but to the inward
life of consciousness.   Conscious feelings and affections, thoughts and purposes, belonging to the
inner world, distinguish the refined and cultivated
member of civil society from the brute or the savage;   and these have the conditions of their developement, not properly in the material objects of
sense, though it be through the medium of sense
and especially by the ministry of words, but in
that which in like manner belongs to, and comes
forth from, the inner world of humanity;   that
world of conscious being, that place of understanding, which, in the language of Job, is hid from the
eyes of all living, and kept close from the fowls of
the air.   If the true character, and outward relations
of what has been thus exhibited, be borne in mind,
it may serve in many ways to aid our conceptions
of the leading subjects before us.

With the aid of these illustrations, then, let us
follow up the inquiry, what is that in the character
and condition of men, on the ground of which he
has need of Christ?   What powers are to be unfolded, and what wants to be supplied, which are
not yet provided for by the rich and abundant
blessings which are thrown around us, as we have

seen, in the material world, and in the society of
our fellow men? The difficulty of answering
these questions arises chiefly from the fact, that in
most men the powers and capacities referred to
are not so fully awakened and called into action
that they are distinctly conscious of their need.
Instead of opening their minds to the contemplation of those higher and ultimate ends which are
prescribed by the original law of their being, and
in reference to which the need properly exists,
they limit their view to those worldly and selfish
ends which they have proposed, and are striving
moreover to satisfy the partial cravings of which
they have become conscious, in the pursuit of an
inferior and worldly good. They are ignorant of
what they *are*, in respect to the highest dignity
and capacity of their being, and consequently ignorant, both of their wants, and of the appropriate and
abundant provision which here too is made for
their supply. But let us endeavor, with all earnestness, to understand the meaning of our Saviour, when, disparaging, as it were, those abundant provisions for the supply of our various wants,
which we have been contemplating, as well as the
human pageantry around him, he directs us to himself for the supply of our most urgent need. This,
indeed, as in regard to our more temporary and
superficial wants, we cannot do fully, unless our
minds are awakened to a practical sense of that
need. Yet, by a reference to those powers and
capacities of our nature of which I have before
spoken, and to that which every one will recog-

nize in his own consciousness, we may see that
we have within us a still higher, and, if I may use
the expression, more inward power, and that this
too requires its corresponding object, and seeks its
proper end. Strictly speaking, no man is unaware
of the power to which I refer. We recognize its
presence in ourselves, and in our fellow men, as
paramount to the powers of nature, even of our
own human nature, and connecting us with a
higher sphere of being. We cannot but be familiar indeed with its existence, and its essential
character ; for it is not only the most inward and
central principle of our consciousness, but manifests its presence in all the outward relations of
man. It is only because it is one with our personal
being, strictly identified with the individual consciousness of every man, that, like the pulsation of
our hearts and the unconscious breathing of the
breath of life, it escapes our notice, and is so difficult to be apprehended aright. But however unconscious we may be of its inherent necessities,
and blind to its own proper end, we yield to it
still in a certain sense the prerogative which it
claims, and submit all our other powers to its control. For it is that in us which is capable of having, and claims to assert, a purpose of its own, in
distinction from the subject appetites and propensities of nature, and in distinction, too, from those
social and intellectual tendencies to which I have
referred. It is that to which we habitually refer
and impute the deliberate acts and purposes of a
man, as the controlling principle within him. It

is the man within the man. It is that by virtue
of which we are capable of self-cultivation, of self-
knowledge, and self-control. It is, in a word, that
principle, whatever we may call it, of free, self-
conscious and *personal* being, by which man is
placed in connexion with the spiritual world, and
has wants which cannot find their appropriate objects in the world of sense and in the compass of
nature. It is that which is properly meant by the
spirit in man, in distinction from all that pertains
to his sensual nature and the world of sense. Now
the point I wish, if possible, to make clear to your
apprehension, is, that what we here speak of, is
truly a distinguishable and higher power, in its relation to those which find their adequate objects in
the world around us, and requires at the same time,
according to the meaning of our Saviour and the
general principle before illustrated, a good out of
itself, and adapted to its higher wants. The powers of our sensual nature, we have seen, have their
appropriate objects in the material world. The
appetites of hunger and thirst, by which the wants
of organic life are manifested, eagerly seek their
appropriate supply in the objects of sense, and in
the enjoyment of these rest and are satisfied, as
with their proper good. So, too, in the higher
sphere of our natural human affections, and of all
those powers of human nature which find their
proper objects in the corresponding powers and
affections of our fellow-men, the same principle
holds true. In the confiding intercourse of friends,
in the free interchange of thought and of social

66

affections, but especially in the relations of the domestic circle, the mind rests and is satisfied, as with objects suited to its nature. But what is that power, and its true objects and ends, by which, in the exercise of a still higher prerogative, we control these powers and capacities of our nature, and indulge or repress, use or abuse them, at will ? Our natural appetites are easily satisfied, and, left to the law of their own nature, act in accordance with, and rest in, their proper end.   But the epicuro pampers and stimulates his appetites, that he may make them the instruments of his self-proposed and capricious enjoyments. The demon of ambition sweeps away from its path the affections and charities of social and even of domestic life, represses the instincts of nature, and makes human life itself subordinate to an arbitrary will, Nay, for all purposes, of good as well as evil. man asserts the authority and control of his personal will over the powers and affections of his nature. In the strength of its high prerogative he makes them the obedient ministers of its purpose, and subject to its law. He excites and urges on the storm of unbridled passions, or arrests its course, and says to their warring elements, Peace, be still. The strong agonies of nature are hushed by his mandate, and the humble Christian in the midst of consuming fire can hold its outbreaking terrors in quiet submission to his will. It was the martyr at the stake who doomed his own right hand to the hottest flame, and cried with his last breath, as he held it unfaltering there,

This hand has offended, this wicked hand has offended.

But this power itself, the man in the energy of that personal will which thus imposes its immitigable law upon a reluctant but subject nature, and makes the highest ends of nature subservient to its own, what are *its* ends, and the means of attaining them? With what scope and for what purpose does it employ its higher energies, and those subordinate powers which obey its mandate? Is it to seek and find these, in that very sphere of nature over which it claims such a prerogative? But the ends of nature, with the outward means of attaining them, as they become known in our experience and consciousness, are, as we have seen, various and manifold. Every distinguishable power and affection here has its own appropriate craving, and in the fulness of that world which God has so amply stored for our use, it finds its distinct and proper object and consequent gratification. Are the ends and the objects of that supernatural power, then, identical with these, equally numerous and diverse? But as a personal and self-conscious power, it places itself, as it were, in distinct and indivisible unity, at an equal remove from all these; *present*, indeed, in a certain and important sense, to *all*, but becoming *identical* with *none*. Can we, then, as personal beings, choose among the endless solicitations and propensities of nature, and arbitrarily *make* to ourselves an end which we can steadfastly pursue? And will this be our *true*, our destined and *ultimate* end? Or can we attain our own proper end, through the appointed means, by yielding to every solicitation of natural appetite, and thus losing ourselves in the infinite dispersion and manifoldness of nature?

These questions are forced upon us by what we see of the actual condition and conduct of man. For, turning away from the one only true and ultimate end to which he was destined, and in which alone the powers of his spiritual and personal being can rest, he seeks his changing and inconstant purposes, and strives to find an end that may satisfy him, among the appetites, the passions and propensities of his nature. Disappointed in his search, in perpetual disquiet and vexation of spirit, and changing his self-proposed ends with the ever-varying solicitations of appetite and passion, he remains fixed to no end; and if he were, it is still within the sphere of his lower nature, and his spirit is in bondage to its law. Thus estranged from his true end, and blind or indifferent, as he must be, to that spiritual good which is the outward condition of its attainment, he regards and pursues only that which is fitted to satisfy the inferior wants, and minister to the sensual or at most to the social gratifications of nature. These he covets and accumulates with ceaseless anxiety. Still restless and unsatisfied, he still cherishes his delusion, and strives to satiate the inward cravings of his soul for a higher and enduring good, with the fleeting phantoms of sense, and the unsubstantial possessions and enjoyments of that world, the fashion whereof passeth away.

But neither in the ends nor objects of the natural world can the spirit of man rest. Though fallen from a right apprehension and pursuit of its true end, and too often unconscious and consequently undesirous of that which constitutes its appropriate good, it yet finds by experience, that what it actually seeks, falls short of its aspirations; and that no finite and worldly good can fill the compass of its desires. How should it indeed be otherwise? The inherent tendencies and wants of animal life are not satisfied, nor do its powers find their appropriate objects and sphere of action, in the obscure form of vegetable life, to which, in the first months of its existence, it is limited. It must open its eyes to the light, and its ears to the music of sounds. It must expand its own lungs to the vital air, reach forth its hands to that which its eye sees, and walk abroad in this world of sense. Neither, as we have already seen, can the powers of that higher life by which our human nature is distinguished from that of the brute, find their proper objects and the conditions of their existence in the mere life of sense. They seek in the higher sphere of humanity the objects which correspond to their own nature, and in and by these they live and attain their predestined ends. Equally impossible is it that the spiritual power of which we are speaking should find its needed good and attain its proper end in a sphere below itself, or in the whole compass of the life of nature. It has its own distinct and proper end, which no capricious and arbitrary purpose of its own can ever

change, fixed by a law which it cannot annul. In
the inward principle of its being, it is essentially
above the powers of our animal nature; and the
end towards which it is borne, is equally above and
beyond the sphere of our worldly life. How then
can it gain that end, and find the rest and happiness, which, by a law of inward necessity, it still
seeks, while grovelling in a lower sphere, groping
for light in the thick darkness, and hunting through
the realms of nature for that which shall give rest
to the spirit? The depth saith, it is not in me;
and the sea saith, it is not with me. It cannot be
gotten for gold, neither shall silver be weighed for
the price thereof.

There pertains, then, to the soul of man, a spiritual power and essence, which transcends the
powers of our inferior nature, having its own distinct and necessary end; and that end cannot be
attained within the sphere of sense, nor by means
of those outward objects which are the conditions
of our natural and worldly life. In turning away
from nature, then, and distinguishing itself from
those inferior powers which seek in the objects of
this world the conditions of their existence, can it
find *in itself* that which it needs for the attainment
of its end? Can it place itself, in the confidence
of stoic pride, aloof from nature, and claim to have
in the resources of its own inward being a self-
sufficing good? In the strength of its own self-
reliance, can it exclude and repel the sense of all
outward dependence, and attain its end by its
own self-productive and unnourished energies?

To these questions, reason and experience, so far as our conscious experience can reach the case, give the same answer. Though we may be unconscious of our need, as the brutified savage is ignorant of any wants but those of his physical existence, there is yet a need there, without the supply of which the life of the spirit is but a living death, a mere negation of its true spiritual life. It is a ceaseless hungering and thirsting, an aching void, a hollow depth of inward poverty and want, which only its own suitable and infinite good can supply. For what we need, must be an adequate and suitable good. It must be that which has a specific relation to our inward necessities, and to our proper and ultimate end. And how imperative, whether we know it or not, how inseparable from the inward law of our spiritual being, is that necessity, which commands us to go out of ourselves, to forsake the resources of our own strength, to deny the pride and self-reliance of our own self-wills, and to seek the conditions of blessedness in that which is more and higher than man! Thus, in accordance with the universal law before illustrated, the finite spirit of man, like all other finite and creaturely existences, is insufficient of itself for its own end. According to the distinctive character of its inward being, it needs, and must have, that which is suited to call forth and feed with food convenient for it, its powers of spiritual life. For, as the life of sense does not truly exist, till we breathe the air and behold the light of this world of sense, and as we have the empty capacity,

but not the actual possession and enjoyment of our
higher social and human affections, without the
surrounding aspects and influences of humanity, so
till we are raised above the life of nature, till we
are awakened to a higher life by the objects of
that spiritual world to which we properly belong,
and by which in our inward consciousness we find
ourselves forever environed, we have only the
capacity, not the possession, of true spiritual life.
For what is the mere naked and arbitrary will of
man, uninspired and unarmed with inward and
spiritual strength, however terrific it may be by the
accidental possession and control of vast physical
power ?   It may, indeed, for the time, and so long
as its physical resources continue, excite the wonder and admiration of those who look only at the
world of sense ; but it has no inward life, no true
spiritual vigor, no enduring power, and accom-
plishes nothing that can endure.   The will and
the cherished purposes of the most powerful and
crafty of despots, so far as they are unsustained
by a higher principle of abiding truth and righteousness, can be effective only for a limited time
and to the extent of his physical arm.   Strip him
of his outward physical force, and in that very day
his thoughts perish.   Thus the true life and power
of the spirit must be an inward life and power ;
and to attain this, it must be fed and nourished
with appropriate food, must breathe the air and
walk in the light of the spiritual world.   As our
human affections are developed and strengthened
by that which is human, so the life of the spirit is

nourished and sustained by that alone which is
spiritual. Here, then, is the inward ground of
that need to which our Saviour refers, when he invites us to come unto him and receive the waters
of life.

But however clearly we may be convinced of
our need, the question may still very naturally
arise, Why should we go to Christ for its supply?
What is there in the distinctive character of the
wants of our spiritual being, so far as they are indicated in our conscious experience, that should
lead us to expect in and from him a corresponding
good? These questions find indeed a partial answer, yet one, for the most part, of only a negative character, in the views already presented.
What more distinct indications do we find in our
inward experience, to determine the specific character 'of our wants? Here, again, it is obvious
that only in proportion as we are excited to earnest reflection, and to a full and practical sense of
our need as a matter of our own experience, can
we be made to understand clearly what it is, or
what Christ is as suited for its supply. Yet there
are facts in the consciousness of all men, abundantly sufficient to make known to them their necessities, and to guide them to Christ. The law,
says St. Paul, is our schoolmaster to bring us to
Christ; and the same apostle asserts that all men
have a knowledge of that law. The law revealed
in the conscience of every man, is for us the necessary condition of all spiritual knowledge. How
much, too, of spiritual truth, and of what infinite

67

moment for us, is manifested in the simple fact of
conscience ; so simple, yet so central and so full of
light !   By it we know ourselves, and in its authoritative law we have the essential and immutable law of our own spiritual being, and that which
prescribes its true and ultimate end.   What is it
but this law, consciously revealed in the soul of
every man, that makes for us the absolute and immutable distinction between right and wrong, and
commands us to do right, to obey the truth, to
love holiness ?   But to come nearer the point at
which I was aiming, it is undeniable, and a truth
of highest import, that the consciousness of a holy
and perfect law, in proportion as it is reflected
upon and becomes practically efficient in our minds,
fills them at the same time with apprehensions of
God, and an inalienable conviction of his existence, as a just, a righteous and holy God.   It
opens, as it were, the eye of the soul to behold
the light of the spiritual world, and directs it to
the contemplation of God as the Sun of that world,
the eternal centre and source of its light.   Thus,
in prescribing the law of our spiritual being, and
in it the ultimate end for the attainment of which
it imperatively commands us to strive, the conscience directs us to God.   For what is our end,
as prescribed by the law of conscience, but to be
Godlike ?   Thus the ideas of a holy God, and of
our own duty and end, are inseparable from each
other ; and it is the first and great commandment,
that we love the Lord our God with all our hearts,
with all our souls, and with all our mind.   There

is and can be no higher or holier law than this. To contradict this law, to resist that in which our inmost consciousness reveals and affirms itself as absolutely and immutably good, is sin, is spiritual evil. A sense of our imperative obligation, therefore, to obey and to fulfil this law of righteousness, to realize in our own personal and spiritual being that truth and holiness which we contemplate as the glory and perfection of God, points us to our true end, and is intimately connected with our need of Christ.

But let me remark again, as another fact, already contained in what was before said, but more practically revealed in our consciousness, that the light of conscience makes known to us our own character as sinners. For in turning ourselves away from our true end, and subjecting our spiritual being to the law of our sensual nature and to the world of sense, as was represented, we have estranged ourselves from God, and live in the violation of his law. The law commands us, and enforces its authority with fearful forebodings, to love God, and to serve him in spirit and in truth. But our hearts are by nature averse to God, and choose none of his ways. Thus we find ourselves at the same time responsible to God, and violators of his law. We find ourselves guilty and miserable sinners, estranged from God, and in need of reconciliation to him. This we learn by the law ; but neither that law nor the devices of our own hearts can justify us to our consciences, or in the sight of God. We are in bondage to the world, enslaved to the law and service of our inferior natures. We need to be delivered from that thraldom, that we may freely obey the inward law of the spirit. We are without true spiritual life, our eyes not yet opened to a direct beholding of the things of the spirit. We need the quickening of a spiritual power, we need the bread and the water of spiritual life, that our souls may live. And what is that which can thus nourish and promote the growth of our spiritual life, but that to which our spiritual being is preconformed? What is it but manifested truth and righteousness; that which has in it the power and the life of the spirit? This it is, inwrought and received, as the inwardly nourishing and sustaining power and life of our personal being, that can alone satisfy our wants, make us at peace with ourselves, and reconcile us unto God. By contemplating these particulars in respect to the nature of our wants, we may understand, in some measure, what objects are suited for their supply, and appreciate the blessings that are proffered in Christ.

Once more I remark in this connexion, that as our needful good, and the condition of spiritual life in our souls, we require, in the object of our spiritual intercourse and contemplation, a personal being. If, in relation to our human affections, as pertaining to social existence, it is the expression of self-conscious and personal intelligence, and of moral qualities as connected with a personal will, which essentially fixes our regard and nourishes our human powers and affections, much more, in the highest concentration of our spiritual energies upon their highest object, must that object be personal.   It is the inalienable law of conscience, that we love God with all the heart, and soul, and mind. It is the first and great commandment.   Has he then no heart ?   Has he no personal and self-conscious existence ?   If not, then is prayer but a mockery, and conscience a dream.   But we are told that truth, and goodness, and holiness, are the objects of love ; and by the contemplation of these, we are to be nourished and attain the end of our being.   What then are these, and how are they possible objects of contemplation and love, except as pertaining to the personality of Him that is true, of Him that is good, and of Him who alone is holy ?   Can we pour out our supreme affections, and pay the devout homage of our hearts, to a homeless abstraction ?   Can our souls cleave with inward affection to a law of central forces, and love the power of gravity ?   Shall we, then, seek these objects of devout and religious contemplation in our own personal being, and in that of our fellow-men ?   Alas ! could we but find them there, and not rather a lie in their stead.   Away, then, with the hollow and profane delusions of Atheism, and let us, with St. Paul, love, and worship, and adore the God and Father of our Lord Jesus Christ.

But these views are designed more especially to demonstrate our need of Christ, according to the second and less obvious meaning which I ascribed to his language in the text.   Would that I could awaken that actual sense of need, and that con-

scious longing and thirsting for the waters of life,
to which his gracious invitation had a more direct
reference. Except as it awakens the mind to reflection, and so leads to this, all speculative truth
in religion is indeed but an empty show, and all
preaching vain. In what I have said in the previous parts of this discourse, I have endeavored to
show, that the earnest and loud cry of our Saviour,
as he stood upon the threshold of that temple, and
in the ears of that vast multitude, was not without
cause. I have endeavored to make it evident, on
no superficial grounds of conviction, that he who
thus claimed the attention of men, knew what was
in man. I have aimed to render in some degree
intelligible, the inward ground and reality, and
something of the character of those wants which
should lead us to Christ, as the truth and the life,
as the suitable and adequate good for their supply.
But it is, after all, chiefly by looking into your own
hearts, by listening to the voice of your own consciences, and turning your eyes to the light of
spiritual truth, which is always radiant there, that
you are to know, and understand, and receive the
truth, so as to be benefitted thereby. There, if
you are faithful with your own souls, and banish
all false delusions from your minds, you will find,
that you are truly in need of Christ. You will be
conscious of the hungering and thirsting of your
inmost spirit after that spiritual good, which alone
can fill the capacious void. You will there learn
more than all books can teach you, of that root of
bitterness in the heart, which the divine power of

Christ alone can extract; of that disease of the
will, which he alone can heal. It is only there
that you can fully know, and there only by slow
degrees, the depths of your guilt and alienation
from God; that you can truly understand the relation to your crying necessities of that glorious provision which is made for their supply, and be
awakened to any due sense of grateful acknowl-
edgement, that the same God whose hand supplies
the daily and hourly wants of our bodies, and
whose higher care has surrounded us with provisions for the larger capacities of our nature, has
here too appeared in the highest manifestation of
his love, to deliver our souls from death. Would
that we might all so feel and understand our own
lost and ruined condition, the depth and the character of our poverty and want, as to adore that
love which passeth knowledge, and rightly to appreciate and desire the riches of the glory of that
inheritance which is laid up in Christ for all them
that believe. And let us remember that this will
soon be not only our chiefest, but our only want.
These eyes will soon cease to require the light of
the sun, and the vital air will be nothing to us.
Nay, the higher wants of our human nature, those
connecting us with our fellow men, by the noblest
and the strongest ties of mere human affection,
must cease, and their objects no longer be sought.
For, in the expressive language of the apostle,
This I say, brethren, the time is short. It remaineth, that both they that have wives, be as though
they had none; and they that weep, as though

they wept not; and they that rejoice, as though they rejoiced not; and they that buy, as though they possessed not; and they that use this world, as not abusing it; for the fashion of this world passeth away. But when shall we cease to need those objects which are connected with the attainment of our highest and ultimate end, as spiritual and personal beings? When will the inward eye of the soul cease to require the presence of Him who is the light of the spiritual world? All those powers that properly belong to our nature, have their growth and decay, their highest point of developement, their revolving periods, and their appointed bounds, which they cannot pass. But what periods are determined, and what bounds are appointed, in the possible existence of that supernatural and self-conscious being in respect to which we are said to be made in the image and after the likeness of God? Who shall assign limits to the capacity for its appropriate good, and the need of its continual supply, or to the destined enlargement and expansion of that soul whose thoughts not only wander through, but essay to grasp and comprehend immensity and eternity, and whose desires can be filled with nothing less than God?

How happy, then, yea, how blessed of God are they, who, awakened from the lethargy of sense, to a consciousness of what they are, and of what they need, and quickened to spiritual life, have sought for and have found an adequate spiritual good, and suited to their now conscious desires!

It is then only, indeed, according to the language
of the apostle, that we can know the things that
are freely given to us of God, when we have received the spirit which is of God.   It is only by
the power of a higher spiritual principle of life
within, that we can either rightly apprehend, or
truly desire and appropriate to ourselves, the abundant spiritual blessings which are so freely proffered for our acceptance.   But those in whom this
power is awakened as an actual living power in
the soul, necessarily desire and seek for and recognize its corresponding good.   Where spiritual
life exists, in other words, there is a consequent
hungering and thirsting for spiritual food.   There,
too, is a just and true apprehension of those objects that correspond to our spiritual wants, as
suited to nourish and unfold the powers of spiritual
life, as being indeed the highest and only absolute
good.   The natural man receiveth not the things
of the Spirit of God, neither can he know them;
but he that is spiritual, judgeth all things, and has
his senses exercised to discern both good and evil.
Thus, with appropriate agencies inseparable from
the existence of spiritual life in the soul, those who
are born of God open the eye of faith to apprehend the objects of the spiritual world, and not
only need, but consciously desire and long for spiritual good, as the proper nourishment of that inward life.   To satisfy its cravings, no sensual or
worldly good can suffice.   Nor is it the mere
vague desire of happiness, which is inseparable
from all conscious existence, that distinguishes

68

them. They seek for truth as their proper object,
as the eye seeks for the light of the sun. They
hunger and thirst after righteousness, as having
the same relation to the inward life of the spirit,
which bread holds to the outward life of the body.
As the powers of spiritual life also transcend, in
their essential character and destiny, the powers
of our natural life, so should the desires which
grow out of them and the conscious necessity of
attaining the proper objects of those desires be
more intense and prevalent than all the cravings
of our inferior nature. Thus it would seem but a
matter of necessity that in the awakened consciousness of spiritual life, the soul should cleave
to the things that are spiritual, whatever other
objects of desire might be torn from its grasp. It
cannot but desire and strive for the possession of
these, with more earnestness of purpose than for
all that pertains to the sphere of our worldly life.
In the awakened energy of that higher principle
which cometh from above, and is now received as
the inward principle of its life, it breaks through,
as it were, and dissipates the forms which pertain
to the outward life of sense, dissolves or trans-
forms into its own image and likeness all the bonds
of natural interest and affection, and with the eye
of faith still contemplating its appropriate objects,
desires and pursues them as of paramount and indispensable necessity. These it must have, though
to attain them it should encounter evils from
which all the powers of our nature shrink with
amazement and terror. These it must have, though

it deny father and mother and wife and children ; though not merely a right hand and a right eye should be sacrificed, but the body be doomed to the rage of wild beasts or to the consuming flame. And these are the objects of desire, for the attainment of which Christ invites us to himself in the language of the text : If any man thirst, let him come unto me and drink. He that cometh unto me shall never hunger, and he that believeth on me shall never thirst.

3. With these views of the grounds of our relation to Christ, as they exist in the inherent character and condition of man, and of the specific indications of our need which manifest themselves in the different states of our inward life and consciousness, I proceed, as was proposed in the third place, to consider more directly what Christ is, as corresponding to that relation and suited to our spiritual wants. To this we are directly led by the terms of his invitation as already explained. For he not only refers to our need of a higher and spiritual good, but directs us to himself for its attainment. He proffers himself as a fountain of living waters, able to quench that thirst which the waters of Siloa could not allay. He claims to possess and hold forth for our acceptance, provisions for that spiritual need which we have been contemplating, and for which, as we have seen, the realms of nature furnish no adequate or appropriate supply. If, then, that need be such and so great as I have endeavored to show it, we may well inquire, with all earnestness, who and what is

Christ, his hidden treasures of wisdom and knowledge, and the resources of his power, that he should thus direct us to himself, and that we should trust in and obey his word? What are the attributes of his character, and under what form are they manifested to meet the essential and universal wants of our spiritual being? What is he relatively to our wants as fallen beings, as sinners under bondage to the law of nature and in a state of spiritual death? By what mysterious and regenerating power of divine love working in Christ, are we to be renewed and reconciled to God? And again, for those who are born of the Spirit, and by faith brought into spiritual communion with Christ, what are the provisions to be found in him that they may grow in grace, and that in their creaturely dependence and conscious insufficiency of themselves for the attainment of their prescribed end, he may become the substance of their spiritual strength, the bread of life to their souls?

In answering these questions, I shall aim, as the general method of the discourse requires, to show what Christ is, simply with reference to those wants, the inherent grounds of which I have already exhibited. It is only, indeed, in their immediate and specific relation to each other, that the objects corresponding to those wants, or even the wants themselves, can be distinctly and truly known. For as we could not know the distinctive character of the wants that pertain to the faculties and organs of respiration and of seeing, nor the nature of air and light as the outward condi-

tions of their exercise and the objects corresponding to those wants, otherwise than by the experience of their specific relations to each other, so
here we can have a distinct knowledge of the
wants that pertain to our inmost spiritual being,
and of Christ as the object corresponding to those
wants, only in their immediate and experienced
relations to each other as manifested within the
sphere of our consciousness.   They are what they
are, as objects of knowledge and of interest for
us, by virtue of those relations.   In showing what
Christ is, therefore, in relation to our spiritual
wants, as we may recognize his presence in different states of our inward consciousness, the nature
of our wants also will be made more distinct than
when separately considered.

In the first place, then, I remark, that in the
earliest dawn of our self-consciousness, or of our
existence as spiritual beings, and at every stage in
the developement of our spiritual powers, we find
ourselves in connexion with a spiritual world, and
the manifested presence in our consciousness of
that which has a necessary relation to our own
spirits.   That in us by which we are raised above
the blind mechanism of instinct and made capable
of a conscious purpose of free and responsible action, truly exists, indeed, in its distinctive and proper character, no otherwise than as that spiritual
presence which is the outward condition of its self-
conscious agency, is manifested to and exists for
it.   In other words, as the faculty of sight can act,
and as we can know that we possess it, only with

the presence of its proper medium, so it is with our spiritual powers. As all men, too, in all conditions of their existence, are still spiritual and accountable beings, so to all is vouchsafed the presence of that which is spiritual. That God, who, as we have seen, has so richly provided for all our natural wants, and who styles himself, in a peculiar sense, the Father of spirits, could not desert us in our highest need; nor has he failed to provide and to manifest in the consciousness of all men, that which constitutes their highest good. On his part is the same infinite freeness and fulness in providing, always and for all, that which corresponds to our spiritual need, as in satisfying our inferior wants. If we fail to recognize its presence and to rejoice in it as the light and life of our souls, we show thereby but the debasement and perverseness of our own wills. That of which I speak as the gift of God and having a specific relation to our spiritual being, is still there in all its fulness and in all its glory, and manifests itself to us as we turn ourselves to it. It is still there, a living presence, unchangeable, while all things change; and the more we open our minds to receive it, the more does it impart to us of that fulness which is sufficient for all and overfloweth. The more we think of it, too, the more do we find it to possess a reality out of ourselves and above ourselves, yet inseparable from our own permanent being.

What I have thus described, every man, who is not wholly void of reflection, will recognize as

present to his own consciousness in that of which
I have before spoken, as the manifested light and
law of conscience. We cannot but find it in that
presence of immutable truth, which, though we
may hold it in unrighteousness, still makes known
to us its existence, and reveals in our consciousness, at the same time, its rectitude, and the perverseness of our wills, its purity and holiness, and
our inward pollution. And what, then, is the presence which we thus recognize, but the spiritual
provision which God has made and manifested to
our inward consciousness, corresponding to the
essential character, and suited to the inherent and
essential wants, of our finite spirits? What is
it, but that true light, which lighteth every
man that cometh into the world? What is it,
but the necessary form in which God manifests
himself to the spiritual intuition of his rational
creatures, as the proper and only adequate object
of desire and love; as that towards which our
souls should turn with unceasing joy, as the eye
turns to the light of the sun? Can we regard it
otherwise than as that divine Word, which was in
the beginning, and by which has still been uttered in the consciousness of every human soul,
the absolute and unchangeable truth of God? Why
should we not regard it as that first-born of the
Father of spirits, wherein is manifested, from eternity, the perfection of his own glory; and which
again, to as many as receive it, communicates of
the riches of that glory, according to their capacity
and their need? So, and so only, can we represent

to our minds the universal and necessary relation
subsisting between our spiritual being and its corresponding and appropriate good.   For that good
is the ultimate, the highest and absolute good of
our souls, and nothing less than God. So only can
we adequately and truly represent it, whether we
look to the immediate testimony of our own consciousness, or to the highest efforts and attainments
of speculative wisdom, or to the revealed word of
God.

Thus we find, as it were, for the original and
essential being and relations of our finite spirits,
their own appropriate and glorious provision for
the attainment of their proper end. The same
God who has provided the various powers and capacities of our animal life with a convenient good,
and surrounded us with objects corresponding to
our human affections, has here too, in the sphere
of our personal and self-conscious being, manifested that light of divine truth, that power of the divine word, that law of righteousness and true holiness, which are, for it, both the means and the
end, the way, the truth, and the life. These, for
every soul of man, as manifested in our inward
consciousness, and proffered for our reception, that
we may grow thereby to spiritual strength, are
free as the air we breathe, more free and more
universal than the light of the sun. As the natural eye, too, by which we look abroad upon the
world of sense, is no sooner opened than it is filled
with light, and sees all things illuminated with its
beams, so that higher power of vision by which we

contemplate a self-conscious purpose, and direct
our minds to the accomplishment of an end, and
act with reference to the absent and the future, by
which we look into the vastness of infinity, and
embrace, in its wide compass and far-reaching
scope, what no finite boundaries can limit nor revolving periods terminate, this power too has its
light, the light of the spiritual world ; and if only
its eye be single, sees it appropriate objects and
is guided to its proper ends, by the clear illuminations of truth and righteousness. Thus should
we walk in the light of distinct consciousness,
obeying with rejoicing hearts that divine Word,
that righteous and holy law which guides us to
our true end, which constitutes the true and essential law of our own spiritual being, and fills our
souls with their proper and all-sufficient good. If,
then, in view of these remarks, the question be
now asked, what is Christ in relation to the original and inherent wants of our being as simply
spiritual and finite? the answer is, that the same
manifestation of the divine being, which, according
to the Gospel of John, was in the beginning with
God; the same Word which was made flesh and
dwelt among us. was, even from the beginning, as
manifested in the consciousness of all men, the
corresponding object, the appropriate good of our
personal being, and the outward condition for the
attainment of our proper end.

But it is only in the original purity and integrity of our spiritual being, that the soul of man could
be represented as turning, of itself, towards what

69

is thus provided for it, and desiring it as its appropriate good. It is only the uncorrupted will, that
whose inward principle and law of action is identical with the divine will, which thus, in its own
original agency, chooses God for its portion and
acts in conformity with his law. Nor without
that integrity and uncorruptness of our own spiritual being, can we conceive the manifestations of
the divine nature to our consciousness to appear
to us in their true character and in the fulness of
their own glory. How little indeed can we understand what would be our intercourse with God,
were there no obstruction on our part to his communications of himself? If, with all our souls, in
the simplicity and integrity of that power by which
we are made capable of apprehending and receiving the things of God, we turned ourselves to that
of which I have spoken, as still manifesting something of his glory to the inward consciousness of
man, how quickly would it degrade in our minds
all the impressions of sense, and the sun itself be
darkened by the brightness of its everlasting light!
Were our minds but freely expanded to receive
them, as the opening flower expands its leaves to the
light and air, what boundless communications of
wisdom and knowledge, of goodness and truth, of
light and life and love, would perpetually flow in
upon us! For to what end were we formed in
the image of God, and capable of spiritual good,
but that he might freely pour forth the treasures
of his goodness for our supply? How, then, would
our souls be filled with the manifestation of his

presence, and at once overwhelmed and upborne
with a sense of his all-pervading and all-sustaining
power. For if it be indeed true that in him we
live and move and have our being, what needs
there but to take away the veil from our inward
eye, that we may see and know how near we are
to God? How infinite his condescension, how
boundless his love to the creatures of his power,
we may see indeed imperfectly by the eye of sense.
But it is only in the immediate manifestation of
his spiritual perfections, as recognized and contemplated in our self-conscious and spiritual intuitions, that we can truly know what God is, and be
prepared rightly to apprehend the invisible things
of God in the order, beauty and harmony of the
material world. In the immediate and free spiritual intercourse with that Word which was life, and
whose life was the light of man, for which we were
formed, how clear then would be our apprehension
of its living power and presence in our own souls,
and in the outward and visible world, as that by
which all things consist! How freely to us would
its informing and sustaining power and life be imparted, awakening, exalting and strengthening all
the spiritual and vital energies of our souls, and
thus securing the attainment of our highest end
in the enjoyment of our only adequate good.

But such, though the original and rightful, is
not the actual relation between the powers of our
spiritual being and that inward manifestation of
God and the things of God which are its proper
objects. We have the evidence in ourselves that

we are fallen beings. We know that we do not
in singleness of heart turn ourselves to the light of
divine truth, follow its guidance with implicit faith,
and long for its greater illuminations. We do not
delight in the voice of the divine Word, which reveals in our awakened consciousness that holy law
and will of God which we should receive as the
rightful law and the true life of our own souls.
We turn ourselves away from these, call in question their authority, and disobey their injunctions.
We trust rather to the impulses and tendencies of
our inferior natures. We confide in the experiences of sense, rely upon the unstable judgments
and limited views of our own understandings, and
thus seek our ultimate end and highest good in the
world of sense and in obedience to the law of our
inferior nature. Hence we are said to hold the
truth in unrighteousness. That true light which
lighteth every man, we are told, was in the world,
and the world was made by him, and the world
knew him not. He came to his own, and his own
received him not. Hence, too, that divine word
revealed in our consciences, which should be at the
same time the inward and living principle of our
own wills, has come to be for us an outward and
constraining law, to which our natural wills are
averse, and thus evidence their own corruption.
Thus the commandment which was ordained to
life, is found to be unto death. We recognize that
law which commands our obedience, as holy and
just and good; but we are fallen from a right conformity to it, and find another law in our members,

by which our personal wills are controlled and
placed in opposition to its holy and divine requisitions. We are estranged from a true confidence
in the manifested truth of God, and cleave to the
idols which our evil hearts of unbelief and our
self-confident but foolish and darkened understandings have substituted in its place. So blinded, indeed, does the mind of the natural man become,
and so absorbed in those objects and pursuits which
lead him away from the light of spiritual truth,
that he denies its reality, or regards it with aversion as false and delusive. His eye is evil, and
the whole body is full of darkness. His will, his
spiritual powers, are become apostate from God,
and have turned away from that gift of God which
is their proper good, and so have fallen into the
darkness of this world. Thus he is in bondage to
the law of sin, and his carnal mind is at enmity
with God. He is doomed by his own apostasy
and the perverseness of his evil will, to seek the
substance in the shadow, and to feed on ashes.
But while thus alienated from God, and lost to all
true desire and enjoyment of spiritual good, he
still retains and cannot change his essential relation
to God. As a spiritual being, he can find no true
rest or satisfaction but in a conformity to Him,
and in the reception of those divine manifestations
by which his own soul is filled with the light of
truth, with righteousness and true holiness. But
even when fully awakened to a consciousness of
his debasement, his guilt and misery, he yet knows
not nor can he apply the remedy to his deep and

fatal disease. He cannot restore the ruins of sin,
nor by his own strength nor skill recover the good
which he has lost. That divine light which should
have guided him, that friendly voice that said to
him, This is the way, walk in it, now serve but to
make known the height from which he has fallen,
and to fill him with self-reproach and remorse.
That light reveals to him the truth of the unchangeable God; but his heart is deceitful, and
there is no truth in it. That voice proclaims to
him the holy and spiritual law of God; but he is
carnal, and sold under sin. Though he has some
right views of what he needs and of what he ought
to be, and in his better judgment approves the law
of God, he still finds another law in his members,
bringing him into captivity to the law of sin.
Helpless, therefore, and conscious at the same time
that the law of truth and of righteousness demands imperatively a right inward principle of
spiritual obedience, and that all his doings originate
in the evil principle of his own natural will, aiming at no higher than merely selfish ends, he can
but despair of any obedience which he can render
in his own strength. He feels that he is indeed
a sinner, not in respect to the accidents and outward circumstances of his character and condition,
but in respect to that out of which, as their original source, his responsible actions flow. He finds
the need of help to effect a change, not in his circumstances, but in himself. He wants not new
appetites, not new instincts or passions, not strictly a new nature, but a new principle of action in

his personal will, by which to control and direct
the powers and propensities of his nature to their
rightful end.   These he now governs more or less
adequately.   But from what principle, and to what
end ?   Reflection now teaches him that it is from
a principle not in accordance with the original and
inherent requisitions of his personal being, but bor-
rowed from that nature itself, and limited by its
conditions.   He finds that the end at which he
aims, consequently, and by which all his purposes
and desires and efforts are limited as ultimate and
inclusive of all subordinate ends and aims, is that
which his individual nature prescribes, and so a
limited and selfish end.   But that divine manifestation of truth and righteousness, which he ought
to have pursued, as at the same time his proper
good and his highest end, and which has now become an accusing and menacing law of conscience,
enforces the sentence of condemnation upon this
debasement of himself.   By its light, he sees and
knows that in thus making himself and his individual interest his ultimate end, he is degrading that
power of his personal being which is essentially
universal in its character and aims, to the sphere
of that which is individual and finite.   He sees
that instead of pursuing whatsoever things are
true, whatsoever things are honest, pure, and lovely, with a free spirit, he has imposed always the
limiting and servile condition of self-interest, and
that his spirit is in bondage to its law.   Truth, as
manifested in the conscience, the proper law of the
spirit, the law of freedom, requires him to love

God supremely, as the only absolute good, and in
subordination to that, his fellow men as himself.
But in looking into his own heart, and the inward
spring of action there, he cannot but see that the
same evil principle limits and pollutes his regard,
not only for his fellow men, but for God, for his
truth, his holiness, and his glory. He is now convinced that under the dominion of that principle,
he has set up himself in the place of God; that
he has made his own selfish interests paramount to
the interests of truth and righteousness. That
holiest and most imperative law, the first and great
commandment, he constantly violates; and the
wrath of God, which is revealed from heaven
against all ungodliness and unrighteousness of men,
now encompasses him with its terrors; for he cannot
but confess that he too has changed the truth of
God into a lie, and worshipped and served the
creature more than the Creator, who is blessed
forever. That idol, self, is between him and the
ever-blessed God. On it his affections centre, and
cannot rise to freely expand themselves upon those
objects which he yet knows to be alone worthy of
supreme regard. However he may control the
impulses of his nature, and subject them to the
law which he imposes; however he may strive to
bring them into subordination to the divine law,
he still finds that the ultimate motive and end are
the same. He is only more consistently and prudently selfish, and has not yet escaped from the
bondage of evil. Yet he is now fully conscious
that it is evil, and that it has its root in his own

heart. He finds that he is himself guilty, perverse in his own will or personal being, and under the condemnation of a righteous law. He now recognizes his need of deliverance from the bondage, of redemption from the slavery, of sin. He abhors himself as an apostate from truth and from God, and dares not so much as lift up his eyes to heaven. He is weary and heavy laden with the oppressive sense of guilt and condemnation, and in the bitterness of his spirit cries. out, with the apostle, O, wretched man that I am! who shall deliver me from the body of this death? What divine power will interpose to redeem my personal being from its state of bondage and spiritual death, and restore it to liberty and life? Who that is all-powerful to save, will break through the strong bonds of sin, take away the pollution of guilt, make me at peace with God, and bring me into the glorious liberty of the children of God?

Thus, as was said more briefly under the previous head of discourse, the truth, as revealed in the conscience, applied to the motives of our actions, and so the condition of our self-knowledge, has become a law for us, and our schoolmaster to bring us to Christ. It makes known to us our lost condition as sinners, and our need of his redeeming power. But I have resumed and dwelt upon this point here more at large, with a view to the great question, What is Christ in relation to our wants as sinners? I have represented the mind as awakened to reflection, and becoming more and more conscious of these wants, both as to their intensity and their

70

distinctive character.   I have endeavored to show,
in some measure, as revealed in the conscience of
the awakenned sinner, the oppressive burthen and
guilt of sin, and the necessity there is of a power
out of himself, as the condition of his deliverance.
It is only in the awakened consciousness of our
character and condition thus represented, that we
can understand or appreciate our need of Christ,
and what he is for us as the Redeemer and re-
storer of fallen man.   It was obviously because of
our fallen condition, of our state of spiritual death
and alienation from the light and life of God, that
the great work of divine love and mercy manifested in the incarnation of the Son of God, became
necessary for our salvation.   It is because we are
sunk in sensuality, in bondage to the elements of
the world, and under the condemning sentence of
the holy law of God, that the knowledge of that
law, as revealed in the consciences of men, is no
longer adequate to procure our spiritual obedience
and happiness, and can only make known to us the
evil of our hearts.   It is in the sense of guilt and
condemnation which that law awakens, and in the
conscious terrors which it inspires in view of our
relation to a just and holy and heart-searching God,
that we are prepared to apprehend Christ as the
necessary mediator, in and through whom God is
reconciling the world unto himself.   By the nkowl-
edge in our own souls, of the deep mystery and
malignity of sin, and by that alone, can we rightly
measure and apprehend the love of God, and that
great mystery of godliness, God manifest in the
flesh.   That manifestation of divine light and truth

in the common consciousness of men, before
spoken of, pertains to the original and essential
relations of our finite spirits to the spiritual world,
and to God as the Father of spirits.   But here we
have, as it were, a condescension to our fallen condition, a love and mercy that follows us in our
guilty self-ruin and alienation, and reveals to us
the same divine Word incarnate in the world of
sense, and in the form of our own humanity, that
he might redeem us from the condemnation and
power of sin, and bring us back to spiritual life,
and to peace with God.   God so loved the world
that he gave his only begotten Son, that whosoever believeth in him should not perish, but have
everlasting life.   But time will not permit a farther developement of the answer to the question
before us.   Let me then, in concluding the present discourse, inquire, in reference to the general
view which has been given, whether we have so
heard the word of God, and so reflected upon our
need of Christ as sinners, as to appreciate the
character in which he is revealed to us in the gospel of his grace ?   Have we become so conscious
of our own guilt and condemnation, as to feel our
need of that reconciliation to God which can be
found only in Christ ?   Are we so deeply impressed with the sense of our own poverty and helplessness, as to be prepared, with all the remaining
strength of our souls, to flee to Christ as the only
Saviour of sinners?   Let us examine ourselves,
whether we be in the faith, and seek for spiritual
life from Him who is able to save, even to the
uttermost, all them that come unto Him.

ADDRESS

AT THE INAUGURATION OF THE AUTHOR
AS PRESIDENT OF THE UNIVERSITY OF
VERMONT, NOVEMBER 28, 1826.

Under circumstances like the present, I should have seemed to be disappointing your expectations, as well as violating the proprieties of time and place, if I had selected a subject for discussion unconnected with the occasion which calls me before you. I could not, moreover, while preparing to enter upon the duties of a station of much responsibility, and requiring immediate attention, have consistently diverted my own thoughts from the objects thus placed before me, to foreign or more abstract speculations; and, although these might have commended themselves more perhaps to all of us by the attractions of novelty, I could not on the whole wish to be freed from the necessity which urges the business and interests of education upon our regard. This subject, however it may have been exhausted, as to its general and theoretical principles, by eminent writers of both ancient and modern times, and rendered trite in its details by the daily discussions of our own periodical press, has still, like that of religion, a hold upon our attention, that can be lost only when we are no longer capable of improvement. Like that, it mingles itself with the sweetest charities of domestic life, and is second in importance only to that in its relation to communities and nations. It comes home to the heart of every father and of every mother, as they contemplate the future character of a son or a daughter, and in the minds of the wise politician and philanthropist is associated with their dearest hopes and most labored efforts for the improvement of society. It is practically connected with our daily and most interesting duties ; and its principles can never be too well understood, or too faithfully applied, by those who wish well to the happiness of their country.

But aside from the more general claims which this subject has upon all men, there are circumstances, if I mistake not, in its relation to the people of this country, which give it additional claims upon our attention ; and perhaps the present occasion cannot be more appropriately employed, than in contemplating *some of the peculiar advantages which we enjoy, as a people, for giving efficacy to the power and influence of education, and some of the higher results, in the general cultivation and well-being of society, which we may reasonably expect it to accomplish, or towards which at*

*least our efforts in relation to it should be di-
rected.*

I am well aware, that on subjects of this kind
there is great danger of being seduced by the delusions of self-flattery, and of indulging hopes that
are never to be realized ; that we, in this country
especially, have been charged, and perhaps not
without sufficient cause, with exhibiting an unusual degree of these weaknesses by drawing upon
the day-dreams of futurity for the gratification of
our national vanity. But, if there is danger of
yielding to the extravagancies of hope, and of ven-
turing in our anticipations too far beyond the sanctions of experience, there is in our circumstances,
perhaps, no less danger of limiting our views of
what is possible in the conditions of society too
much by our knowledge of what has been accomplished, and of thus having our active virtues paralyzed, and our well-grounded and self-realizing
hopes of the future withered, by coming under the
fascination of the past. In discussing the subject
of education especially, we cannot be too often reminded, that we are making an experiment upon
its efficiency, as yet untried in the progress of
human society. It is not that we profess to know
more of the principles or practice of education, as
an art, and in its individual applications, than was
known by Quintilian. So far, it may have been as
well understood and as effectually applied under
the dominion of the Ptolemies and the Cæsars, as
it is, or is likely to be, among us ; but in its more
extended influence on the condition and well-being

of community, and so of its members in their
social relations, it is accompanied and rendered
effectual by political and moral principles which
had not then dawned upon the world ; principles,
too, of mightest energy, and of intensest interest
to the general mind, which, among other nations,
are cautiously hushed to repose in the dormitory
of the soul, or, if partially aroused, are held in
durance by the chains imposed in their sleep, but
which among us have been active and unrestrained from the first landing of our pilgrim fathers ;
which have given birth to the ideas of society now
realized in our institutions of government and religion ; which are to us as free and as vital as the
air we breathe, and attest their vivifying presence
by the comparative enlargement and elevation of
soul which every where pervade our population.
What these are comparatively, and what is the
special importance of the principles to whose influence I have ascribed them, in giving efficacy to
the means of knowledge and improvement, is best
known to those who have had opportunity to compare the spirit of society among a free people with
that which prevails among a passive and humbled
peasantry, hopeless and therefore thoughtless of
improving their condition ; or to those benevolent
but unfortunate individuals, who, knowing the value of knowledge and of character to men in every
condition, have labored to impart them to the
minds of their slaves. These principles, our common birth-right, and the experience and knowledge
of ourselves, the feeling of independence, and

sense of personal responsibility in the performance of duties which our institutions impose alike upon all, and to which we unavoidably grow up, form a common substratum of general character, on which each individual more easily and more permanently lays the foundation and erects the superstructure of his own ; they constitute a living and life-giving root, on which the homogeneous principles of truth, of knowledge and of social improvement may be engrafted, and thus yield a more abundant harvest. For they are not merely proclaimed with imposing solemnity in our declarations of right and our constitutions, thenceforward to serve no other purpose but that of a dead-letter introduction to our statute books ; but reflected back from every page that follows, and infusing their spirit into all the actual forms and positive institutions of society, they impart to all a higher degree of practical efficiency, and are felt in their all-pervading influence by thousands who are unconscious of their power, as the vital principle of the atmosphere gives warmth and life to those who are ignorant of its nature.

But perhaps their legitimate character and effects are no where so clearly revealed as in that remarkable institution, to which we are interested more especially to attend, the institution of common schools. In the minds of those by whom our principles and our form of society were bequeathed to us, the maxim that all men are alike independent and have the same right to act in the various relations of society, awakened of necessity the idea of so providing for the instruction of all, that they should be qualified to act well. Hence, at a very early period after the settlement of New England, free schools were established ; and a system, unknown in every other country, which provides that the property of all shall be taxed for the education of all, under some varieties of form, now every where prevails. The object or the effect of this is not, indeed, to give very eminent attainments to any ; but to accomplish what the spirit of benevolence is now aiming at in other countries ; to implant the great principles of knowledge, of morality and religion, and to elevate the condition and character of the great body of the people. It goes among us to establish and secure forever the principles of equality, from which it sprung ; to secure the lower from the insults of the higher, and the weak from the oppressions of the powerful. It prevents, therefore, all those evils, which, in other countries, have arisen from the opposing interests of different classes of the community, and obstructed the progress of general improvement. Instead of limiting our thoughts to a few only, it extends our hopes and our designs of improvement to all the members of the body politic, while it presents them to us in a condition best suited to receive the benefit of our labors.

It might be said, perhaps, in regard to the superiority which we are here claiming, that, although in a different way and by a different mode of instruction, the citizens of Athens were as intellectual, as highly cultivated, and as jealous of their liberties,

71

as we are. But even admitting that in their theatres, at their public games, and in their academic groves, they exhibited more acuteness and activity, more cultivation, if you please, of the intellectual powers, counterbalanced, as these were, by a dissoluteness of morals almost beyond our belief or conception; we shall, as christians, and with our views of social happiness and cultivation, be little disposed to retract our claims of superiority of condition and of promise, when we consider, that in the whole population of Attica, these proud distinctions, and that lofty independence of spirit of which they boasted, were confined to a few thousands, and, in perfect accordance with the political and moral principles which then prevailed, were purchased at the expense of more than twelve times their number of slaves in a state of physical and moral degradation, by the unprincipled oppression of strangers among themselves, and by the frequent ruin of their colonies abroad. Nearly the same remarks may be made with justice of the inferior and less general cultivation of the Romans. To them, the idea of extending liberty and instruction to all, to those who performed the labor as well as to those who enjoyed its fruits, to the poor as well as to the rich, had never occurred as even possible. Not only the sensual epicurean, but the stoic philosopher and speculative statesman had no higher conceptions of a perfect form of society; and their most ideal theories of a free state took for granted the necessity of the citizens being supported by the labor of slaves, that they might have leisure to cultivate their minds and attend to the concerns of the public welfare. Even in modern times, indeed, and under the influence of christianity, till a comparatively late period, the means and principles of education were confined to a very small number. Comparatively a few only, constituting for the most part the higher ranks of society, enjoyed its advantages personally, or felt much of its indirect influence, in any country. Even in those countries most distinguished for literary privileges and attainments, the great mass of the population, whether in the condition of slaves or vassals, were not only placed, in fact, but believed to be placed of necessity, beyond the reach of instruction, and remained, to almost as great a degree as the slaves of antiquity, at a hopeless distance from every form of intellectual improvement, ignorant of letters, and unknown to history.

Since the Reformation, indeed, there has been in Europe, and, of late, through the efforts of benevolence, in other parts of the world, a gradual extension of the blessings of knowledge to all classes of the people. In the Protestant countries on the continent of Europe, and in Great Britain, schools are established for the more or less general diffusion of knowledge; but no where are they made, as they are here, an important and leading object in the policy of government, or supported on the same sure and liberal principles which have been adopted in this country.

And even if they were universally established and supported, there is by no means that entire community of privileges and excitements to exertion, which has so great an influence in giving efficiency to our system. The same prevailing opinions which formerly operated to exclude the body of the people entirely from the means of improving their condition, still operate, though in a less degree. The existing and established forms of society still have their influence; and even in England, amidst the great and benevolent efforts now made for the instruction of the laboring classes, the political expediency and safety of such a diffusion of knowledge are to this moment disputed by no small portion of the privileged classes. The efforts of the wise and the benevolent are baffled by the apathy of humbled ignorance on the one hand, and by the officiousness of proud ignorance on the other. In this country alone is the experiment undergoing a fair and unprejudiced trial, of placing all classes and all individuals theoretically and politically upon the same level, and providing for all the same system of free, public instruction. Here alone, among civilized nations, is political aristocracy entirely abolished, and the aristocracy of nature permitted and assisted to grow up, unrestrained by artificial relations and forms of society. Our advances in general improvement are neither frowned upon on the one hand by a privileged nobility, jealous of their rank, and cautious lest the toe of the peasant should come too near the heel of the courtier, nor on the other our efforts retarded, our energies of mind exhausted, and our resolutions and hopes dissipated, by a sensual and degraded race hanging upon our skirts, from whose minds the gladdening rays of knowledge are excluded alike by our precaution-ary measures of self-defence, and their own incrus-tation of sensuality. In the development of our form of society, the only collision that can arise from the cultivation of any or of all classes, must concern individuals only, and arise from the free and fair competition of talents in the general strug-gle for advancement. This competition it cher-ishes, and renders subservient to the general improvement, while it furnishes security against its evils. But no class of society can hope to ren-der their condition more secure or more happy by repressing the aspiring efforts of another. If evils, real or imaginary, result from such a system, they are trifling compared with its beneficial effects,— are felt under every form of society, and are such as will accelerate that general progress of cultiva-tion, in which they will find their remedy. If a little knowledge renders men self-confident and presuming, the only method of curing their folly is, to give them more. If the refined taste and fas-tidious feelings of the cultivated are scandalized by the necessity of holding intercourse with those of grosser habits, our state of society provides but one remedy, which is, to awaken and cherish the feelings of modesty and docility, by giving them clear conceptions and living examples of more perfect character, and with all patience and long-suffering to teach them refinement.

But while we observe with gratitude such tendencies to improvement, and find so much to encourage our efforts and give them a permament effect, in our frame of society and in the principles for which our fathers contended, we should do injustice to ourselves, if we did not associate them, as they did, with other principles of a still more elevated and more sacred character. We can never forget, nor can we be too careful to remember, that religious liberty, the right to worship God according to the dictates of their own consciences, was the great object, for the sake of which they at first asserted their political rights. In their minds, it was the power of religion, — the profound and abiding conviction of its divine principles and its obligations, that gave their highest importance to the rights and forms of human government. It was their views of eternity, and of its interests, that exalted and substantiated the interests of time. It was the power of faith in the objects of another world, that sustained their spirits, and enabled them to undergo hardships and accomplish enterprizes, the consequences of which have formed a new era in this. It was, in a word, the BIBLE and the great ultimate principles of human reason which it announces, that had taken possession of their minds, and kindled up there an enthusiasm which no earthly power could subdue. From these originated the new and sublime ideas of human government and human society which they cherished, and which their posterity have so far realized. From their

practice, as well as from their theoretical principles and their order of precedence in their own
minds, it followed too by an easy inference, that
the principles of religion, being of higher importance and antecedent authority, could not, in any
of their developements, be subjected to those of a
political nature. Thus the principles which Milton proclaimed to unbelieving Europe, were put in
practice here, and history now furnishes an argument for their confirmation, which the genius even
of Milton could not discover. While the nations
of Europe, even those which are Protestant, have
still endeavored to control the power of religion
by human institutions, and to give efficacy to its
divine authority by the enactments of human legislation, and still believe their establishments necessary to its support, our experience furnishes, by
its contrast with theirs, ample proof that the effect
of their system has been only to overbody and en-
cumber the spiritual energy of religion with worldly interests and intermixtures ; of ours, comparatively, to give it a wider expansion, and its own
divine efficacy in subduing the hearts and forming
the characters of men. For, notwithstanding the
many faults in public as well as individual character, which good men have deplored, and the temporary effects of the revolutionary war, and the ab-
sorbing interest of politics that succeeded it, perhaps no people have ever felt the influence of the
Bible so permanently, so efficaciously, and so universally through all ranks of society, as the descen-
dants of the pilgrims. There has been less of that

passive acquiescence in its truths, which neither
implies nor produces the exercise and conviction of
the understanding, than prevails where religion is
more connected in the minds of the people with
their worldly interests. The sublime principles
and ideas every where proclaimed in the Old and
New Testament, even where they have not gained
an habitual control over the heart, have more universally called into vigorous exercise the rational
and moral powers, and produced a speculative
faith. The sense of religious obligation and the
authority of conscience have consequently a greater
influence on the intellectual character, and the
fears and hopes which a consciousness of responsibility and the revealed sanctions of religion awaken, exert a more powerful influence over the popular mind. The inference from all this is, that
we have not only more already accomplished in
the moral elevation and well-being of society, but
a more sure foundation in the religious as well as
in the intellectual character of our population, on
which to erect the superstructure of future improvement, than can be found among any other
people. For as religious principles were the starting point and the source of all those ideas which
we have realized in our institutions, so the influence of religion on the moral character and the
intellectual habits and acquirements of the great
mass of our population is still the foundation on
which those institutions rest. Thus, while poli-
ticians in Europe consider it an essential part of
civil government to support religion, we have re-

versed the order, and look to our religion as the
only effectual support of our government; not indeed as a part of the political system, associated
and become one with it, as seems to have been
the original design, but the basis on which it rests
in the hearts of the people. For it is not only
withdrawn, more than in any other country, from
all secular interferences, but abstains from directly
interfering with all secular interests. It sustains
itself in and by its own spiritual life and energy;
and while it is independent of all aid from human
institutions, and claims connexion only with heaven
and the hearts of men, as its appropriate home and
abiding place, it still sends forth its energizing and
quickening spirit through all the complicated forms
of society, building up the ruins that are fallen
down, uniting and organizing anew the elements
of good, which the warring passions and interests
of men had torn asunder and scattered abroad,
and budding and blossoming forth with rich luxuriance in the refined and pure affections of social
life, and in the nobler enterprizes of benevolence.
In the character and condition of the great body
of the people, its influence is visible, even to the
passing stranger, in the appearances of comparative
decency and regularity, which so generally prevail;
and let it never be forgotten, when, in passing
through our country, we look with pride and joy
from the summit of some lofty mountain upon the
rich and splendid landscape beneath us; upon the
varied tokens of wealth, and prosperity, and happiness; upon the cultivated and glowing fields, and

72

the thick clustering villages, which impart by their
presence a human interest to the mountains that
hang over them and the rivers that wind around
them, O, let it never be forgotten, that the talis-
man which has called up before and around us
this more than "*phantom* of delight," this vision
of substantial beauty, is no other than those taper-
ing spires, which in every direction we behold
rising among the hills, and pointing to heaven.
That fervent and holy communion of men's hearts
with the objects of another world, which they
indicate, imparted an unearthly character of dura-
bility and progressiveness to their doings in this;
it awakened those deep-rooted principles that
actuated them, and gave birth to those sublime
ideas of beauty and perfection which were a light
to their understandings, and have not only realized
what we may behold from a distant elevation, but
in each and all of those numerous villages have
stirred up a spirit of active beneficence, and scattered along their shaded streets the schools of
knowledge and industry, have diffused the blessings of order and domestic comfort through all
their dwellings, and from their outmost borders,
and far up among the hills, have banished from the
view of the traveller the disgusting haunts and
deformities of vice.

And while we rejoice, with more of thankful-
ness than of pride, in such fruits of the piety and
wisdom of our fathers, we are encouraged in all
our labors by the belief that the same productive
energies still exist in all their fulness and vitality,

and that our labor shall not be in vain. While, in
other countries, the efforts of those who are be-
nevolently aiming at the general diffusion and increase of knowledge and social happiness are baffled and retarded in their effect by the conflicting
passions and interests that are connected with an-
tiquated but unyielding forms of society, and by
the fears of even good and wise men, in most
countries, lest disorder and revolution should be
the consequence, we have the way of improvement
open and plain before us; a population already intelligent, and therefore more conscious of their
wants, and more capable of advancement; so
skilled in the arts of life, as with all the labors of
society upon their own hands to find leisure and
inclination for still higher attainments in knowledge, and capable, as those arts shall be still farther improved, of indefinite progression; under a
form of society and of government established
upon general principles so simple and so powerfully
commending themselves to the understanding and
reason of all men, and withal so conclusively approved in practice, as to be perplexed with no fears
of change. In pursuing the great object, indeed,
of improving our condition as a people, through
the influence of education, and of attaining, or approaching at least, all those forms of ideal perfection in society at which our religion teaches us to
aim, we feel ourselves delivered from the slavery
of fear, and given up unshackled to the promptings
of hope; and if it be indeed true, as we are compelled to admit from the facts of history, and as

the most philosophic historians have believed, that the religion of the Old and New Testament has been mainly instrumental in raising the Christian world to its present comparatively high degree of knowledge and civilization; if it be true that our pagan ancestors of the North of Europe were elevated far above the debasing horrors of their own paganism by the awakened hopes and fears of Christianity, in its then corrupt and sensualized forms; if it be true that the power of the same religion delivered the Protestant nations of Europe from the thraldom of Papal superstition and tyranny, and, recovering still more of its native divinity from the burthen of sensuous and cumbrous ceremonials, inspired our fathers with faith to seek on these shores an asylum for the more free developement of its spiritual energies, and secure their influence upon "those who should come after;" and if, in that more spiritual form, it has already produced an elevation of the great mass of the people, in their moral and intellectual character, above the condition of any other people, and well nigh delivered us from the fear and the power of human laws, by giving to society "a power of moral efficiency above and beyond the law;" then may we with good reason hope, that, in the farther developement of its spiritual and heavenly powers, it will bear us onward to yet higher degrees of social happiness and perfection.

Nor is this animating hope discouraged, on a nearer view, by the existing state and prospects of religion among us. We have had sufficient expe-

rience to be convinced, notwithstanding all we
may find to lament, that religion will best sustain
itself, in its spirituality and efficiency, in the independent condition in which we have placed it.
We have proof of it in our multiplied and increasing voluntary associations for every purpose of religion and charity. We have proof of it, and of
its increasing effect in promoting the intellectual
and moral improvement of the people, in the dis-
tribution of Bibles and Tracts, in the establishment of Sabbath Schools and Sabbath School Libraries. In all these, indeed, we may find ground
to hope for far more than we have yet experienced,
in the efficacy of the public system of instruction,
and in the general character of the popular mind.
And even in its influence on the higher forms of
knowledge and cultivation, we have much to hope
from the increasing enterprise and more clerkly acquirements of our clergy, from their more general
and more habitual recurrence to the original sources
of religious knowledge, and an apparent inclination towards the higher ethics and more spiritual
philosophy of our ancient divines. In all things,
as well in relation to society at large as to individual character, indeed, the spirit of the Gospel, and
the nature of the ideas to which it gives birth,
teach us to go on to perfection. And why may
we not, without the charge of presumption, indulge
the hope, that by its all-powerful aid, and the more
efficient application of the means within our reach,
the universal standard of intellectual cultivation
may become far more elevated than it has yet

been, and the power of moral principle increased, till every family and every individual shall feel to good purpose the influence of motives, far nobler and purer than the fear of human laws. To realize all this, indeed, to a very eminent degree, it seems only necessary to carry into general operation the methods of instruction already introduced and partially exemplified in their effects in some of our cities and villages. These methods, securing to so remarkable a degree the essential article of economy, and applying the general principles of instruction with a practical effect so entirely beyond what is attained in our common schools, and withal so capable apparently of universal application in a state of society constituted like ours, seem to afford a sure presage, that our children are destined to a far higher degree of improvement, than has fallen to the lot of their fathers — that the ability to read and write, which was itself but a few centuries ago classed among the "arts magicall" by the majority of our ancestors, will soon be no longer the object of congratulation and boasting, as the universal attainment of our population. The results actually realized in some of our infant schools, and in others, where still the expense both of time and money falls within the limits of our general system of public instruction, and the redemption from moral degradation and crime, said on the highest authority to be so thoroughly effected by the influence of Sabbath Schools among the most exposed population of our cities, seem to give the sanction of experience to anticipations that a few years ago would have been deemed chimerical ; and, with fidelity on our part, as parents, as citizens, and as christians, to promise, at no distant period, a waking up of the dormant energies of reason and intellect, an intensity of action in the popular mind, that shall give to our social life " a being more intense," and diffuse, through all classes of society, a kind and degree of moral and intellectual enjoyment hitherto known only by the few.

Our views of intellectual improvement, however, and of acquired knowledge among the great mass of community, we know and admit, must have their limits. We cannot expect, that all men will be philosophers. We cannot hope that every farmer's son will exhibit the genius of Robert Burns, or that every votary of the awl and last, like a master-singer of Germany, will leave to posterity his half-score of folios, and never make a shoe the less. But with such methods of early instruction as have been just now alluded to, and the aid of such institutions for the improvement of the laboring classes as are rapidly going into operation in some parts of Europe and of this country, and of those village libraries and associations, the advantages of which can be so easily enjoyed among us, we may hope for the diffusion of the rich treasures of English literature, and so much of practical and scientific knowledge among all classes, that every artist shall understand the principles of his art, and the labors of the agriculturalist be not altogether empirical,—that each shall be so well ac-

quainted with the sciences immediately connected
with his daily occupation, as to be prepared to
adopt or to invent the most useful and scientific
methods of accomplishing his ends. The advantages to be expected from such practical and scientific attainments may be estimated best, by those
who have observed the superiority in the state of
the useful arts, and in the conveniences of domestic life, which the general diffusion of intelligence
has already given us over those countries in which
the laboring classes are untaught. It is not merely that with instruments adapted to their purpose
and skill in the use of them, more labor is performed with the same expense of time and strength;
but more leisure from the laborious duties of life
is secured to a large portion of the community for
the acquisition and enjoyment of the higher sources
of happiness. That habit of mind, moreover,
which a diffusion of such knowledge would tend
to cultivate and render more extensively useful, a
habit almost unknown to the laboring classes in
other countries, is already strikingly characteristic
of ours, and the source of many of those interesting and important improvements and inventions in
the arts which have been multiplied among us. It
is a habit, too, of higher dignity and importance,
in an intellectual point of view, than we might at
first imagine ; for the mind that is accustomed to
the free and bold use of its own inventive powers
in the methods of accomplishing its own daily
purposes, and, looking beyond the experience of
the past, has learned to aim at ideal improvements

in its ordinary pursuits, is of the same class with that of the theorizing politician; and the power of intellectual vision, that in the rude implements still made use of in most other places, could discover the form and adaptation to its purpose of the ordinary scythe or rake even, with which the grass is gathered from our meadows, or which seeks for ideal perfection in the form of an inkstand or of a cooking stove, may claim some kindred with that which discovered the possibility of the steam engine in the rise and fall of a pot-lid, or even with that ethereal vision, which, in the fall of an apple, saw the constructive principle of the material universe.

In regard to the higher objects of a system of education in the pursuit of the sciences, and of that general cultivation of the mind which qualifies men for the business of a professional and literary life, it would be difficult to say, with any considerable definiteness, to what points our efforts may be consistently and safely directed. It must be admitted, I fear, that the general spirit of our institutions does not, as yet, so much favor the pursuit of those higher attainments which from the nature of the case must be confined to a small number, as of those which may be common to all. The consequence is, especially in the present infancy of our schools of learning, that, in the pursuit of objects requiring for their attainment so large and costly an apparatus of books and implements of science, our efforts are often frustrated and our hopes discouraged, by the want of advan-

73

tages which the European scholar can every where
enjoy. We have, however, no reason to doubt,
that, with the growing value of those donations of
land which have in fact been already liberally given
in this and most of the other states, and the rapidly increasing conviction of the importance of
such attainments to the general welfare of society,
this evil will be gradually if not speedily removed.
In the mean time, in order to arrive at the highest
results that may reasonably be expected from the
excitements to excellence which our state of society furnishes, we cannot be too well aware, especially in this State, that economy in the dispo-
sal of our resources is indispensably necessary.
We cannot hope, from what we now know of the
sources from which they are to be derived, that
we shall ever be able to compete with most of the
other States of the Union in the pursuit of either
public or private wealth. We could not even ask
our Legislature to bestow its hundreds of thousands upon the buildings of our University; nor
have we many individuals who could, if they were
so disposed, bestow their tens of thousands upon
our libraries and philosophical collections. Nor
are we able, as in some other States, to derive
revenues to our higher schools from those who
enjoy their instruction. If we would encourage
and cherish the love of science and literature
among our population to any considerable extent,
we must bring them within the means of attainment by offering them cheap. Under all these
disadvantages, it was not to be expected that we

should very much abound in men of scholarlike attainments. In the higher departments of science and literature, consequently, it must be confessed that our scholars are, as a body, inferior to the scholars of Europe, though much has needlessly been said to vindicate our character in this respect. It is more correct, and more to our credit, too, to say, that the infancy of our establishments, and our very limited means for making such attainments, rendered them impossible ; and that, if we have not had scholars, we have had men who in our circumstances were far better ; men, who, in a state of things entirely novel, and such as would inevitably have led the *slaves* of knowledge and experience into the grossest practical anachronisms, had judgment and skill to shape their own course ; men who had a heart to prompt, a head to contrive, and a hand to execute; of large round-about sense and cultivated reason ; who, with no guide but the knowledge of our common nature, and the general principles which their own reason furnished, without the aid of book or precedent, could form ideas of unknown and untried institutions, and prove their practicability by giving them actual existence. Of such men we have had, and still have many ; and, while we acknowledge, with regret for the fact, that in the higher attainments of a systematic education we are inferior to the scholars of European Universities, and that our degrees in the arts are not indicative of as much sound book-learnedness as theirs, we still hope that the difference may justly be ascribed, not to the imperfect form of our social institutions, so much as to their imperfect developement; and when we shall have acquired something more of practical skill and efficiency in our systems of elementary instruction, and shall have had time to accumulate at our Collages and Universities the same means of giving and receiving instruction in the higher departments of knowledge; when our master minds can be withdrawn from the great work of completing the developement of our social institutions, and we can assemble in our cities and villages, and gather around our seats of learning, men whose minds have received a more manly discipline, and who are thus prepared for that reciprocal action of mind upon mind, which is after all the life and soul of a nation's literature; then, as we trust, may we hope to rival our transatlantic brethren in the extent and variety of our individual attainments, in the vigor and clearness of the light that emanates from our halls of science, and the glory that encircles the high places of our literature, philosophy, and religion. Then will our marts of literature, and our scholastic retreats also, be furnished with all the abundance and variety of the literary craft. We shall have an ample supply, not only of men of learned lore, the useful and laborious race of critics and lexicographers, but the numberless enthusiasts of natural science; those whose highest ambition will be gratified by giving name to an undescribed flower or fossil, and who will find matter for infinite congratulation in the discovery of a beetle or a butterfly which had escaped their predecessors. We, too, shall be thronged, in our own due time, by men of minute attainments ; by antiquarians, and topographers, and bibliographers, and the whole catalogue of German subdivisions. And, if we may safely hazard our auguries of the future from the present appearances in our literary horizon, we shall have no want of more popular writers; of those who shall weave the rich material existing in the strange facts of our early history, and in the original, enterprizing and bold characters of our early adventurers, into the variegated tissue of their own beautiful and sublime fictions, and by the power of their enchantments over the popular mind, shall evince our affinity in peculiarities of talent, as well as in our common ancestry and language, to the great sovereigns of the human heart ; of those who may claim relationship with that peculiar but powerful race, who rule with undisputed sway over the minds of our elder brethren, and who have extended the dominion of Britain, where her regal sceptre can never reach ; whose unobtrusive but fascinating voice is heard along the shores of our lakes, and among the recesses of our mountains, and leads in unresisting captivity the hearts of men who would not obey the imperative thunders of her navy.

Then too, if not till then, we may hope to have our men of poetic genius,

"men of highest gifts,
The vision and the faculty divine;"

men, who, drinking deep at the well-springs of human knowledge, enriching their intellectual stores, and building up their moral being, by daily and nightly communion with the great men of every age, and with that Spirit who enricheth with all gifts of knowledge and of utterance, shall mould the elements thus collected into the bright and imperishable forms of their own creative imagination, a monument at once to their own fame, and to the honor of their country ; men who, by that magic power which language imparts to the genius of the poet, shall give life to the inanimate, and permanency to the fleeting forms of the material world around us, and shall transport our beautiful lakes and majestic mountains in vision of glory to the people of other lands and of other tongues, and make them to glow in our own imaginations under a new and more brilliant veil of vernal splendor, of which no blighting frost shall divest them, and which can never again be hidden from our view by the gathering snows, or the lengthening darkness of winter.

We, too, like the nations of Europe in ancient and in modern times, may hope to have our philosophers, and those worthy of the name ; men of deep and mysterious thought ; men who, escaping from the thraldom of the sensuous and the present, and with large discourse of reason looking before and after, shall form their minds to the discovery and apprehensions of ultimate principles ; the ventriloquists of human reason, uttering forth her untold mysteries, and

"truths that wake
To perish never;"

who, learning to see all things in the laws of their existence, and thus the future in the present, and to divine the fate of nations from the principles that actuate them and govern their policy, shall look through the vicissitudes of coming years, and be the wise men and prophets of their day; men who, by the depth and justness of the principles which they announce, the living and productive energy of the ideas which they promulgate, shall impart wisdom to our teachers, and give laws to our legislators, thereby exerting a controlling power over the minds of their countrymen, and the future destinies of their country; who, treasuring in their minds

"the sayings of the wise,
In ancient and in modern books inroll'd,"

shall put to flight the phantasms and hollow abstractions of an unfruitful and lifeless system of speculation, shall lead us to the true knowledge of ourselves, and of that living and spiritual philosophy, which elevates knowing into being, which is at one with the truths of the Gospel, and which, beginning with the fear of God, terminates in the adoring love and holy participation of his divine nature. Such we may be permitted to hope will be the inspired and inspiring oracles of our academic groves, the philosophers who shall be honored and followed by the studious and choice spirits of their time, and in the language of a living writer not unlike themselves,

" Piercing the long-neglected, holy cave,
The haunt obscure of Old Philosophy,
Shall bid, with lifted torch, its starry walls
Sparkle, as erst they sparkled to the flame
Of odrous lamps, tended by saint and sage."

DISCOURSE.

NECESSARY AGENCY OF RELIGIOUS TRUTH IN THE CULTIVATION OF THE MIND.

[Delivered at the Dedication of the Chapel of the University of Vermont, 1830.]

O, SEND OUT THY LIGHT AND 'THY TRUTH; LET THEM LEAD ME; LET THEM BRING ME UNTO THY HOLY HILL, AND TO THY TABERNACLES.—Psalm xliii. 3.

To God it becomes us, in every enterprise, first to direct our thoughts. To recognize our dependence upon him, and in all our ways to acknowledge him, is our obvious duty, not as christians only, but as men. Nor is it the superintending control of his providence alone, that claims our regard. We are taught also to look to that inward agency of his Word and Spirit, whereby he hath wrought all our works in us. He knoweth our frame, he remembereth that we are dust; and it becomes us to remember that all our springs are in him. It becomes us to ask of him according to our need in the varying circumstances in which his providence

74

may call us to act, that his strength may be perfected in our weakness, that his light may illuminate our darkness, that his unchanging truth may dwell in and establish our inconstant hearts. Especially should we feel the propriety of doing so, while engaging in those enterprises which in their character and tendency are nearly related to the operations of his Word; and the accomplishment of which, both from their nature and their magnitude, is, in a more peculiar sense, his own prerogative. In devising means for diffusing the light of knowledge, for sustaining and unfolding through successive generations the intellectual and moral energies of a free people, and thus carrying them onward, both as individuals and as a body politic, to the ultimate ends of their being, we ought unaffectedly and unceasingly to pray to God with the Psalmist: O, send out thy light and thy truth; let them lead me; let them bring me unto thy holy hill, and to thy tabernacles. In the prosecution of such objects, the light and truth of the divine Word are not only necessary to direct our labors in the employment of other means, but are themselves the most efficient, and an indispensable means of operation.

The connexion of these sentiments with the present occasion, I trust, will appear obvious to all. The institution within whose walls we are assembled, is intimately connected with the interests of education in the community to which we belong. The character and consequences of our doings, and of the principles we adopt in its organization and management, concern not private interests, not the interests of one generation only, and not merely the personal advantage of the comparatively few who in successive generations may come under the immediate influence of its instructions. All that pertains to a literary institution, especially among a free people, is public in its very nature, and affects the character and happiness of the whole community. Such was the design, indeed, with which this institution was originally established; and it is destined, as we trust, to hold an important place in that system of means by which the people of this State are seeking to provide for the intellectual and moral interests of themselves and of the generations that shall come after them. We contemplate it as an instrument for promoting among us some of the higher and more important objects of mental cultivation, of literature and science, of philosophy and religion; as a price put into our hands and the hands of our children to get wisdom; as capable at least of becoming an agent of great power for the diffusion of light and truth, an abiding and active principle of intellectual life in the community to which it belongs. With these views of its character, of its designs and its possible influence, and of the ultimate ends with which it is connected, as an important part of our general system of means for eliciting and directing the powers of intelligence among us, we recognize the propriety and the necessity of associating with it, in the essential principles of its organization, the efficient influences of divine light and divine truth.

It is not, therefore, in conformity with established usage alone, that this place has been provided within its walls, or as a customary formality, merely, that we are assembled to consecrate it to the duties and influences of religious homage. *We wish distinctly to recognize the truths and duties which concern our relation to God, as intimately and essentially connected with the appropriate objects of such an institution.* We would hereby express our conviction, that in this and in all institutions that are concerned in the proper business of educating the minds and forming the character of a free people, the influences of religion, the light and truth of the divine Word, are essentially necessary to the attainment of the end. Such, it is to be presumed, is the general conviction among the people of this State; and by them, we trust, the principle will be recognized in its application to our whole system of public instruction. It is not, however, wholly free from contradiction, or so easily understood in all its relations as to leave no room for misapprehension. It implies, moreover, for those who admit it as a principle of action, corresponding obligations, upon which it becomes us to reflect, and of which we cannot be too distinctly conscious.

Let us proceed to inquire, therefore, (as the occasion invites us to do,) *what is the practical and necessary agency of religious truth in the cultivation of the mind, and what are some of the inferences to be drawn, with regard to the method and the obli-*

*gation of employing it in connexion with our gen-
eral system of instruction.*

In attempting to give a satisfactory answer to
these inquiries, as to many others relating to the
subject of education, the difficulties arise chiefly
from the vague and contradictory notions which
prevail, with respect to the nature and proper objects of an education. We cannot of course determine, in any case, the fitness and propriety of
the means proposed, unless we have distinct and
correct apprehensions of the end which they are
designed to accomplish. We cannot rightly appreciate the labors of an instructor, and the suita-
bleness of the means which he employs, so long as
we mistake the object at which he is aiming. It
seems proper, therefore, to remark in few words,
that the legitimate and immediate aim of education, in its true sense, is, not by the appliances of
instruction and discipline to shape and fit the powers of the mind to this or that outward condition in
the mechanism of civil society, but, by means corresponding to their inherent nature, to excite, to
encourage, and affectionately to aid *the free and
perfect developement of those powers themselves.*
We do not seek, in devising methods of instruction
and selecting the means of mental excitement, to
ascertain what will qualify the subjects of it for a
predestined routine of occupations, but what is the
character of their minds, and what will best serve
to stimulate their growth, to elicit and cultivate
their latent powers. The question is not what
will make them skilful lawyers or adroit politi-

cians, but what will make them men. Nor is this a distinction of trivial importance. It affects not only our speculative views of an education, but to a great extent also our practical methods of instruction. It should be added, that in nothing pertaining to an education is its practical importance so great, as in that to which our present inquiry relates. If, in providing for the instruction of the young, our guiding purpose be, as it too often is, to prepare them for attaining some worldly end, we make them, in fact, subservient to that end. If their whole education be conducted with an ultimate reference to their success in the world, as merchants, for example, or civil engineers, or as professional men, the results will be such a cultivation of their minds only as will shape them to the particular relations in which they are to act. The aim will be to make their powers *serviceable* for attaining the outward object, rather than to provide for their harmonious and perfect developement. The inherent claims of the mind itself, in its own proper being, its inward seekings and tendencies, are disregarded, or forcibly subordinated to some object of worldly interest or ambition. If we have right views, on the other hand, of the purposes of education, instead of aiming at some object alien to the nature of the mind itself, we shall contemplate with reverence those awakening energies that so truly claim our reverence, and carefully inquire, what is their own proper tendency and ultimate end. The great question will be, not to what worldly purpose can the mind be made serviceable, but what are the inherent claims of the soul itself; to what does it tend in the essential principles of its own being ; what constitutes the perfection of its being, and by what methods and means of education can we promote its attainment. If we distinctly apprehend and admit this view of an education, we shall be prepared in some measure to understand and appreciate the means proposed for its attainment.

Especially shall we be prepared to contemplate with growing interest that regard which we owe, in our systems of education, to the higher claims and tendencies of our being. That indeed would alone be a perfect education, according to this view of it, in which all our powers, both physical and intellectual, were cultivated and unfolded in their due proportions. But if, in aiming at the essential interests of our whole being and our highest perfection as men, we reflect upon our various faculties in their relation to the end which we have in view, we cannot but admit that the cultivation of all is by no means equally important. Thus the surprising physical powers which are cultivated by the exercises of the gymnasium, contribute in their proper place, if rightly understood, to the general perfection of our complex being. But when compared with a well cultivated understanding, how little do they add to our estimate of the man! A similar remark may be made even of those faculties of the understanding which the occupations of society lead us to cultivate with most care, when compared with those higher powers of reason and reflection. We may be convinced of this, if we contemplate them as they are sometimes manifested alone, or accompanied with little exercise of these higher faculties of the mind. The Indian hunter in the pursuit of his game, or warrior in the stratagems to which he resorts, exhibits a keenness of perception, an accuracy of discrimination, and a degree of skill in adapting his means to the accomplishment of his end, seldom surpassed by those who have enjoyed the advantages of education. Again, in the opposite extreme, among the over-civilized nations of the East, we may find men, in all the various occupations of civilized society, as well prepared to fill them, so far as the faculties of the understanding which they call into action are concerned, as in Christian nations. The native merchants and lawyers of Calcutta are not deficient in foresight or adroitness for the accomplishment of their ends. Why then are the accomplished Indian hunter and the well-bred Hindoo lawyer to be ranked so far below the well-educated man of our own Christian land? Nay, why is the most crafty and the most eloquent of all the sons of the forest, or the most far-sighted and adroit politician of an Oriental court, placed, as he unquestionably is, and ought to be, in our general estimation of his character, far below a man of plain understanding, who has grown up under the light of the gospel? Is it not because the powers which they have cultivated, however useful for the attainment of their worldly ends, are essentially, in every degree of cultivation, of

an inferior order, belonging to man in common
with the brutes ; while in a Christian land there is
among all classes a comparatively greater developement of a higher power ?   In them we may
find even more, perhaps, of that which is merely
useful with reference to the subordinate worldly
ends of civil society ; but among ourselves, more of
that which constitutes inherent and essential worth,
self-consciousness and reflection upon the ultimate
ends of our own being. Contemplate, if you
please, in their highest degree and most perfect
developement, those powers which the warrior and
the politician would think it alone necessary to
cultivate for the pursuit of their ambitious ends ;
and how far do they come short of that at which
we ought to aim in the education of our children !
Let them be the powers of a Napoleon or a Tal-
leyrand ; and suppose them, as they unquestionably
may be, to have been so exclusively cultivated as
to constitute their highest claims to our regard ;
and however they may excite, as beings of vast
power and forethought, our admiration, they cannot and should not command our esteem and veneration as men.   Contemplate, on the other hand,
a man whose powers of understanding are comparatively feeble and but imperfectly cultivated,
but who, instead of rushing eagerly and unreflect-
ingly into the pursuits of worldly interest and ambition, has turned his thoughts to the knowledge
of himself; who has communed with his own heart
and cherished the powers of reason and self-consciousness ; and we cannot but acknowledge a new

75

and higher claim to our regard. The man who has been taught to reflect upon the ultimate ends of his being, to contemplate with steadfast eye the fixed and eternal principles of reason and right, whose soul is filled and expanded with the ideas of immortality and of God, and who, at the same time, elevated and awed by the contemplation of these, walks reflectingly with a sense of religious obligation and reverence, he is the man in whom we recognize essential and inherent worth. In him we find unfolded the true and distinctive principles and characters of our humanity. We recognize in him the dawning of that light which breaks in upon us from the spiritual world. We contemplate in him, not merely powers that are serviceable as means for the attainment of an outward end ; but that which has a worth of its own, and not only deserves but commands our reverence for what it is in itself. We discover the awakening of those energies by which our humanity is allied to eternity and to God. And shall the cultivation of these be forgotten or disregarded in our methods of instruction ? Shall we neglect to unfold those powers which are of highest worth, those powers of self-knowledge and self-control which connect us with the spiritual world, while we exert our skill and exhaust our means in cultivating those in the perfection of which, after all, the brutes may be our superiors ? Show me rather the youth whose soul has been wakened up and aroused from the thraldom and lethargy of sense, from the fascination of the present and the world-

ly, to the contemplation of spiritual truths, to a
near and earnest communion with the secrets of
his own being, with the indwelling and humanizing
law of his conscience, with the self-revealing ideas
of responsibility and of God, and I will show you
one who, though unskilled it may be in the occupations of the world and undisciplined to the routine of the merchant, the warrior or the politician,
has nevertheless, in a higher sense than either, the
education of a man in the great essentials of his
humanity, of a man in the image of his Maker. It
is this waking up and actuating of the essentially
human and the spiritual in man, which we are
bound to consider the highest aim in the education both of individuals and of the community.
It is hardly necessary to add, that for the accomplishment of this, we must look to the influence of
religious truth. What other power has been found
among the arts and knowledges of civilized society,
in ancient or modern times, that could dissipate the
darkness of the understanding, by kindling up the
light of reason; that could so fully emancipate the
truly human from the domination of the animal in
man? Nor is it by a mere arbitrary agency, that
it produces such an effect upon our minds. All our
powers are actuated and unfolded by agencies corresponding to their character; and the natural light
is not more perfectly correspondent to the power
of vision and essential to its exercise, than the
presence of divine light and truth, to the developement and exercise of our rational and spiritual
powers. It is indeed the essential correspon-

dency and preconformity of our minds to the ideas
and truths of religion, that constitutes our humanity. Conceive them divested of the ideas of God,
of eternity, of freedom and absolute truth, and we
leave the animal merely, but the man has vanished.
There remains, indeed, a creature more subtle than
any beast of the field, but likewise cursed above
them all; upon its belly must it go, and dust must
it eat all the days of its life. No, the great and
commanding truths of religion with which we are
blessed, and which we have the privilege of employing as means of mental cultivation, are no outward framework of propositions for the understanding alone, and proposed as the arbitrary instruments of discipline and outward conditions of
intellectual improvement. They are rather inherently and essentially the correlatives of our inward being. They are an expressed and outward
manifestation to our understandings of that which,
by reflection, we are to unfold in our own self-consciousness and reason. No other truths can have
the same power, because no other truths have the
same relations. It is because we recognize these
relations, that we feel and cannot resist their
power. It is because they commend themselves to
our reason and consciences, as reflections of that
same light which in them, too, has its dawning,
that we cannot dispute their authority. It is because of this, that they seize with such energy
upon the minds of all men, and not only unfold and
call into action those powers of thought to which
they are more immediately addressed, but extend

their quickening energies to all the germs of intelligence, and give "unity and the circulating sap of life" to our whole intellectual growth.

If such, then, be the inherent character and necessary relations of that religious truth with which we are concerned, and such its practical influences upon the developement of the human mind, may we not draw some very obvious but important inferences with regard to the use of it as a means of education? If those specific effects which it produces are of a higher kind, and more indispensable to the well-being of the whole man, in relation to his ultimate end, than the effects produced by any other means of instruction, can it reasonably be omitted in the choice of those means? While we make provision for every other object in the education of our children, shall we leave that which, considered, as it now is, with reference to the perfection of an education merely, is more important than all others, to the operation of chance, or the general and uncertain influences of society? Or shall we entirely separate this from the inferior objects and means of education; and, while we make other and distinct provision for its attainment, exclude the exhibition and influences of religious truth from our seats of learning? To all these questions, the answer seems to me very deducible from the views which have already been given. To exclude the light and truth of the divine Word from the minds of those whom we profess to educate, and to provide in no way for securing their appropriate influence, to say nothing of its more criminal character in the eye of the christian, is the grossest absurdity to the view of an enlightened philosopher. However we may cultivate other faculties, if the higher and religious tendencies of our being are neglected, we do but educate the animal man. We may make him, indeed, a well disciplined and serviceable animal; but his true humanity is yet latent. Cheated of its prerogative, and shrouded in those webs of worldly knowledge and those inventions of an unenlightened understanding which serve but to exclude the true light from heaven, it manifests its being and its tendencies in the form only of groping superstition and idolatry, and becomes the blind and gloomy prompter of those inhuman observances which flow, even in the most civilized countries, from the "dark heart" of paganism. That the same outward results do not follow in christian countries, with regard to those whose religious education is neglected, or from whose minds the truths of religion are wilfully and so inhumanly excluded, proceeds from the fact, that, where the light of truth pervades the community, no perverted ingenuity can wholly prevent it from illuminating the minds of all. Such general illumination, in a community like our own, will indeed do much; and it is this diffusive and holy light, beaming upon our towns and villages and penetrating to every sequestered cottage among our mountains, that, without any conscious effort of their own, tends, more than all other agencies, to elevate the general character of the people, and saves even the most worldly and degraded from the gloomy abominations of paganism. But how far short is the general influence thus exerted, of the effect that might be expected from the direct and habitual and personal application of religious truth to the minds of all!

Nor is the effect at which we aim, considered as a part and the most essential part of our human education, one that can be separated, in the pursuit and in the use of the appropriate means, from the other objects and means of intellectual culture. The influence which religious truth exerts and the energies which it calls into action, are essentially connected, as was already remarked, with all our powers of knowledge and all the products of intelligence. It is not so much a distinct and separable part of what should be taught in a system of instruction, to be learned and stored up in the mind for future use, as a pervading and life-giving presence and power that should act upon the mind in every stage and process of its developement, and bring all the powers of the soul, as they are unfolded, under its holy and humanizing influence. It is not by the critical investigation of religious truth, that its great and indispensable influence as a means of education is chiefly to be secured. Most of those great truths to which this influence is to be ascribed, have little need of the aid of speculation in order to their proper effect. They are such as address themselves immediately to the intuitive perceptions of reason and conscience. They need but to be distinctly exhibited and they carry their own evidence with them. And however the evil and perverse will may place itself in opposition to the duties and obligations which they imply or impose, the effect, so far as the specific purposes of general education are concerned, is forever secured. These are " truths that wake, to perish never." When so presented and contemplated as to waken up the corresponding powers of our inward being, they become in fact identified with them. When once the ideas of God and of moral responsibility, for example, are distinctly contemplated and unfolded in our minds, no sophistry of the understanding, and no perverseness of the will, can ever dislodge them from their place, or entirely divest them of their influence. We must first cease to be rational, before they will cease to form a living and indwelling principle and power within us. It is the habitual exhibition and present influence, therefore, of the great truths of the divine word, from which the effects aimed at, by their means, in a system of education, are chiefly to be expected. In this way, at least, not only the Christian, but every rational man, who will reflect for a moment upon the nature of religious truth and its relation to the human mind, must admit that its light and power ought to accompany all our general systems of education, and pervade our schools of knowledge.

But if the energy of the divine word be as I have represented it in its relation to our powers of intelligence, an all-pervading energy; if it be as the sap of life to the living tree of our knowledge, will it not, and should it not, extend its influence, in a greater or less degree, not only to the mind of the scholar directly, as an accompaniment to other means, but as a directing and modifying influence to those means themselves, and to the subject and material of our systems of instruction? While we employ it as a primary agent in cultivating the powers of intelligence, ought not the whole system of means which we employ, to be in harmony with its influence? We must not, indeed, confound the objects and methods of a *general* system of education, either with those of a professional education, or those of the Christian ministry. It is not its purpose to teach a system of theology, nor, in the same manner as the ministry of the gospel, to concern itself with the spiritual character and condition of its subjects. But, while it is directed to its own distinctive and appropriate objects, should we not be careful that there be no contradiction and inconsistency in the means and influences which it employs? The powers of reason and intelligence, all those powers which it is the proper business of education to unfold and cultivate, belong to the same mind. Though differing from each other, and unfolded by different means, suited to the character of each, they are not contradictory and subversive one of the other. The perfection of mental development results in the united and harmonious action of all our intellectual powers. A perfect system of education would consist in the systematic agency of all such means as may conspire for the accomplishment of that end. Com-

76

mon sense would teach us, therefore, that we cannot, with propriety and consistency, combine in our
system of instruction the truths and principles of the
divine word, and other principles and influences of
contrary tendency. Our powers of intelligence are
not only without contradiction in their relation to
each other, but they instinctively tend, under the
control of reason, to systematise and reduce to consistent and harmonious principles the whole complex body of our knowledge. The mind is one,
and truth, in its relation to the mind, is one. The
power of intelligence admits of contradiction, neither in its being nor in its knowing. The more
deeply we reflect, the more distinctly shall we be
conscious that such is, and by a necessity of reason
must be, the case with every rational intelligence.
Thus the commanding power and influence of religious truth, where it is fully admitted, must especially tend to bring into harmony with its own
spirit the whole system of instruction. Nor can
any one deny that such *ought* to be the result.
Such will and ought to be the case, more *especially*
in those higher institutions of education, in which
not only the teachers, but the pupils, may be supposed capable of reflecting upon and systematising
the knowledge which they acquire. In this case,
even more latent inconsistencies would be liable to
detection ; and, whether detected or remaining latent, their influence must be injurious. Do not
the interests of *education*, therefore,—and it is
with these only that we are now concerned—do
not the interests of education, as well as those of

religion, require that we teach nothing incompatible with those great truths and principles of the divine word, which are themselves fitted to seize with such power upon the mind? Especially should all appearance of contradiction be avoided here, in that stage of an education when the mind is becoming more distinctly conscious of its own energies, and of the grounds of truth in its own being. The systems of philosophy taught usually in our higher institutions, even where they do not immediately relate to the truths of religion, call into action powers of thought and form principles of reasoning, which cannot but be applied to all our views of truth and the ground of our convictions. The spirit of philosophical inquiry, and the tendency to reduce our knowledge and our opinions to the unity of a system, consistent and harmonious in itself, cannot be restrained in its application, even if it were desirable that it should be. Is it wise, therefore, as in the Scottish Universities, to attempt to draw a line of separation between the truths or doctrines of religion and the results of philosophical inquiry?

If the principles of religion are true, and hold such a relation to truth generally and to our intellectual being as I have represented, must they not be such as philosophy also is bound to recognize? Whether we consider the truths of religion, or the truths of philosophy, indeed, as the foundation in the architecture of our minds, the *superstructure* can be such only as the foundation will sustain. The entire upbuilding of our intellectual being must spring from the same foundation of eternal truth. It must be a living temple, animated and adorned by the light and power of truth, and consecrated to the God of truth, or it will prove but the fancy-work of vanity, or the more solemn mockery of error and delusion. It was from a deep conviction of this, produced by that perception of the essential relations and interdependency of all the principles of truth which similar circumstances in the history of the human mind have always occasioned, that, in the fervor of the Reformation, so deep an interest was felt in the whole system of intellectual discipline and instruction. Thus we find, in the latter part of the sixteenth century, the most powerful minds which the excitements of the Reformation had called into action, engaged in earnest controversy on the introduction of a new system of Logic into the Protestant schools of Europe. Is it because we are wiser than they, and understand the principles of education better, that we have no Logic, and do not concern ourselves with relations of this sort? I dare not believe it. A system of education must be one system, a united and consistent whole, referable, in all that it teaches, to harmonizing first principles; or it must contain, however they may be latent for a time, the elements of distraction, of error, and of dissolution.

Such a system, consistent with itself, in unison with those principles of religious truth which concern the essential constituents and the ultimate end of our being, and irradiated by the light of the

divine Word, we are bound to aim at, in all our
plans of general education. We are under obligations, not as christians merely, but as men and
as members of a body politic, to give to the power
of divine light and truth the place which it so man-
ifestly claims, in providing for the education of our
children and the members of the community to
which we belong. Other and more mechanical
methods may give to men that partial and relative
discipline of their faculties which is more immediately sought for, with reference to the different
occupations of civil society; but only that which
forms them with reference to their ultimate end,
can make them *men*, or fit members of a *free community* of men. The means of instruction and
discipline employed in the despotic government of
the East, may, as they have done for centuries,
make those subjected to them *civilized;* may shape
and mortice them, that is, to the places, and fit
them for the special services, assigned them in the
mechanism of civilized life; but can never make
them, in the distinctive sense, *cultivated*, or give
them that self-knowledge or self-control under the
authority and law of reason, which are essential to
the enjoyment of rational liberty. We are bound,
therefore, so far as it is possible, by the influences
of religious truth in our system of education, to
cultivate and unfold the higher and distinctive principles of humanity. We are bound to do so, as
men linked by the common bonds of humanity to
our fellow men. As members of the great community of persons, of rational and accountable

beings, we are under obligations, even paramount to those which bind us to the interests of a worldly state, to promote the higher interests of our own and the common humanity. From these obligations, no mere worldly interests and no state policy can absolve us; because all worldly ends are subordinate to those which reason prescribes as the alone fixed and ultimate end of our rational being. I make this distinction, because where the State exists, with a fixed constitution and determinate worldly ends *as a State*, those ends are not identical or always coincident with the personal and ultimate ends of the individuals who compose it. Thus, in the civilized states of the East, the ends of the state are answered, when, in the division of labor and diversities of rank which the organization of society renders necessary, every individual is fitted to the place assigned him, however unfit he may be for attaining the ends of his own personal being. In this sense, indeed, the people of the East have reduced civil society to a more complete organization, in other words, they are more civilized, perhaps, than the nations of Christendom. Every individual is fixed in his place, and taught the precise duties which belong to it. It is only for the occupations of a state so organized, that a system of education designed for the attainment of particular worldly ends exclusively, can prepare its subjects. The two things, indeed, are nearly related to each other; and the perfect idea of a state formed of such subjects, and for the attainment of its own ends, with entire disregard of personal and individual ends, seems to have been conceived in the earliest periods of hoary antiquity. By the division into castes, not only the individual with respect to himself, but the parent with respect to his children, is deprived of all power and privilege, both in the choice of an object and the mode of pursuing it. All are *predestined* to fill certain stations and perform certain services in the mechanism of society, marked out for them with the greatest possible precision ages before their birth. Such is the highest perfection of state policy and state craft.

But for us and our children, in the providence of God, a better inheritance is provided. We are not the subjects of such a state, nor predestined to be mere working instruments for attaining the subordinate and worldly ends which the thraldom of civilization imposes upon us. We can hardly, indeed, be said to be subjects of any state, considered in its ordinary sense, as a body politic with a fixed constitution and a determinate organization of its several powers. But we are constituent members of a community, in which the highest worth and perfection and happiness of the individual free persons composing it, constitutes the highest aim and the perfection of the community as a whole. With us there is nothing so fixed by the forms of political and civil organization, as to obstruct our efforts for promoting the full and free developement of all our powers, both individual and social. Indeed, where the principle of self-government is admitted to

such an extent as it is in this state, there is in fact
nothing fixed or permanent, but as it is made so
by that which is permanent and abiding in the intelligence and fixed rational principles of action in
the self-governed. The self-preserving principle
of our government is to be found only in the continuing determination and unchanging aims of its
subjects. Its principle of unity exists only in the
unity of an all-pervading law of reason and conscience. Our obligation to the state, therefore,
as citizens, is simply an obligation, as men, to preserve and transmit to our children that condition
of society, in which the highest perfection and
well-being of the individuals composing it, is identical with the highest aims of the Commonwealth.
The rational idea of such a Commonwealth in its
full developement, permit me to add, would be
realized, where the powers of reason were unfolded
in all the members of the community, where all
were self-controled by the indwelling law of conscience, and where the personal well-doing and
well-being of each results in the harmonious co-
agency, the ever-living combined energy and social
happiness of all. But this, I am well aware, is
an idea which belongs either to poetry or to religion. It can be contemplated only in the ideal
creations of the poet, or in the city of God. Let
us rather dare, in the power of a Christian's faith
and hope, to contemplate the latter; to look forward to the time when, by the free and living
energy of that Word which we are privileged to
employ, our land shall become indeed the city of

God, a mountain of holiness, and a dwelling-place of righteousness.

If in any way we can be honored and privileged to be co-workers in realizing an idea so far beyond the results of past experience, and the designs or even hopes of the mere politician, it must be chiefly by promoting the cultivation of the community. If we would promote that cultivation in its distinctive and proper sense, as the developement of the truly human in our complex being, it must be chiefly by employing the more than human power and efficiency of divine light and truth. With these, should all our systems of instruction be accompanied, and by these should our schools of knowledge be always irradiated. It is from a conviction of this truth that the place in which we are assembled has been prepared in this institution, and that we have come to consecrate it to the worship of God and the influences of his word. The God who claims our homage, is wonderful in counsel and excellent in working. It is the same God who worketh all in all. Most devoutly then would we invoke his presence ; and most solemnly do we consecrate to him and his more immediate service, this place of cur daily prayers. May he ever vouchsafe to dwell in it, and make manifest his presence here by the light and power of his word. May those who teach, and those who learn, in this institution, as they assemble here for their morning and evening devotions, receive with meekness the ingrafted word, and be all taught of God. In all the appropriate duties of this place, in the whole

77

organization and instruction of this institution, and from year to year and from generation, may the quickening and elevating and humanizing influences of divine truth be experienced. From this place may a light and power emanate from age to age, pervading and informing the mind of this whole people, raising them from the slavery of ignorance and vice to the freedom of knowledge and virtue, unfolding those powers of their humanity by which they are most nearly allied to the divine nature, making them capable and worthy of those blessings of liberty which are yet untold, but which God, in his providence, has placed before us and our children. May his light and his truth be sent forth to give power and efficacy to all our institutions and means of improvement, that we may have wisdom and understanding in the sight of the nations, and that a voice as from heaven may be heard saying, Behold the tabernacle of God is with men, and he will dwell with them, and they shall be his people, and God himself shall be with them and be their God.

TRACT ON ELOQUENCE.

ON THE DIFFERENCE BETWEEN THE ESSAY
STYLE AND THE STYLE OF ORATORY.

The character of style denoted by the essay
style, is not, I believe, very distinctly defined. An
essay, according to Johnson's definition, is "a
loose sally of the mind, an irregular, indigested
piece." The style naturally to be expected in such
a production would of course be easy and inarti-
ficial, varying with the momentary fluctuations of
thought and feeling, as in the essays of Montaigne
and Goldsmith. The writer proposes to himself
no fixed object, no definite end, to which he shapes
his thoughts ; but allows himself to be guided by
the natural train of association. The style, consequently, adapts itself to the thoughts as they
rise. It may be elegant, polished, harmonious,
energetic, or sublime ; it may possess all the variety of expression which Cicero would place at the

command of his ideal orator; but that variety is undesigned and casual, not moulded, by the modifying power of the imagination and the regulative power of the understanding and will, to a unity of purpose and harmony of effect. All its movements are prompted from within by the successive evolutions of thought and feeling, and are in no regard prospective. In this point of view, the essay and the oratorical style differ from each other in a manner very nearly analagous to that which Schlegel, in his "Poesie der Griechen," has pointed out between the Homeric epic and the tragic style. The one is absolutely general and indefinite in its aim, seeking only to mould to a harmonious form and movement the successive images and feelings, as they present themselves in the mind of the poet; while in the other, the tragic style, the poet seeks not merely harmonious movements, but harmony and absolute unity of effect. He has a fixed object, a definite and preconceived result, to which every thing is made to converge. He aims to make his work an organized and harmonious whole, in which all the parts are modified and assimilated to a coincidence with the ruling spirit and purpose of the whole. If this view of the subject be admitted, it will be manifest at once that the characteristic feature of the oratorical style is, not that it employs exclusively or eminently any one of the multiplied forms that succeed each other in the indigested essay, but in that shaping and conformation of the parts to the whole which belongs to it as a work of art, as a production of creative imagination. In order to render intelligible my views of this peculiarity, I must be allowed to go more at large into the theory and some of the fundamental principles of the art.

It will be seen, from what I have already observed, that I consider oratory as belonging to the circle of the arts. As such, it is dependent for its characteristic peculiarities on the same powers of mind, or in the language of Brown, on the same species of mental action, as the dramatic or other forms of poetry. The process of mind which gives to all these their form and colors, is synthetic; and thus contradistinguished from the process of scientific inquiry, which is analytic. This latter, especially in pure *a priori* science, is, for the most part, analytic. It begins with separating intellectually and classifying ideas that exist in our minds. It is purely an intellectual process; and not only does not require, but for the time being and in proportion to the degree of its action, is incompatible with the presence of emotion. The farther and more accurately the distinctions and analysis are pursued, and the less this exercise of the mind is disturbed by the blinding influence of feeling, the more purely and characteristically scientific is the process. I do not mean to be understood as saying that this power of mind, the power of analysis, is unnecessary to the artist. On the contrary, the more penetrating this power is; the more he analyses to their primary elements the complex ideas and feelings which present themselves, the more rich and varied will be his materials for accomplishing the reversed and synthetic processes of creative genius. I say only that the creative process of the imagination, which belongs appropriately to the artist, is in itself directly the reverse of the other, and that they cannot have a coexistent exercise in the mind. He must dissolve, diffuse and dissipate; but it is only *in order* to his appropriate business as an artist, that he may reproduce what Schiller would call the elements* in new and ideal forms, that the blending and modifying power of the imagination may more easily imprint upon its material its own character, and mould it into its own harmonious creations. A clear apprehension of the generic distinction between these two modes of mental action, I conceive to be essential to a right understanding of all that is distinguishing in the productions of the arts, and no less of oratory than of poetry. In their proper place and appropriate exercise, they both belong to the artist; but in the mode of their operation they are as diverse, and as to the possibility of their co-existent exercise as incompatible, as the powers of dissolution and creation, or as the apotheosis of these powers in the Vishnoo and Siva of Hindoo mythology. Analytical speculation, with memory and fancy, are necessary to supply him with materials; but as yet they may be compared to the ʻυλη of the old philosophers,

* See his piece on the introduction of the Chorus into the Modern Drama, prefixed to his Braut der Messina.

being without form or quality; and it is in the exercise of his peculiar synthetic power, that he shapes them into beauty and harmony. It is the creative power of imagination that bodies forth " forms of things unknown, and gives to airy nothing a local habitation."

The exercise of this power not only admits, but presupposes, the existence of emotion in the mind of the artist. I cannot but consider it, indeed, the essential aim of all general arts, not only of oratory and poetry, but of the plastic arts, to embody and give expression to feelings, or to those states of mind, which Brown* has classed together under the head of emotions. An excited state of mind, an emotion, whatever its nature may be, not only gives an impulse to the imagination, but is continually present with it, and indeed constitutes perhaps an essential ingredient of its creative energy. It is not necessarily, to be sure, the individual personal feelings of the artist. It may be entirely aloof from every thing personal. It is sufficient for my present purpose to say that it co-exists in the mind with the efforts of creative genius, and that those efforts are employed in clothing it with a body which gives it its appropriate expression. The first process of the artist's power is, to conceive that state of mind which he wishes to embody in the materials of his art; that form of thought or feeling, which he aims to express or to lodge in the minds of others. It is a secondary process to

* See Brown's chapter on the classification of the powers of mind. Vol. I., p. 259.

adapt the means to the end, — so to embody the
primary conception as to give it an exact and perfect development. A work exhibits the perfection
of art, and so is classical, when this latter process
is complete, or, in the metaphysics of Coleridge,
when the secondary imagination fully and perfectly
re-echoes the primary. It is the purpose of these
remarks to show what I consider essential to a full
understanding of the subject; how the primary
conception and main purpose of the artist must
necessarily shape and modify the whole, and even
the minutest part of his production. In its external structure and conformation, it must be moulded
to the character of the conception, the form which
it is designed to embody. I shall not, I hope, be
thought to frustrate my own design, if I refer, in
order to illustrate my ideas, to the system of philosophy to which I have already alluded. The
animating and energizing forms of the Peripatetics,
as they represent them, have an agency in nature
precisely analagous to that which I ascribe to the
conceptions or forms of the artist's mind in the
productions of art. They consider those forms as
living, efficient powers ; and to the diversity of
these powers, the diversity of organization in the
corporeal world has reference. These organiza-
tions are precisely adapted to the forms which
they embody, as means to ends. Thus the mild
and gentle instincts of the lamb led to an organization suitable to its wants ; the ferocity of the
lion, to one alike appropriate ; and every soul,
says Aristotle, must have its proper body. The

aptness of this illustration to the plastic arts of painting and sculpture will be obvious at once ; and but little reflection, I think, will be necessary, to see that it applies equally well to those productions in which the poet and the orator embody their ideal creations. Here as well as there, every soul must have its own body. From the simple lyric ode of Anacreon and the sonnet of Petrarch, in which a single and momentary movement of the soul is developed, to the sublime and more varied harmony of the Oedipus Tyrannus, and the immensely complicated movements of the Shakspearean drama, and from the brief eloquence of Homer's heroes to that " which thundered over Greece, to Macedon and Artaxerxes' throne," we shall find the same principle apply. There is the same subordination of the means to the end, and of the parts to the whole. Both the poét and the orator, having once distinctly conceived the things to be expressed, the end to be accomplished, chained every power of the mind strictly to the point. The shaping and modifying power of the imagination, of which I have spoken, was ever active and was everywhere present, raising and depressing to the exact point of appropriateness, every lineament of the organized whole. Every part was so arranged as to give the highest possible unity to the structure, and harmony to the result. It is very much to my point here, that Cicero*, in the work of his old age, has referred to the inventive power, not

* See his Dialogue de partitione oratoria, c. 1.

the discovery only, but the collocation both of things and words. By that secondary exercise of the imagination, they must all be placed and modified with a reference to the whole.

Both the votaries and the critics of ancient art, were equally nice in regard to the exact appropriateness of language and imagery to the form and degree of emotion to be expressed. The το πρεπον was with them a thing all important. This was the point in which, by the consent of antiquity, Demosthenes far surpassed all his competitors. The means, the instruments of his art, were so perfectly at his command, that he not only expressed every form and degree of emotion, but expressed them in language exactly fitted to them, and without ever violating the strictest propriety. Thus Hermogenes,* in describing the style adapted to the multiplied characters, or forms of emotion, which he considers the elements of an oration, as well as in the account of that mixture and blending of them which constitutes the harmony and perfection of the combined whole, constantly refers to Demosthenes as the perfect model in all. All superfluity of language or imagery, all that was above or beyond the exact requirements of the thing to be expressed, was banished from the style of Demosthenes ; and if Cicero sometimes overstepped the modesty of nature in his youth, he lamented and corrected his errors in riper years. It was not the partial splendor and pomp of single passages, which the ancient artists aimed at, but

---

* See his book De formis oratoriis, passim.

the grand and combined effect of the whole. A French dramatist or orator seeks to be clapped and applauded at every paragraph or every line; while the genuine artist would be filled with indignation at so absurd a discord in the deep and harmonious movement which he was laboring to impart to the minds of his audience. It may be inferred from what I have already said, that I conceive it to be the business of the orator, as well as of the dramatist, to impart such movement to the minds of his audience, and not only to impart but to preserve it unbroken; to introduce nothing so directly and purely speculative and analytical* as

* Here the distinction between science and oratory cannot be too carefully observed. Thus Aristotle makes a distinction between him who seeks what is persuasive as an orator, and him who seeks abstract truth. Rhetoric, he says, teaches to present an enthymematic view of a subject, but to present it in a way fitted to persuade. The orator reasons and uses both kinds of logic, the inductive and syllogistic; but he uses them in a form peculiar to himself: not in that in which the simple inquirer after truth uses them. An *example* is a rhetorical induction, and an *enthymeme* a rhetorical syllogism. So the logic of rhetoric differs from that of science, and assumes a form capable of falling in with and increasing the current of passion. So we find it in the great masters of Greek and Roman eloquence. In his oration for the crown, Demosthenes must have had as cumbrous a satchel as any bearer of the green bag in our courts of law. He brings forward a great mass of testimonies, written and oral laws of Athens, decrees of foreign towns and of the Amphictyonic council, and records of history, all exhibited and discussed with the utmost force and clearness. But through the whole process, there is an under-current and moving power of passion and eloquence that carries us forward to a final and unavoidable result. It is as though we were embarked upon a mighty river. All is animation and energy around, and we gaze with a momentary reverie upon the deep and transparent waters beneath. But even while we admire, the current grows deeper and deeper, and we are

to be incompatible with its existence, and so disturb and interrupt the impulse that should be given. Thus, of the four parts into which Cicero divides an oration, he has appropriated the first and the last especially to the communication of an impulse to the minds of the audience (ad impellendos animos). The narrative and argumentative parts that intervene, go to substantiate and realize the movement already given.

Thus far, I have purposely classed oratory and some other forms of art together, and have treated of them only in regard to those principles which, from the general and essential nature of the arts, they possess in common. But there is one point, in which oratory is not only distinguished, but contradistinguished, from those to which I have alluded. I mean, the nature of the faith which it requires, and the consequent nature of the effect produced. The work of the dramatist is professedly ideal; and we require of him, as the conditions of submitting to the effects which he would produce, only a dramatic probability, and a harmony and unity of parts conformable to the natural and necessary principles of the art. He does not ask us to be awake and believe; but if he perform these conditions, we voluntarily surrender ourselves to illusion, and indulge in a waking dream. We suffer his magic power to transport us now to Athens, and now to Thebes; and to stir up every emotion of our souls, for the mere pleas-

unconsciously hurried onward with increasing and irresistible power.

ure with which he repays us. But then, in this case, "our judgment," to use the words of another, "is all the time behind the curtain, ready to awake us at the first motion of our will." We submit to the power of the artist, just so long as his pageantry suits our convenience or our pleasure ; and then we dissolve the charm, and step out of his magic circle.

The orator makes no such contract with the judgments of his audience, nor suffers them to make it. What is professedly ideal in the creations of the dramatist, is substantiated and realized in those of the orator, by the power of the understanding. Every part of his work must bear the impression of truth and soberness ; and, instead of soliciting the voluntary and negative assent, command the positive and involuntary conviction of the audience. He must lodge his propositions firmly within the intrenchments of our reason and judgment, before we surrender ourselves fully to the movement that he requires of us. Till our understandings are taken captive, we withhold the homage of our hearts. Thus, in Cicero's division, he has appropriated the second and third, the narrative and demonstrative parts of an oration, to the conviction of the understanding, ad faciendam fidem ; that the audience may thus admit and follow on the impulse and direction given in the first. The conviction must not only be awakened, but continued unbroken, that what we listen to, is not merely dramatic but absolute truth. We must be convinced, too, that the orator be-

lieves it, and is the subject of the emotions that
he would awaken in us.   In short, we must be
out of the ideal world altogether, and in that real
world where there is no illusion.   If he seeks to
move our passions without first persuading us that
he does it on just and true grounds, he confounds
two acts that are essentially distinguished.   It was
on this ground that Aristotle* found fault with the
rhetoricians who preceded him.   By teaching
their orators to move the passions, without teaching them how to discover what was fitted to persuade and convince, they made them mere theat-
rical stage-players.   Again, we must be convinced
that truth, or rather an effect founded in truth, is
the sincere and only aim of the orator.   To this,
as the form which he is embodying, every thing
must be strictly and entirely subordinated.   The
least overstepping of the vanity of art, or of self-
display, is like the tongue of flame and the serpent
eyes in Christabel; it reveals to us the withering
secret, that we are the silly dupes of the artist.
This, from the representation of all the rhetoricians who have given an account of them, was, as
might from the nature of the case have been expected, " the main head of their offending," who
first taught and practiced oratory as an art in
Greece.   They became so vain of the art, as to
make the display of it their main object.   They
forgot to subordinate it, as they should have done,
as means to an end; and so degenerated them to
what Plato has denominated them, to men λογο-

* See his Ars Rhetorica, cap. I.

δαιδαλοι. The consequences were such as might be
expected. The auditors listened to their productions as specimens of only ingenious, artificial display. Thus the paranomasia, the antithesis and
finely-balanced sentences of Gorgias, the rhythm-
ical cadences of Theodorus and Thrasymachus,
and the rich and varied rhetorical artifices,* pomp-
pæ quam pugnæ aptius, which Isocrates was so
fond of displaying in his younger, but which he
abandoned in his riper years, were all heard, not
for the sober truth they conveyed, but, like the
exhibitions of the theatre, for the mere gratification of the fancy and the ear.† Even Plato is se-
verely criticised by Dionysius,‡ not only for his
dithyrambics, but for his labored antitheses; and
the great prince of orators, Demosthenes, first
learned to use the artifices of the middle style
without ever abusing them.

* So Quintilian, palæstræ quam pugna magis accommodatus.

† The style of eloquence here described had its origin in the
Greek colonies of Magna and Grecia, or perhaps rather with Empedocles, who taught rhetoric in Sicily 444, B. C. Lyscias and
Corax, however, are generally allowed (see Quin. B. 3. C. 1. and
others) to have been the first who laid down rules for it. These
were followed by Gorgias of Leontium, a scholar, as it is thought,
says Quintilian, of Empedocles. They taught and had followers
in Athens and other parts of Greece. Gorgias taught also in
Thessaly and other places. But the strength and energy of Athenian eloquence had a different origin. It was born amid the con-
tentions and revolutions of that free republic, and nourished in the
assemblies of the Athenians. Pericles and Cimon were not indebted to the western rhetoricians for the power that swayed
those turbulent mobs. Demosthenes owed to them his art, but his
sublime power and energy was of Athenian and republican growth.

‡ De ad miranda vi dicendi in Demosthene, cap. 23—24.

Many of the preceding remarks, I may be allowed to say, apply with full force to the style of composition and the effect of sermons. The basis of all sound eloquence, at least of all that is appropriately such, is the truth of Scripture, the authority of revelation. The whole superstructure must stand, and be seen by the hearer to stand, on that immovable foundation. If room is left in the interpretation, or the argument, to throw in a doubt, or a query, it is so much clear loss to the eloquence of the production. If it is to be highly splendid and poetical, I may, if I choose, voluntarily surrender myself to the illusion, and enjoy the loveliness of the song, but both the production and my own mind, in that case, entirely change their condition. *That* is no longer eloquence; and it is no longer my *conscience* that is addressed. I remember, for example, reading, not long since, a splendid sermon of one of our most popular New England divines. The language was eloquent, and the theory magnificent, but he had not secured his outworks. My judgment stuck at this interpretation, and I wrote Ichabod upon the sermon; for its glory had departed. In such cases the merit of a work, as a mere production of imagination, is not altered, but we must prize and enjoy it in a character entirely different from that which it was intended to possess. Jeremy Taylor has much poetry, where we could wish there had been eloquence; and the sublime and magnificent conceptions of the Theoria Sacra of Burnet, though designed to be eloquent, are now read only as poetry.

Notwithstanding, then, all that has been and may be said of the deadening influence of a critical system of interpretation, it is a necessary and indispensable prerequisite to all genuine pulpit eloquence.*

From all this, I gather the full conviction that it is not so easy a matter as we may have been led to imagine, to acquire the style and the art of oratory. It is not true that the mere purpose, blind and headlong as it generally is, will make man elo-

---

* Strictly speaking, the orator needs only to produce conviction in his audience, by *whatever* means. If he succeeds in doing it with false interpretations and inconclusive reasoning, he is indebted to the incapacity of his audience, and not to his own wisdom. The degree of critical accuracy, therefore, necessary to the effect, will depend very much on the character of the audience. Though the theory of eloquence developed in the text is there applied only cursorily to the eloquence of the pulpit, it is believed that it actually applies in nearly its whole extent, and that to fill the perfect *ideal* indeed of sacred eloquence on any principles of art, is far more difficult than to fill even the " aures avidæ et capaces " of Cicero himself. To sustain the impassioned and divine enthusiasm of St. Paul, and clothe it in forms of human language and human art, requires the learning and inspiration of Paul. What is said in the text of the variety and extent of the requisite qualifications for an orator, also, might be defended at any length in its application to the sacred orator. The following brief summary is from the Ecclesiastes of Erasmus, a work more worthy the attention of the student, and certainly more capable of inspiring him with enthusiasm, than those most likely to fall into his hands : quisquis præparat huic tam excellenti muneri, multis quidem rebus instructus sit oportet, sacrorum voluminum recondita intelligentia, multa scripturarum exercitatione, varia doctorum dictione, judicio sano, prudentia non vulgari, sereno fortique animo, præceptis usuque dicendi, et parata linguæ copia, qua dicendum est apud multitudinem, aliaque, quæ suo loco commemorabimus; mea tamen sententia, nihil illi prius aut majori studio curandum est, qui tam excellenti muneri sese praeparat, quam ut *cor, orationis fontem, quam purgatissimum reddat.*

quent. The ignorant wish for the power, with the design of attaining some sinister and forcing purpose by the use of it, will never lead to the acquisition. Students are told, for example, that they *must* be orators, that it is absolutely necessary to be orators, that their reputation depends on it, that learning is useless without eloquence, &c. So they resolve to be orators, they read or hear the story of Demosthenes, of the letter ϱ, and the pebbles; that action is the *first* thing, the *second* thing, yea, and the *third* thing; and then they go and *act*, and pronounce their words trippingly on the tongue. But pray, what has all this to do with the eloquence of Demosthenes? Before we are worthy to name *that* eloquence, we must have learned and habituated ourselves more " deeply to drink in the soul of things," and raise to " loftier heights our intellectual soul." We must learn in *idea* what eloquence is, and have imbibed a *genial* love for it, before we are prepared for its attainment. There must be enthusiasm; the whole power of the mind must be enlisted, and the soul must be all a-glow with that *aliquid immensum infinitumque*, which inspired the youthful ardor of Cicero, and, after reducing him to the brink of the grave, raised him to the summit of human glory.*

* Since writing the above, I have fallen upon the following passage in Quintilian: " We are apt to cloak our indolence under the pretext of difficulty, for we are not very fond of fatigue. It generally happens that professors of eloquence court her for vile purposes and mercenary ends, and not because of her own transcendent worth and matchless beauty. I desire my work may be read by none who shall sit down and make an estimate of the

With such a preparation, we may begin to advance
in the path of genuine eloquence. But O, even
then, though we might utter our most fervent *uti-*
nam that it were otherwise, we shall find it no business of a man's leisure hours, no holiday sport, to be
an orator, and a true one. The necessary requisites
are too various and too great to be thus attained.
The diversified powers of language, and the Pro-
teus versatility of style, which Dionysius * has
described by a dozen and a half of successive epi-
thets, as the style of Demosthenes, and which
formed so essential a qualification of Cicero's ideal,
is not the accomplishment of a day. Even in the
imperfect degree to which, by his own confession,
Cicero had attained it, but on which he valued
himself so highly, it cost him long and unremitting
labor. † We need but to study his conception of
a perfect orator, or even the account of his own
studies, to feel our littleness. ‡ The laborious
pursuit of dialectics and philosophy, the daily repeated and never ceasing efforts of the voice
and the pen, under the best masters, in Latin and
in Greek, at Rome, at Athens, in Asia and at
Rhodes, omnia sine remissione, sine varietate, vi
summa vocis, et totius corporis contentione, omni

expense of time and application. But give me the reader who
figures in his mind the idea of eloquence all divine, as she is ; who
with Euripides gazes upon her all-subduing charms ; who seeks
not his reward from the venal fees for his voice, but from that
reflection, that imagination, that perfection of mind, which time
cannot destroy, nor fortune affect. See at the end of B. 1.

   * De admiranda vi dicendi in Demosthene, cap. 8.

   † Orator.

   ‡ Brutus, cap. 91—93.

genere exercitationis, tum maxime *stilo*,—such are
the means to which the Roman orator submitted
to attain the object of his love. We can never
hope to attain it by efforts less varied and laborious. The study of that technical and analyzing
species of criticism and rhetoric, which concerns
itself only with the external dress of oratory, without communicating its spirit, can never make us
eloquent. We might study such works as that
ascribed to Demetrius Phalarius, and labor through
all the minutiæ of rhetorical figures and elocution,
till our gray hairs told us what we should soon
enough learn, that art is long and life is short. It
is the most eloquent lesson they will ever teach
us. We must begin, where Aristotle and Cicero
direct us to begin, with the knowledge of things.
We must have eloquence of soul, before we have
eloquence of tongue. If we would speak in the
language of Demosthenes, we must learn habitually to breathe his spirit. We must read his works
till we love them, and then study them with the
intensity which they deserve. We must read
them till we catch the fire that lives and burns in
his eloquent pages. For it is only by the habitual and yearning contemplation of the great masters of eloquence in the magnificent proportion of
their own monuments, that we can hope to attain
a sympathy with their minds. We must be content to rise step by step, with a humble but upward
and ardent gaze, till they unroll around us their
mighty gradations, "and growing with their
growth, we thus dilate" "our spirits to the size
of that they contemplate."

TRACT ON EVANGELISM.

[Read before an Association of Ministers, 1837.]

~~~~~~~~~~~~~~~~~~~

IS IT EXPEDIENT TO EMPLOY EVANGEL-ISTS IN CHURCHES FURNISHED WITH THE STATED AND ORDINARY MEANS OF RELIGIOUS INSTRUCTION?

~~~~~~~~~~~~~~~~~~~

In treating of this question, I shall inquire, to some extent, into the purpose of the stated ministry, and its relation to the church and the community ; and then point out some of the effects to be apprehended from the introduction of a distinct class of religious teachers, such as we understand by the term Evangelists in the question before us.

I. What, then, in the first place, is the proper function of the established and regular ministry, in its relation to the church and to the community at large ?

The general answer, of course, is, that they are appointed to preach the gospel and administer the ordinances of the gospel. They are set apart as a distinct body of men, necessary to the ends which God in his word and in his providence prescribes. But why necessary; and what are the qualifications which are to distinguish them from other christians, and on account of which the necessity for them exists? Obviously, they are required to have a knowledge of divine truth, an intellectual insight into spiritual things, a systematic and comprehensive acquaintance with all that is necessary for the right and the effectual teaching of divine truth and the application of the word and power of the Gospel to the minds of men, which does not belong and is not expected to belong to other men. They are the appointed, and, if they are what they ought to be, the divinely appointed and authorized spiritual guides and guardians of the flock. It is their business and their duty to be thoroughly instructed in the things pertaining to the kingdom of God, and able to teach others whatever is necessary to their salvation. There is a kind of knowledge requisite to fit them for their duty, which is not necessary to the private christian in order for his salvation. They must have a theoretical and speculative and a systematic knowledge of those truths which need only be known practically and in their immediate relation to the individual conscience, in order to have a saving efficacy for the individual. Take, for example, the doctrine of original sin. It is only necessary for the individual, in order to its practical effect on himself, to admit, with an inward undoubting conviction of its truth, the fact that he is a guilty, self-ruined and helpless sinner, all whose thoughts and purposes are evil ; and that in Christ alone is his help and the power to overcome evil. The more simplicity, the more immediate and unquestioning assurance there is in the reception of this fact on the simple authority of conscience, the less of speculation and of speculative doubt about it, the better for the ends of the gospel in the application of all its truths. So, generally, the more the minds of those whom we would save by the word and spirit of the gospel are kept to the plain and simple practical application of the truth to the conscience, the more they can feel that it is purely a matter between God and their own hearts, and their minds kept free from doubtful and agitating questions, either about essential truths and duties or about matters in themselves indifferent, the better is the opportunity of the preacher to bring home the gospel to the heart with power and the Holy Ghost and an elevating and transforming efficacy. But how is this simplicity of mind, this humble and undoubting reception of the fundamental truths and principles necessary to the saving efficacy of the gospel in the heart and conscience of the private individual, to be secured ? By the supposition, and from the nature of the case, it cannot be the result of speculation in the great mass of the people. It must be from the immediate agency of reason and conscience, enlightened and actuated by the Word and Spirit of God ; and it is the business of the ministry to

know how to apply the rightly understood and interpreted words of divine truth so as to produce
this result; and instead of goading the people into
speculative difficulties and doubts, to aid their consciences, and be co-workers with the Spirit of God
in bringing them into practical obedience to the
truth. But what will be the result, if there be no
settled and consistent system of instruction on the
part of those who are looked to as spiritual guides;
but if, on the contrary, the effect of their teaching
is to turn away the minds of the people from the
immediate truths of reason and conscience,—those,
I mean, which the unsophisticated practical reason
and conscience of all men will approve, — and to
lead them into speculations beyond their depth,
and the exercise of a faculty which they are unqualified to employ on subjects of a spiritual kind?
Will it not tend to unsettle their conviction of essential and fundamental truths which immediately
and practically concern their own inward being,
and unfit them for being benefitted by the simple
preaching of the gospel?

The clergy, then, the stated and established ministry, I maintain, must be, in order to the accomplishment of the purpose for which they were
appointed, a body set apart by their knowledge
and ministerial qualifications, and recognized and
respected by the people, as guides and teachers in
spiritual things. They must, as a body, respect
and govern themselves, with all humility, indeed,
as the servants of Christ, and with a deep sense of
their responsibility as the guides of the flock and

instructers of the ignorant, but without losing sight
of their place and office in the church.   It is their
duty to be *guides;* to understand many things
speculatively, which can be taught to the people at
large only *practically,* and so far as they practically affect their hearts and consciences.   How can
they perform the duties for which they are set
apart and ought to be qualified, if they yield, on
all occasions, to those who are unqualified to act
upon them, the decision of those very questions
which they have themselves been specially qualified to act upon and decide?   How can they shift
off the responsibility which, by virtue of their
office, devolves upon them, without a dereliction of
their most solemn duty?   As a distinct body holding this common relation to the church of which
they are ministers, they ought to agree together in
regard to the great and fundamental doctrines
which they preach, and in regard to the measures
which they adopt for the promotion of the interests
of truth and the well-being of the church of God.
They ought, as a body of qualified spiritual guides
and teachers, to settle among themselves all those
doubtful questions which they are supposed qualified to understand and decide, but which, from the
nature of the case, the people at large cannot understand, and therefore cannot decide aright.   They
must be responsible to each other and to the ecclesiastical bodies in which they are united, and
must, I say, in order to the best practical effect of
their ministrations, understand and maintain this
common relation to the people of their care ; nor is

80

it possible for them in any other way to discharge
the trust committed to their hands. Such was the
purpose of ecclesiastical organization, in all the different denominations of Christians which would be
regarded as of any authority here. What else is
the proper end of our organization in this body,
but to secure unity of action and agreement among
ourselves in doctrine and in practice, so far as regards the relation we hold to the church and the
modes we adopt for advancing the cause of truth?
What can be expected as to the practical advancement of religion in the churches and among those
who are to be taught and guided, when the guides
are at variance, and lead in different and opposite
directions? It is unquestionably a matter of the
highest import, that the clergy, at least of the same
denomination, understand each other, and be responsible to each other for unity of action, in regard
to all those matters which it is their proper business to examine and decide. It is important, and
a part of their responsible and especial duty, to
keep from the people all those agitating questions
which the people cannot act upon intelligently, and
leave their minds, as far as possible, unexcited by
them. In this case, a body of clergy, such as they
ought to be, truly *reverend* for their upright and holy
conversation, their sound knowledge and wisdom,
standing forth as the ministers, and speaking as
becomes the oracles of God, will be *revered* by the
great body of the people, and will have with them
that spiritual authority which will prepare their
minds to receive with simplicity and meekness the

ingrafted word ; to apply it practically and immediately to their own consciences, with all its reno-
vating and redeeming power.

Now let us suppose a body of clergy aiming at
or having attained this position in relation to the
church and people of their care ; responsible to
and watchful over each other, as brethren ; understanding the principles upon which they act, and
working together in the same spirit, for the same
end. Suppose this as that which either is, or
ought to be the fact ; and then I am prepared to
show, in part at least, in the second place, my
views of the probable, or at least possible, effect of
the present mode of employing evangelists.

1. They may come into their sphere of action
from a distance, authorized to preach by they
know not whom, and wholly irresponsible to them
as a body. In this case, so far as they have any
settled and understood principles of action for the
promotion of religion, they are liable to be broken
in upon, and the minds of the people turned away
from the practical application of truth to their own
consciences, to the consideration of the changes
made, and the debating of questions which belong
not to them, and which they are unqualified to understand. All the advantages of union and consistency among themselves are lost, and the people are agitated by matters that belong to the
clergy. The whole purpose of ecclesiastical organization is prostrated ; the clergy appear before
the people, at variance among themselves ; and
even supposing the diversity to be incidental, and

of little moment in itself, it tends to direct the attention to other things than those which immediately and practically affect the heart.

2. They may more directly interfere with the relation subsisting between the established body or clergy and the people of their charge. I have said that this relation ought to be, and must be in order to its proper end, one of watchful superintendance and guidance and spiritual authority on the one side, and of confiding and reverential docility on the other. This is liable to be broken up, by a course that withdraws confidence from the established clergy in regard to those very questions which it is their business and duty to settle, and teaches the people to judge and decide for themselves what they are wholly unqualified to determine. When this is done, it has precisely the same effect in the church, which the prevailing radicalism of the day has in politics. It puffs up the ignorant and inexperienced with a vain confidence in their own understandings or their own fancied experience in spiritual things, and leads them to undervalue, perhaps to censure and deride, those to whom they ought to look up with humility and reverence. It leads them to engage in speculations wholly beyond their reach, from want of discrimination to confound truth with falsehood, to unsettle all fixed principles in their minds, to make them regardless of the most sacred distinctions between truth and falsehood, and leave them the sport of every new doctrine, or the dupes of every new form of fanaticism. This is the case

not only in regard to individuals, but to churches. They become broken off from the ministry which God has ordained, and heap to themselves teachers who will flatter their self-confidence and be governed by their ignorant and delusive notions. Again, by seducing the churches from their proper relation to their spiritual guides, it tends to seduce from the truth and from the plain path of duty the clergy themselves. It places them under the strongest temptation to yield up their own principles and those of the order to which they belong, to place knowledge under the control of ignorance, and to subject the established order of the gospel to the caprice of self-willed arrogance and presumption. It leads to the habit of referring to laymen, and to those necessarily ignorant of the matter, subjects and questions which belong properly to the clergy, and ought to be decided in ecclesiastical bodies. In a word, it tends directly and inevitably to strip the clergy of all their rightful prerogatives, held as they are, too, and delegated solely for the benefit of the church. In other words, the clergy are led to yield that which it is their solemn duty to retain, and responsibly to exercise for the end for which they were qualified and put into the ministry.

3. From the nature of the case, where the church is thus seduced from its confidence in the established clergy, we are exposed to the incursion of evangelists who are themselves wandering stars, undeserving of personal confidence, and from their erratic character irresponsible to any ecclesi-

astical body ; ignorant, conceited and fanatical. Such an one, with his petty scheme of empiricism, with a boastful proclamation of his numberless conversions and testimonies to their genuineness, like a medical empiric with his marvellous cures and long list of certificates, and with the same want of discrimination both as to the nature of the disease and the employment of the rightful remedies, with the same self-complacency as to the superiority and wonderful effects of his own petty inventions, the same contemptuous treatment of those who profess to have any other and better knowledge, and still farther, with the same cautious avoidance of that inspection or publicity which might perchance expose his shallowness, will yet find admittance into our churches, break up all established order, degrade and disgrace the services of the sanctuary, diffuse a spirit of fanaticism within the church, and of contemptuous infidelity without, and then leave the tumult of disorder to settle as it may, while he practises the same arts in other regions, with the same lamentable and disastrous results.

How different is all this from the calm and silent, but laborious and persevering inculcation of the truth, by a learned, a wise, a holy and revered body of men, in whom the people confide, and from whom, with docility, with simplicity and meekness, they receive the ingrafted word, which is able to save their souls! And how vastly different is the result upon the intellectual, the moral and spiritual character of the community at large;

upon the order and decency, the dignity and propriety, the purity and sacredness, of all the ministrations of religion! Yet, as evangelism is now
conducted, it cannot consist with that relation between the people and the ministry of the gospel
which is essential to this state of things, and to the
best interests of the church. Its tendency is to
disorder and irregularity, to the discredit of sound
and healthful instruction, to the dishonoring of the
Word and Spirit of God, and to the substitution
of the devices of the human understanding and of
men; will-worship for that worship which is in
spirit and in truth. I would not charge upon this
alone, by any means, all the evils which exist in
the moral and spiritual condition of our churches.
But I maintain, that the more superficial, the more
dead to spiritual things, the more in need our
churches are of a true and genuine reviving of the
power and graces of the Spirit, the more danger is
to be apprehended from the employment in them
of eccentric and self-confident and irresponsible
men. The excitement so produced is not the
awakening they need, and only aggravates the disease it is intended to cure. There is no cure for
it, but the patient and laborious and persevering
application of the truth, in its nakedness and simplicity, to the hearts and consciences of men, by
a ministry whom they know; in whose simplicity
and honesty and godly sincerity they confide; by
men who have renounced the hidden things of dis-
honesty, not walking in craftiness, nor handling
the word of God deceitfully; but, by manifesta-

tion of the truth, commending themselves to every man's conscience in the sight of God. By such a ministry, as the appointed and authorized instruments of and co-workers with the Spirit of God, the churches may be truly revived, so as to become not revival but living churches, and be no longer exposed to that "sad mixture of fanaticism and knavish imposture" into which the "art of revival-making" is ready to degenerate, in the present mode of getting up and "conducting" and "managing" revivals.

From these considerations, it seems to me perfectly clear, that it will always be unsafe to employ evangelists at all in the way in which it is now done, out of the sphere of the ecclesiastical bodies with which they are properly connected and to which they are responsible. If they are employed in any way, the nature of the case seems to dictate that it be only in correspondence and in unison with their own association or presbytery, and within their proper limits. Under such limitations, they may, perhaps, be employed in the destitute churches, and be occasional helpers of those who are in the more stated labors of a settled pastor, without danger of disruption and the many evils which attend the course of an erratic and transcendent evangelist.

These views I value chiefly as assigning, according to my humble estimate, their proper and rightful place and dignity and spiritual authority, in relation to the church and the world, to the regular and established clergy. This is the position, which, according to divine appointment, and in view of the best interests of the church, they unquestionably ought to hold; and whatever interferes with and dissolves this relation between them and the people, is both inexpedient and wrong. An established ministry, qualified for their place and performing their duties as becomes their sacred office, deserving the respect and the confidence of the people by all those qualifications which belong to their high and responsible station, are entitled to that confidence, and may rightfully, nay, must, under the highest responsibility, exercise those prerogatives with which they are invested, as the shepherds of the flock. To what end are the schools of the prophets, and all that laborious discipline, by which, as a matter of duty, the minister of God prepares himself, with the aid of God's grace and the teachings of his Spirit, for the discharge of his high trust, if his judgment is to be yielded on all subjects to untaught ignorance or presumptuous folly? To what purpose are our associations and conventions, our ministerial intercourse and our talk of the vast responsibility that rests upon us as having the care of souls, if, after all, every question that we are to decide, individually or collectively, may be decided for us by those who feel no responsibility, and have never qualified themselves for the task? No, brethren; we cannot divest ourselves of our responsibility. He who is ordained to the care of souls, is and must be responsible for the doctrines which are preached in his pulpit; for the measures, whether

81

of order or confusion, that attend, under his charge, the ministrations of the sanctuary. He is bound to see that nothing be there taught or done, inconsistent with the established doctrines or orderly ministrations of the ministerial brotherhood to which he belongs, and with whom he is a co-worker, in the unity of the faith and in the order of the gospel. On this ground alone can there be any unity, or the existence and continuance of that relation of the ministry to the church, which is indispensably necessary to the performance of duty, on the one side, and the reception of the appointed blessing, on the other. The manifold blessings flowing to the church and the world, from a ministry thus qualified, thus organized, thus responsible, can never be secured by the labor of irresponsible and irregular dispensers of truth or error, as the case may be; and when its ends are frustrated by such men, no power on earth can remedy, no human wisdom foresee, the evils that must be the inevitable result.